Spirituality and Liberation

Books by Robert McAfee Brown
published by The Westminster Press

Spirituality and Liberation:
Overcoming the Great Fallacy

Saying Yes and Saying No:
On Rendering to God and Caesar

Unexpected News:
Reading the Bible with Third World Eyes

Religion and Violence, Second Edition

Making Peace in the Global Village

Theology in a New Key:
Responding to Liberation Themes

Is Faith Obsolete?

The Pseudonyms of God

The Collect'd Writings of St. Hereticus

The Hereticus Papers
(Vol. II of The Collect'd Writings of St. Hereticus)

The Significance of the Church
(Layman's Theological Library)

The Bible Speaks to You

P. T. Forsyth:
Prophet for Today

Spirituality and Liberation

Overcoming the Great Fallacy

Robert McAfee Brown

The Westminster Press
Philadelphia

Book design by Gene Harris

First edition

Published by The Westminster Press®
Philadelphia, Pennsylvania

PRINTED IN THE UNITED STATES OF AMERICA

9 8 7 6 5 4 3 2 1

Library of Congress Cataloging-in-Publication Data

Brown, Robert McAfee, 1920–
    Spirituality and liberation.

    Bibliography: p.
    1. Spirituality. 2. Social action. 3. Liberation
theology. 4. Sociology, Christian. I. Title.
BV4501.2.B7668 1988   233   87-29425
ISBN 0-664-25002-5 (pbk.)

Theology is not a provable accumulation,
like science, nor is it a succession
of enduring monuments, like art.
It must always unravel and be reknit.
                    —John Updike,
                        Hugging the Shore

Contents

Acknowledgments

This book, several years in the making, creates indebtedness to many people. I must thank some of them, while simultaneously absolving them of responsibility for shortcomings that slipped through the cracks.

Among individuals, special thanks to my sons, Peter and Mark, who took the photographs that are discussed in the Transition after chapter 3, with the hope that more and more of their artistic vision will rub off on me; to Sydney, whose gentle and firm attempts for forty-five years to keep me theologically honest ("Do you really mean that?") account for whatever integrity the text possesses; to Denise and John Carmody, Jim and Wilys Claire Nelson, Donald Gelpi, S.J., Karen Lebacqz, and Janet Walton, who have all made special contributions to my understanding of spirituality and liberation; to Judy Dunbar, who demonstrated that "friend" and "critic" are not mutually exclusive terms; to Elie Wiesel, whose commitment to liberation for all people has a hardly won spirituality within it, whether he would call it that or not; to Sr. Joan Delaplane, O.P., for a quotation from Augustine (used to begin chapter 10) that has empowered me ever since I heard her use it; to members of the Religion Department at Carleton College, valued colleagues while the manuscript was being revised, and especially to Professor Anne Patrick, without whose counsel (and typewriter) the book would still be languishing; to Leslie Argueta-Vogel, living in El Salvador, for many third world materials; and, in ways beyond all telling of them, to Gustavo Gutiérrez, whose influence will be noticeable at every crucial point in the argument.

I owe special thanks to students in a class in the Network Program of the Graduate Theological Union, in which we developed a course on "Prayer and Social Justice"; to Professor Bernard Adeney of New College, Berkeley, with whom I team-taught a course at the Graduate Theological Union on "Spirituality and Justice," and to Sr. Clare Ronzani, S.N.D., for opportunities to explore portions of the material with participants in the Institute for Spirituality and Worship at the Jesuit School of Theology.

Four books were especially helpful during the actual time of writing: Walter Brueggemann, Sharon Parks, and Thomas Groome's *To Act Justly, Love Tenderly, Walk Humbly;* Donal Dorr, *Spirituality and Justice;* Elizabeth O'Connor, *Journey Inward, Journey Outward;* and Roger Haight, *An Alternative Vision.*

Material from these pages formed the basis for the Snuggs Lectures at the University of Tulsa, Tulsa, Oklahoma; for the Ecumenical Chair in Theology Lecture series at Xavier University, Cincinnati, Ohio; and for talks at the Hennepin Avenue Methodist Church, Minneapolis, Minnesota, and the Lutheran Theological Seminary in Philadelphia. I benefited greatly from the discussion elicited on each of these occasions.

Most of the material appears in print for the first time, with the exception of a few pages and paragraphs from my chapter in Lee Cormie and Richard Snyder, eds., *Theology and the Struggle for Liberation: Responses from the Mainstream* (Maryknoll, N.Y.: Orbis Books, 1988), and articles on "Spirituality and Liberation" published in the *Sewanee University Journal of Theology* and *Worship* (published at St. John's Abbey in Minnesota), and, as "Espiritualidad y liberación," in *Vida y Reflexión* (Lima, Peru), 1983. A few of the comments on Henri Nouwen first appeared in *National Catholic Reporter.*

ROBERT MCAFEE BROWN

Northfield, Minnesota

Introduction

An Episode, a Few Distinctions, and Some Clarifications

Prayer is not the first thing that a person does. Before praying one experiences an existential shock.
—Leonardo Boff, *The Lord's Prayer*

To clasp hands in prayer is the beginning of an uprising against the disorder of the world.
—Karl Barth

[I have been learning] a beautiful and harsh truth, that the Christian faith does not separate us from the world but immerses us in it; that the church, therefore, is not a fortress set apart from the city, but a follower of the Jesus who loved, worked, struggled, and died in the midst of the city.
—Archbishop Oscar Romero, shortly before he was shot for interfering with life "in the midst of the city"

June 16, 1985, started out like any other Sunday. Children were scrubbed and prepared for Sunday school, choirs got together early to practice the morning anthem, ministers looked over their manuscripts, wishing they had devoted more time to sermon preparation. And in many churches that day, when eleven o'clock finally rolled around, the pastors, acknowledging that these are troubled times and that in troubled times people are in special need of God's help, read a statement that had been circulated to the churches throughout the nation, entitled "A Theological Rationale and a Call to Prayer . . . ," urging a renewed dedication to devotional life, all preceded by a biblical and historical "rationale," complete with fourteen footnotes.

Ho-hum.

The pious could be pleased that the church was once again attending to its "real job." Church officials could feel encouraged that their denominations were rallying together under the banner of prayer. And government officials could breathe more easily, now that the churches were "looking inward" once again, rather than messing around with politics and social action.

But it didn't work out that way. All the expectations were dashed. The pious were greatly agitated, upset that prayer had been used for partisan political ends. Church officials were deeply divided, some describing the "Call" as "presumptuous" and others as "contrary to scripture and tradition." And government officials were apoplectic, furiously charging that the church had intruded into areas where it didn't belong, engaging in what amounted to acts of treason. Prayer as an act of treason. The newspapers were full of it for weeks.

All this furor simply over a call to prayer? What could be more appropriate than for churches to commend a deeper prayer life to their constituents?

But the furor was real. For the country was South Africa; the date was the anniversary of the Soweto Uprising of June 16, 1976, when government troops had entered this black township of Johannesburg and opened fire on black children; and the full title of "A Theological Rationale and a Call to Prayer . . ." was "A Theological Rationale and a Call to Prayer *for the End to Unjust Rule.*" Excerpts:

> We now pray that God will replace the present unjust structures of oppression with ones that are just, and remove from power those who persist in defying his laws, installing in their places leaders who will govern with justice and mercy. . . .
>
> The present regime, together with its structures of domination, stands in contradiction to the Christian gospel to which the churches of the land seek to remain faithful. . . .
>
> We pray that God in his grace may remove from his people the tyrannical structures of oppression and the present rulers

in our country who persistently refuse to hear the cry for
justice. . . .
   We pledge ourselves to work for that day.

(Cited in Allan A. Boesak and Charles Villa-Vicencio, eds.,
When Prayer Makes News, pp. 26, 29; Westminster Press, 1986)

Strong meat.
   The "Call to Prayer" was not blanketed with smooth
generalities or bland exhortations. It stated without equivo-
cation that the situation in South Africa was an offense to
God and consequently an offense to God's people, that the
present government was responsible for this offensive state
of affairs, and that its leaders must therefore be replaced by
new leaders committed to "justice and mercy." It not only
pleaded with God to bring these changes about, it served
notice to God and the state that those who offered the
prayers were not going to leave it to God alone but were
themselves pledged "to work for that day." No wonder that
the published report of these events was entitled *When
Prayer Makes News.*
   Should prayer "make news"? Is it the job of church people
to pray for the overthrow of their government? Does religion
have anything to do with politics? Can one's private faith in
God be enlisted as a vehicle for changing public policy? Were
those church folk right to propose a change of government
within a service of worship? Aren't "spiritual" matters (like
prayer) and "liberation" matters (like politics) meant to be
kept separate?
   It is questions such as these, particularly the last, that are
addressed in this book.

   The questions are not new. They have been front and
center ever since Pharaoh unsuccessfully tried to persuade
Moses that religion had nothing to do with Egypt's domestic
policy on the status of nonindentured servants. God rather
aggressively got into the act on Moses' side, and Pharaoh
wound up a distant second in a field of two.
   The structure of the argument should be clear from the
Contents and from the brief introduction to each of the three

parts. Instead of repeating it again, let us reposition the question by brief comments on the two chief words of the title.

The book intends to offer an alternative to ongoing attempts to compartmentalize life into, roughly, the "sacred" and the "secular" (the former being "good" and the latter "evil"). One can ask why the terms "spirituality" and "liberation" were chosen to carry the weight of the argument. The answer is unedifyingly simple: These are the words most frequently used in current discussion, and they are usually invoked in such a way as to suggest that they are mutually exclusive. One can be "into spirituality," as many people have always been, or "into liberation," as increasing numbers of people appear to be. But the notion that one could be "into" both, or that the dichotomy itself is suspect, are not notions that are entertained with generous affection.

In Latin America, Asia, and Africa, there are millions of people who once assumed that they were trapped in unfortunate situations with no option but to accept their lot and hope for a better deal after death. But a dream of liberation from all kinds of oppression, especially political and economic, has seized them and become the guiding star in their firmament. Things can be different, here and now.

The impulse is not only nurtured abroad. Within the United States, a self-conscious embrace of the liberation message has empowered blacks to work for freedom from the various bondages imposed on them, and the same has been true of liberation movements in the lives of women, native Americans, gays, lesbians, Asian-Americans, and a host of others.

Many of these liberation movements have arisen in, or been nurtured by, the church, and in all parts of the world "liberation theologies" have appeared, to provide religious grounding for the struggle.

In the commonly held understanding, liberation is pursued chiefly to establish a new social order that will wipe out the oppressive structures to which disadvantaged people have been subjected and create a society where all, and not just some, can live creative lives.

Similarly, there are millions of people with a vision described by the word "spirituality." They do not necessarily look on political and economic structures as unimportant, but they do not see them as primary vehicles of redemption. For them, spirituality is a state of being, frequently approached through "spiritual exercises" and acts of discipline that put them in touch with realities, or a Reality, not discernible in ordinary experience. Deepening a relation to that Reality is what life is all about.

This is not a new movement in the way that widespread concern for liberation is a new movement. Nor is it found chiefly or exclusively within "western religions," in the way that many liberation movements are prominently identified with Christianity. Much of the wisdom about a life of spirituality has been nurtured in Buddhist and Hindu settings, as well as in the mystical traditions of Judaism and Sufi Islam.

It is significant that within our own upwardly mobile and success-oriented culture, the appeal of such a spirituality is on the rise. Finding no lasting fulfillment in the rat race of modern capitalist society, many outwardly successful people seek ways to overcome the competitive pressure and attain a measure of serenity that will fill the emptiness and counterbalance the chaos that appears eager to destroy them.

These descriptions (which will need not only fine-tuning but considerable overhaul as we proceed) suggest two impulses of the human spirit so apparently foreign to each other as to reinforce our earlier suggestion that they are mutually exclusive. This is certainly how many of their proponents see them, and much of the difficulty of relating them is attributable to their deeply ingrained suspicion of each other. It will be the purpose of this book not simply to dispel some of those suspicions but, finally, to suggest a different approach altogether.

It remains only to clarify three sources of possible misunderstanding.

First of all, these pages are not a how-to manual for the practice of either spirituality or liberation. They should not be consulted in the hope of finding techniques for approaching Reality in zones of quiet or for rebuilding the earth in the name of justice. There are plenty of books that do both, and some are listed in the bibliography. The aim is more modest. It is to provide an approach through which spirituality and liberation can begin to be seen as two ways of talking about the same thing, so that there is no necessity, or even a possibility, of making a choice between them.

My own personal story has led me along the route of liberation concerns that I increasingly perceive as including all that spirituality truly means, a route that is undoubtedly reflected in the way the argument develops. But others may come to that identical conclusion from the opposite starting point. Let not such persons feel slighted in these pages; let them write their own accounts for the edification of us all.

If the theme of the book seems obvious, or its development laborious, I can only congratulate the reader for having escaped a debate that seems to flourish with renewed vigor every few years, as those who want to keep the dichotomy alive mount their battle stations once again. This book is only one in a long chain of efforts to reclaim territory unjustly seized.

Second, I want to anticipate another possible misunderstanding. It will soon be clear that the *bête noire* of these pages is dualism, or dividing the world into two separate compartments, and that my concern is to deny the legitimacy of such division. In making my case, however, I may sometimes appear guilty of excessive authorial zeal by following too exclusively what the British writer Charles Williams called the way of "the affirmation of images," according to which every created thing partially reveals God and can lead to God, human love being the most obvious example. But according to Williams, who exemplified this approach in most of his writing, there is another way, called "the negation of images," that reminds us how paltry are the insights we can derive from images in a fallen world, and how unreliable are any conclusions reached in that way. Adherents of such a position usually feel confident only to say what God is not, since positive images become idols and do not sufficiently acknowledge the remaining unlikenesses. It was Williams's contention that we must practice both ways, since each protects against the excesses of the other. The way of affirmation makes certain claims possible; the way of negation safeguards against claiming too much for the claims. While human love is a pointer to God's love, for example, it is not the same as God's love, and there are many things done in the name of human love that it would be manifestly wrong to offer as analogies to God's love. The unlikenesses must not be glossed over. Let the principle be invoked by the reader whenever the author is observed transgressing it.

Third, while this is manifestly a book written by a Christian, it is not written solely for Christians. It is written for all people who are concerned about its subject matter, and especially those on whom the Christian tradition is most dependent, the Jews. Whenever possible, and especially at points that seem to separate Christians and Jews from one another, I have tried to indicate points of contact and sharing. What I have tried *not* to do is mute my own perspective, since that only fuzzes the issue. When there is a Christian insight to be made I try to make it, aware that for those moments at least the interest of others may wane (though I hope they might at least be curious). My own *rebbe,* Elie Wiesel, says that the more clearly he writes as a Jew, the more clearly he communicates to non-Jews, and my experience in reading him confirms that this is one of the secrets of his communicative power. The posture I adopt here tries to be a mirror image of his, save that by comparison my glass is cracked and tarnished. But I will be happy if I can succeed one tenth as well as he does, in building bridges between our two communities.

PART ONE

Deconstruction

WHEREIN *an effort is made to clear the decks so that a new proposal can be launched;*

WHEREIN *it is shown that the Great Fallacy (long though it has flourished and impressive though its credentials may be) errs in dividing life into two separate compartments;*

WHEREIN *it is further shown that previous attempts to overcome this separation likewise err, either by demolishing one of the partners in the discussion or attempting (with initial attractiveness) to synthesize them;*

WHEREIN *it is next proposed that the imagery of "withdrawal and return," while appearing to reinforce the Great Fallacy, creates a threshold for approaching life in a more unified way;*

AND WHEREIN, *finally, by employing the insights of two photographs, a transition is provided to more constructive efforts in Part Two.*

1

The Great Fallacy:
Variations on a Single Theme

The body is the prisonhouse of the soul.
        —Many Greek philosophers
        before Aristotle

*The spiritual regimen that emerged from an essentially dual-
istic definition of human nature was a simple one: things were
bad; the body was bad; suffering was good. If-it-hurts-it-must-
be-holy became the standard of all activity.*
        —Sr. Joan Chittister, O.S.B.,
            describing the earlier mentality of the church

The subject matter of this book is not the Great Fallacy.
But its proper subject cannot be attended to until the theme
of the Great Fallacy has been examined. Just when we think
we have pushed it out the front door of our minds, it sneaks
in the back door, all the more powerful for being more subtle.
It is a formidable foe, present in many forms and variations.

Variations first, theme later

Let us consider some of the variations, as a way of approaching the theme.

> IRATE PROTESTANT LAYPERSON: Pastor, you've got no
> right to bring the election into the pulpit. It's not your job
> to deal with political issues. Just remember, religion and
> politics don't mix.

IRATE CATHOLIC LAYPERSON: What are those bishops up to anyway? First they write a pastoral letter on nuclear weapons, and now they've done one on the economy. If they're so keen on writing pastoral letters, why don't they do one on prayer?

HARASSED PARISHIONER: I have enough of a problem simply getting through a week at the office. I don't come to church to be reminded of still more problems; I come to church to be reinforced for next week. If I want to hear about conditions in Central America I'll go to a rally.

CALM PARISHIONER: We all had a truly spiritual experience being off in the woods on retreat, far away from all the mess of the world we live in most of the time. For the first time in months, I felt really close to God.

ACTIVIST PASTOR: Our government is doing such terrible things in Nicaragua that I can hardly bear to train Sunday school teachers, call on the elderly, and conduct worship. Instead of singing hymns we ought to be sitting in at the Senator's office.

TROUBLED TEENAGER: I've got problems. What do I do about drugs? Is sex okay? How am I going to get a job when I get out of high school? I'm tired of getting dragged to church to sing boring hymns and pray to God.

TROUBLED TEENAGER: I've got a problem. How can I believe in God when there's so much evil in the world? That really bothers me. Can't God stop it? But the only thing the youth group wants to do is plan ski weekends.

IDEALIST PHILOSOPHER: God is Eternal Being, unchanging and therefore unaffected by what happens to us. If we want to enter the realm of Eternal Being, we have to clear our minds of earthly distractions and seek God through detachment.

IDEALISTIC REVOLUTIONARY: The only God I can believe in is one who helps us get the supplies we need to bring down our tyrannical government and set up an era of peace and justice for everyone.

THEOLOGIAN (who just might be an old-style Lutheran): The church's task is to initiate us into the spiritual kingdom where we can find salvation. God has decreed that politicians and businessmen and soldiers should run the earthly kingdom. As long as they don't interfere with our kingdom, we won't interfere with theirs.

All these variations point to a single theme: Life is divided into two areas, two spheres, two compartments, and if we know what's good for us we'll keep it that way.

What are these two areas? The words we use to describe them are legion. Here is a sampling, with space for still more.

A Handy Checklist of Opposites We Encounter in the Real World (in No Particular Order)

sacred	vs.	secular
prayer	vs.	politics
faith	vs.	works
withdrawal	vs.	engagement
church	vs.	world
eternity	vs.	time
theory	vs.	practice
religion	vs.	ethics
soul	vs.	body
personal	vs.	social
spirit	vs.	flesh
holy	vs.	profane
heaven	vs.	earth
otherworldly	vs.	this-worldly
divine	vs.	human
meditation	vs.	agitation
mysticism	vs.	humanism
saint	vs.	sinner
spiritual	vs.	material
contemplation	vs.	action
God	vs.	humanity
inner	vs.	outer
love	vs.	justice
creeds	vs.	deeds
priest	vs.	prophet
evangelism	vs.	social action
abstinence	vs.	sex
immortality	vs.	resurrection
Greek	vs.	Hebrew

"verticalism"	vs.	"horizontalism"
transcendence	vs.	immanence
liturgy	vs.	legislation
Jesus the Christ	vs.	Jesus of Nazareth
theonomy	vs.	autonomy
spirituality	vs.	liberation
_____	vs.	_____
_____	vs.	_____
_____	vs.	_____
_____	vs.	_____

All of us identify some of these items. We know there is a difference between saint and sinner, prayer and politics, faith and works, and a few others. Some of us can't identify all of the terms. Unless we have gone to seminary we have not lost much sleep worrying about the differences between theonomy and autonomy or verticalism and horizontalism.

Not to worry. One virtue of the list is that if we can identify even a few of the polarities, we have already gotten the point: Whatever words we use, we keep dividing life into two realms.

Some of the separations seem valid even if others do not. This is because they are deeply grounded in our cultural as well as our religious life. We use terms like "soul" and "body" all the time, for example, even if we're not quite sure what they mean, and we're bombarded with the notion that there are important distinctions between the "things of the spirit" (whatever they are) and the "things of the flesh" (with which we have detailed acquaintance).

It is the contention of this book—to be up front about it from the very start—that these separations are not only awkward, inaccurate, and unhelpful but that they are, in almost all cases, just plain wrong. They do not add meaning to our lives or give us good interpretive tools; on the contrary, they distort our lives and lead us to faulty understandings of who we are and what the world is like. That is why the attempt to insist on such divisions is called the Great Fallacy. A fallacy is not just a trifling error; it is a huge deception.

The Great Fallacy is nothing new

The Great Fallacy has been around a long time, despite the fact that Judaism, out of which Christianity grew, was never seduced by it. On the contrary, Judaism has always had a positive view of the importance and sacredness of the created order and all who inhabit it. Indeed, one of the most robust resources for Christianity in combating the Great Fallacy is deeper immersion in its Jewish roots.

One problem for the early Christians was that they found themselves living not in a predominantly Jewish culture but in a culture that was dominated by a Greek worldview. To get a hearing in the Greek culture, they had to employ Greek terms and employ a Greek way of thinking. And for many Greeks of that time, the Great Fallacy was the Great Truth. They believed that the body was evil and the soul good, that time was corrupt and eternity pure, that earth was to be shunned and heaven sought, that flesh was the seat of impurity and spirit the seat of blessedness.

To be "saved," in this kind of situation, was to disengage from the evil world. The message was clear: Scorn the body for the sake of the soul, forsake earth for the sake of heaven, stamp out the flesh for the sake of blessedness.

At two crucial points the church resisted this message. It rejected a view known as Docetism (from the Greek *dokeo,* meaning "to seem or appear to be"), which argued that Jesus only "seemed" to be human, since pure deity could not dwell in impure flesh; and it also rejected a more complicated position known as Gnosticism, which held that salvation could come only from "inside" information or wisdom (*gnosis*) that was discovered by turning one's back on the world.

Nevertheless, as Christianity developed and spread, the temptation to cut the Christian cloth to fit the Greek pattern proved almost irresistible. The "desert fathers" and other monastics, for example, retreated from the world and its blandishments, feeling that only in isolated places could God be truly found; and Jesus, who had first been known as a very flesh-and-blood Jewish rabbi, was more and more described as a celestial Being who could best be encountered not in the midst of a flesh-and-blood world but in a celestial realm. (Docetism lurked in every nook and cranny.)

Two ways of living a Christian life emerged. There was the A+ way, which meant taking vows of poverty, chastity, and obedience and turning away from the evil world to live in seclusion in monasteries, nunneries, and hermitages; and there was the B− way, which meant remaining in the evil world as a butcher, baker, or candlestick maker, counting on the prayers of the A+ Christians to get the B− Christians into heaven.

By the Middle Ages, there were two ways of attaining virtue, "The Spiritual Works of Mercy" and "The Bodily Works of Mercy," as follows:

The Spiritual Works of Mercy	The Bodily Works of Mercy
Converting the sinner	Feeding the hungry
Instructing the ignorant	Giving drink to the thirsty
Counseling the doubtful	Clothing the naked
Comforting the sorrowful	Harboring the stranger
Bearing wrongs patiently	Visiting the sick
Forgiving injuries	Ministering to prisoners
Praying for the living and the dead	Burying the dead

All these works were admirable, but they were very different kinds of works.

An even more telling example of the Great Fallacy is a devotional classic from the late medieval period, Thomas à Kempis's *The Imitation of Christ,* the full title of which is *The Imitation of Christ and Contempt for All the Vanities of the World.* The world was not seen as an arena for human fulfillment and Christian living, but as an arena so fraught with temptation that Christians should shun it and choose the divine realm over the earthly. "He who loves God," Thomas advises, "despises all other love," a conclusion that leads him to assert that love for neighbor, love for one in need, and love for a spouse are all to be spurned so that love may center exclusively on God. "Worldly" things such as food, clothing, and shelter must be used "without desire," and a similar distancing from persons is urged; God looks with favor on those who "for the love of virtue withdraw themselves from their acquaintances and from their worldly friends." It is a sign of religious devotion "seldom to see others."

The Great Fallacy made its way into the liturgy. A phrase in the baptismal service, still used by some denominations, asks the sponsors, in the name of the child, to "renounce the world, the flesh, and the devil," the world and the flesh being understood as the arena in which the devil holds sway.

While the Reformation was on one level a protest against this two-tier view of reality, the above baptismal formula reminds us that Protestants soon introduced their own versions of the Great Fallacy. The traditional Lutheran doctrine of "the Two Realms," postulating an earthly realm (presided over by the state) and a spiritual realm (presided over by the church) was a reinforcement of its medieval forebears. Protestant hymnody became a fertile seedbed for dualism. Phrases such as "Let sense be dumb, let flesh retire" and references to "A joy to sensual minds unknown" have their parallels in gospel hymns:

> Earthly pleasures vainly call me,
> I would be like Jesus;
> Nothing worldly shall enthrall me,
> I would be like Jesus.

Music itself was a mixed blessing, because of its association with the sensual, the earthy, the seductive, and some Protestant groups went so far as to remove organs from their churches, fearing that the beauty of their tones would distract worshipers from the beauty of the Divine Being. In Calvinist Geneva, the organ pipes were once melted down to provide ammunition for the defense of the city—a curious inversion of the biblical commandment to turn swords into plowshares. Others, not going quite that far, allowed only unison singing, fearing that the aesthetic pleasure of harmonizing would cause worshipers to stand in awe before the wonder of the human voice rather than the thunder of God's Word.

It took the wisdom of the Lutheran Johann Sebastian Bach to cut through such dead ends and fashion his most deeply moving chorale, *O Sacred Head, Now Wounded,* out of the melody of a drinking song he had heard in a local tavern. But Bach was both a genius and an exception.

Why the Great Fallacy is so appealing:
A conspiratorial view

Why does the Great Fallacy persist? Some would argue that the thesis of this book is exactly backward, and that the Great Fallacy persists because it is actually the Great Truth; life really *is* dualistic, and no attempt to argue otherwise can finally win the day. "Truth crushed to earth," as we learned in grammar school, "will rise again."

Another reason for the persistence of the Great Fallacy is that it has become so embedded in the tradition (as we have already seen) that it never occurs to people to challenge it. Traditions die hard; anything that has lasted so long must be right.

But there is another, less benign, explanation of the ongoing appeal of the Great Fallacy. Much of the support for it comes because it is in the interest of those with power—whether political, economic, ecclesiastical, or all three—to retain that power, free from challenge. To such persons, a religion that centers attention on "the realm of the spirit," removed from the nitty-gritty of life, is a boon, while a religion that insists on dealing with the world of hunger, exploitation, and dehumanization is a bane. To believe, in the words of Juan Luis Segundo, that "the world should not be the way it is" is to issue a call for change, and those who benefit from "the world as it is" are going to feel threatened whenever they hear declarations of discontent.

Third world dictators want "the masses" insulated from notions of political or economic liberation, since such notions might challenge their power. They reward those within the church who preach a message to the poor that goes: Accept your lot, find "spiritual" liberation in the midst of physical hardship, don't rock the boat, and God will reward you in the afterlife. When Chilean bishops challenge General Pinochet for violations of human rights, he responds that they should be in church praying.

It is not only third world dictators who feel this way. Many conservative first world Christians likewise want religion to concentrate on "spiritual" things and stay away from challenges to political or economic injustice. To opt for "spirituality" means to them that things as they are need not be challenged, whereas to suggest that the love commandment means reexamining social structures that allow people to starve is, among other things, "unwarranted interference," a distortion of the gospel, a reduction to mere politics, a replacement of Jesus Christ by Karl Marx, a humanistic rather than a theocentric faith. Many businessmen, for example, are upset by the Catholic bishops' letter on the economy, because it suggests the need for changes in the capitalistic system of free enterprise.

In sum, the appeal of the Great Fallacy is that it frees us from having to face challenges to the present state of affairs. It is a way of opting for the status quo.

Now "opting for the status quo" might not be a bad thing if the status quo were only a little more just. Those who opt for it are going to be those who most directly benefit from it. But if we look realistically at the world, we find that the beneficiaries are few in number compared to the victims, who have every reason to seek change and even more reason to be suspicious of those who refuse to do so. Those who feel the urgency of change, who believe that "the world should not be the way it is," can never rest content with the Great Fallacy; they look for ways to overcome it.

Warning: Overcoming the Great Fallacy may be hazardous to your faith

But let us not proceed too fast. Overcoming the Great Fallacy, and rejoining things falsely severed, provides no automatic victories. In some cases, the cure may be worse than the disease. This is particularly true in the relation of religion and politics.

The early Jews were under no temptation to equate their religion with the dominant politics of the time, since they were always the persecuted minority under attack, kicked this way and that, enslaved, imprisoned, bought, and sold. They could not have equated their Jewish faith with Pharaoh's politics even if they had wanted to. However, when they finally did establish a divinely approved monarchy of their own, generations later, things went to seed so rapidly that the dream of a society in which there was an equivalency between God's will and the king's decrees was a short-lived and ill-fated nightmare.

The early Christians, all originally Jews, were likewise a tiny minority at first, and it took four centuries before religion and politics became so intermingled as to be almost indistinguishable from one another. The Emperor Constantine, discovering that he couldn't lick the Christians, decided to join them and with a single stroke of the stylus made Christianity the "official religion" of the Roman empire. State policies now began to receive religious sanction, and wars of conquest were now fought under the sign of the cross. The taste for power was so heady that for a time even the papacy had an army and fought its own wars, likewise under the sign of the cross.

When Constantine's "Christendom" began to unravel, at the time of the Reformation, there emerged the extraordinary spectacle of Europe being divided into areas whose religious affiliations were determined by the religious affiliation of their king, on the principle of *Cuius regio eius religio* (meaning roughly that if a king is Lutheran his subjects are Lutheran, ditto a Calvinist, Catholic, or Anglican).

Calvin's rule in Geneva (which often gets a worse press than it deserves and included many social programs for the care of the sick and poor) was enforced by those fully persuaded that they knew the minutiae of God's will and could apply them to the minutiae of civil government. Michael Servetus, fleeing persecution in Catholic Europe because of his heretical views (he held that Jesus was *a* son of God but not *the* Son of God), was burned at the stake in Protestant Geneva, just as he would have been burned at the stake in Catholic Florence, in order that God's will be done.

Fanaticism, in other words, is not something from which religious people are automatically immune. Indeed, they are particularly susceptible. One can believe that religion and politics *do* mix without being persuaded that every "mix" is a good one.

This helps us understand the new situation in the United States. During the 1960s, when "liberal" Christians were involved first in civil rights demonstrations and later in protest over United States involvement in Vietnam, many "conservative" Christians challenged the appropriateness of such activities by invoking the familiar rubric, "Religion and politics don't mix." And yet, within a decade, many of the same conservative groups were lobbying, registering voters, and vigorously pushing political agendas of their own, such as prayer in the public schools, antiabortion legislation, and the need for a bigger defense budget. The earlier cry, "Religion and politics don't mix," was replaced by the claim that "Religion and *your* politics don't mix, but mine do."

The real issue goes: Since religion and politics *do* mix, what is the nature of the mix? What sort of religion, what sort of politics? A religion that claims, according to one Southern Baptist leader, that "God does not hear the prayers of the Jews" will have important political consequences, since if Judaism is a spurious religion, its adherents can appropriately be excluded from public office in the building of a "Christian America," an agenda dear to the hearts of many religious conservatives.

With this caution in mind, we can examine some attempts to overcome the Great Fallacy.

2

Attempts to Overcome
the Great Fallacy:
Plan A and Plan B

What we must reconquer and reform is our entire world. In other words, personal conversion and structural reform cannot be separated.

—Fr. Pedro Arrupe, S.J., 1975,
while head of the Jesuit order

We have a problem. We have discovered that we apparently live in two very different kinds of worlds, worlds that can be contrasted in at least thirty-five different ways. This renders us uncomfortable. We want lives that are unified rather than fractured.

In this situation we can do one of two things. (1) By neglect or caricature or outright annihilation, we can deny the legitimacy of one of the two partners in the discussion, thus procuring victory for the other. This tactic we will call Plan A, the reduction seduction, or the "nothing but . . ." approach. Or (2), we can acknowledge that there is sufficient truth in each position so that neither one can be disposed of as easily as proponents of Plan A propose, and that the wisest course will be to bring the two positions together, in order to combine their best features. This tactic we will call Plan B, the way of synthesis, or the "if you can't lick 'em, join 'em" approach.

Let us examine each plan in turn.

Plan A: The reduction seduction, a "nothing but . . ." approach

Concern for "spirituality" renders many people nervous, particularly when it is understood as something that "really religious" people have in abundance, so that those lacking it are felt to be religiously inferior. The natural reaction in the face of such a put-down is to want to devalue spirituality, to reduce it to "nothing but . . ." an unappealing caricature that need not be taken seriously. (This is a handy device in politics as well: e.g., "Capitalism is nothing but organized greed" or "Teddy Roosevelt was nothing but a jingoist.") The tactic may not be worthy, but it is widespread enough to require brief exploration. A particularly convenient put-down is to lump together everything in the practice of religion that seems distasteful, along with a few things that are exemplary, and define the result as "spirituality." William Stringfellow offers a marvelous example of this technique:

> "Spirituality" may indicate stoic attitudes, occult phenomena, the practice of so-called mind control, yoga discipline, escapist fantasies, interior journeys, an appreciation of Eastern religions, multifarious pietistic exercises, superstitious imaginations, intensive journals, dynamic muscle tension, assorted dietary regimens, meditation, jogging cults, monastic rigors, mortification of the flesh, wilderness sojourns, political resistance, contemplation, abstinence, hospitality, a vocation of poverty, nonviolence, silence, the efforts of prayer, obedience, generosity, exhibiting stigmata, entering solitude, or, I suppose, among these and many other things, squatting on top of a pillar.
>
> (Stringfellow, *The Politics of Spirituality,* p. 19)

As an accurate description of spirituality, this gallimaufry (look it up) surely misses the mark, as Stringfellow intended. But as an accurate description of the way many people view spirituality, this combination of a little truth and a lot of error is discouragingly on target.

Employing the "nothing but . . ." technique a little more systematically, we discover that those who want to discredit spirituality usually offer one or another or all of four overlapping charges:

1. *Spirituality is otherworldly.* It finds meaning in some world other than the world in which we dwell. It thereby encourages dualism (the Great Fallacy itself) by downgrading the importance of earth for the sake of heaven or exalting the sacred as superior to the secular. Thus it is escapist, for it promises salvation by extrication from the messy human condition rather than energizing us to clean up the mess.

2. *Spirituality is individualistic.* It represents the "privatization of religion" and ignores the communal dimension that relates human beings to one another. The focus is on God—a remote God somewhere else—who is to be sought singlemindedly without regard for the neighbor. It is *my* needs, the state of *my* soul, how *I* can get right with God that has priority.

3. *Spirituality is an endeavor often reserved for the elite.* It is the saints, the "holy" people, those who are withdrawn from the world, who can have the luxury of cultivating "spiritual" lives—monks, contemplatives, hermits, or people with sufficient material resources not to have to worry about where their next meal is coming from.

4. *Spirituality produces no impetus to work for change.* Since the world is evil to begin with, and salvation is found by escaping its clutches and getting attuned somewhere else, the important thing is to concentrate on that "somewhere else" and forget the world. As a result, people who are "into spirituality" aren't usually socially concerned. At best they support the status quo by default and take little or no responsibility for those who are being hurt by it, such as the two thirds of the human family who go to bed hungry every night.

If the above seems like a caricature, which it is, we need to remember that a caricature always contains enough truth to be worth attention. In order to be fair, however, we must expose "liberation" concerns to the same kind of scrutiny. In this area as well, the "nothing but . . ." approach has been employed in devastating fashion. Indeed, we can construct an almost mirror image of the appraisal of spirituality.

Concern for "liberation" renders many people nervous, particularly when it is understood as something that people who are really "with it" have in abundance, so that those lacking it are felt to be morally inferior. The natural reaction in the face of such a put-down is to want to debase concern for liberation, to reduce it to "nothing but . . . ," an unappealing caricature that need not be taken seriously. (This is a handy device in politics as well: e.g., "Socialism is nothing but a denial of individual human rights" or "Franklin Roosevelt was nothing but a Communist.") The tactic may not be worthy, but it is widespread enough to require brief exploration. A particularly convenient put-down is to lump everything in the practice of social concern that seems distasteful, along with a few things that are exemplary, and define the result as "liberation." Since William Stringfellow does not provide a second example of this technique, we will have to create our own.

> "Liberation" may indicate capitulation to atheism, a biblical perspective, gun-toting guerrilla priests, a "preferential option for the poor," horizontalist heresy, militant activism, reductionism, commitment to the revolutionary process, belief in praxis, dependence on social analysis, leaving the church or changing the church or using the church or destroying the church or redeeming the church or all of the above, prophetic realism, Marxism with a socialist veneer, socialism with a Christian veneer, naive utopianism, materialistic obsession, solidarity with the masses, class struggle, political engagement, belief in violence, creation of "base communities," mendacity, integrity, a willingness to die for justice, and a belief that God takes sides.

As an accurate description of liberation, this gallimaufry (did you look it up?) surely misses the mark. But as an accurate description of the way many people view liberation, this combination of a little truth and a lot of error is discouragingly on target.

Employing the "nothing but . . ." technique a little more systematically, we discover that those who want to discredit liberation usually concentrate on one or another or all of four overlapping charges:

1. *Liberation is this-worldly.* It reduces religion to ethics, and debatable ethics at that, glorifying violence and class struggle. It forgets the "vertical" dimension of relationship to God and concentrates exclusively on the "horizontal" dimension of relationship to people. It thereby encourages dualism (the Great Fallacy itself) by downgrading the importance of heaven for the sake of earth, or exalting the secular as superior to the spiritual. It uses concern for the here and now as a way to escape from God.

2. *Liberation is so communally oriented* it loses sight of the importance of the individual. It is willing to sacrifice persons for the sake of a future new social order. It replaces the Gospel of Mark with the gospel of Marx. The focus is so exclusively on the need for "systemic change" that individual personal conversion is downplayed and in the struggle for the "good society" God is ignored.

3. *Liberation becomes so much an endeavor by "the people"* that the contributions of those who are not part of "the masses" are not taken seriously. A reverse elitism operates. To be poor seems to be the prime qualification for social insight, and the rich (or even the moderately well off) are scoffed at. To know where one's next meal is coming from disqualifies one from being anything but an "oppressor."

4. *Liberation puts so much emphasis on impetus for change* that it leaves no place for the inner life. In a naive belief that the world can be radically transformed, proponents of liberation concentrate so much on external structures that they forget only changed people can create a changed society. Too much stress on the needs of the body leads to neglect of the needs of the soul. Until spiritual poverty can be overcome, the stress on human self-sufficiency will only lead to burnout and disillusionment.

Plan B: The way of synthesis; or, "If you can't lick 'em, join 'em"

It is unlikely that proponents on either side of the Plan A skirmish are going to emerge victorious. But the very form of setting out the argument offers another possibility, with more hope of leading to a creative resolution. Since each position possesses (with whatever attendant errors) a portion of the truth, and the two portions appear to provide a fuller whole than either one can provide by itself, surely the wise thing would be to draw truths from each into a comprehensive synthesis that will give us the best of both worlds. Plan B, therefore, might have two parts and look like this:

1. Spirituality is basic to the religious life, but it can be enriched by the contribution of liberation.

The only place we can really begin is with ourselves, with what is going on inside of us. If we haven't got our own act together, we are never going to be able to reach out and help others. It will simply be the blind leading the blind. We need to develop resources that will put us in touch with all that God can be for us, which means prayer and meditation and a disciplined devotional life. If we will take sufficient time to be open to the leadings of the Spirit—through the Bible, through the lives and examples of the saints, through times on retreat, through consultation with a spiritual director— God may be able to break down some of the walls we build to keep God out.

This is a long and arduous journey and one that will never be completed in our lifetimes, but it is absolutely essential to be on that journey, if we are to know who we truly are in God's eyes, and therefore in our own. Only in this way can we become instruments that God can use for the fulfillment of the divine purposes.

As long as we are seriously trying to keep our spiritual lives in order, then *of course* we must turn outward toward others, especially toward those in need, to share what we have found. We are not to share only one-on-one, or limit our concern to the spiritual lives of others. We need to explore the social implications of our faith, to deal with the physical as well as the spiritual needs of our neighbors, to find ways to join with them in their liberation struggles. We need to listen to them, as well as hope that they will listen to us, so that we can put our two different understandings of faith together in a whole that is more complete than either part can be alone.

But we must insist on the priority of the spiritual as the basis and resource out of which our social concerns can grow, and not succumb to premature and grandiose attempts to "change society" overnight. It is not the basic job of church or synagogue to change society. The basic job of church or synagogue is to create the individuals who can do so. A changed society will come as a result of the sustained efforts of changed individuals, and changed individuals will come to the extent that we cultivate the life of the spirit as our true contribution to human liberation. We must not succumb to the temptation T. S. Eliot describes in *The Rock,* of "dreaming of systems so perfect that no one will need to be good." We must keep insisting on the need to establish spiritual depth as a basis for all social change.

2. *Liberation is basic to the religious life, but it can be enriched by the contribution of spirituality.*

We live in the midst of a world that is really hurting. Unless we are willfully blind, we know that there are myriad problems confronting the human family, and unless they are solved pretty soon there will be no human family at all. We face a world of hunger, unemployment, child abuse, political tyranny, economic exploitation, torture, sexual harassment, and the specter of a nuclear war our political leaders seem willing to risk if our "national honor" is assaulted.

These and other threats are not going to go away unless we decide to attack them. Our task, therefore, is to become informed, find others who share our informed concerns, mobilize, and organize. Otherwise it will be the bland leading the bland.

It is morally indulgent to postpone our engagement in the liberation struggle until we feel good enough about ourselves to stop turning inward. We belong in the midst of the struggle. People who are dying have to be helped to stay alive; people who are hungry have to be empowered to find food and work. If we stand idly by in the midst of such situations, we become complicit in their ongoing misery.

As we are involved, *of course* we need to be open to, and actively seek, the kind of resources that the spiritual quest can furnish us. We need to discover ways in which a closer relationship to God can put us into a closer relationship with our neighbors. Indeed, if we fail to do this, the immensity of the social tasks will overwhelm us and we will become dispirited, discouraged, and potential or actual victims of burnout. So while we must not diminish our social passion, we need to deepen and enrich it by the contributions of spirituality.

But we must insist on the basic responsibility of all religiously minded people to be at work on the social scene, and not let the spiritual quest deflect us from that task. People can have all the spirituality in the world, but if they don't have food and clothing and shelter and medical care, not all the spirituality in the world can compensate.

Shortcomings of the synthesis

Shortcomings? Haven't we just bridged the gap between the two polarities? Hasn't the Great Fallacy been laid to rest? What is the matter with where we've gotten?

"Where we've gotten" is certainly better than where we were. We do not have so divided a world, and the two viewpoints have more in common than we imagined. I must confess that when I began thinking about the problem of spirituality and liberation, "where we've gotten" thus far in chapter 2 is where I anticipated we would be at the end of the book: spirituality and liberation are two different realities, but we have managed to relate them significantly to one another. Mission accomplished.

Unhappily for such anticipations, the mission has self-destructed and a further verdict is called for: *The Great Fallacy has not been overcome, it has been reinforced.* If Baudelaire was right that the devil's cleverest wile is to persuade us that he does not exist, the Great Fallacy's cleverest wile is to be present though undetected. For what we have done, however well-meaning our attempt, has been to accept the premise of the Great Fallacy—that there are two separate worlds to be brought together—work within the assumptions of that premise, and frame a conclusion confirming the Great Fallacy rather than displacing it. We remain walking examples of religious schizophrenia, engaged in an unending series of attempts to maintain a precarious balance between two warring elements.

This will not do. We cannot settle for a solution that merely restates the problem.

3

A Clarification: "Withdrawal and Return"

[Jesus] withdrew to the wilderness and prayed.
    —Luke 5:16

"Und now ve vill haf some yotz."
    —Albert Schweitzer
    to J. Seelye Bixler

[Persons] cannot be fully active except they be partly contem-
plative, nor fully contemplative (at least on earth) without
being partly active.
    —*The Cloud of Unknowing,* a fourteenth-century
    tract on spirituality

Let us try another tack. There is a long tradition, by no means confined to Christianity, that stresses the importance of "withdrawal and return." The tradition reminds us that it is sometimes important, and even necessary, to engage in "withdrawal" from the clutter and ambiguity of our day-to-day existence so that, by getting in touch with deeper realities that elude us in the everyday world, we can gain not only a new realization of who we are but a deeper realization of who God is—gifts we can then take back with us in our "return" to the immediate demands of life.

On the face of it, such a proposal seems to reinstate the Great Fallacy in spades, suggesting that there *are* two diverse realms between which we oscillate, and furthermore that the "other" realm is the really important one.

But let us not reach too premature a judgment. It may be that without reinforcing the Great Fallacy we can discover insights in the movement of "withdrawal and return" that help us relate spirituality and liberation more creatively.

Our experience

Albert Schweitzer, playing Bach on a piano in the Lambaréné forest for an American visitor, J. Seelye Bixler, realizes that even unrelieved Bach can become too much of a good thing and proposes, as a brief respite, an interlude of contemporary jazz ("yotz"), before returning to "The Well-Tempered Clavichord." Professor Bixler reports that the change of pace worked wonders in his appreciation of the concluding portion of the informal concert.

Living on a less elevated level than Bach partitas and fugues, the rest of us frequently need the refreshment of a fishing trip, or a World Series game, or a day off, or a vacation, or a movie with absolutely no redeeming social significance, simply to provide a time of relaxation before returning to the sterner stuff of daily life.

This is true of the overall rhythms of our lives as well, including the life of worship. There was great wisdom behind the provision in the Ten Commandments for a day of rest, the Sabbath, on which no work was to be done. Each week had six days for labor (a provision much of the world has since reduced to five), and the seventh day was designed to be devoted to the worship of God (a provision much of the world has since revised, transforming the "holy day" into a "holiday"). But in whatever use is made of the Sabbath, or "the long weekend," we see further examples of the principle of "withdrawal and return."

The biblical experience

The biblical accounts of withdrawal are many; the experiences of Moses and Jesus provide sufficient material with which to work.

Moses, who has "withdrawn" into the desert by himself

(not exactly by choice, since he is being sought in connection with a murder charge), is accorded the privilege of a theophany, or manifestation of God—a burning bush that is not consumed and from within which the voice of God is heard (Exodus 3). He is told to take off his shoes, for the place on which he stands is "holy ground." Later on, the same Moses, no longer solitary but leader of a vast throng, is called by God to a solitary mountaintop experience on Sinai, where he gets some orders directly from the deity's mouth.

The same pattern is present in Jesus' life. He frequently goes apart to pray: in the wilderness (Luke 5:16), on a mountaintop (Luke 9:28), in a garden (Luke 22:41), by himself (Luke 9:18), in the company of others (Luke 9:28). The most significant clarification of his mission occurs in the desert (Matt. 3:1–11), and the moment when his disciples discover who he really is comes when they have withdrawn to the far north to figure out their next steps (Matt. 16:13–20).

In all these biblical examples, the "withdrawal" is temporary; it is valuable in itself yet is also for the sake of "return." In Moses' case, the mystical experience of the burning bush is not an end in itself, for the voice in the midst of the bush orders him back to Egypt to persuade an unrelenting dictator to free the slaves. As for his mountaintop experience on Sinai, the purpose of the "withdrawal" is to enable Moses to "return" as the bearer of the Ten Commandments.

In the case of Jesus, each instance of "withdrawal" is the vehicle for a "return" to new levels of activity—healing lepers and epileptics, getting in trouble by claiming to forgive sins, creating a "movement" that is bound to get him in even greater trouble, clarifying his messianic vocation in disturbingly new directions, and confronting the secular authorities in Jerusalem in ways that lead to his being trussed up on the first-century equivalent of an electric chair.

These instances are reminders of an important truth: The "withdrawal" does not seem to be an end in itself but is for the purpose of "return." Moses does not stay on Mount Sinai thinking, Now that I've found God, I'll stay up here and build a condominium. He goes down the mountain to a scene that must have made him wonder if he didn't reject the

condominium option prematurely, for things have deteri-
orated badly in his absence and worshiping a golden calf has
become the top priority.

Nor does Jesus remain in the wilderness, or on the mountaintop, or in the garden. When he climbs Mount Tabor with
a few disciples and they are accorded a mystical vision, Peter
wants to stay there and, going Moses one better, suggests the
construction of *three* condominiums in which they can settle,
rather than going back down into a scary world. Jesus will
have none of it, and they return to a series of unpleasant
encounters that range from dealing with an epileptic boy (see
Luke 9:28–43) to getting impaled on a cross.

Arnold Toynbee, who deals extensively with withdrawal
and return in *A Study of History,* is right to underscore this
point. "A transfiguration in solitude can have no purpose
and perhaps even no meaning, except as a prelude to the
return of the transfigured personality into the social milieu
out of which he [or she] had originally come" (p. 217, Somer-
ville edition).

A single world seen two ways

But Toynbee is not fully right, and our discussion thus far
might suggest that true meaning, or God, is to be sought
preeminently in that other realm of "withdrawal" and
brought back into the immediate realm of "return." If so, it
would appear that the Great Fallacy has triumphed once
more. So two further clarifications are in order.

1. We must recognize that what happens in the experience
of "withdrawal" *can* have meaning in and of itself. That is
to say, it is not to be valued only in terms of its utility for
a subsequently invigorated life. It will no doubt have utility;
if we experience God's love despite our unworthiness, that
should lead us into a new love for persons, despite their
presumed "unworthiness" in our eyes. But whether or not we
respond to the divine love in that fashion does not negate the
ongoing reality of the divine love, however much it may
highlight the limitations of our human love.

2. The best way to understand "withdrawal and return," therefore, is to see it not as an oscillation between two different worlds, but as a way of *concentrating for a time on a part of the single world we inhabit.* That single world is too spacious in its totality for us ever to embrace it fully, even in our highest moments of ecstasy or our most earthy moments of immediate awareness. And so we try, from time to time, to bring certain parts of it into clearer focus, persuaded that the clarity achieved at one point will enable us to understand the whole more adequately. The traffic can go in many directions; a single act of human forgiveness may tell us something, hitherto hidden from our eyes, about compassion on a cosmic scale, while an act of adoration of God may unexpectedly stab us with the utter worthwhileness of a personal relationship we had been neglecting.

The point of "withdrawal and return," then, is not to "find God" somewhere else and bring God back into the here and now so that it may be invested with a meaning it did not previously have, but rather to engage in the exciting discovery that the God we thought was only "out there" is *already* "in here," and it was only our previous dimness of vision (or our sin) that kept us from such awareness. "Withdrawal and return" provides us with a fresh perspective on our world, seeing it from a different angle of vision, so that what is already here can be discerned more clearly than before. And since our vision is always faulty, the rhythm of "withdrawal and return" is an ongoing component of our lives.

A musical coda

My own experience of withdrawal and return comes not so much from retreats or long sessions of private prayer as from playing the cello, a form of spiritual exercise I regrettably did not begin to cultivate until my sixtieth birthday. There are occasions, however rare, when a phrase, or even a single note, is played well enough (perhaps even as the composer intended it) for me to experience a sense of spiritual fulfillment.

As I reflect on this specific experience in my own life, I find a number of analogies to the overall theme of withdrawal and return.

1. I frequently need reminding that the "spiritual" experience is not as withdrawn from everyday experience as I might think. A moment of musical beauty is impossible without the help of such mundane objects as a bow (made from the hairs of the tail of a horse) and strings (made from the entrails of deceased cats) over which I must draw the bow. Only in partnership with these earthy and aesthetically unappealing objects (horsehair and catgut) can beauty be created.

Score one for the unity of God's creation, not two worlds but one.

2. In the midst of a frenetic life, there is undeniable refreshment and renewal from putting the hectic pace on hold and becoming involved in something utterly different. Furthermore, I not only revel in those moments while they are happening, I have the further pleasure of anticipating them ahead of time and recalling them when they are over. They do not exist simply in themselves but in relation to what went before and what comes after. When I leave or reenter the pressure cooker of modern existence, it is with new resources that those moments apart have provided. While I do not desire to play the cello all the time (or at least not *quite* all the time), I am convinced that I can subsequently push a pen or operate a typewriter or relate to my grandchildren more creatively in the light of those musical moments than I would be able to otherwise.

Score another for the interweaving of the various aspects of God's creation.

3. I suggested that the moments of making music do not exist simply in themselves but in relation to what went before and what comes after. That is the truth, but once again it is not quite the whole truth. For, however infrequently they may occur, there are moments that *do* have meaning simply "in themselves," a meaning that is not dependent solely on serving the utilitarian function of gearing me up to speak more effectively at the next anti-*contra* rally. They have meaning not only because of what they are used for but also,

quite simply, because of what they *are*. It is good that we can occasionally create beauty as an end in itself, and we should rejoice when that opportunity is given us. It is an added grace when such moments, complete in themselves, can also nourish us for times when beauty will be far away unless we are its carriers.

Score yet another for the unexpected gifts that come to us in the midst of God's creation.

4. Although this particular musical withdrawal, like most withdrawals, begins in solitude (for demonstrably good reasons, I try to practice only when no one is home), it does not end in solitude. Playing alone, I soon discovered, was not enough; music is a communal experience and must be shared. So the next step was to find friends with whom to play, and I was graced to find a pianist and violinist who were close enough friends to tolerate my flagrantly amateur status. After some months of playing trios together, we made the communal discovery that it was not enough just to play for ourselves. We needed to play for others, not only to share what we had come to love but also because we needed the symbiosis, the interdependence and give-and-take that is part of what it means to be human: if we gave a little to them in playing, they gave much to us in listening and carried us along by the sheer fact of their presence.

Members of the Guarnari String Quartet (to leap into a totally different musical universe) have testified that they do not like to make recordings, because for acoustical purposes they must play in an empty studio where there is no audience response, no symbiosis, to carry *them* along, such as they receive in a live performance. There, too, individual experience (practice) leads inexorably to the need for communal experience (shared performance).

Score one finally for the fact that in God's creation, however solitary we may be at the beginning, we are drawn into community at the end.

TRANSITION

Meditation on Two Photographs

In the midst of the hectic presidential campaign in 1940, a relatively unknown candidate named Wendell Willkie challenged an unbeatable incumbent named Franklin Delano Roosevelt. Whatever Willkie's strengths or weaknesses, for one breathtaking moment he offered voters a new vision of reality, encapsulated in the title of his book *One World.*

Willkie's vision, farfetched at a time when World War II was being waged, was that we could no longer describe our situation by saying that we lived in a multitude of competing worlds—the world of American initiative, the world of resurgent German nationalism, the world of British colonialism, the world of emerging Russian power, the world of Asian aspirations for independence. However useful such terms were, they had become too provincial to communicate our actual situation—the fact that we were all part of *one* world, the world of shared humanity.

Almost half a century later, the vision still seems too farfetched to elicit wide acceptance, and yet, if anything has become clear between Mr. Willkie's time and our own, it is an increasing realization that whether we like it or not we *are* part of a single human family, and that our survival (or destruction) depends on how deeply, how radically, we appropriate that fact and take the new kinds of actions it demands of us.

In similar fashion, we have been looking at our lives as a struggle between two apparently competing worlds—for which the terms "spirituality" and "liberation" are descriptive—and we have discovered that we must find our own counterpart for a vision of one world rather than two or (as in Mr. Willkie's case) half a dozen.

So crucial is this transition to a new kind of perspective that we can receive our greatest initial help by moving to a different mode of communication, meditating on the two photographs in this chapter, one by Peter Brown and one by Mark Brown, which state visually what the rest of the volume will try to state verbally.

What we see initially in Peter's photograph of the wall is a wonderful play of light and shadow, delicate, almost unearthly. There are no recognizable "objects" to distract us, only random disembodied patterns with a minimum of structure, patterns that delight us by their ethereal quality. The photographer has ushered us into what many would call the realm of the spirit.

If that were the whole picture, we would feel unambiguously uplifted, grateful that for a moment we had transcended the petty stuff of our hectic daily lives and been marvelously nurtured—before the inevitable return to those hectic daily lives.

But that is *not* the whole picture. The photographer does not give us the luxury of such a painless aesthetic experience. Instead, alongside the visionary foreground he has included an excessively ordinary background, featuring that most banal artifact of our materialistic culture, a TV set. The only way to drive the point home more incisively would be to wire the photograph for sound, so that as we were looking at the beauty of the transfigured wall we were being forced to listen to . . . a deodorant commercial.

Faced with this disturbing juxtaposition, our initial reaction is surely: Why didn't the photographer crop off that jarring and intrusive left-hand sliver, thereby excluding the TV set, with its reminder of the banal, and allow us the "pure" enjoyment of unalloyed beauty?

The response, of course, is that he could have done so and chose not to. For to have done so would have been to falsify. The fact is that we do not get our beauty unalloyed, or our

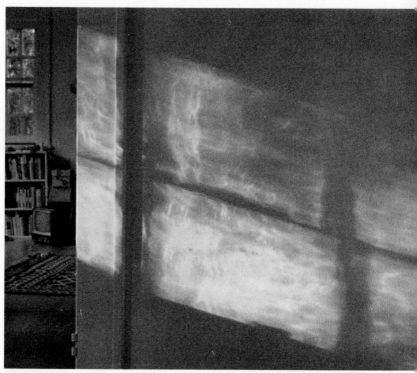

Peter Brown
Houston, Texas, 1979

ethereal experiences unsullied by "the world." To whatever
degree manifestations of the spirit are a possibility in our
lives, it is right in the midst of the world of TV sets and
deodorant commercials that such a possibility is located.
There is no "pure" realm into which we can flee. If we do
not have a complete picture by blocking out the disturbing
left-hand portion, no more can we have a complete picture
by blocking out the beneficent right-hand portion and pre-
suming to label either one of them "reality."

That may sound like bad news. But there is another side
to it. If the spirit can be experienced in the trappings of our
day-to-day world, then there is no place in that world in
which the reality of the spirit cannot appear. We can anticipate the possibility of such a presence wherever we are,
and—since the world is full of surprises—the presence may
be here one moment and somewhere else the next. Five
seconds after the photograph was taken, the wall may once
again have been an "ordinary" wall, devoid of the play of
light and shadow. Part of the trick of living, it would seem,
as well as of photographing, is to be on the alert for things
to happen when and where we least expect them.

There is yet another thing to learn. Most photographs are
counterparts of the left-hand portion only, which is, after all,
what cameras normally record. But after seeing this particular photograph, with its special reminder that the two portions comprise a single whole, we can see photographs of the
world of TV sets in a new way; they can remind us of what
the wall communicates to us, even without the presence of
the wall itself. A good photograph showing only what (since
our vocabulary limps) we call the "ordinary" world will
henceforth cause us to ponder: What lies behind it all?
Whence the particular color of the particular rock? Why
does the shade of blue in the sky cause us to rejoice? What
is the status of the beauty when no camera is recording it?
Why does recorded squalor fill us with resentment and recorded beauty have the capacity to bring tears to our eyes?

What happens in such cases is that we are led beyond the
photograph—or, better, *through* the photograph—to ponder
the meaning of our lives. It is "ordinary" things that intro-

duce us to the extraordinary realities, just beyond our view. The fullness of our lives includes the presence of the intangible within the framework of the tangible, so that we never have one without the other and come to realize finally that they are not two but one.

The second print, by Mark Brown (which is also a photograph but one that has been subjected to a series of darkroom and hand-drawn adaptations known as the photointaglio and relief printing processes), reminds us that when we see a photograph (or a statue or a painting), we do not simply receive from it, we also contribute to it. There is an interplay; the viewer must participate. Different viewers will, of course, see different things in this particular photograph, sometimes far beyond what the artist may have consciously intended.

My own reading of Mark's print, for example, is to see it as a nativity scene—a conviction that gradually emerged out of repeated viewings (and also, I imagine, because I am a theologian always looking for help wherever I can find it). I see a cast of characters assembled in some kind of overarching cave. They are very different—tall, short, nondescript— but there is a unity-in-difference because the scene has a focal point. We are not immediately sure what is happening at the focal point but, stimulated by an atmosphere of mystery in what the artist offers us, we can use our imaginations. We keep asking ourselves, "What is going on here?", for the lines are suggestive rather than definitional.

For me the focal point suggests a manger and a mother, with the rest of the folk straining to see. What I like best is a sense of ecstasy expressed by hands reaching up over heads in gestures of joy and abandon and maybe even gratitude. Something wonderful is happening, and they are caught up in its wonder.

Were we there, we might feel awed to silence, experiencing a joy too deep to utter, requiring physical gestures in place of sounds. On the other hand, the cave might also be ringing with our shouts and cheers, our uninhibited recognition that something of great moment and great goodness was happening, and we were just lucky enough to get in on it. "Joy to the world," we might all be singing, "the Lord is come!"

Mark Brown
In Waves of Dreams (State Two)

So much for speculation. What is the picture "actually"? What was going on when the shutter was snapped? I happen to know the answer to that question. What was going on when the shutter was snapped was that on a California beach on a Sunday afternoon a group of artists were holding on to the strands of a huge parachute that a cooperative gust of wind had just inflated for them.

This extraordinary disparity between the "actual" subject and the wealth of imaginative possibilities that the viewer can bring to bear on the subject is another instance of how life is all of a piece and not a lot of unrelated pieces. In theological language, this is sometimes called "the sacramental principle," which means simply that a piece of ordinary stuff can be the carrier and communicator of an extraordinary reality—"an outward and visible sign," as Augustine defined a sacrament, "of an inward, invisible grace." As we will explore later, "an inward, invisible grace" (forgiveness, empowerment, a sense of God's presence) can be communicated to us by "an outward and visible" and very ordinary sign (a piece of bread, a sip of wine, a drop of water). The same principle is operating here: The birth of God's Son is brought into view by a photograph of folks enjoying a fantastically successful beach party.

If bread can confront us with God's presence, parachutes and lenses and film baths can confront us with human (and divine) birth. By caprice, it seems, connections are made— not to pull two different worlds together but to remind us that there is only one world, a world we so frequently and falsely sever.

And who knows? Perhaps deliverance from that misunderstanding is finally not caprice but providence.

PART TWO

Clues for Construction

WHEREIN *the Great Fallacy is further interred by examining aspects of its denial in Jewish and Christian history that lead to the possibility of an alternative;*

WHEREIN *the alternative begins to take shape through an examination of the earthiness of both the form and the content of scripture;*

WHEREIN *the argument is advanced by recalling the story of God's involvement in the world of the flesh, as it is variously told in Judaism and Christianity;*

WHEREIN *the understanding of liturgy as encompassing all of life is acknowledged, and the sacraments ensure that "sacred" and "secular" remain inseparable;*

AND WHEREIN *the gift of sexuality is affirmed as inseparable from the gift of spirituality, and it is possible to anticipate drawing these discoveries together in Part Three.*

4

A Clue in the Confusion:
Scripture

The Hebrew word erets, *meaning earth, occurs at least five times as often in the Bible as the word* shamayim, *meaning heaven.*
         —Abraham Heschel,
         Israel: An Echo of Eternity

This is what Yahweh asks of you, only this: to act justly, to love tenderly, and to walk humbly with your God.
   —Micah 6:8
   Brueggemann, Parks, and Groome,
   To Act Justly, Love Tenderly, Walk Humbly

How does the Great Fallacy fare as a way of understanding scripture? Not well at all.

The earthiness of scripture

Some people who believe in the Great Fallacy assume that a "holy" book or a "sacred" scripture will be utterly different from all other books, exempt from the limitations of an earthly perspective, so lofty in its conceptions that it will direct our eyes away from earth toward heaven, from which it presumably descended in its present form.

The only ones who can sustain this illusion are those who do not bother to examine the book itself.

If they do bother, even for a few pages, they will suffer a

rude shock. For they will discover a very earthy hodge-podge—another gallimaufry, no less:

a little philosophy but not very much
a lot of gossip, rumor, and speculation
some lofty poetry and some turgid prose
more lofty poetry and some magnificent prose
too many genealogical lists
conflicting accounts of such important items as the creation of the world
a few saints alongside a rogues' gallery of stunning proportions
a collection of 150 sacred songs almost cheek by jowl with an erotic love poem
firsthand reports of military campaigns
visions . . . and dietary laws
exacting rules of behavior
generous promises of forgiveness and new life
snippets from personal letters
lengthy bits of correspondence
floating ax heads
exhortations
help for the beleaguered
challenges to kings
support for commoners
murder, rape, and adultery
consolation, hope, and incredible possibilities
boring legislation
consistent concern for the oppressed
myths . . . and census reports

In short, the Bible encompasses and illustrates *all* the dimensions of life—spirituality and liberation wrapped so deftly in a single passage that there is no conceivable way of separating them. This book has been cited as an authority for everything from burning people alive who were suspected of being witches to forgiving enemies and turning the other cheek when assaulted.

This is the book that Jews and Christians acclaim as the source of their knowledge of God. It is not a "spiritual" book confronting an "earthy" readership. It is as earthy as anything its readership could dream of, and then some. Conclusion: It is by means of a very human vehicle that God confronts us. No encouragement at all for the Great Fallacy.

The God of scripture, ". . . in our midst"

What is true of the structure of the Bible is true also of its message. That message is not about a remote God contemplating the divine essence in self-sufficient solitude, but about an active and vigorous God who is found in the midst of all those "earthy" things of which the Bible is so full.

The Greek gods, by contrast, could be described by the word *apatheia,* remoteness or disinterestedness, qualities we associate with our English word "apathy." The opposite of *apatheia* (arrived at in Greek by removing the initial letter) is *pathos,* which means to be active, engaged, involved. And the God of the Bible, rather than being a god of apathy, is the God of *pathos,* one who is "active, engaged, involved." Rabbi Abraham Heschel, who has written compellingly on this subject, defines the divine *pathos* as "combining absolute selflessness with supreme concern for the poor and the exploited" (*The Prophets,* p. 271).

There could be no better way to emphasize the Bible's repudiation of the Great Fallacy than such an understanding. On the one hand, it indicates God's presence in the midst of human struggle on behalf of victims, thereby demolishing any notion that God dwells exclusively in a separate "sacred" realm. On the other hand, it makes clear that the true index of belief in such a God will be the attempt of believers to embody that same quality of *pathos,* exhibiting in their own lives "supreme concern for the poor and exploited."

Where, then, according to scripture, is such a God found? The answer is unequivocal: right in the midst of what is happening on earth—siding with the Jews against Pharaoh; empowering a country boy, a "dresser of sycamore trees" named Amos, to get up in the busiest intersection of the city of Bethel and denounce the government for cheating the poor and exploited; placing a burden on everyone to give

special help to the "widows and orphans," the most oppressed and exploited people in the ancient world; making "a
preferential option for the poor" (as Roman Catholic bishops
in North and South America encapsulate the biblical message); prodding Nathan to call King David to account for
committing adultery; assuring Shadrach, Meschach, and
Abednego that they need not worship pagan gods even if a
fiery furnace is waiting just offstage; using the voice and life
of Jesus of Nazareth to point out that the way to serve God
is to serve those in need; using the pen and life of Paul to
empower people to believe that "neither death, nor life, nor
angels, nor principalities, nor things present, nor things to
come, nor powers, nor height, nor depth nor anything else
in all creation" can separate them from God's love, and that
in the face of promises like these they can throw themselves
into the human struggle with a little more trust and abandon
than they customarily display.

God's message is never: Turn away from the sinful world
and find me somewhere else. God's message is always: Im-
merse yourselves in this sinful world that so desperately
needs words and acts of healing, and you will find you are
not alone, for I am already there, summoning you to help me.

The Bible is a very earthy book because God is a very
earthy God.

The message of scripture, a new/old view of salvation

It can hardly be contested that the basic message of the
Bible is salvation. What *can* be contested is what it means
to say that the basic message of the Bible is salvation.

At least two important emphases in the biblical understanding of salvation have slipped through the cracks in most
contemporary discussion. The first is that salvation deals
with the *whole person,* not with some presumed "spiritual"
portion of the whole; and the second is that salvation is a
communal rather than an individual reality.

When someone approaches us and says, "Brother [or sis-
ter], are you saved?" the odds are high that neither of the
above biblical understandings is inspiring the query. The

question either translates into "What is the state of your soul?", with the clear implication that the state of your body is unimportant, or into, "How are things between you and God?", with the clear implication that how things are between you and your neighbor is unimportant. In either case, the questioner is exemplifying the Great Fallacy and reintroducing a dualism that is foreign to the biblical perspective.

These misunderstandings of salvation are so widespread that we must dig into the basic meaning of the word, in order to recover a more adequate biblical understanding.

The Latin root of our English word "salvation" is *salus, salutis,* and its basic meaning (to our initial surprise but eventual gratification) is "health" or "wholeness," along with derivative meanings such as "beneficial," "salutary," and "wholesome." (Salus, it is worth noting, was the goddess of public safety in ancient Rome, and anyone who has ever tried to weave through traffic in modern Rome has, however unknowingly, offered fervent supplications to this pagan deity for sheer survival.) The Hebrew word *yesha',* which we usually translate "salvation," has a similarly wide meaning, standing for such diverse things as happiness, wealth, prosperity, victory, and even peace.

It is this fundamental connection with "health" and healing that enables us to recapture the biblical understanding of salvation as dealing with the *whole person.* Paul Tillich, who has written widely on this point, sees salvation as the healing that overcomes brokenness and division within our lives: "Healing means reuniting that which is estranged, giving a center to what is split, overcoming the split between God and ourselves, ourselves and our world, as well as the splits within ourselves" (Tillich, *Systematic Theology,* vol. 1, p. 166, slightly modified; Chicago: University of Chicago Press, 1951).

Here is a perfect rendering of the fact that salvation is an overcoming of the divisions, the "splits" as he calls them, that the Great Fallacy perpetuates.

The New Testament does not talk about "spiritual" salvation, as though the salvation or health of the body were unimportant. Indeed, one of the distinguishing characteristics of Jesus' healing miracles is that they can be seen simultaneously as restoring physical health and manifesting the forgiveness of sins. To be concerned about human salvation in a biblical sense, therefore, means to be concerned not only about what is usually called "the state of the soul" but also with whether or not the persons involved have soles on their shoes.

The other misunderstanding of salvation is just as much in need of correction. This is the assumption that we are "saved" when we have worked out a private relationship with God. It cannot be contested that relationship with God is at the heart of the meaning of salvation, but it must be insisted that such a relationship is achieved *in community*—community as the milieu in which new health or wholeness is received, and community as the milieu in which the new life is lived out in relation to the neighbor.

The Bible does not tell us that God bestowed salvation on individuals—on Abraham or Sarah or Amos or Deborah—and then moved those individuals into a community. On the contrary, the Bible tells us that God called a people, a community, into covenant relationship, and that individuals—Abraham or Sarah or Amos or Deborah—found the fullness of who they were by virtue of relationship to that community.

That is not, of course, the end of the road but only the beginning, for experiencing salvation in this way carries with it the responsibility of reaching out to others in ways that both image and nurture the newfound wholeness. When Jesus challenges the unscrupulous Zacchaeus, a functionary of the Palestinian Internal Revenue Service, to mend his ways, Zacchaeus does not say, "I now see the error of my ways so I'll go on a retreat and start developing a rich prayer life," though somewhere along the line that might be a good idea. Instead, he says, "Lord, I realize I've been ripping off the people with this little tax racket of mine, so what I'll do is give every one of them a four-hundred-percent return on what I extorted from them in the first place."

And it is only when Jesus sees this recognition by Zacchaeus that his relationship to God means a new relationship to the community, based on justice and the restoration of stolen property, that he says, "Today salvation *[sic]* has come to this house" (Luke 19:9).

Putting the spotlight on Micah 6:8

The diverse strands we have been collecting can be woven into a single pattern, thanks to the major contribution of a minor prophet named Micah. The adjective "minor" is a quantitative rather than a qualitative judgment; the biblical prophets are classified as "major" or "minor" according to the extent of their productivity, which is a long way of saying that Micah wrote a short book. By any qualitative measurement, however, Micah is definitely in the big time.

Micah is a small-town boy from a farm about twenty-five miles southwest of Jerusalem. As he grows up, things are falling apart both domestically and internationally—a state of affairs that almost always inspires someone to prophetic utterance. Not only is the powerful Assyrian empire breathing down the neck of every country on the horizon of the ancient world, Palestine included, but back on the farm Micah has discovered that the city folks are grabbing power and defrauding the peasants as agribusiness takes over the small farms—a baleful story he recounts in some detail in the early chapters of his book. As a result, the rich are getting richer and the poor are getting poorer. Injustice rules not only in the marketplace and the law court but in the houses of worship as well, where everyone is trying to bargain his or her way into God's favor by the cheapest possible route. Overt bribes, sharp maneuvers, and sneaky calculations are the order of the day, with the inevitable result that human relationships are shattered in the process.

Micah is not pleased with this state of affairs, and he has good reason to believe that God is not pleased either. So Micah and God begin to collaborate. They make quite a team.

At the beginning of chapter 6, our focal point, Micah joins the issue through the imaginative device of summoning Israel to stand trial in the court of the Almighty. Interestingly enough, the mountains and the hills are designated as judges in the assize, an ominous foreboding for those today who commit ecological rape against the environment without fear of reprisal. There will, apparently, be a similar day of judgment for them as well.

Throughout the preceding chapters of Micah's book, a relentless and devastating case has been built up against Israel, so that it is no surprise to be informed that "the Lord has a controversy with [Israel]" and will bring an accusation against the people (v. 2). What is surprising is the yearning, almost gentle voice with which God mounts the accusation. No fire and brimstone here, but rather a grieving deity who has lavishly poured out love only to have it repudiated. There is a swift historical review—all the way from leaving Egypt to entering the land of promise, in two breathless verses— that centers on Israel's *failure of memory.* Israel has forgotten "the saving acts of the LORD" (v. 5). Remember . . . remember . . . is the theme of these verses. They stand almost as a paraphrase of George Santayana's remark that "Those who cannot remember the past are condemned to repeat it." And since it is clear that Israel has *not* remembered, certain consequences are bound to follow, if a verdict of guilty is returned by the court.

The mood changes as the accused respond (vs. 6–7). They do not try to deny the charge. Their tactic is as old as the earliest court of law: Can we bribe the prosecutor? Can we buy off the one who is bringing the charges? Everyone has a price; what is God's? Maybe we can settle out of court by offering our best calves for sacrifice, thousands of sheep instead of hundreds, endless streams of olive oil rather than a few jars, the sacrifice of our firstborn sons in exchange for having the charges dropped.

It doesn't work. There must have been a resounding "No!" that shook the rafters of the court. And hard on its heels, an alternative is proposed. Its bite has been dulled to our ears by over-familiarity; everybody knows Micah 6:8. So let us approach this verse as though for the first time and bring to it our particular question: What does it say to us about spirituality and liberation?

"You are confused about what has gone wrong, and how to set it right?" the prophet asks. "Then listen. This is what Yahweh asks of you, only this: to act justly, to love tenderly, and to walk humbly with your God" (Micah 6:8, adapted).

This is not the outline for an article in *Reader's Digest* entitled "Three Easy Steps on the Way to Moral Rehabilitation." The prophet is *not* saying, "God asks three things of you. First, you are to act justly. Second, you are to love tenderly. And third, you are to walk humbly with your God."

What *is* the prophet saying? A helpful way to explore this question is to return to the musical image of theme and variations. A composer will often present a theme, usually a fairly simple melody, and then follow it up with a series of variations in which the theme, still recognizable, is presented in a sequence of different forms: in a minor key, in syncopated rhythm, in the bass clef with musical embroidery above it, and so on. When the piece has been completed, the original theme has a richness and depth we had not previously recognized.

Applied to the Micah passage, the analogy at first appears to limp badly, for while we clearly have three discernible variations, Micah seems to have forgotten to clue us in on the overall theme itself. We can turn this apparent liability into an asset, however, by noticing that any one of the three phrases can serve as the overall theme, with the other two phrases serving as variations. We do not have *three different assertions* being made, but one assertion being made in *three different ways*.

A strange but compelling logic is at work here. We cannot talk significantly about any one of the three phrases until we have talked about all three of them; and yet by the time we have talked about all three of them, it is sufficient to talk

about any one of them, since we now perceive that it includes
the other two.

Put visually:

To act justly = to love tenderly = to walk humbly with God.

Or another way:

> *to act justly* means to love tenderly and to walk humbly with
> God
> *to love tenderly* means to walk humbly with God and to act
> justly
> *to walk humbly with God* means to act justly and to love
> tenderly

Any starting point will do, so long as it is clear that the
starting point will make no sense until its meaning includes
the other concerns as well.

We could decide that *to act justly* is the place to start, a
"liberation" concern if there ever was one. But acting justly
is not possible unless we also *love tenderly,* for justice without
love is cold and harsh and can unwittingly be the vehicle of
fresh injustices (out of a concern for justice for everybody,
one might say to an individual, "I will decide what is best for
you"). Empowerment to act justly and love tenderly comes
from *walking humbly with God,* the God whom we know to
be precisely a God of love and justice, in whom our own
commitments to love and justice must be grounded if they
are to avoid becoming instruments for our own power and
domination over others.

Or we might decide that *to love tenderly* is the place to
start, since love is always the bottom line of a truly creative
life. But we would soon discover that loving tenderly is not
possible unless we also *act justly,* since love without justice
is sentimental and naive; we can hardly be said to "love"
victims of economic deprivation if we are not working to
create economic structures in which their exploitation will
no longer be possible. And even with the best will in the
world, such attempts will founder unless we believe that love
and justice are at the heart of things, grounded in a God

whose very nature is to act justly and to love tenderly, things we are likewise empowered to do as we *walk humbly with God.*

Finally, lest it seem that the God part is only an add-on, we could decide that *to walk humbly with God* is the place to start—a concern of spirituality if there ever was one. But if we take seriously what that means, we will find that instead of removing us from the world, such a commitment will engage us where God is, in the midst of contemporary events, as we discovered earlier in this chapter. Furthermore, the God with whom we seek to walk humbly is the God of justice who therefore empowers us *to act justly,* and the God of love who therefore desires us *to love tenderly.* And since love and justice are not two separate things in God's life, they cannot be two separate things in our lives either. So to walk humbly with God is the equivalent of acting justly and loving tenderly, and they, in their turn, are equivalents of each other. Full circle.

There is a lot of repetition in the above three paragraphs. That is exactly as it should be, since they are all talking about the same thing. Which is the whole point.

The Great Fallacy cannot even get a toe in the door.

The introduction to the verse provides a conclusion to the chapter: "This is what Yahweh asks of you," Micah begins, "*only this.*"

First reaction: relief. Micah has pared everything down to three lines, and we have pared the three lines down to one idea. How splendid to have achieved simplicity in the midst of such apparent complexity.

We had better enjoy the relief while we can, however, for it is likely to be short-lived. The most exacting demands usually come in the smallest packages: "Don't be frightened," "Love your enemies," "Be faithful to your spouse," "Be perfect as God is perfect." Augustine got it down to six words: "Love, and do as you please," which sounds like a cinch until we reflect that if we *do* "love," many of the things we would otherwise "please" to do are now out-of-bounds.

So also with Micah. If the "only" thing we have to do is, let us say, to love tenderly, that is easy counsel only until we are tempted (perhaps five minutes from now) to love exploitatively or (perhaps before reading the next paragraph, which is coming up *very* soon) confront someone whom it is difficult for us to love at all, let alone tenderly.

So the passage is no simple shortcut to sanctity. But it is a base from which we can go forth and make our stumbling efforts, and to which we can return when we have stumbled once too often and need to check our directions afresh.

5

The Clue Comes to Clarity: Incarnation

By virtue of the Creation, and still more of the Incarnation, nothing here below is profane for those who know how to see.
—Teilhard de Chardin

The Word became flesh and pitched his tent in our midst.
—John 1:14, adapted

We found this man subverting our nation, opposing the payment of taxes to Caesar, and calling himself the Messiah, a king.
—Luke 23:2–3, NEB, adapted

We have discovered that the Bible is an earthy book because its subject, God, is an earthy God, present "in our midst," in the here-and-nowness of our lives. That is a considerable claim, and we must spell it out in more detail.

The goodness of creation

In the Hebrew scriptures, the claim that God is "in our midst" emerges out of the struggle of the Jews to make sense of their own history, with its frequent tragedies and its infrequent triumphs. Over the centuries they became persuaded that the God who was part of their ongoing life—"in the midst" of droughts, wars, deportations, and forced marches through the desert—had created the world in which that ongoing life took place. This was a speculative conclusion (nobody was on hand to observe the creation of the world), reached after centuries of living and dying. Our natural inclination is to assume that since the creation stories come first in the Bible, they must have come first in Hebraic reflection about God. But a good author, we need to remember, often writes the first chapter last.

The affirmation of God as Creator is a late development in Jewish reflection about God, but it is an affirmation that has persisted, centrally and powerfully, ever since. In our own discussion, this means at least three things. It means that since creation is God's handiwork, *creation is good* rather than evil; that since creation is God's handiwork, *God loves it* rather than despising it; and that since creation is God's handiwork, *clear signs of God's activity will be found within it.*

What these claims have in common is a repudiation of the Great Fallacy. Creation is *not* evil, so we must not downgrade it; creation is *not* repudiated by God, so we must not repudiate it either; creation is *not* devoid of God's presence, so we must not turn away from the world to find God. On the contrary, God is seeking us within creation.

This message, firmly lodged in the Hebrew scriptures, has had continuing vitality in all strands of postbiblical Judaism. One such strand, the Hasidic movement of Middle European Jewry, is especially insistent that witnesses to God's ongoing presence can be found everywhere. It is only a matter of knowing where to look. Elie Wiesel writes:

> Every woodcutter may be a prophet in disguise, every shoemaker a Just Man [one of the thirty-six who, according to Jewish tradition, preserve the world from destruction], every unknown the Ba'al Shem [the founder of Hasidism] . . . A shepherd plays a tune—the Ba'al Shem relates him to King David. A stranger in rags provokes laughter—the Master refers to him as Abraham.
>
> (Wiesel, *Souls on Fire,* p. 33)

Such claims illustrate the basic message of Hasidism, Wiesel insists, that "God is not indifferent, and man is not His enemy" (*Four Hasidic Masters,* p. 15). We are to love God by loving one another. To celebrate humanity is to celebrate God. "Who loves, loves God" (*Souls on Fire,* p. 31).

Such claims are based on a belief that the world, as God's creation, is good, that God is still at work within it, and that God calls on us to affirm creation's possibilities and keep it going, since the creation process did not come to a halt after the six days of intense divine activity recorded in Genesis.

Conclusion: Life here and now has fantastic possibilities.

The messianic hope

But to lots of people the whole idea seems farfetched. The created order, they point out, is a far cry from being "good." It is a mess. Evil, rather than good, is in the saddle. How can Jews, history's most targeted victims, be so naive?

Naive the Jews are not. Nor are they blind to the dark side of history, since they experience more of it than any other people on earth. They realize early on that the anomalies, the contradictions, the defeats, are not going to be overcome by closing their eyes to evil or assuming that with just a bit more effort they can push it off the scene.

Recognizing that they are called to struggle mightily on the human scene, they also see with utmost realism that if there is going to be redemption for a world which, if once good, is now evil, that redemption will finally be God's doing rather than theirs. And so hope begins to take root in the ashes—hope in an "anointed one" whom God will send to set things right, a *māshīah* (rendered in English as "messiah").

There are centuries of conjecture about what the messiah will be like. Some insist on a warrior king who will annihilate the hosts of wickedness; others anticipate the return of King David or, at the very least, someone who springs from the Davidic line; a few believe that an idyllic pastoral shepherd type can transform the aforesaid hosts of wickedness into forces for good; and later on, the initially curious notion of a "suffering servant" messiah makes its way into the tradition.

For the moment, however, the fact *that* a deliverer will

come is more important than exactly *who* or *what* the deliverer will be like. The promise is that "the anointed one," in whatever guise, will enter into the human situation to *transform* it, rather than leading his followers (after the fashion of the Pied Piper of Hamelin) away from the messiness of history. The messianic hope is a long-shot gamble that the mess can be cleaned up, and that God cares enough about the place where the mess has accumulated to send a messiah to work right there for its transformation rather than its destruction. Instead of scrapping the created order as a divine miscalculation, creation will be remade.

Bad news to believers in the Great Fallacy, who have already written off the created order and started looking elsewhere. But potentially good news to everybody else.

The incarnation

Things frequently get so bad in Jewish history that belief in the imminent coming of the messiah reaches a fever pitch. A group of Jews see an individual stride onto the scene so powerfully and appealingly that they think, The messiah has come at last! In almost every case, the hope is dashed: the presumed messiah gathers no followers, or his ideas go sour, or he is rudely defeated, or he turns out to be a charlatan.

On one occasion, however, a tiny group of Jews gathers around an itinerant rabbi—much like themselves, without significant schooling or cultural polish or connections in high places—and even though he meets a tragic end after a couple of years of public life (the political authorities execute him as a "subversive"), the manner of his life, the nature of his teaching, and a conviction that not even death can destroy him convince this handful of friends and associates that he is indeed the messiah they have been waiting for. His name is Joshua ben Josef or, as we now say, Jesus, son of Joseph, and they increasingly feel that in the life of this teacher from the boondocks of Nazareth—a life that includes tears and hunger and disappointment and betrayal—God has been incarnate.

The word "incarnate" is key. What it means is stated in the prologue to the Fourth Gospel, which contains some real surprises. It starts out nonthreateningly enough with an abstract claim that "In the beginning was the Word," "Word" being an unfortunate translation of the Greek *logos. Logos* is a word that has had many meanings. To first-century readers living in a Greek culture—the Gospel's most likely target—it seems to have represented a mediating principle between the eternal realm of goodness and the temporal realm of evil. If so, the Gospel's readers were in for some surprises, for the author immediately claims that the *logos* was not only "with God" but "was" God. And after several verses of equating the activity of the *logos* with the activity of God, the author then takes an unexpectedly new tack and asserts unequivocally that the *logos* became flesh and pitched his tent in our midst (John 1:14), which means that the *logos* took up habitation among us, became like us, shared our plight.

Nothing could have been more shocking to the first readers of the Fourth Gospel. Believing that the world was impure and that "flesh" was the seat of its impurity, they could not have conceived of anything divine becoming "flesh." And yet that is exactly what the author of the Fourth Gospel asserts. The Latin word for "flesh" is *carnis* (from which we get words like "carnivorous," meat-eating or flesh-eating, and "carnal," which we associate with "desire," which, when preceded with "carnal," we associate with the risqué). Incarnation means "in the flesh," and to say that God was incarnate is to say that God was "in the flesh"; that is, in a human life fully like ours, no exemptions granted.

Incarnation, in other words, is not about a divine masquerade, in which God appears to live a human life but really doesn't. It is about a God who is found in the midst of life in the flesh, in a human life like ours, subject to all our limitations, frustrations, and anxieties. We need not seek God elsewhere, for God has already sought us right where we are.

So we can no longer speak of God without speaking of humanity, since it is in a human life that we see God most clearly; and we can no longer speak of humanity without speaking of God, since humanity is where God's tent is pitched.

This claim that the messianic hope was fulfilled in Jesus of Nazareth divides Christians and Jews, and we must take note of the tragic history that has resulted.

The first "Christians" were a tiny group of Jews who gave Jesus the title of "Messiah" (for which the Greek equivalent is "Christos"). Most first-century Jews did not share this belief, and the Christians soon turned to the Gentile world to expand their fellowship. But as soon as they began to get a little clout on the political scene, they started making things extremely rough for Jews who did not agree with them. In the name of one who came preaching love, they practiced hate, calling Jews "Christ killers," a "deicide race," "apostates," and a good many other things less esoteric and more blunt. They subjected Jews to ghetto life, torture, forced conversion, and death.

This is a scandalous legacy. Not only must Christians repudiate it, but they must begin to look at the relation of Jews and Christians to the messianic claim in a new way.

Jews and Christians still share a messianic faith. That has not changed. What has changed is that (if one may so put it) they now have different timetables: Christians await the "second coming" of a messiah who for Jews has not yet appeared once.

Jews have waited millennia for a messiah. Their ongoing, agonizing question is, "Since the world is so evil, why does the Messiah not come?" With every reason to give up hope, they persist in affirming that, though he may tarry, yet will they wait for him.

Christians have frequently responded to Jews in the following manner: "You have a problem? Fortunately for you we have a solution to your problem. The Messiah *has* come. All you need to do is become Christians and believe the good news." This approach has led to an escalating Christian "triumphalism" that finally ends up vilifying Jews for their persistent disbelief.

Christians are not entitled to operate this way. For if Jews have a problem with messianic faith, so do Christians. The traditional Christian "answer" engenders a question of its own, the opposite of the Jewish question, that goes: "Since the Messiah has come, why is the world so evil?" Christians have assumed that the cosmos got tidied up around A.D. 30 and that the message ever since has been one long victory communiqué. Christians need to learn that the redemption of the world is not so evident to Jews (and many others) as it apparently is to some Christians. "We taste its lack of redemption on our tongues," states Martin Buber.

There are no cheap triumphal choruses for Christians—or for God. Auschwitz put an end to them. So, long before, did the first unjust death of a child.

Jesus of Nazareth

The claim *that* there was an incarnation is a further nail in the coffin of the Great Fallacy. But we must press on to explore briefly *who* was incarnate and *what* the incarnate life was like.

Let us suppose for a moment that we do not know the Jesus story, and that we are asked in what kind of life we would expect an incarnation of God to take place. We would be likely to assume that it would occur in the most impressive manner possible, in someone well enough placed in public life to assure maximum exposure to the claim, and in a place where the most people with the most influence could spread the word around.

But according to the biblical story, it didn't happen that way at all. Jesus was born in a tiny town off the beaten track, in a barn rather than a hospital. His mother was under suspicion of having had an affair, and it was rumored that his "father" was not the biological father; the "parents" came from a working-class background, and both of them were Jews, a scattered group well toward the bottom of religious census charts. Not a very prepossessing set of claims.

Consider now the cover of this book and ask, "Where are the signs of God's presence in the picture?"

Some might respond, "In the beautiful world of nature—the lake, the cloud-flecked sky, the islands, the invisible power of the wind that the sailboat suggests."

Someone with an eye to symbolism might respond, "In the bird flying in the sky, a dove, symbol of the Holy Spirit."

Another, sensitive to a different kind of symbolism, might say, "In the carpenter's square on the post, which represents the order and stability of God's universe."

Still another, schooled in certain ways of picturing God, might respond, "In the man with the beard, who is obviously in charge of the whole operation and is issuing the orders."

Hardly anyone would be inclined to answer, "In the little kid with the long hair, sandals, purple shorts, and T-shirt." The idea seems almost offensive.

Add the further "offense" that the scene of the painting is Nicaragua—the land to which an American President has sent massive shipments of arms that kill children like the child in the picture—and we get a further sense of the way the Jesus story breaks the limits of anything we can anticipate or control. About the only thing that could make the story more unlikely would be to portray the Messiah as a woman—as does a gripping modern portrayal of the crucifixion entitled *Christa*. And if that proposal seems farfetched to some people today, we need to reflect that it is no more farfetched than the proposal that the Messiah was the son of a Jewish carpenter seemed back then.

The Messiah did not come in the way people expected. Anybody writing the script in the first century would surely have done it differently. There would have been none of this "particularity" of a Jew, a working-class type, a man getting hungry and thirsty. There would have been a messiah who transcended all that, who was exempt from suffering and change, as befits a god, who gave gentle maxims and helped people immunize themselves against the hurts and passions of the world—a reassuring phantom from another world who could give directions for shedding this world and entering the one from which he came.

In the face of such a proposal, there is one thing of which we can be sure: The kid in the carpenter's shop is not an otherworldly phantom; when he misses the nail and hits his finger with the hammer, it hurts. And when it becomes clear to him, about thirty years down the line, that he has some kind of special mission to perform, he is simply himself so fully that God can be seen through who he is and what he does. People see a rabbi who somehow personifies the God he talks about—a God who forgives, a God who heals, a God who comforts, a God who chastizes, a God who challenges, a God who gives, a God who shares the human lot. That single unified life is not a fusion of two dissimilar things but an integrated whole. All that we mean by "spirituality" at its best is present in him; all that we mean by "liberation" at its best is present in him, and they cannot be separated. This is a consistent pattern throughout his ministry. For example:

1. Early on, Jesus and his followers come to a field of grain. They are hungry. But it is the Sabbath. A dilemma: No work can be done on the Sabbath, and plucking grain counts as "work"—a splendid occasion to drive home a "spiritual" lesson about the observance of ritual law. But Jesus, who believes that human beings are "the temple of God," tells his followers to fill their stomachs, Sabbath or no. Seeking to explain this unforeseen decision, Frei Betto, a Brazilian priest, comments:

> There is nothing more sacred than [a person], the image and likeness of God. The hunger of [a person] is an offence to the Creator.... A religion that cares for the supposed sacredness of its objects but turns its back on those who are the real temples of God the Spirit, is worthless.
>
> (Betto, *Fidel and Religion,* pp. 53–54)

2. Midway through his ministry, during a "retreat" of five thousand people, far from any supermarkets or delicatessens, it is suddenly suppertime and everybody is ravenously hungry, particularly the kids—a great opportunity for Jesus to say something like, "Let us ask God for strength to rise

above our rumbling stomachs and show our true devotion to 'the things of the spirit' by fasting all night long." But instead of such an exhortation he enlists the help of the kids and busies himself with finding ways to provide an evening meal.

3. Almost at the end of his ministry, Jesus gathers his closest followers in an upper room for the celebration of the Passover. How should they prepare for such a time of solemn worship? Prayer, meditation, fasting, interior examination are traditional exercises. Which does Jesus propose? None of the above. Instead, he gets a towel and a basin of warm water and makes the rounds of the room, washing the dirty, smelly feet of sandal-shod disciples who moments before had been walking through dust and donkey dung—a demeaning task that must have seemed curiously out of keeping with the exalted service of worship that lay just ahead.

Since we don't *wash* feet in public anymore, the closest analogue in our experience would be to massage the feet of our dinner guests, or do whatever else was appropriate for their physical comfort. Whatever we did, it would indicate that nothing is so important that physical realities lose their importance. "At the end of his life," as Juan Luis Segundo puts it, "Jesus found nothing of greater value than to kneel at the feet of these poor men, his friends" (Cited in Alfred T. Hennelly, *Theologies in Conflict,* p. 148; Maryknoll, N.Y.: Orbis Books, 1979).

Dealing with cracked toes becomes an act of worship.

These three randomly selected examples from Jesus' ministry all turn out to involve food. Joseph Grassi can go so far as to say of one of the Gospel writers, "Luke is almost obsessed by the centrality of food and drink in the ministry of Jesus" (*Broken Bread and Broken Bodies,* p. 55). We can go farther than that: The whole Bible shares this "obsession," from the disastrous eating of the fruit of the tree of the knowledge of good and evil, in the book of Genesis, to the final triumphant messianic banquet in the book of Revelation. The highest moment in the worship of God comes when bread and wine are passed around. And one of the ultimate tests of an authentic life, according to Jesus' moral calculus, is whether or not we gave food to the hungry person.

This unwillingness to separate the human being into two parts ("body" and "soul," or "spirit" and "flesh") is evident not only in what Jesus did but also in what he said. Both the *way* he taught and *what* he taught illustrate this, as we discover in his teaching about God's realm.

Jesus' *way* of talking about God's realm, particularly in his parables, does not involve his saying, "If you want to understand God's realm, close your eyes and turn your back on the world, since it can only confuse your vision. Put out of your mind all the images of ordinary living, and then maybe you can get an inkling of what I'm talking about."

His method is just the opposite. The images he uses to describe God's realm are always drawn from the world around him:

> God's realm? Well, imagine yourself getting all geared up to buy a piece of real estate. Remember how that feels? . . . And that widow down the block who thought somebody had stolen her Social Security check. Remember how happy she was when it turned up? . . . And that father in Perth Amboy whose youngest son flew the coop and blew the whole trust fund, principal *and* interest, that his father had created for him. Remember how the father used to go down to the bus terminal every day, just to see if by chance his son had returned? And how ticked off the older brother was when his younger sibling did return, flat broke, and the old man threw a party for him? . . . And remember that middle-management executive trying desperately not to get fired, by doctoring the books, currying favor with the boss in order to avoid a hostile takeover? We can learn even from that misguided zeal.

If it's clues you want about the nature of God's realm, Jesus tells us, start looking right in front of your noses, because it is out of the bits and pieces of what you find there that you'll get whatever clues there are. So take it seriously, he might go on, when you see people reunited with children they thought they had lost forever, or when someday, somewhere, somebody—maybe even you—recovers something precious that had gotten lost, or you put the leftover Chablis in the bottle of Chenin Blanc and it doesn't work. The pointers don't mean that God's realm has come in all its fullness, but they do mean that it is breaking in here and there—and that when it *does* come in all of its fullness, those pointers will turn out to have been the best previews in town. Never forget, he might conclude, that you saw it here first, in the kitchen or out in the garage or just around the corner.

Even more important than the *way* Jesus taught is *what* he taught. The content reinforces the claim that God's realm, like God, is "in our midst." From the moment in Mark's Gospel when Jesus bursts abruptly onto the scene, he has stunning news on his lips. First recorded utterance: "God's realm is at hand," which can also be translated: "is in your midst," "has broken in," "is right here and now." The world isn't suddenly transformed into God's realm the moment he speaks those words, but from that moment on the world has to be looked at in a new way, not as alien territory to be shunned or only warily entered but as a homeland to be embraced in joy, since it is the arena of much more than meets the eye, and all the ordinary things going on around us are full of a significance we had not previously imagined. Joan Chittister captures the new mood perfectly in the *National Catholic Reporter:* "The journey to God becomes less a process of tiptoeing through a minefield in snowshoes, and more a pilgrimage in spring."

"You want to talk about God's realm," somebody back then might tell us, "then talk about sheep, or widows, or wineskins, or patched-up coats, or people working on a construction job. The signs are all around you. Open your eyes! Open your ears! Open your hearts!"

That's not the whole message, of course. God's realm is not just an extension of our realm, presented in living technicolor on a wide screen. For the other side of the message is that the further creation of God's realm is a vast reconstruction project, already under way, in which we are God's concern. Jesus did not come to bless our failings, but to let us in on the ground floor of what one of his later followers called "a more excellent way." The word in Mark after the announcement that "God's realm is at hand" is "Repent!", which means, "Turn about, start all over again, make a clean break with the past." There is a shattering as a condition of rebuilding.

We need to notice one other troubling thing about the message Jesus brings. Who are the people to whom the good news is particularly directed? The answer can only be sobering to people who read (and write) books like this, for the message is particularly directed to the poor, the outcast, the people who have AIDS, the laid-off workers, the women, the folks on welfare. They all appear likely to make it into God's realm considerably before the rest of us. Rich young rulers are also welcome, of course, but some strings are attached to their entrance; they—read "we"—have more encumbrances to get rid of first.

Our carefully contrived social barriers, for example, skillfully erected to keep us at a good distance from those of a different race or social class or economic background, collapse like a house of cards the minute we take seriously the announcement that God's realm has broken in. And all the efforts that have gone into creating those barriers—economic systems based on greed, nuclear weapons based on fear, privileges for the few based on self-concern—likewise crumble and have to be replaced.

It's enough to make one wish the Great Fallacy were true. Then at least we wouldn't have religious leaders interfering in our lives.

6

Acting Out the Clue:
Liturgy and Sacraments

They beheld God, and ate and drank.
     —Exodus 24:11

When I give people food, they call me a saint. When I ask why there is no food, they call me a communist.
     —Dom Helder Câmara,
      archbishop of Recife, Brazil

Only those who cry out for the Jews have the right to sing Gregorian chant.
     —Dietrich Bonhoeffer, during the persecution
      of the Jews in Germany

[The liturgy] turns our hearts from self-seeking to a spirituality that sees the signs of true discipleship in our sharing of goods and working for justice.
     —U.S. Catholic bishops' pastoral letter,
      paragraph 331

  Liturgy. We feel relieved; here at last is a topic removed from activism and exhortations to change the world. For a moment we can leave the bustle, seek nourishment, and ground our lives in communion with God, before returning to the fray. Right?

Liturgy as "the people's work"

Wrong. Or, at most, only partly right. For if there is any portion of our faith that challenges the Great Fallacy (lurking behind every word in the previous paragraph), it is a true understanding of liturgy.

Our English word "liturgy" is a transliteration of the Greek word *leitourgia,* which in turn is a combination of two Greek words, *laos* (from which we get "laity" or "the people") and *ergon* (from which we get "erg," a unit of work, as we all learned in high school physics). "Liturgy" therefore is simply "the people's work," or "the work that people do." When first used, it had nothing to do with religion or theology or church or worship. It meant "the work that people do *wherever they are.*"

Paul, for example, uses the closely related word *leitourgoi* (meaning "servants" or "ministers") to describe the pagan tax collectors (Rom. 13:6). They were not servants or ministers in the church, but in the government, and their service or ministry—their "work"—was not to lead the Wednesday evening prayer meetings but to run the Internal Revenue Service of the Roman empire as efficiently as possible.

"Liturgy," then, describes what people do in a place of business, in a shopping center (whether buying, selling, or just looking), in the defensive backfield of the San Francisco Forty-niners, in a physics laboratory, giving birth to a child, being a track coach, writing a book, hauling garbage to a dump site, serving in the state legislature, or being a yeoman third class in the U.S. Navy.

Gradually, in what must be viewed as a succession of linguistic impoverishments, this original meaning of the word was narrowed, until it came to mean what it means today in the popular mind, "the work people do *in church,*" whether praying prayers, singing hymns, preaching sermons, distributing communion, receiving communion, or struggling to stay awake.

This kind of narrowing breathes new life into the Great Fallacy, for it legitimates a tidy distinction between what happens "inside church" and what happens "outside church." There is a sacred realm and a secular realm, and never the twain shall meet.

Only by recapturing the original meaning of liturgy can we avoid such a mistake and validate our contention that life is all of a piece and that "worship" and "action" are finally only different ways of talking about the same thing.

Worship and worth-ship

Before proceeding full steam ahead with this discovery, however, we need to take account of a possible wrong turn. It would be misleading to leave the impression that worship is an activity designed solely to energize us either for social change or inner contentment. This is the "filling station" view of worship: we need a full tank of gasoline once a week to keep us moving along life's road, and we need to have the battery checked in order to see the road clearly, particularly in the dark. The purpose of Sunday is to keep us fit Monday through Saturday.

There is some truth to this view. We do get tired and our vision does falter, and we need help wherever we can get it. But such a utilitarian view of worship reduces it to little more than a device or gimmick, which, if we were strong enough, we could probably get along without.

So we need to remember that the fundamental reason to worship God is that God is worshipful. "Worship," after all, simply means "worth-ship"; worship is an acknowledgment of the worth-ship of God. Whether it yields tangible "returns" or not, worship is a significant human activity. Part of what distinguishes human beings from other forms of life is not only that we make tools (*homo faber*), play (*homo ludens*), work for a living (*homo laborans*), make lifetime commitments with partners (*homo amans*), and use our analytical minds (*homo sapiens*), but also that we worship (*homo adorans*).

Confusion arises, however, when we see "work" and "worship" as two quite different "liturgies," rather than seeing them as two expressions of the same "liturgy"; that is, as the work we do wherever we are at the moment, part of which may be done in church and part elsewhere. Jesus' picture of the Last Judgment makes clear that feeding hungry persons is a way of worshiping God (Matt. 25:31–46). And in the Sermon on the Mount, he makes the point that if we approach the altar fresh from an unresolved spat with a brother or sister (meaning anybody), we cannot make an offering to God under those circumstances; we must put the gift down, leave the altar, and be reconciled with the brother or sister (still meaning anybody) before we can return and offer the gift to God (Matt. 5:23–25). To honor one made in the image of God (by patching up the quarrel) is already to honor God; to be in right relationship with God (by offering a gift at the altar) necessitates being in right relationship with brother and sister, which means already to be in right relationship with God.

The argument sounds circular; it is a glorious circularity.

Reclaiming old forms in new ways

So isolated has much worship (in church) become that it is tempting to suggest taking a new liturgical broom, sweeping clean, and starting all over again. Jesus, however, warns us of the perils of the "empty house"; just as we are disposing of all the debris out the front door, seven devils are sneaking in at the back (Matt. 12:43–45). Newness is no guarantee of improvement.

We can never make a fully clean break with the past. Such things as who our parents were, the good and the bad in our upbringing, the culture into which we were born (without being consulted) indelibly shape us. Some events from the past need to be repudiated, some affirmed, and not a few reinterpreted. This is true of worship as well. Bad hymns can be replaced by good hymns, droning prayers by vital prayers, actions that ignore the world by actions that affirm it. Sometimes even preaching can come alive.

This recuperative power can be illustrated by observing

how an act of individual "devotion," the Roman Catholic stations of the cross, can be invested with new life and show us that spirituality and liberation are two sides of the same liturgical coin.

Early Christians in Jerusalem used to reenact Jesus' carrying the cross from Pilate's court to Golgotha. Churches elsewhere gradually began to provide facsimiles of the stages, or "stations," on the journey ("Jesus falls the first time," "Jesus is nailed to the cross," and so on), by depicting them on church walls. Individuals would stop before each of the fourteen stations for appropriate prayers and a time of private nurturing.

This would hardly seem the stuff out of which the relationship of worship to social transformation could be reestablished, and yet Leonardo Boff, a Brazilian Franciscan, has created a new setting of the stations that not only focuses on the "then" but relates it vividly to the "now."

His treatment of the sixth station ("Veronica wipes the face of Jesus") provides an example. Back "then," a woman named Veronica, an early follower of Jesus in Jerusalem, broke through the crowd of soldiers and gently wiped the sweaty and bloody head of Jesus in an exemplary act of human compassion. Worshipers kneeling in front of this depiction would feel gratitude that she was on the scene, perhaps meditate on the need for similar compassion in their own lives, and then move on to the seventh station ("Jesus falls the second time").

Boff lingers. While he is there, he pulls the "then" into the "now." He first reminds us of our conventional question, "Where do we find God? and our conventional answers: in prayer, the interior life, asceticism, the church, the sacraments, loving encounters with neighbors. But there is a more important question: "Where does God want to be encountered by human beings?" Boff offers two answers. First, God chooses to encounter us in Jesus Christ, a conventional enough answer until we realize that in this very station Christ is being portrayed as "a frail, powerless human being." We must be "scandalized" at the thought of God being in such a situation. But there is more to come:

> Second, we encounter God
> in the lives and faces
> of the humiliated and downtrodden.

What is the new mindset of "the humiliated and downtrodden"? It is an unwillingness any longer to accept their lot passively. These people, with whom Jesus identifies himself,

> raise a protest:
> This situation contradicts the will of God,
> and is unacceptable to any human being
> who has preserved the least trace of humaneness.

But in addition to raising a cry of protest, the downtrodden are also

> the bearers of a great hope
> which manifests itself as a demand of justice.

They expect "to recover their trampled dignity," and they claim God's support:

> God considered this hope and this demand of justice so ineradicable
> That [God] identified with the oppressed.
> In their faces we find the face of God.

What has all this to do with Veronica and our own response to what she did?

> If we want to serve the true God . . .
> then we must do as Veronica did.
> We must break out of the circle of self-absorption
> and pay heed to the bloodied face of our fellow human beings.
> For they are the great sacrament of God,
> the signs and instruments of authentic divine reality.
> If we do not share life with the oppressed,
> we do not share life with God. . . .
> When we wipe the face of our fellow human beings
> who are suffering life as a painful passion,
> we are wiping the face of Jesus.
>
> (Boff, *Way of the Cross—*
> *Way of Justice,* pp. 42–48)

Boff is not arguing only for individual gestures of compassion after the damage has been done. To wipe the face of our fellow human beings means examining why our fellow human beings are suffering; discovering what political, social, and economic structures cause their suffering; exploring what kinds of systemic changes will be needed to ensure that the suffering does not continue; reflecting on how we can avoid slipping back into the old oppressive structures once the zeal for change abates. Such concerns are mandatory for Christians, since the story of Jesus' suffering and the story of all human suffering are part of the same story.

The title of Boff's book reads *Way of the Cross—Way of Justice.* Maybe the "—" should be an "=" sign.

Sacramental subversion

"Subversion" is a scare word in our vocabulary. It calls to mind spies, cloak-and-dagger operations, covert plans to overturn a government. The word literally means "to overthrow (*vertere*) from below (*sub*)." Where we least expect it—from below—movements may be generated that bring about radical change in the ordering of society.

But surely such movements will not be generated around a communion table. What could be more remote from "liberation" than a kind of "spirituality" in which a bunch of people are eating morsels of bread and taking little sips of wine? Here is a place where the sacred and the secular appear fully insulated from each other. No "overturning" is going to be initiated here.

Those who so believe need to look again. For the time at which the Christian community proclaims (with whatever differences of interpretation) the "real presence" of Christ is not a time of ignoring the world outside but of incorporating it by making use of its creations. This "sacred" experience cannot even occur without the use of earthy objects from the here and now: namely, bread and wine. And the bread and wine are available only because there has been planting, cultivating, harvesting, gathering, fermenting or baking, storing, transporting, distributing, buying, and selling—in short, all those things we identify with the life of economics and politics. The so-called "sacred" is not realized without the help of the so-called "profane." There is no point at

which the attempt to separate them has more difficulty than
right here.

The process works both ways. While we do not live "by
bread alone," as Jesus informed the tempter in the wilderness, neither can we live without it. To say "We are not saved
by bread *alone*" is an appropriate reminder to those with full
stomachs. To say "We are not saved *without* bread" is a
necessary acknowledgment of the claims of those with empty
stomachs, and a rallying cry to find ways to procure the
needed bread.

The Eucharist (as Tissa Balasuriya points out in *The Eucharist and Human Liberation*) was originally a celebration
of the political and economic liberation of the Jews from
Egypt. The early church had a vigorous view of the relationship between liturgical integrity and commitment to the
poor. Hear Basil the Great (A.D. 330–379):

> The bread in your cupboard belongs to the hungry [person],
> the coat hanging unused in your closet belongs to the [person]
> who needs it; the shoes rotting in your closet belong to the
> [person] who has no shoes; the money which you put in the
> bank belongs to the poor. You do wrong to everyone you
> could help but fail to help.
>
> (Cited in John Ryan, *Alleged Socialism of the Church
> Fathers,* p. 9; St. Louis: B. Herder Book Co., 1913)

Back then, it would have been self-evident that food on the
Lord's Table cried out for a world in which there was ample
food on all other tables.

Later Christians, however, tamed and domesticated the
event, so that rather than remaining a celebration of full
liberation for all people, it was pressed into the service of the
status quo and became a resource for inner calm rather than
outer change. This "social conditioning of the Eucharist" has
relieved the consciences of leaders of repressive regimes from
any necessity to act on the radical social consequences of a
meal that is supposed to pave the way for adequate food for
all, rather than insulating comfort for a few. The potential
for prophetic action was turned into nonthreatening inac-

tion. Colonialism and industrialization later increased the distance between the eucharistic table and other tables and rendered the Eucharist more and more irrelevant to the lives of the poor, who saw the liturgy supporting those in power and speaking no word of admonishment to them.

From such a perspective, the latent explosive power at hand when the Eucharist is celebrated is beyond calculation. Dictators, who have tried to suppress preaching as politically dangerous and Bible study as potentially subversive, have often let the church go on celebrating the apparently innocuous rite of the breaking of the bread. In terms of their own self-interest, they are making a great mistake, since the "simple" act of breaking bread at the Lord's Table empowers people to engage in the more complex act of breaking structures of oppression that perpetuate the lack of bread elsewhere.

Paul's difficult warning that we can eat and drink at the Lord's Table to our own damnation (1 Cor. 11:27–29), has been the object of centuries of speculation. The foregoing discussion suggests that one way of eating and drinking to our own damnation may be to accept food from the Lord's Table without making sure that there is food on other tables.

The usual interpretation of sacrament goes like this: We go through our daily, dreary, ordinary routines, and every once in a while there is an unusual or extraordinary event—a baptism or a Eucharist with a special meaning—that for the moment intrudes the presence of the unusual, the extraordinary, into the daily routine. And after that we settle back into the routine, glad for our momentary respite.

But surely it is the other way around: The sacramental moments are meant to be the normative moments, that show us what ordinary life is meant to be and usually is not. On this reading, it is all of life that is included in the "real" moments, the sacramental moments. The Lord's Supper is not meant to be the extraordinary meal but the *ordinary* one, the meal that is the model for all other meals. The way bread is shared on this occasion is the way bread is meant to be shared on all other occasions. The dynamics of the occasion say to us:

You can't afford to pay for the meal? Come anyway, there is
no charge. You don't usually meet the sort of people who are
gathered here? Come anyway, for there are no distinctions
here between upper and lower classes, rich and poor, male
and female; everyone is on the same footing, and the equality
is an equality of need. You haven't done anything to earn the
right to be here? Come anyway, for neither has anybody else.

And when someone replies that it isn't really like that, since
at many tables women cannot yet preside, or minorities
aren't really welcome, let it be said that such a recognition,
loudly noted, is itself an important step on the way to closing
the gap between what is and what is meant to be.

Discovering that one moment has potential for all other
moments is by no means limited to the sacraments. Other
kinds of special moments, often fleeting, are pointers to what
all moments could become. Couples in love give flowers to
one another. The simple act expresses in that moment what
is meant to be true of all the other moments; namely, that
life is a giving and receiving, preeminently the gift of each self
to the other, which the flowers symbolize. The flowers will
fade and die; that does not really matter. What matters is
that for a moment they have expressed what will not fade and
die—the love of two persons for each other, and their affirmation that all moments are meant to contain the sort of
giving and receiving symbolized in that particular moment.

The play within the play: Help from *Hamlet*

The sacraments, as the supreme expression of this, have a
significance similar to the significance of the play within the
play in *Hamlet.* In Shakespeare's drama, things get all mixed
up. No one is quite sure who the heroes and villains are, who
should be trusted, who should be doubted, what has "really"
been happening. And so Hamlet decides to present a play
within a play. He will put on a dramatic production for the
king that will reveal what is *really* going on. The play within
the play becomes the moment of truth, as a result of which
the other moments can be seen with fresh clarity.

So, too, with the sacraments. While *Hamlet* shows us what

is evil, the sacraments show us what is good. They represent those moments of truth that tell us, confused as we are by all other evidence, what is *really* going on, what the nature of life is meant to be. And the nature of that life, we learn, has everything to do with justice and nothing to do with injustice; everything to do with possibilities for the *whole* person and nothing to do with dividing persons into bodies and souls so that liberation can be neglected for the sake of spirituality, or vice versa; everything to do with "calling into the present" one who comes, in the words of an Advent hymn, with a clear agenda of liberation:

> He comes to break oppression,
> To set the captive free,
> To take away transgression,
> And rule in equity.
>
> He comes with succor speedy
> To those who suffer wrong;
> To help the poor and needy
> And bid the weak be strong.

Full-blown subversion.

7

A Case Study: Spirituality and Sexuality

And I wanted to cry out at her that I could not put the body apart from the soul, and that the comfort of her body was more than a thing of the flesh, but was also a comfort of the soul, and why it was, I could not say, and why it should be, I could not say, but there was in it nothing that was ugly or evil, but only good. But how can one find such words?
> —Pieter van Vlaanderen, in Alan Paton,
> *Too Late the Phalarope*

Pieter's wife is unable to believe that human sexuality can be a good thing. By seeking to distinguish between the soul (goodness) and the body (evil) she is affirming the Great Fallacy without knowing it and demonstrating its baleful consequences. In so thinking, she is not alone, for there is a strain of Christian teaching (to which she has obviously been exposed in her upbringing) that conditions her to feel this way and ultimately contributes to the tragic destruction of her marriage.

A fresh look at spirituality and sexuality can help us see some further consequences of the Great Fallacy and also provide resources for overcoming it.

Spirituality and sexuality at odds:
A long history

When it comes to sex, Christianity has had a bizarre history. The Hebrew scriptures, which Christians inherited, do not contain the negative view of sex that has clouded much Christian history. The Song of Songs, for example, is a collection of oriental love poems with considerable erotic imagery. Later Christian interpreters tried to disguise its real subject by suggesting that it was really an allegorical poem about Christ's love for the church—a notion that would have startled its original authors, since they wrote at least three hundred years before Christ's birth.

The basic Jewish view (which took a back seat when Christians started interpreting the Jewish scriptures) can be found in the creation story: After each specific act of creation (earth, vegetation, sun and moon, birds and sea monsters, cattle and creepy-crawlies) there is the refrain "and God saw that it was good" (see Gen. 1:10, 12, 18, 21, 25). But after creation has come to its culmination in the creation of male and female, after sexuality has appeared, the editorial evaluation escalates: "and God saw everything that [God] had made, and behold, it was *very* good" (Gen. 1:31, italics added).

So the later equation, "sex=sin," did not enter Christian history from the Hebrew scriptures, where sex is viewed as a gift of God, but from the Greek culture in which the Christians found themselves, where a dualistic view, splitting soul from body, prevailed. If, as many Greeks maintained, the body is the prison house of the soul, then a low view of the body (and especially of its sexual functions) will naturally prevail, and the goal of salvation will be extrication from the evil body so that the pure soul can once again be free. (Many Christians unwittingly sustain this version of the Great Fallacy when they talk about eternal life exclusively in the imagery of "the immortality of the soul.") This view increasingly dominated Christian thinking, displacing the inherited Jewish view that the body is "the temple of the Lord" and therefore sacred rather than evil.

Augustine (A.D. 354 – 430) played a central role in the creation of this legacy. A talented philanderer before his conversion, Augustine had great difficulty getting his own sex life under control, a fact he was honest enough to acknowledge in the prayer, "O God, give me chastity, but not yet." Once he had seen the light, however, Augustine developed a negative Christian ethic of sex with all the zeal of a true believer and bequeathed to the subsequent tradition a conviction that sin had entered into the human condition through the sexual union of Adam and Eve, not only causing their downfall but leaving all—repeat, all—of their descendants tainted with sin as a result. Sex was therefore an evil, even though a necessary evil, since the continuation of the human race depended on it. Augustine walked the tightrope of this dilemma by concluding (a) that sex belonged only in marriage, (b) that it could be engaged in only for the purpose of having children, and (c) that it was to be tolerated under conditions (a) and (b) only so long as the partners got no enjoyment from it. Married people populate earth, he grudgingly conceded, but virgins populate heaven.

Building on such conclusions, the church decreed that one of the signs of true sanctity was virginity, and that all who were set apart for priestly functions must be celibate—one of the less popular decisions in the two thousand years of Christian history. In the resulting male-dominated church, women (unless they entered holy orders and took vows of celibacy themselves) were looked upon not only as unclean but as sources of temptation. The demeaning of sex carried with it the demeaning of women, and Christian literature is full of put-downs of the seductiveness of feminine charm, warnings about the carnal desires that women arouse in men, and the exclusion of women from roles of leadership in the church. This demeaning persists in Roman Catholicism today, where women are still excluded from leadership roles, where teaching about sex reiterates that the chief function of intercourse is procreation, and where artificial means of birth control, making marital sex possible for mutual enrichment as well as procreation, are forbidden.

This baleful history is an example of the Great Fallacy writ large. Had the Jewish-biblical view prevailed, the goodness of all that is earthy, immediate, and sexual would not have been downplayed for so many centuries.

Spirituality and sexuality intermingled: A longer history

What is therefore needed is a rejection of this view and the recovery of an understanding of the unity of the human person—frequently described as a "psychosomatic" understanding. Etymology can help us with this difficult but important word. The Greek words *psyche* and *soma* mean, respectively, "soul" and "body." When we put them together they become *psychesoma* ("soulbody"), from which we get our transliteration "psychosomatic." It is significant that this is one word rather than two, for it underlines the fact that there is a unity rather than a duality to the human person. We are not talking about a good soul trapped in an evil body, but about a total being who can do many different things— think, fight, remember, love, anticipate, pray, copulate, sing, laugh, imagine. *All* the activities can be used for good ends, all can be abused and turned to evil ends.

This suggests that spirituality and sexuality, rather than being understood as opposites, should be understood as intimately and inextricably bound together, two expressions of a single basic reality rather than two different realities.

In the light of this, let us take a second look at the "tampering" that was done to the Song of Songs, the Jewish canticle to sensual human love. Christians, as we have seen, tried to allegorize the poem by transforming the images describing the love of two human beings for each other into images of the love of Christ for the church. What the original authors saw as good, Christians saw as prurient, and so they tried to exclude sex from the purview of their highly susceptible readers.

Suppose, however, that we let the analogy of the Christian redactors stand for the moment, not because, like them, we wish to deny the reality of sex but because, unlike them, we wish to celebrate and affirm it. In that case, we would be saying one of two things or, better still, both of them. We would be saying, first:

> If we want an image for the highest love of all, God's love for us (in this case, Christ's love for the church), then the best image we can employ is an image of the highest love we can know in human terms, the love of human beings for each other.

Or we would be saying, second:

> If we want an image for the highest love that human beings can have for one another, then the best image we can employ is an image of the highest love of all, God's love for us (in this case, Christ's love for the church).

Or, finally, if we were to try to say both things simultaneously, we would be saying:

> We cannot make a clear-cut distinction between God's love for us and our love for one another. While they are obviously not totally alike, they are so much more alike than they are unlike that reference to either will cast light on the other. We understand divine love better by reference to human love, and we understand human love better by reference to divine love.

In coming to such conclusions, we would not be doing violence to other parts of the biblical tradition but exemplifying them. The place where this is seen most clearly is in the story of the prophet Hosea. On first reading, there seem to be two stories in Hosea: the story of Hosea's love for his wife, and the story of God's love for Israel. But they are actually one overall story, in which each part is needed in order to understand the other.

The Hosea part of the story goes like this: Hosea falls in love with Gomer; they marry and have three children. Gomer becomes a prostitute. Hosea is directed by law and custom to throw her out of the household and make a public spectacle of her. But almost in the moment of doing so, he makes the astonishing discovery that he still loves her, despite all that has happened, and keeps her as his wife. The relationship is restored.

The God part of the story goes like this: God loves Israel and enters into a relationship with her called a covenant, that lasts many years. But Israel, too, becomes a prostitute—in the pungent language of the King James Version, she goes a-whoring after false gods—the idols, the Baalim, of the fertility cults. God, by the terms of their agreement, is entitled to throw Israel on the scrap heap, and there are moments when the divine anger is so kindled that that seems likely to be the result (see Hos. 6:5–7, for example). But then comes the astonishing discovery that the divine love cannot be quenched. Despite all that has happened, God still loves Israel and cannot cast her out. The relationship is restored (see Hos. 11:8–11).

Query: Did Hosea have his own experience of ongoing love in spite of betrayal, and then decide that if he could love Gomer despite her unfaithfulness, so could God love Israel despite *her* unfaithfulness? Or did Hosea, aware of God's ongoing love for Israel despite Israel's infidelities, decide, when faced with a parallel situation in his own life, that he should emulate God's ongoing love for Israel by his own ongoing love for Gomer?

Answer: (a) We don't know for sure and (b) it doesn't really matter.

What does matter is that the author of the book of Hosea intuited a deep truth: that love between two persons and love between God and persons are so much alike that they can be thought of almost interchangeably. There are more similarities than dissimilarities. The result is that the experience of human love helps us understand divine love, and the experience of divine love helps us understand human love. Each illumines the other. Neither is really full or true without the other.

Spirituality and sexuality revisited:
An updated history

So far the biblical story. But for many people today the biblical story doesn't work anymore. It seems offensive because it is based on stereotypical sex roles: man as the aggrieved partner who has been wounded by his wife's infidelity; woman as the seductress who takes on other lovers and flaunts those relationships before her husband. How can anyone today learn from such a skewed scenario?

Let us accept the legitimacy of the grievance. Could we tell the story of Hosea in modern dress by reversing the sex roles? Without attributing any such intention to her, we can see enough of the Hosea story in Nora Ephron's novel *Heartburn* to make the experiment worth trying. In her version, contemporary counterparts of Hosea and Gomer are married and have children, and then Hosea enters into a long-standing affair with one of Gomer's best friends, which, it turns out, is only the most recent in a series of long-standing affairs and one-night stands. Gomer, appropriately indignant, leaves Hosea and holds him up to public ridicule by writing a novel that is only a thinly veiled account of the whole story. The account ends as Gomer, with exquisite marksmanship, throws a pie that hits Hosea in the face during a public banquet.

Of course, if this modern story were a consistent retelling of the biblical story, the account would not end there. Gomer would discover that she still loves Hosea, despite his long string of infidelities, and out of her valid anger in the pie-throwing episode she would move to forgiveness, and after some transforming work on both sides the relationship would be restored.

One can imagine the furor that might have resulted had Nora Ephron employed such a twist of plot. Her book would have been described as one more instance of how men have their cake and eat it too, in a male-dominated world where women (the "weaker sex") crawl back, almost asking for further humiliation.

Fair enough. But the retort helpfully clarifies something else that is going on in the biblical version. For if our modern Gomer would be seen as spinelessly capitulating to a wily male, so much the more would the biblical Hosea have seemed craven and weak in terms of the expectancies of his time—a time when men were not supposed to be manipulated by fallen women but were expected to dominate and control them with all the appropriate macho and Rambo-like responses. Hosea defied all that when he took Gomer back, breaking with custom for the sake of love.

The point of the story survives, whether it is the woman who stumbles and the man who picks her up or the man who has the roving eye and the woman who restores his vision. In either case, compassion is operative. Human love is not evil; it is where we gain our knowledge of God's love.

Kierkegaard fumbles and Buber recovers: A recent history

This is even clearer in the contrasting attitudes toward the relationship of human love and God's love in the thought of Søren Kierkegaard, a nineteenth-century Danish theologian, and Martin Buber, a twentieth-century Jewish philosopher.

Kierkegaard, who wanted to give himself unreservedly to the love of God, wooed a young girl, Regina Olsen, for several years before finally prevailing upon her to say yes. No sooner had she done so, however, than Kierkegaard had second thoughts and decided that to marry Regina would distract him from loving God unreservedly. Out of loyalty to what he considered a "higher" love, he decided to relinquish the "lower" one. "In order to come to love [of God]," he wrote, "I had to remove the object [i.e., Regina]."

Martin Buber comments on Kierkegaard's decision in a marvelous way:

> That is sublimely to misunderstand God. Creation is not a hurdle on the road to God, it is the road itself. We are created along with one another and directed to a life with one another. Creatures are placed in my way so that I, their fellow-

creature, by means of them and with them, find the way to God. A God reached by their exclusion would not be the God of all lives in whom all life is fulfilled. . . . *God wants us to come to [God] by means of the Reginas [God] has created, and not by renunciation of them.*

> (*Between Man and Man,* p. 52, italics added;
> New York: Macmillan Co., 1965)

Buber's words are appropriate not only in response to Kierkegaard but in response to all attempts to sever love of God and love of creatures. Bianco da Siena (c. A.D. 1367) would have merited a similar response. Writing about the Holy Spirit, she prays, movingly,

> O Comforter, draw near,
> Within my heart appear,
> And kindle it,
> Thy holy flame bestowing,

words that are unexceptionable, save that she then goes on:

> O let it freely burn,
> Till earthly passions turn
> To dust and ashes
> In its heat consuming.

That, too, "is sublimely to misunderstand God."

Martin Buber is widely known for reflections on what he calls an "I-Thou" relationship between two human beings, in which each treats the other as a subject with whom there can be full reciprocity and sharing, in contrast to an "I-It" relationship, in which the other is reduced to an "object" (as Kierkegaard described Regina) who can be manipulated and used and is thus depersonalized from a "thou" to an "it." So much is well known. What is less well known, but equally important, is Buber's claim that any real "I-Thou" relationship points to, and is grounded in, the Eternal Thou. Truly to enter into relationship with another human being is to enter into relationship with God. From this perspective, also, we are to come to God by means of the Reginas and not by renunciation of them.

But before we erase all distinctions, we need to remember Dietrich Bonhoeffer's blunt statement that for a man to be

thinking about God while embracing his wife is, to say the
least, in bad taste—a sentiment with which the wife might
be inclined to agree. If we so fully equate love of God and
love of a human partner that when we love the human partner we are thinking only of God, we are dangerously damag-
ing both relationships. No person, after all, wants to be loved
merely as a symbol of something else; we want to be loved
for who we are, with our distinctive strengths and weaknesses.

It is seldom the case, however, that we obliterate the presence of the one we are embracing and experience the occasion as nothing but a time of the presence of God. We are
more likely to be so enchanted by the immediacy of the
human love that God comes in a distant second. Yet even so,
the paradox remains that in the midst of passionate sexual
embrace, that very "I-Thou" relationship is also rooted in
God, whether or not God's reality is consciously acknowledged by the lovers.

It might seem, from the above, that the only location for
recognizing the interrelatedness of divine and human love is
heterosexual marriage, and it is true that in Christian theology this has been a consistent theme. But it is also true in
human experience that relationships between two women, or
between two men, or between men and women not married
to one another have been channels of divine grace, and the
same thing can be said for relationships in which age or
physical impairment have made sexual relations impossible.

Many issues are raised here that are beyond the scope of
this particular book; the point at issue is simply that we
cannot arbitrarily create boundaries around the ways God's
love and human love can intersect.

"Where love is, there God is": An enduring history

There is no formula to which all these matters can be
reduced, but we can begin to realize that the co-mingling
of divine and human love is more possible than we had
imagined. The presence of the Eternal Thou can enrich
our relationship to a human thou, as Buber promised, and

invest immediate moments and enduring relationships with new depth. If *eros* (in which the other is attractive and desirable to us) is the basic stuff of human relationships, it is still true that *agape* (love offered without counting the cost) is crucial if the relationship is to deepen. Lynn Rhodes helpfully expresses the intermingling of spirituality and sexuality:

> Our love is embodied in our feelings, our touch, our passion, and our care. If spirituality loses touch with its roots in sexuality, it loses power to form and inform our deepest selves. When sexuality is separated from spiritual development, it becomes something we use to manipulate, control, and harm what we profess to love. When spirituality is separated from our sexuality, it loses the power of personal connection and becomes lifeless—it cannot move us to passionate care for this world.
>
> (Rhodes, *Co-Creating: A Feminist Vision of Ministry,* pp. 64–65; Philadelphia: Westminster Press, 1987)

A musical refrain from the liturgy of the Taizé Community in southern France reinforces the point:

> *Ubi caritas*
> *et amor,*
> *ubi caritas*
> *Deus ibi est.*

We can translate this roughly as "Where there is love, God is present" or (using the title of a short story by Tolstoi), "Where love is, there God is also." The refrain reminds us that there can be no final separation between God's love and human love, since love constitutes the deepest possible sharing between persons, and shared love constitutes the very nature of God. When love is present, God and persons meet; the Eternal Thou is there.

The insight did not originate at Taizé. The First Letter of John says it best:

> Beloved, let us love one another; for love is of God, and the one who loves is born of God and knows God. Those who do not love do not know God; for God is love.
>
> (1 John 4:7–8, adapted)

The author is not talking only of sexual love, but he is not excluding it either. Just as love of God is expressed in love for human beings, so love of human beings expresses love of God. To be dazzled by the fact that another person loves us, when there are so many good reasons not to, is to experience the quality of divine love, since it too is a gift, similarly undeserved and yet given anyhow. Divine love and human love do not work at cross-purposes; they are reminders of the sheer wonder and unity of our existence.

PART THREE
Radical Reconstruction

WHEREIN *it is shown that a "radical" approach to spirituality and liberation, discovering the "root" of their various meanings, establishes that each, truly understood, includes what is meant by the other;*

WHEREIN *some of the implications of this conclusion for both our acting and our speaking are explored;*

AND WHEREIN, *finally, recognizing the danger of cerebral solutions, we observe a variety of persons and events, which, taken together, validate the equivalency of spirituality and liberation more convincingly than any book can do.*

8

Plan C:
An Exercise
in Redefinition

If I am hungry, that is a physical problem; if my neighbor is hungry, that is a spiritual problem.
> —Nicolai Berdyaev, who, without quite escaping
> the vocabulary of the Great Fallacy,
> is still on the right track

In our age, the road to holiness passes through the world of action.
> —Dag Hammarskjöld, General Secretary
> of the United Nations

There are few words more dangerous than "spiritual."
> —George McLeod, founder of the Iona Community

Twin dangers and the need for a radical approach

George McLeod is right, in two very different ways. First of all, a superficial understanding of the word "spiritual" that equates it with otherworldliness is indeed dangerous. It allows us either to dismiss the notion of spirituality as irrelevant to our immediate lives, or to attach so much importance to it that it preempts the legitimate attention we ought to give to our immediate lives.

But "spiritual" can have other meanings than superficial ones—meanings that render it "dangerous" in more significant ways. For if we understand "spiritual" in its deepest sense, we find that it calls upon us to take risks, to change our priorities, to surrender our sense of self-importance, to be more concerned with the doing of God's will than our own will, and many other things that are inconvenient and dangerous to well-ordered lives.

Going George McLeod one better, we could also argue that "there are few words more dangerous than 'liberation.' " First of all, a superficial understanding of the word "liberation" that equates it with the-violent-overthrow-of-existing-governments-by-those-who-give-covert-allegiance-to-Marx-while-overtly-mouthing-Christian-platitudes is "dangerous." It allows us to dismiss the notion of liberation as, irrelevant to our immediate lives, since such proposals strike us as preposterous, or to attach so much importance to bringing about social change that we justify all moral excesses in reaching that goal.

But "liberation" can have other meanings than superficial ones—meanings that render it "dangerous" in more significant ways. For if we understand "liberation" in its deepest sense, we find that it calls upon us to take risks, to change our priorities, to surrender our sense of self-importance, to be more concerned with the doing of God's will than with our own will, and many other things that are inconvenient and dangerous to well-ordered lives.

The preceding chapters have given us the tools to rise above superficial understandings and look for root meanings that will demonstrate that spirituality and liberation are finally two ways of talking about the same thing, as the repetitive style of the above four paragraphs has tried to suggest.

This demands a "radical" approach that we will call Plan C. And the introduction of such an adjective demands an explanation.

The words "spirituality" and "liberation" are so difficult in themselves that proposing to clarify them by using an even more difficult word, "radical," seems a perverse route to illumination. But the proposal of a "radical" approach is a serious one that can shed new light on our terms.

In political life, "radical" is often used pejoratively,

equated with "leftist," describing someone who favors basic change in our sociopolitical-economic structures. From such a perspective, "liberals" are bad enough, sniffing the seductive scent of socialism, but "radicals" are worse, since they are either very smart (covering up their real aims with diversionary rhetoric), or very stupid (letting themselves be "used" by Communists who exploit their naiveté for nefarious ends). This is not the primary sense in which "radical" will be used in the following pages, although we will discover some important political implications before we are through.

The Latin word *radix, radicus* (from which we get "radical") means "root." A radical approach, then, is one that tries to get at the root of things, to dig beneath the surface and discover what is really going on. The dictionary defines it as "going to the foundation or source of something," to what is fundamental or basic. The antonym, or opposite, of "radical" is "superficial" or "shallow." (Peter DeVries describes one of his characters with the words, "Oh, on the surface he's profound, but way down deep he's shallow.")

A description of "radical" from the field of chemistry offers further help:

> A group of two or more atoms that acts as a single atom and goes through a reaction unchallenged, or is replaced by a single atom; it is normally incapable of separate existence.

Spirituality and liberation sometimes appear to be "two atoms"; in the full understanding toward which we are pressing, however, they are replaced by a single atom and are "incapable of separate existence."

A "radical" approach then, is dissatisfied with surface impressions and tries to get at the heart of the matter, whether the object of scrutiny is the Holy Roman Empire, the *Tractatus* of Wittgenstein, the "spirit" of the Renaissance, the non-negotiable demands of a terrorist, or the meaning of spirituality and liberation. And in the last case, we find that when we do get to the root meaning of either term, *the inclusive reality to which each of them points is the same reality.*

The new saints

Let us begin the exercise of redefinition by looking at popular piety in Latin America—a more faithful index than academic treatises—where we discover a new understanding of spirituality emerging. For centuries, it was the custom to look for the "saints" among those who disengaged from the world and sought to contemplate the divine in far-off places, whether desert, monastery, or convent. God was not found in the marketplace; God was as far from the marketplace as possible.

But Latin Americans are beginning to see that the true saints are not those who forsake the world but those who embrace it, involving themselves fully in its ambiguities, power struggles, and trials.

Today, the model for sainthood is someone like Archbishop Oscar Romero of El Salvador, who, in the midst of the political corruption, sadistic violence, and economic exploitation in his own country, did not ignore such realities, or make his peace with them, but challenged them directly in the name of a Lord who likewise lived in the midst of political corruption, sadistic violence, and economic exploitation and challenged them directly. No other posture was possible for Romero, once he saw that the God he served was the God who had taken the side of the exploited Israelites in Egypt and had later entered into the plight of those same oppressed people by sharing their humanity in Jesus of Nazareth, struggling at their side. He realized that only by a similar identification on his part, likewise at risk of death, could the liberating and resurrecting power of God be released in El Salvador.

In the case of both Jesus of Nazareth and Oscar of San Salvador, the attempt to show the indissolubility of liberation and spirituality led to death. Nothing could be more potently symbolic than the fact that Archbishop Romero was gunned down while saying mass. In the crucifixion of Jesus that the mass reenacts, God chose to side with the victim rather than the apparent victors. The one whom God vindicated was not Pilate or Herod but Jesus, and his resurrection attested to the ultimate triumph of God over all that political and economic exploitation could attempt. As in first-century Jerusalem, so in twentieth-century San Salvador, Archbishop Romero affirmed with his words, his life, and his death that the engagement of God in human lives is for the sake of their total healing, a redemption his detractors could neither measure or control. "If I die," he said, only weeks before his death in 1980, "I will rise again in the Salvadoran people."

He has.

The same can be said for three Roman Catholic sisters and a lay missionary—Dorothy Kazel, Ita Ford, Maura Clarke, and Jean Donovan—who likewise gave their lives in El Salvador in 1980. Their commitment to the "religious" life led to their increasing identification with poor and starving people, especially children. For working with "the least of these," for actions with and on behalf of the truly needy, for demonstrating that spirituality and liberation are inseparable, they were ambushed, assaulted, shot, and left in an unmarked grave.

Those in political power could not accept the notion that such lives were authentic. Alexander Haig, then Secretary of State, fabricated a story about the nuns being gunrunners. Jeane Kirkpatrick, then U.S. Ambassador to the United Nations, as much as said that the women got what they deserved. Ernest Lefever, Reagan's rejected nominee for Under Secretary of State, suggested that the four women had violated the meaning of a religious calling by becoming political.

Such rhetoric not only represents a frantic defense of the Great Fallacy in the corridors of power but is also a left-handed tribute to the integrity of Dorothy Kazel, Ita Ford, Maura Clarke, and Jean Donovan, who in responding to the call of Christ were led not away from, but into the midst of, human need. In El Salvador (and also, alas, in Washington), siding with the poor is perceived as politically threatening and worthy of death.

The awesome truth is that for every archbishop, every sister, every lay missionary whose story is known, there are thousands of nameless ones—the new saints who embody the biblical truth that to know God is to do justice (Jer. 22:12–17). They demonstrate that eating and drinking, helping others get enough to eat and drink, struggling for justice, and discovering God in the midst of that struggle cannot be separated.

So a new kind of spiritual exercise is emerging. It involves not withdrawal but engagement; not shutting one's eyes to evil but opening one's eyes clearly to see both the individual and systemic reasons for that evil; not emptying the mind, so that the Spirit can flood into the emptiness, but filling the mind with statistics about who doesn't eat and why not, about where concentrations of wealth (and consequent injustice) are located, about indignities suffered by powerless people, so that the Spirit can be well informed in using the new saints in subsequent assaults on centers of exploitation and unjust privilege.

Meister Eckhart, many centuries ago, knew where the saints should be found. Reflecting on the fact that Paul was once lifted to "the third heaven," he continued: "Even if a man were in rapture like St. Paul and knew of a man who was in need of food he would do better by feeding him than by remaining in ecstasy" (Cited in O'Connor, *Search for Silence,* p. 118). Today we would also feel it important to help the man find a job. But Meister Eckhart is pointing in the right direction.

Redefining spirituality

Spirituality when radically understood includes what is meant by liberation. Recent discussions of spirituality almost always deny that it can be understood in an otherworldly or individual sense. Suppose we were to eavesdrop on a conversation about the meaning of spirituality today, undertaken by those who do not simply speak but embody that of which they speak. There would be some recurring themes:

The participants would insist that *spirituality includes all of life.* It would describe the way in which Christians live every aspect of their existence, including politics and merchandizing as well as prayer and meditation. The fullness of reality would be the reference point, not some isolated aspect of reality. The word "holistic" would figure in the discussion; perhaps John Carmody (author of *Holistic Spirituality*) would remind the others that all the domains of human existence—ecology, economics, health, prayer, politics, sexuality and education—are in the province of spirituality.

Before long someone in the group, perhaps a Latin American priest named Segundo Galilea, would spell this out as involving *simultaneous commitment to God and to persons*. From his perspective, "contemplation would mean that personal encounter with Christ and personal encounter with our neighbor are inseparable." Others would add that our "neighbor" is anyone in need, particularly the poor and oppressed, and a biblical scholar such as Elsa Tamez from Costa Rica might add that the kingdom of God would be realized to just the degree that such concerns as justice and equality were the fruits of this "simultaneous commitment to God and to persons."

If the discussion began to get too complex, Frei Betto, a Brazilian priest, might offer a disarmingly simple definition of spirituality, as no more and no less than *following Jesus*. Soon, however, what seemed disarmingly simple would begin to appear disconcertingly demanding, for it would become clear that just as Jesus became involved in historical conflict, so too would those who were "following" him be expected to do likewise. It would not be sufficient to follow Jesus only to quiet places such as deserts and mountaintops; he had a consistent pattern of going from such places into situations of turmoil. Placid serenity would not be the hallmark of such spirituality. Jesus would be seen as the "dangerous liberator" he was, more dangerous by far than the criminal Barrabas—a fact of which Pontius Pilate, the Roman procurator, was well aware.

Another voice, perhaps that of Jon Sobrino from El Salvador, would press the difference between "imitating" Jesus and "following" Jesus, insisting that since for Thomas à Kempis (as we have seen) *The Imitation of Christ* meant *Contempt for the World*, following Jesus must involve affirmation of the world as the arena in which he is to be followed, since the world is the place in which he decided, in love, to cast his own lot. "Christian existence," Sobrino would insist, "is the following of Jesus in a concrete situation" (*Christology at the Crossroads,* p. 395).

And on that note of specificity, someone would observe that the argument had come full circle, since (point one) "spirituality includes all of life," and "following Jesus" has now been shown to mean following him in "all of life." One of the participants might tie this together by recalling the statement made at a meeting of third world Christians in Brazil, that "in the following of Jesus the spiritual experience is never separated from the liberating struggle," and another would point out that the argument at the meetings had been capped by the subsequent assertion that "prayer and commitment are not alternative practices; they require and mutually reinforce one another. In the spirituality that we want to create, the option in solidarity with the poor and the oppressed becomes an experience of the God of Jesus Christ." (In International Ecumenical Congress of Theology, *The Challenge of Basic Christian Communities,* p. 240.)

By this time, there would be stirrings in the group to summarize their newly forged understanding of spirituality, and their attention would gradually focus on one of their number, Gustavo Gutiérrez, a Peruvian "liberation theologian" who had recently concluded just such an effort in a book called *We Drink from Our Own Wells: The Spiritual Journey of a People.* He would finally be prevailed upon to summarize his summary.

He would begin by reminding them and us that his title comes from a comment of Bernard of Clairvaux, that the place from which our spiritual nourishment comes is the place where we think, pray, and work; we begin our spiritual journey where we are, and not somewhere else. If the Latin Americans' "own wells" are located within the liberation struggle to which they are committed, our North American wells will likewise be found in our own situation, as we struggle, for example, with the affluence we so often use exploitatively. In either case, the life of spirituality will be located in the midst of the world's turmoil, rather than in safe havens of disengagement.

This cannot be done, Gutiérrez would continue, with an individualistic spirituality, and he would call attention to the important subtitle of his book, *The Spiritual Journey of a People,* as a reminder that spirituality must be communal. To show that this conviction is not idiosyncratic to himself, he might cite the comment of John de Gruchy from South Africa, another continent where oppression and struggle are daily companions of the Christian:

> The Christian life, while intensely personal, is always communal. . . . The privatization of piety is not part of the Christian tradition and it undermines the Christian life. . . . Christian spirituality is, therefore, the spirituality of Christian community. But it is not Christian community lived in isolation from the world.
>
> (De Gruchy, *Cry Justice,* p. 25)

Having rooted spirituality in the immediate human situation, Gutiérrez would then explore the riches of the biblical and historical traditions, in order to pave the way for five interconnected marks of the new spirituality of liberation. They are worth some attention, because they are as true for us in our situation as they are in his.

The first of these is *Conversion: A Requirement for Solidarity,* and it involves a break with the past and the setting out on a new path that is both personal and social. Conversion involves both an acknowledgment of individual sin and a recognition that ours is a sinful situation, containing structural causes of injustice. So conversion will involve the option to live in solidarity with those who attack sin on both levels. Hunger for God and hunger for bread go together.

A second characteristic is *Gratuitousness: The Atmosphere for Efficacy* (which we might render in less cumbersome fashion as "Grace: The Basis for Action"). God's gracious love is the source of everything else, including our own ability to love. Such love starts with the concrete need of the other, not with a "duty" to practice love. Drawing on Bernanos's theme that "all is grace," Gutiérrez reminds us that grace provides beauty for our lives, "without which even the struggle for justice would be crippled." Prayer expresses our faith and trust in the gracious God, a "living dialogue" that becomes a touchstone of life. There is always "a twofold movement": a full encounter with the neighbor presupposes the experience of grace, and Christ, as our way to God, is also our way to the neighbor.

The third note is *Joy: Victory Over Suffering.* Gutiérrez does not gloss over the reality of suffering, but he also insists that the last word is "the joy born of the conviction that unjust mistreatment and suffering will be overcome." Such joy can be found even in a time of martyrdom, for to defend the poor easily leads to suffering and death. Martyrdom "is something that happens but is not sought," and Christians must never create a "cult of death." The only joy that can ultimately sustain us is "Easter joy," a joy that "springs from hope that death is not the final word of history." Those who encounter the cross are led to experience the resurrection.

The fourth mark is *Spiritual Childhood: A Requirement for Commitment to the Poor.* The task, as Gutiérrez frequently remarks, is to be "with the poor and against poverty." The demands are severe: One must assume "voluntarily and lovingly the condition of the needy . . . in order to give testimony to the evil it represents." To do so will provoke opposition from the privileged, who are not enchanted when those within the church "disassociate themselves from the injustices of the prevailing system." Commitment to the poor means looking on the world of the poor "as a place of residence and not simply of work," sharing in exploitation, inadequate health care, and all the rest but also making new friends, experiencing a new kind of love, and developing "a new realization of the Lord's fidelity."

The fifth mark is *Community: Out of Solitude.* To be with the poor will mean going through "the dark night of injustice" oneself, enduring ostracization, fear, weariness, cowardice, and despair, not to mention having to make crucial decisions when "nothing is clear." This is when we move "out of solitude" and into community. God does not call us to remain in the desert, but to pass through it on our way to the promised land. As we are drawn more deeply into community, we find foretastes of the promised land, even in the midst of the desert, places where the death and resurrection of Christ are remembered, and where the Eucharist becomes a point of departure and arrival. The mood is celebration.

> Spirituality [Gutiérrez concludes] is a community enterprise. It is a passage of a people through the solitude and dangers of the desert, as it carves out its own way in the following of Jesus Christ. This spiritual experience is the well from which we must drink. Through it we draw the promise of the resurrection.

Throughout, Gutiérrez has been describing spirituality. Throughout, Gutiérrez has been describing liberation.

Redefining liberation

Liberation when radically understood includes what is meant by spirituality. We can make our point by calling once again on Gutiérrez, who, as the practitioner of a life in which spirituality and liberation cannot be separated, has particularly compelling credentials. We need to call attention to only a single point made in his first major work, *A Theology of Liberation* (esp. pp. 36–37 and 176–181). If this point is clear, the case for the inclusiveness of spirituality and liberation has been established. It is Gutiérrez's contention that liberation has three levels of meaning but that no one of them is properly understood unless all three are simultaneously affirmed.

The first level is *liberation from unjust social structures* that destroy people. These structures may be political, economic, or cultural, they may grow out of warped attitudes based on race, class, nation, or sex, and they may also (as Gutiérrez has personal reason to know) be embodied in church structures, operating in concert with any of the others. The attention of liberation theologians has been strongly focused on this level, since it is the most immediate barrier to full personhood that their constituencies face, and it has thrust many of them into conflictive situations.

The second level with which liberation is concerned is more subtle but equally devastating. It is *liberation from the power of fate,* from the sense that one's station in life is foreordained, and that not only is there nothing one can do about it but it would be presumptuous and arrogant even to try. If one is born poor, that is the way it is meant to be; if one is born rich, that, too, is the way it is meant to be. Good news to the rich, bad news to the poor. Result: apathy or despair among the poor, and exhilaration among the rich, who are determined to keep things that way. The counsel to accept whatever cards fate deals serves as a magnificent justification for the status quo, a fact not lost on the rich and powerful.

For hundreds of years, the church played a major role in supporting this position, by the simple device of substituting "providence" or "the will of God" for the pagan concept of "fate." Accept your lot without complaint, the sermons went, and God will reward you in the afterlife.

The liberation message on this second level is that things need not remain the way they are, that the biblical God is working actively for justice and seeks to enlist all people in the struggle. The operative word is hope.

The third level of liberation is *liberation from personal sin and guilt.* This is not an add-on to the liberation agenda, inserted late in the day to forestall the critics, but has been there from the start, as any examination of the literature will show. Critics who fail to see it testify only to their own myopia. If the third level receives less quantitative treatment than the others, this is for the good reason that it has always been the central if not exclusive message of the institutional church, hardly in need of new champions, whereas levels one and two have only infrequently been acknowledged as part of the Christian agenda. Even so, the quantitative as well as qualitative attention given to such matters in Gutiérrez's writings is impressive. Prayer, Bible study, worship, Eucharist, and (as we have seen) grace are central to his understanding of liberation.

The descriptions of the three levels thus far have been put in negative terms, as "liberation from . . . ." But the positive counterparts are clear: Liberation from unjust social structures means liberation *for* participation in creating a just society; liberation from fate means liberation *for* responsible action; liberation from sin and guilt means liberation *for* a grace-filled life, the "gratuitousness" of which Gutiérrez speaks so often.

The discussion is not complete without another reminder that we do not truly understand any of these levels unless we affirm them simultaneously. None has meaning without the other two. No liberation is "merely" political, or "merely" biblical, or "merely" anything else. It is all of them together.

> Our aspirations include not only liberation from *exterior* pressures which prevent our fulfillment as members of a certain social class, country, or society. We seek likewise an *interior* liberation, in an individual and intimate dimension; we seek liberation not only on a social plane but also on a psychological.
>
> (*A Theology of Liberation,*
> p. 30, slightly altered)

He quotes David Cooper approvingly: "If we are to talk of revolution today our talk will be meaningless unless we effect some union between the macro-social and the micro-social, and between 'inner reality' and 'outer reality' " (ibid., p. 31).

And finally, Gutiérrez again in a later work: "Liberation is an all-embracing process that leaves no dimension of life untouched" (*We Drink from Our Own Wells,* p. 2).

It should be clear that such comments do not mean a simplistic equating of the three levels of liberation. Gutiérrez reminds us that all three are necessary, but that they are not exactly the same: "one is not present without the other, but they are distinct" (*A Theology of Liberation,* p. 176). Otherwise we reduce the kingdom of God to nothing but a temporal process.

The interrelationship of the three levels of liberation recalls the interrelationship within Micah 6:8, a verse that, as we saw in chapter 4, presents not three different exhortations but a single exhortation expressed in three different ways. Whether by fate, providence, or sheer coincidence (let the reader decide), Micah's three variants happily coincide with the positive statements of Gutiérrez's three levels of liberation that we have just identified:

To act justly = to participate in creating a just society
To love tenderly = responsible action
To walk humbly with God = a grace-filled life

Throughout, Gutiérrez has been describing liberation. Throughout, Gutiérrez has been describing spirituality.

9

Plan C:
Some Consequences

The affairs of the world, including economic ones, cannot be separated from the spiritual hunger of the human heart.
> —Roman Catholic bishops' pastoral letter on the economy, paragraph 327

Holiness is not limited to the sanctuary or to moments of private prayer... holiness is achieved in the midst of the world.
> —The bishops again, paragraph 327

There is a spirituality that dares to sink roots in the soil of oppression-liberation.
> —Gustavo Gutiérrez,
> *We Drink from Our Own Wells*

If that is all true, then at the very least we have to act differently and speak differently.

Toward a new way of acting

To Juan Luis Segundo, a Jesuit from Uruguay, the starting point for a liberating spirituality, as we saw earlier, is very simple: *The world should not be the way it is.* If you are satisfied with the way the world is, if you feel morally at ease within it, Segundo tells us, you will never understand what we are about, for we are *not* satisfied with the way the world is, and we do *not* feel morally at ease within it. We see too much misery, too much exploitation, too many children with bloated stomachs, too many wretched slums, too many parents unable to provide for their children, too many poor whose lives and deaths are determined by too few rich.

That must all be radically changed, Segundo would argue—at the roots. No tidying up around the edges will suffice. To feed the poor a nourishing breakfast does not deal with the fact that they will be hungry again by suppertime. Within the religious community, too many people either come up with palliatives that do not basically change anything, or assert that such problems are none of their business—a stance they justify by one version or another of the Great Fallacy.

Imagine, however, a group of people who are being forced to face such issues head on and whose reliance on the Great Fallacy is being exposed and discredited. Imagine that the relationship between how they worship God and how they deal with the world needs to be refocused, so that those two concerns become one. How will this change them? What will it do to their politics and to their worship?

Let us look at a typical "worshiping congregation" that has been living comfortably with the Great Fallacy and watch what happens when the divine boom is lowered. Happily, there is a case study already at hand, thoughtfully provided by an unknown Hebrew prophet.

The backdrop of the passage (Isaiah 58:1–12) is that God is highly displeased with the introspective character of the people's worship and instructs the prophet to make the divine displeasure clear beyond any shadow of a doubt: "Cry aloud, spare not, lift up your voice like a trumpet," and confront the people with their sins (v. 1). All the dirty laundry is to be hung out in full view of the neighbors.

This is a shock to the people, who had been under the impression that the newest liturgical detergent had left their religious practices gleaming. After all, they are part of a nation doing "righteousness" and following "the ordinance of their God" (v. 2). The code word in their culture for going the religious second mile is "fasting," a particular spiritual exercise that we can take as a symbol for *any* kind of worship or religious practice designed to curry favor with God.

So when the word of judgment comes in one of those prophetic trumpet blasts, they feel entitled to complain. They have been going out of their way to do the "extra" religious thing, and God hasn't even noticed how pious they are. In that case, why bother?

> Why have we fasted, and thou seest it not?
> Why have we humbled ourselves,
>   and thou takest no knowledge of it?
>   (v. 3)

Ask a question, get an answer. When they fast, God responds, they only do it to get points for being pious. And not only that, but at the very moment they are preening themselves on their spiritual rectitude, they are committing injustice in the workplace:

> Behold, in the day of your fast
> [in the midst of your religious practices]
> you seek your own pleasure,
>   *and oppress all your workers.*
>   (v. 3, italics added)

If they ask another question, "But what has worship got to do with paying the minimum wage?" they will get another answer: Everything. God will not even listen to people who make humble gestures, bow down their heads, and call that a sufficient exercise of their faith: "Fasting like yours this day will *not* make your voice heard on high" (v. 4, italics added). There is scorn as well as thunder in the divine voice:

> Will you call this a fast,
>   and a way acceptable to the LORD?
>   (v. 5)

It's a rhetorical question.

By this time God has built up a considerable head of steam, and it is about to erupt. You want to know my idea of a fast, God continues, you want to know my idea of what is acceptable "worship"? I'll tell you. And God does, in one of the most powerful utterances in all scripture:

> Is not this the fast that I choose:
>   to loose the bonds of wickedness,

> to undo the thongs of the yoke,
> to let the oppressed go free,
> and to break every yoke?
> Is it not to share your bread with the hungry,
> and bring the homeless poor into your house;
> when you see the naked, to cover [them],
> and not to hide yourself from your own flesh?
>
> (vs. 6–7)

And if that's still not clear, God continues, let me spell it out a little more, because you are going to have to make a choice:

> If you take away from the midst of you the yoke [of oppression],
> the pointing of the finger [of contempt], and speaking wickedness,
> if you pour yourself out for the hungry
> and satisfy the desire of the afflicted . . .
>
> (vs. 9–10)

. . . then things will be different, God promises, and a future full of hope can be anticipated—a future spelled out in glowing detail in the next verses.

Note well: *This exhortation to achieve justice in human relations is not part of the social action platform of the local synagogue but is a definition of worship.* This is the "fast," the kind of religious observance that God chooses, and its guiding principle is justice.

Our two apparently divergent definitions of "radical" (cited at the beginning of the last chapter) begin to overlap. For to worship "radically" (in the sense of getting to the root of what God asks of us) is to be thrust into a "radical" political stance (in the sense of working for basic change, rather than a cosmetic touching up of the way things are). We see this overlap clearly in the successive uses of the image of the "yoke" in the passage.

A yoke is worn by a beast of burden and indicates subservience to whoever is driving the beast, one who could well be a harsh taskmaster. To put a yoke on the neck of a person, as the Isaiah passage does, is to reduce that person to the level of a beast, to make that person subhuman. How is this situation to be overcome? The prophet outlines three steps, each more "radical" than its predecessor.

1. *To "undo the thongs of the yoke"* (v. 6): to loosen it, make it less painful, provide some immediate relief from the burden; in other words, to alleviate some of the immediate condition of social evil.

2. *To "break every yoke"* (v. 6), a more demanding challenge: to destroy the social structures symbolized by the yoke, whatever they are, that condemn people to live subhuman lives.

3. *To "take away from the midst of you the yoke"* (v. 9): not even to leave the debris around (that might tempt people to patch it up) but to banish the structures of oppression from the scene once and for all, repudiate them, so that they can never dominate again but can be replaced by structures patterned on justice rather than exploitation.

Not content simply to denounce, the prophet interlaces these comments with a suggestive laundry list of what the new structures will look like. True worship, the "true fast," will involve such things as:

1. The sharing of bread with the hungry, which in this new context will not simply mean making a few of our leftover slices available to those who don't have any, but working to create an economic order in which everyone has direct access to bread and the money with which to pay for it.

2. Bringing the homeless poor into our houses, which will mean not only responding to the immediate situation of the tens of thousands of homeless people in our cities by providing shelter in our homes and churches and synagogues, but also working to create an economic order in which housing projects are built, and jobs provided, so that "the homeless poor" will have homes of their own to dwell in and will not be dependent on the charity of the affluent. In our day there must also be special action on behalf of the "homeless poor" from places like El Salvador and Guatemala, who have fled for their lives from death squads and whose ongoing survival depends on churches and synagogues providing "sanctuary" for them, so that our government is unable to deport them to likely death.

And the agenda continues throughout the passage: clothing the naked, being responsible to the members of one's own family, pouring ourselves out for the hungry, meeting the needs of the afflicted—all of which, by prophetic standards, will have to go far beyond charitable handouts and will involve new structures to replace the old.

Our starting point, provided by Fr. Segundo, that "the world should not be the way it is," has led us in some surprising directions. Not only has it brought the two meanings of "radical" closer together, but it has indicated that our worship is defined by how we act for justice, and that how we act for justice defines our worship.

A new way of acting, indeed.

Toward a new way of speaking

To the degree that we discover that spirituality and liberation are two ways of speaking about the same thing, we will discover that we need a new way of speaking, a new vocabulary. There will need to be some new words, not yet discovered, but in the meantime we can begin to invest some old words with new meaning.

Commenting on Gutiérrez's treatment of spirituality, for example, Henri Nouwen, a Dutch priest, shows that in reappropriating great themes from the past like conversion, gratuity, joy, spiritual childhood, and community, Gutiérrez has given them new meaning for the present:

> These old words sound fresh and new when they have been distilled from the life experience of the suffering of the Latin American church. *Conversion* then emerges as part of a process of solidarity with the poor and the oppressed; *gratuity* as the climate of fruitful work for liberation; *joy* as victory over suffering; *spiritual childhood* as a condition of commitment to the poor; and *community* as a gift born out of the common experience of the dark night of injustice.
>
> (Foreword to *We Drink from Our Own Wells,*
> p. xix, italics added)

Tissa Balasuriya, a Sri Lankan priest, does much the same thing. In a chapter provocatively entitled "Toward a Spirituality of Justice," he takes the traditional notion of "prudence" (which has probably been employed to scuttle more movements for social justice than any other so-called Christian "virtue") and gives it revolutionary content:

> Prudence requires that we not waste our time and energies in unnecessary battles and secondary issues, for this will dissipate the effort even of the well intentioned. Prudence will decide on the issues that are worth fighting for, as well as the means to be used in the struggle. Prudence tells us when it is necessary to bypass an issue and pursue it to the extent of polarization.
>
> Prudence will help us calculate risks so that risks taken will yield results. Prudence decides when to give oneself for a cause, even if it means such extreme sacrifices as imprisonment or life itself. The action of Che Guevara in joining the guerillas may have seemed imprudent in the short term. But in the long term it has made an inestimable contribution to the cause. A spirituality of liberation therefore involves an understanding of risk-bearing and disappointment.
>
> (Balasuriya, *Planetary Theology,* p. 265)

Johannes Metz, the European theologian most sensitive to third world views, has done a similar reevaluation of the ascetic side of Christianity in the light of a "theology of the world." Metz sees asceticism, which has often been interpreted as a denial of the world, not as "flight from the world, but flight 'forward' with the world," an exercise in which another vision of what could be is juxtaposed to what is. Paul, for example, "is critical not of solidarity with the world, but of conformism with it." Asceticism can thus have a "revolutionary quality, as protest against the present for the sake of the future."

From this perspective it is possible to assess mysticism in a new way, since it too has often been associated with "distance" from the world. In a paragraph that defies paraphrase, Metz offers an illuminating corrective:

> Christian mysticism is neither a kind of pantheistic infinity mysticism, nor an esoteric mysticism of exaltation, tending toward the self-redemption of the individual soul. It is—putting it extremely—a mysticism of human bonding. But it

does not proceed from an arbitrary denial of persons and the world, in order to seek to rise toward a direct nearness to God. For the God of Christian faith is found only in the movement of God's love toward persons, "the least," as has been revealed to us in Jesus Christ. Christian mysticism finds, therefore, that direct experience of God which it seeks, precisely in daring to imitate the unconditional involvement of the divine love for persons, in letting itself be drawn into the . . . descent of God's love to the least of God's brothers and sisters. Only in this movement do we find the supreme nearness, the supreme immediacy of God. And that is why mysticism, which seeks this nearness, has its place not outside, beside, or above responsibility for the world of our brothers and sisters, but in the center of it.

(Metz, *Theology of the World,* p. 104, slightly adapted)

New understandings of old words sneak up on us unawares. A commandment like "Thou shalt not steal" embodies conventional wisdom. It is invoked to ensure that I do not rob you. But since what is fair for one is fair for all, I insist on invoking it to ensure that you do not rob me—a reading that appeals to me tremendously, particularly as I am fortunate enough to accumulate more and more goods and thus need extra protection against your covetous eye. I, of course, have no interest in breaking into your modest dwelling for the sake of a few knickknacks, so I am no problem, but society needs a police force to keep watch over your proclivity to try shoplifting in my place of business.

However, if we take seriously the spirituality-liberation connection, we discover disturbing implications, in this apparently straightforward commandment, that have been under wraps for centuries.

1. As far back as the early church fathers, it was noted that if I have more than I need, and you have less than you need, I am already committing "theft" against you and am breaking the commandment not to steal. John Chrysostom defines robbery as "not sharing one's resources," and Ambrose makes caustic remarks about situations in which "a naked man cries out, but you are busy considering what sort of

marble you will have to cover your floors" and pay no heed. Theft.

2. Not only is the accusing finger being pointed at me, but you, as the one in need, are authorized to take from me what you need for your survival, no penalties incurred. In a remarkable passage in "The Church and the Modern World," the 2300 bishops at the Second Vatican Council stated:

> The right to have a share of earthly goods sufficient for oneself and one's family belongs to everyone. . . . *If a person is in extreme necessity, such a one has the right to take from the riches of others what he or she needs.*
>
> (Paragraph 69, italics added)

3. Strictures against theft are targeted not only against individuals but against society. A society with a few wealthy and many poor is a thieving society, and those within it who benefit from such disparities are breaking the commandment "Thou shalt not steal." The remedy comes by appeals not only to individual behavior but to responsible action on the part of society as a whole. The surprising bishops continue:

> According to their ability, let all individuals *and governments* undertake a genuine sharing of their goods. Let them use these goods especially to provide individuals and nations with the means for helping and developing themselves.
>
> (Paragraph 69, italics added)

In a recent work, *On Job: God-Talk and the Suffering of the Innocent,* Gustavo Gutiérrez gives us further help on language by initially distinguishing two ways of talking about God in the book of Job.

Prophetic language stresses God's predilection for the poor. God loves the poor not because they are better than others but simply because they are poor. And this "preferential option for the poor" on God's part must be reflected in a similar "preferential option for the poor" on the part of those who worship God. God's grace and this preferential option go hand in hand.

Contemplative language is supported and reinforced by

prophetic language. "Mystical language" (as Gutiérrez also calls it) "expresses the gratuitousness of God's love; prophetic language expresses the demands this love makes" (p. 95). Contemplative language acknowledges that everything comes from God's unmerited—i.e., gracious—love. But the two languages are linked, as a passage in Jeremiah shows:

> Sing to the LORD;
>   praise the LORD!
> For [the Lord] has delivered the life of the needy
>   from the hand of evildoers.
>
> (Jer. 20:13)

The first two lines are contemplative, the latter two prophetic.

However, the point is not that "two languages—the prophetic and the contemplative—are required" but that "Both languages are necessary and therefore inseparable; they also feed and correct each other" (p. 95). But there is a further point—"they must also be combined and become increasingly integrated *into a single language*" (p. 94, italics added).

As Gutiérrez writes in an earlier essay:

> We need a language that is both contemplative and prophetic; contemplative because it ponders a God who is love; prophetic because it talks about a liberator God who rejects the situation of injustice in which the poor live, and also the structural causes of that situation.
>
> (In Fabella and Torres, eds.,
> *Irruption of the Third World,* p. 232)

Without denying the importance of the words we speak directly to God in prayer, either in public or in private, we can begin to see from our new perspective how deeds themselves can be forms of prayer. A prayer of intercession may be a trip to the city jail to provide bail for someone wrongly arrested because of having the wrong skin color; an act of praise of God may be the affirmation of a Laotian child's success in the English as a Second Language program; an act of contrition may be persuading a Congressional representative to vote against aid to the Nicaraguan *contras;* a Hail Mary may be involvement in a political group trying to implement the concern for the poor that is celebrated in the Magnificat; a choral response may be joining in the cheers at a rally to reverse the arms race; a blessing may be the gift of time and money that enables a woman victimized by sexual harassment to secure legal help; a prayer of adoration may be the formation of a political coalition to fight a specific injustice at city hall.

Conversely, a word spoken to God in private may be the condition for a deed done for a victim in public; an inner impulse, empowered by grace, may generate a political conviction; a meditation on scripture may inspire an act of civil disobedience; hearing a sermon about Nathan challenging David may focus the need to challenge the Immigration Service or the State Department.

Laborare est orare—to work is to pray—was how the medieval monks put it. We are only beginning to catch up with them.

There is a trap into which we could fall, and it will take a final chapter to avoid it. The trap consists of implying that our discovery of the overlapping of spirituality and liberation is mainly a matter of the intellect.

Faithfulness to our subject matter compels us to acknowledge that this will not do. The recovery of the unity of spirituality and liberation must be exhibited in the day-to-day events of human lives rather than in the line-to-line sentences of human books.

We need not definitions but examples, not victories of logic but victories of love. And these are what we will seek in the final pages.

10

Showing by Deeds
What Cannot
Be Shown by Words

Hope has two beautiful daughters. Their names are anger and courage: anger at the way things are, and courage to see that they do not remain the way they are.

—Augustine

Whenever an angel says "Be not afraid!" you'd better start worrying. A big assignment is on the way.

—Elie Wiesel, in conversation

Unfortunately no single word communicates the single reality we have identified. To write "spirituality/liberation," or "liberation/spirituality" works technically but remains awkward. Words already available carry enough accumulated baggage to invite misunderstanding. *Praxis* comes close, since it means the interrelationship of reflection and action, but it is so closely associated in our minds with "practice" that it is likely to distort as much as illumine. *Shalom,* a beautiful Hebrew word, points to the wholeness of life, but it has been so widely employed as a synonym for "peace" that its meaning is too narrow for our purposes.

There is another way to communicate, however, that may be more faithful to our subject matter than seeking a new word. This is to use words that point not to definitions but to deeds—to episodes or persons or events that enact what our speech, by itself, cannot communicate.

There is good biblical precedent for this, most notably in

the Letter to the Hebrews, where the unknown author is trying desperately to communicate something of the meaning of the word "faith." Let us assume that the author is a woman. She tries her hand at a formal definition: "Now faith is the substance of things hoped for, the evidence of things not seen" (Heb. 11:1, KJV). Pretty abstract. She offers a historical generalization: "For by it [those] of old received divine approval" (v. 2). Not much better. Maybe cosmology will clarify: "By faith we understand that the world was created by the word of God"—her readers' faces are still blank. In desperation she turns to epistemology—"so that what is seen was made out of things which do not appear" (v. 3), a sentence destined to confuse rather than clarify.

By this time a gnawing question is working its way up into the author's consciousness: "Will this fly in Dubuque?" It is her considered—and correct—judgment that it will not. Dubuque couldn't care less.

Nothing to do, then, but start all over. First question: "How to explain faith?" Second question (which is an answer to the first question): "How about telling stories about people who exemplify faith, describing events in which faith is on the scene, lining up a cast of very different characters, ranging from harlots to heavenly beings, who have at least in common that faith is written all over who they are?"

It works. The next forty verses (spilling over into chapter 12) are as exciting as the first four are dull. She calls up Abel, Noah, Abraham, Sarah, Rahab, Isaac, and Joseph, among others, and one whom she describes as the "pioneer and perfecter" of the faith; she takes her readers on hikes through the wilderness; she lets them participate in crossing a body of water without getting wet; she describes battles and tumbling city walls, resurrections, torture scenes, duels—a vast historical kaleidoscope that replaces definitions with deeds.

Dubuque is listening.

We will take our cue from the author. Although we will not range as widely as she did, or assume that our efforts will one day be enshrined in Holy Scripture, we will likewise forsake further formal definition and offer a contemporary kaleidoscope of events distinguished by the fact that within them spirituality and liberation are cut from the same cloth. Using terminology from her letter, we will call it:

A cloud of witnesses

There is a Dutch priest named Henri Nouwen, and for many years Henri Nouwen has been "Mr. Spirituality"—or, more properly, "Fr. Spirituality"—not only to many Catholics but to many other Christians as well. They turn to him for devotional reading, for suggestions about what to do "on retreat," for help in deepening their prayer life. Through his writings and his person he is a tutor to the human spirit; in the realms of the personal, the individual, the inward, his role as a spiritual director is grace-filled and sustaining.

And then one day Henri Nouwen discovers that he must test a prompting that has come to him in his own devotional life. Perhaps he has a vocation to settle in Latin America and live among the poor, seeking to combine a life of prayer with a sharing in their ongoing struggle for justice.

As he goes to Latin America, no lights flash and no bells ring, but he realizes immediately (as he records in his journal, *¡Gracias!*) that "Prayer and work with the poor belong together" (p. 10) and that the need to pray increases when people are confronted with oppression and exploitation. His reading of the Bible and his discernment of the contemporary world begin to inform one another: "I try to remember that Jesus was killed as a subversive . . . under the accusation of being an enemy of the ruling class" (p. 29). And again: "[The words of the Magnificat] today have taken on so much power and strength that, in a country like El Salvador, they are considered subversive and can be a cause of torture and death" (p. 68).

Events in the liturgical year take on new relevance in the context of living among the poor. The Feast of St. John of the Cross, for example, reveals the intimate connection between resistance and contemplation: "[St. John] reminds us that true resistance against the powers of destruction can only be a lifelong commitment when it is fed by an ardent love for the God of justice and peace" (p. 72).

Whatever the final outcome of Henri Nouwen's quest, he realizes that it is no longer possible to be a contemplative without taking political revolution into account, and that praying in the future may mean praying in the midst of a revolution rather than at a distance.

Henri Nouwen's new engagement in the struggle for social justice is an expression of his prayer life, not an alternative.

There is a splendid sign in the chapel of Temple Emmanuel Shalom in Burlingame, California, which in addition to the sign also contains a pulpit, an ark, the Torah, and all the other normal accoutrements of Jewish worship. The sign is a public declaration from the local fire department indicating maximum legal occupancy under a variety of conditions.

The sign is interesting in that—like most such things—its message is unexpected. It does not stipulate "62 Persons for Prayer Services," "47 Persons for Bar Mitzvahs or Bat Mitzvahs," or other ceremonies usually associated with chapels. The sign simply says that the maximum legal occupancy in this place of worship is

26 DINING
55 DANCING

There is a marvelous recognition that "earthy" things like having meals and throwing dances—celebratory events—are not only not excluded from places of worship but are expressions of what places of worship are for. How do we celebrate God's reality? Give a party!

Somebody has finally caught up with that curious passage in Exodus we have already noted: "They beheld God, and ate and drank" (Ex. 24:11).

Peggy Hutchison stands in the United States District Court in Tucson, Arizona, Judge Earl Carroll presiding, waiting to be sentenced. She has been found guilty of conspiracy in violation of Title 18, United States code 371. In less abstract language, she has been convicted of helping political refugees escape from death squads in El Salvador and Guatemala, so that they can find sanctuary in the United

States until it is politically safe for them to go back home.
Has she anything to say "by way of mitigating evidence"
before sentence is imposed?

She has.

She tells the court that her family and the United Methodist Church both helped to shape her values and taught her
that beliefs didn't mean anything unless she put them into
action. Her church enjoined her in its Discipline to be part
of "a witnessing and serving community." As she worked
with political refugees on both sides of the border, she soon
realized, as she informed Judge Carroll, that "they have fled
torture, they have fled imprisonment, civil war, and death,"
and that to turn her back on them would make her complicit
in actions that would imperil them all over again.

She discovered by bitter experience that the immigration
courts, the procedures of the Immigration and Naturaliza-
tion Service, and the policies of the Border Patrol were con-
spiring to make it impossible for political refugees to escape
deportation. She reminded the judge that the United States
had reacted with similar callous disregard to the plight of
Jews seeking to emigrate to the United States after the rise
of Hitler, and that "never again" must that happen. She
came to the conclusion that our immigration laws were not
being fairly administered, and that the lives and deaths of
people must be her paramount concern.

As she had said before the trial, her political involvement
was heightened not just by her study of the law but by her
study of scripture. Passages like "Do not mistreat foreigners
who are living in your land. . . . Love them as you love
yourselves" (Lev. 19:33, adapted) jumped out at her. Jesus'
admonitions, as she summarized them, to "feed the hungry,
clothe the naked, welcome the stranger, take care of the sick,
visit the imprisoned" (cf. Matt. 25:31– 46), seemed to have
been written for the precise situation in which she found
herself, and they could not be ignored.

In the face of this conflict between human law and divine
gospel, she reports that she "spent time in meditation, reflection, and prayer." Rather than providing relief from her
political dilemma, the meditation, reflection, and prayer con-

fronted her with a series of options, from within which she knew she had to choose: "I could collaborate with the United States government, which helps sponsor the torture of thousands of people; I could learn to live with atrocity; or I could stand with the oppressed and persecuted Salvadorans and Guatemalans and respond to these sojourners in my midst."

The consequence of making the latter choice not only heightened her political activity (until her arrest) but simultaneously deepened her faith—a not surprising consequence, since in her life "political activity" and "faith" are not two but one.

And there was a gift as well. She learned that the refugees to whom she was ministering were ministering in turn to her. It was from them, she reports, that she discovered how to live in the midst of exploitation, destruction, and death and still affirm hope, resurrection, life . . . and change.

No one who tries to understand Peggy Hutchison's experience will be tempted to separate her life into a "spiritual" compartment and a "liberation" compartment.

No one, perhaps, except a district court judge, who, after hearing the "mitigating evidence," sentenced her to five years' probation.

Rabbi Abraham Joshua Heschel was a professor at Jewish Theological Seminary in New York City until his death in 1972. He had come to the United States from his native Poland shortly before Hitler's forces invaded his homeland and destroyed all the Jews they could find.

One of the most remarkable things about Heschel's years at Jewish Seminary was his title. He was not just an ordinary "professor"; he was—in a title that was a clear consequence of divine inspiration—Professor of Mysticism and Ethics.

Many people find mysticism a topic beyond their comprehension, and at least as many people, in this relativistic era, find ethics equally baffling. Join them—mysticism and ethics—suggesting that they belong together, and the mystery is compounded beyond apparent resolution. Hard enough to be a professor of either, but to be a professor of both?

Those who knew Heschel found nothing incongruous in

the title. It was simply a description of who he was—never just the mystic, never just the ethicist, but an authentically integral human being in whom the two were one. He could write a beautiful book on the Sabbath and march in civil rights demonstrations at Selma, Alabama, saying, "Today we are praying with our feet." He could simultaneously inveigh against the immorality of the U.S. action in Vietnam and invoke the mercy of God, whether in pulpit or public square. He could glory in the tasks of scholarship and give his energy to improving relations between blacks and Jews. He could meet with popes to alter the course of Jewish-Christian relationships and instruct young rabbis in Torah. The one whose presence could remind others of the majesty of the prophets, and of the God to whom the prophets witnessed, could also enjoy a good cigar.

In his later years, Heschel formed an abiding friendship with the Protestant theologian Reinhold Niebuhr, a neighbor in New York City, of whom he wrote, in words that are a perfect description of Heschel as well:

> His spirituality combines heaven and earth. . . . It does not separate soul from body, or mind from unity of our physical and spiritual life. His way is an example of one who does justly, loves mercy, and walks humbly with his God, an example of the unity of worship and living.
>
> (Heschel, *The Insecurity of Freedom,* p. 147)

Sometimes it takes one to know one.

It is my first communion service after ordination. It is taking place on the after gun turret of a U.S. Navy destroyer during World War II, and I am there because I am a navy chaplain. There is only room for three communicants at a time to come forward and receive the elements. The first three to respond to the invitation are a lieutenant commander, captain of the vessel; a fireman's apprentice, about as low as one can be in the ordinary naval hierarchy; and a steward's mate, who, because he is black, is not even included in the ordinary naval hierarchy; all blacks can do in the then–Jim Crow navy is wait on the tables where the white officers eat.

An officer, a white enlisted man, a black enlisted man—day by day they eat in separate mess halls. There are no circumstances in which they could eat together at a navy table. But at the Lord's Table, not even navy regulations can dictate who eats with whom. For this one moment—as is true during no other moments on shipboard—they are equals, and they are at the same table. Here is the one place where hierarchical statutes do not prevail. To make the point, I serve the black enlisted man first, the enlisted man second, the commanding officer last.

Holy Communion is usually described as the highest "spiritual" experience Christians can have. That particular Holy Communion was a "liberation" experience as well—liberation for a moment from the structures that otherwise separated those three men, and a liberation enacting in advance the kind of new structures that would someday prevail even in the U.S. Navy.

Spirituality, liberation. No separation.

Many communions later I am helping to celebrate at the General Assembly of the Presbyterian Church of Southern Africa, in the city of Durban. The black and white members of that denomination worship separately for fifty-one Sundays a year. During the week of General Assembly, however, they meet together, study together, eat together, worship together.

We distribute bread and wine to the deacons, who will partake before serving the congregation. They are lined up before the Lord's Table—black, white, black, white, white, black, white, black, black, white—a random selection. The bread is passed from hand to hand, and each hand, whether black or white, breaks off a piece to give to his or her neighbor. No hesitation. No problem.

And then a common cup—a single chalice—is passed down the line, lifted first to black lips, then to white lips, then to black lips. No hesitation. No problem.

I, a visitor to that land, would not have believed it possible. The "spiritual" act of sharing the body and blood of Christ becomes an occasion of "liberation" for all those people—

liberation for a moment from bondage to the fierce laws that on all other occasions legislate the separate sharing of food and drink by black and white. One day the fierce laws will change and the exception, enacted in that service, will be the rule. Much more blood—Christ's blood in Christ's children, both black and white—will be shed before the day when it is so, and that is a great tragedy. But it *will* come, in part because the distance between Christ's Table and all other tables can no longer be tolerated, and that is a great hope.

Spirituality, liberation. No separation.

The steps of the Federal Building, San Francisco, December 4, 1967. The occasion: a draft card turn-in by young men who are declaring that they will not fight in an immoral war. A political act. And an act of worship.

Each participant comes forward and places his draft card in the offering plate, symbolizing the offering of himself to oppose the killing. The cards are then lifted up—eighty-seven that day, as it turns out—blessed, placed in a large envelope addressed to the Office of Selective Service in Washington, and mailed by the participating clergy, who, in "aiding, counseling, and abetting" the draft resisters, place themselves in the same legal jeopardy as their younger compatriots.

When those cards were first mailed to their original addresses, they were messengers of *death,* summoning the addressees to participate in killing Vietnamese peasants. In the liturgical act of their gathering and remailing, they are transformed into messengers of *life,* declaring that their former owners are unwilling, no matter what the cost or inconvenience, to enlist in the service of death. Outwardly, the cards have not changed; inwardly, they are totally changed—from messengers of death to messengers of life.

I reflect that this is about as close as I, a Protestant, will ever come to understanding the ancient doctrine of transubstantiation—the belief that in the Roman Mass the bread and wine, while outwardly unchanged, become, after the words of consecration, the actual body and blood of Christ.

On the steps of the Federal Building in San Francisco, a "spiritual" experience of common worship is an act of "liberation" for eighty-seven young men, freed from bondage to the powers of death, freed for a future in which they can "choose life, so that they and their descendants may live." Spirituality, liberation. No separation.

Members of the Iona Community, a movement for reform within the Church of Scotland, believe (as we have previously suggested) that "liturgy" is *all* the work we do, both inside and outside the church. They have developed a daily way of issuing this reminder.

When they gather each morning for worship, they engage in a fairly conventional service, with scripture, hymns, and prayers, but the service ends unconventionally; there is no "benediction," no conclusion. Instead, they go directly from the chapel to whatever tasks they will be doing that day— helping to build a new dormitory, baking bread in the kitchen, mixing cement, rounding up cattle that have gotten loose. That is their continuing "liturgy," their work, until it is time to return to the chapel in the evening. Once again they engage in a fairly conventional service, with scripture, hymns, and prayers, but the service starts unconventionally; there is no "call to worship," no beginning, since they have been "at worship" all day long and what is happening now is simply a continuation of that worship in another form. The whole day is their "liturgy"; their work in church and their work outside are interconnected varieties of the one work. Only at the very end of the full day, when all the tasks are completed, is there a "benediction," a blessing for the day and a prayer for rest during the night.

Latin America is a land of martyrs, famous people (as we have seen) and thousands whose names we will never know, from villages, cities, barrios; priests, lay people, women, children, men. The blood of thousands of them is on U.S. hands, because of the part our nation has played in supplying munitions and arms and training to those who kill. The martyrs, while unknown to us, are heartbreakingly known to their wives and fathers and husbands and mothers and grandparents.

Their deaths are celebrated in sorrow but also in hope. When there has been the massacre of a family, or the burning of a village, or a "visit" by a death squad, or an ambush of coffee pickers, or an attack on a child care center, the people gather, when it is safe to do so, for a memorial service. The names of those attending are read out one by one, and each responds *¡Presente!* (I am here!) And then the names of the murdered victims are read out one by one, and after each name, the people with one voice respond for them: *¡Presente!*

> Raphael, killed by a land mine . . . *¡Presente!*
> María, machine-gunned in the child care center . . .
>   *¡Presente!*
> Juan, shot defending the hospital . . . *¡Presente!*
> José, killed by a sniper . . . *¡Presente!*

Meaning: "He is here . . . she is here . . . they are here . . . *in us.* We speak for them, since they can no longer speak for themselves. We take on their tasks, we will stand where they stood. Teresa will be at the child care center, Pedro will help defend the hospital. If necessary, we will fall as they fell, and if we do, then our names will be read out at another service, and the rest of you will say *¡Presente!* for us, and the struggle will go on until no more guns have to be fired, and we are free."

Sometimes the roll call is even more extensive:

> Archbishop Romero . . . *¡Presente!*
> Ita Ford . . . *¡Presente!*
> Victor Jara . . . *¡Presente!*
> Camilo Torres . . . *¡Presente!*

And a prayer will be offered: "Lord, keep alive in us the subversive memory of the martyrs from our people. Let them live in us, and we in them."

Political, or the communion of saints?

No separation.

At the height of the "unrest" on the campuses during the Vietnam War, the chaplain of Yale University, William Sloane Coffin, Jr., was indicted by a federal grand jury for "aiding, counseling, and abetting" young men who felt that they could not fight in a war they perceived as immoral.

This was the last straw for certain red-blooded sons of Eli Yale, who felt it was not the job of "a minister of religion" to be opposing the policies of his government, running around the country "agitating," "fomenting unrest," and counseling others "to break the law." Realizing that Coffin was up for reappointment, the alums organized a campaign to bring sufficient discredit on him so that no reappointment would be forthcoming. They hoped, by extensive interviewing, to show that Coffin had become so deeply involved in "secular" matters elsewhere that he was failing to mind the "religious" store at home.

The results of their not-so-impartial survey, however, came up with such a different profile of Coffin's activities that the movement to deny him reappointment collapsed. He was, to be sure, "running around the country," speaking, marching, occasionally getting arrested. But a look at Coffin's calendar showed that he was equally busy, if not more so, doing such things as conducting weddings and funerals, preaching the gospel, leading Bible study classes, visiting the sick in the university infirmary, baptizing the children of Yale faculty and students, presiding at the Lord's Table on communion Sunday, putting in many hours of counseling each week on a myriad of topics besides Vietnam, praying in public (and presumably also in private), and sharing in panel discussions on everything from sex education to Christian-Jewish relations.

Had he been asked how he kept these two sides of his life together, Coffin would have responded (with an appropriate *bon mot*) that that was the wrong question. There were not "two sides." People worrying about Vietnam have babies and want them baptized; the morality or immorality of public policy is a fit subject for prophetic preaching; making personal decisions about the future can be aided by Bible study; turning points in people's lives often lead them to private prayer and public worship; a student about to turn in his draft card may wish to receive Holy Communion. "If we spend years trying to educate young people to use their consciences," Bill Coffin had long ago decided, "we may not desert them in their hour of conscience."

All of a piece, all of a peace.

During the controversy over apartheid at the University of California at Berkeley in the spring of 1985, a massive rally was held at Sproul Plaza, at which six or seven thousand students gathered to demand that the university divest its holdings in companies doing business in South Africa. The nine theological seminaries up the hill from the university ("Holy Hill," as it is called locally, with varying inflections of affection or disdain) were invited to participate by marching down to Sproul Plaza dressed in ecclesiastical vestments, to give visible witness to the presence and support of the church. Since so many churchy types were to be present, the leaders of the rally decided to depart from custom and begin this particular rally with a prayer, and since I taught at one of the seminaries, I was invited to deliver it.

I worked long and hard on a text that could be delivered over a PA system within the allotted three minutes. (There is a theory on many university campuses that God is either hard of hearing or has a short attention span—and another more credible theory that even if the divine attention span is enduring, the human attention span is pretty short. "Three minutes at most," was the instruction.) When it was time for the rally to begin, I was on the podium as instructed, but the legions of the Lord's anointed had not yet put in an appearance, apparently inflicted with the same penchant for tardiness they so deplore when their lay constituencies practice it on Sunday morning.

There was nothing for it but to begin without them, hoping that their late arrival would not be interpreted as lack of commitment. I was scarcely well launched into my plea to the Almighty when there began to be interruptions from the crowd, with a significant enough decibel rating to make me wonder if public prayer at a rally was being looked upon with disfavor by the overwhelmingly "secular" crowd. But the scattered interruptions soon coalesced into a roar—a mighty cheer that made any attempt on my part to continue a futile gesture at best and an arrogant action at worst. I stopped and looked up, intending to wait for silence to be restored, so that I could continue to offer God my carefully crafted prose— and saw a line of hundreds of seminarians, dazzlingly be- decked with their tokens of office (the Episcopalians always come off best), spilling into the crowd, which was acknowl- edging their arrival with shouts of approval. Their cries, while not the biblical "Hallelujah!" were an adequate mod- ern rendering of that word: "Right *on!*"

As the noise subsided and I prepared to return to my utterance, it was given to me (in one of those rare visitations of the guiding hand of providence) to realize that I not only need not complete my prayer but that I should not do so. It had already been completed by the action of my colleagues, the solidarity of whose physical presence was spelling out, better than words could ever do, their commitment to this particular issue. *Their deed was their prayer.* They were pray- ing, as was Heschel at Selma, with their feet.

The deed, we are told, authenticates the word. Sometimes, as on this occasion, the deed *becomes* the word.

Elizabeth O'Connor exercises a variety of ministries.

She has been on the staff of the Church of the Savior, in Washington, D.C., since 1953; she has been a "spiritual di- rector" to thousands of people; she occasionally teaches and leads workshops; and she writes penetratingly about prayer, meditation, Bible study, and the uses of silence. Presently she is involved in the creation of Sarah's Circle, a ministry to and with the inner-city elderly poor. She is, in sum, a kind of Protestant Henri Nouwen—a comparison that honors them both, so long as we add immediately that Henri Nouwen is a kind of Catholic Elizabeth O'Connor.

Elizabeth O'Connor, then, guides people on what she and members of the Church of the Savior call "the journey inward." But that is not a sufficient description. What makes her contribution so special is her realization that there must simultaneously be a "journey outward," always in company with others. Neither journey alone is sufficient for church or individual.

> While it is a crucial mistake to assume that churches can be on an outward journey without being on an inward one, it is equally disastrous to assume that one can make the journey inward without taking the journey outward.
>
> (O'Connor, *Journey Inward, Journey Outward,* p. 9)

So when one joins the Church of the Savior, in addition to the inner disciplines of engagement with self, God, and neighbor there is a "fourth discipline": to become part of a "mission group" and work on a specific project—outreach into the halls of Congress, helping to run a coffeehouse, giving support to a health care center, focusing on "health advocacy for the poor, empowering the powerless to care and to seek care for themselves."

A brochure describing Wellspring, the church's retreat center, reminds those going on retreats:

> We share a way of being church that includes two simultaneous journeys—the journey inward and the journey outward. On the inward journey we become more deeply engaged with ourselves, with God, and with others. On the outward journey we join Jesus at a particular point of his ministry to the world, confronting the structures that perpetuate poverty and injustice . . . whatever they may be.

There is a care for balance in dealing with the two journeys, but when the chips are down the priorities are clear. Referring to Meister Eckhart's conviction that it is more important to feed a hungry person than to remain in spiritual ecstasy (a quotation pirated from Elizabeth O'Connor's writings and used in chapter 8), she continues:

> If we had to choose in any given moment between prayer and joining in the struggle of the hungry poor, we would turn from our praying.
>
> (O'Connor, *Search for Silence,* p. 118)

Two journeys. . . . But since neither can proceed without
the other, and both must be undertaken simultaneously, one
journey.

The Nicaraguan Minister of State, Miguel d'Escoto, also
happens to be a minister of the gospel. As a Catholic priest
and member of the order of Maryknoll Missioners, he par-
ticipates in the liturgy which is the Roman mass for many
years. He gradually comes to recognize, however, that there
is a wider "liturgy" in which he must also participate, the
liturgy of working to redeem the social order. And so, leaving the safety of North America where he has lived for
several years, he returns to his native land to participate in
the people's uprising against a dictator. After the triumph of
the revolution, he accepts appointment to the "secular" position of Minister of State. Along with several other priests, he
feels called to be both a "minister of God" and a "minister
of the people." There is no incompatibility, only complemen-
tarity.

The church authorities, however, disagree and discipline
Fr. d'Escoto and his fellow priests by removing their "facul-
ties": their right to celebrate mass, to hear confession, and
so forth. While this saddens them, it does not deter them, and
they continue to believe that the "liturgy" to which God calls
them includes their work for the state, as the means by which
they can best serve the people and thus serve God.

Realizing at one point that options for Nicaraguans and
citizens of other countries have been reduced to choosing
between various kinds of violence, and believing profoundly
in the power of nonviolence, Fr. d'Escoto does a most
unusual thing for a Minister of State. He goes on a public fast
for peace, to spark an "evangelical insurrection" and remind
the Nicaraguan people and the rest of the world of the need
for "a more excellent way." An ancient and usually private
liturgical action, fasting is reinvested with meaning as an act
of social witness.

The next year, as the Lenten season approaches, Fr. d'Escoto goes to the northern border of Nicaragua near Jalapa,
target of many U.S.-sponsored terrorist *contra* raids, and

begins walking south to Managua, the capital city, reenact-
ing, with hundreds of Nicaraguans who accompany him, one
station of the cross each day of the journey. Fr. d'Escoto
takes the private journey outdoors and makes it a communal
pilgrimage, through which many people can share in Jesus'
final struggle and discover new meanings that it might have
for them in the future.

These are quite extraordinary happenings, but we will miss
the point if we see Fr. d'Escoto's religious vision reflected
only in fasting and marching, although a religious vision is
certainly present in both actions. The really extraordinary
thing is the integrity by which he invests the ongoing daily
acts of political office with a clear sense that to work for the
people in their struggle for social justice is to work for God.

Amen.

Getting onstage ourselves

The author of the Letter to the Hebrews has a final gift for
us. After all the action-crammed lines, the extraordinary
characters, the frightening and faith-filled episodes about all
the folks "back then," she unexpectedly shifts gears. Instead
of letting her readers remain on the sidelines, spectators to
what is happening on the playing field, she draws the readers
out onto the playing field themselves, or (to put it differently)
she draws them into the story.

"Therefore," she writes at the end of her historical recital,
pausing to catch her breath, therefore . . . but she does not
go on, "let us be glad that so many of them ran the race so
well." No, the words after "Therefore" are, "since *we* are
surrounded by so great a cloud of witnesses . . . let *us* run
with perseverance the race that is set before *us*" (Heb. 12:1,
italics added).

A little later, saying, "Consider [Jesus] who endured from
sinners such hostility against himself," she does not interpo-
late, "How proud his parents must have been!" No, she
writes, "Consider him who endured from sinners such hostility against himself, *so that you may not grow weary or faint-
hearted*" (Heb. 12:3, italics added). The story does not end

back there. The writer informs us that we are now in the story ourselves. It is no longer only *their* story, it is also *our* story. Welcome onstage.

The deeds that proclaim spirituality/liberation, liberation/spirituality, praxis, shalom—whatever—are not there just to be admired. They are there as signs and pointers to us. This is the way to come, they are telling us. You can't just watch from the sidelines. You have to come onstage. You are part of a community now. You have to venture, to risk. You are needed. After all, the life you save may be someone else's.

An Eccentric Bibliography

"Eccentric" does not necessarily mean strange. It means off center, a little off track, headed in slightly unexpected directions.

The brief bibliography that follows *is* a little off center. It is not carefully balanced. Any attempt to catalog the significant literature on spirituality or liberation with something like equal time for each would soon outstrip the confines of this or any other volume. So what most of the works cited below have in common is that they are attempts, from an initially "liberation" perspective, to develop an understanding that is inclusive of "spirituality" as well. Many come from the third world, which is appropriate at a time when most of us need to begin by listening.

Latin America

Avila, Rafael. *Worship and Politics.* Tr. by Alan Neely. Maryknoll, N.Y.: Orbis Books, 1981.

Betto, Frei. *Fidel and Religion.* Sydney, Australia: Pathfinder Press, 1986.

Boff, Leonardo. *The Lord's Prayer: The Prayer of Integral Liberation.* Tr. by Theodore Morrow. Maryknoll, N.Y.: Orbis Books, 1983.

———. *Saint Francis: A Model for Human Liberation.* New York: Crossroad, 1982.

———. *Way of the Cross—Way of Justice.* Tr. by John Drury. Maryknoll, N.Y.: Orbis Books, 1980.

Cabestrero, Teófilo. *Ministers of God, Ministers of the People: Testimonies of Faith from Nicaragua.* Tr. by Robert T. Barr. Maryknoll, N.Y.: Orbis Books, 1983.

————. *Mystic of Liberation: A Portrait of Bishop Pedro Casaldaliga of Brazil.* Tr. by Donald D. Walsh. Maryknoll, N.Y.: Orbis Books, 1981.

Câmara, Helder. *The Desert Is Fertile.* Tr. by Francis McDonagh. Maryknoll, N.Y.: Orbis Books, 1981.

Cardenal, Ernesto. *The Gospel in Solentiname.* 4 vols. Tr. by Donald D. Walsh. Maryknoll, N.Y.: Orbis Books, 1976–1982.

Challenge of Basic Christian Communities, The. See under International Ecumenical Congress of Theology.

Fabella, Virginia, and Sergio Torres, eds. *Irruption of the Third World: Challenge to Theology.* Maryknoll, N.Y.: Orbis Books, 1983; esp. Elsa Tamez et al., "Worship Service: This Hour of History," pp. 181–187.

Galilea, Segundo. *The Beatitudes: To Evangelize as Jesus Did.* Tr. by Robert R. Barr. Maryknoll, N.Y.: Orbis Books, 1984.

————. *Following Jesus.* Tr. by Helen Phillips. Maryknoll, N.Y.: Orbis Books, 1981.

————. "Liberation as an Encounter with Politics and Contemplation." In Claude Geffré, *The Mystical and Political Dimension of the Christian Faith,* pp. 19–33. New York: Seabury Press, 1974.

Gutiérrez, Gustavo. *On Job: God-Talk and the Suffering of the Innocent.* Maryknoll, N.Y.: Orbis Books, 1987.

————. *A Theology of Liberation: History, Politics, and Salvation.* Tr. and ed. by Sister Caridad Inda and John Eagleson. Maryknoll, N.Y.: Orbis Books, 1972.

————. *We Drink from Our Own Wells: The Spiritual Journey of a People.* Tr. by Matthew J. O'Connell. Maryknoll, N.Y.: Orbis Books, 1984.

International Ecumenical Congress of Theology. *The Challenge of Basic Christian Communities.* Papers from the Congress, Feb. 20–Mar. 2, 1980. Ed. by Sergio Torres and John Eagleson. Tr. by John Drury. Maryknoll, N.Y.: Orbis Books, 1981; esp. Gutiérrez, "The Irruption of the Poor in Latin America and the Christian Communities of the Common People," pp. 107–123; Meesters, "The Use of the Bible in the Christian Communities of the Common People," pp. 197–210; "Worship," pp. 217–227; and "Final Document," pp. 231–249.

Libañio, J. B. *Spiritual Discernment and Politics: Guidelines for Religious Communities.* Tr. by Theodore Morrow. Maryknoll, N.Y.: Orbis Books, 1982.

Nouwen, Henri. *¡Gracias! A Latin American Journal.* San Francisco: Harper & Row, 1983.

Pironio, Eduardo, et al. *Liberación: Diálogos en el CELAM.* Bogotá: CELAM, 1974; esp. "Sentido caminos y espiritualidad de la liberación," pp. 17–25.

Segundo, Juan Luis. *The Hidden Motives of Pastoral Action: Latin American Reflections.* Tr. by John Drury. Maryknoll, N.Y.: Orbis Books, 1978.

———. *A Theology for Artisans of a New Humanity.* 5 vols. Tr. by John Drury. Maryknoll, N.Y.: Orbis Books, 1973–74, esp. vol. 2, *Grace and the Human Condition,* and vol. 4, *The Sacraments Today.*

Sobrino, Jon. *Christology at the Crossroads: A Latin American Approach.* Tr. by John Drury. Maryknoll, N.Y.: Orbis Books, 1978.

Elsewhere

Balasuriya, Tissa. *The Eucharist and Human Liberation.* Maryknoll, N.Y.: Orbis Books, 1979.

———. *Planetary Theology.* Maryknoll, N.Y.: Orbis Books, 1984.

Brueggemann, Walter, Sharon Parks, and Thomas H. Groome. *To Act Justly, Love Tenderly, Walk Humbly: An Agenda for Ministers.* New York: Paulist Press, 1986.

Carmody, John. *Holistic Spirituality.* New York: Paulist Press, 1983.

Crosby, Michael H. *Spirituality of the Beatitudes: Matthew's Challenge for First World Christians.* Maryknoll, N.Y.: Orbis Books, 1981.

De Gruchy, John W. *Cry Justice: Prayers, Meditations, and Readings from South Africa.* Maryknoll, N.Y.: Orbis Books, 1984.

Dorr, Donal. *Spirituality and Justice.* Maryknoll, N.Y.: Orbis Books, 1985.

Grassi, J. A. *Broken Bread and Broken Bodies: The Lord's Supper and World Hunger.* Maryknoll, N.Y.: Orbis Books, 1985.

Haight, Roger S. *An Alternative Vision: An Interpretation of Liberation Theology.* New York: Paulist Press, 1985.

Heschel, Abraham. *The Insecurity of Freedom: Essays on Human Existence.* New York: Schocken Books, 1972.

———. *The Prophets.* New York: Harper & Row, 1963.

Kavanaugh, John F. *Following Christ in a Consumer Society: The Spirituality of Cultural Resistance.* Maryknoll, N.Y.: Orbis Books, 1981.

Meehan, Francis Xavier. *A Contemporary Social Spirituality.* Maryknoll, N.Y.: Orbis Books, 1982.

Metz, Johannes B. *Theology of the World.* Tr. by William Glen-Doepel. New York: Herder & Herder, 1969.

O'Connor, Elizabeth. *Journey Inward, Journey Outward.* New York: Harper & Row, 1975.

————. *Search for Silence.* Waco, Texas: Word Books, 1972.

Sider, Ronald J. *Rich Christians in an Age of Hunger: A Biblical Study.* New York: Paulist Press, 1977.

Stringfellow, William. *The Politics of Spirituality.* Philadelphia: Westminster Press, 1984.

Wiesel, Elie. *Four Hasidic Masters and Their Struggle Against Melancholy.* Notre Dame, Ind.: University of Notre Dame Press, 1978.

————. *Souls on Fire.* New York: Random House, 1972.

Praise for LIFE OF PI

"Although the book reverberates with echoes from sources as disparate at *Robinson Crusoe* and Aesop's fables, the work it most strongly recalls is Ernest Hemingway's own foray into existentialist parable, *The Old Man and the Sea*."　　　　—*The New York Times Book Review*

"Readers familiar with Margaret Atwood, Mavis Gallant, Alice Munro, Michael Ondaatje and Carol Shields should learn to make room on the map of contemporary Canadian fiction for the formidable Yann Martel."　　　　—*Chicago Tribune*

"Fantastic in nearly every sense of the word, *Life of Pi* is a gripping adventure story, a parable about the place of human beings in the universe and a tantalizing work of metafiction.... Laced with wit, spiced with terror, it's a book by an extraordinary talent."
　　　　—*San Jose Mercury News*

"[A] fantastical tale."　　　　—*USA Today*

"Each chapter is a well-polished pearl. ... [*Life of Pi*] is an exhilarating story of gut survival, of strange islands with people-eating trees and flying fish that appear like manna."　　　　—*Seattle Times*

"If this century produces a classic work of survival literature, Martel is surely a contender."　　　　—*The Nation*

"By the time Martel throws Pi out to sea, his quirkily magical and often hilarious vision has already taken hold. . . . Beautifully fantastical and spirited."
—*Salon*

"A bit of seafaring, more than a hint of magical realism, and a wallop of sheer storytelling genius characterize Martel's novel."
—*New Jersey Star-Ledger*

"*Life of Pi* may not make you believe in God. But it will make you believe in literature."
—*The San Diego Union-Tribune*

"Nothing short of miraculous. It's an adventure tale so filled with love for the animal kingdom that it ought to roar."
—*Denver Post*

"One of the strangest but most approachable novels in years . . . *Life of Pi* mixes yarn, fable, and morality tale."
—*The Economist*

"A brilliant tale of survival and faith . . . The world for the reader of this novel, for a time, consists only of a young boy, a lifeboat, a tiger, and the wide blue ocean."
—*New Orleans Time-Picayune*

"Think: comic strip 'Calvin and Hobbes' with an overt religious theme."
—*Wall Street Journal* (Editor's Pick)

"A fabulous romp through an imagination by turns ecstatic, cunning, despairing and resilient . . . Martel displays the clever voice and tremendous storytelling skills of an emerging master."
—*Publishers Weekly*

"A work of wonder . . . Martel is a limpid stylist with a flair for the poetic. Mainly, however, he's a storyteller—and a brilliant one."
—*Book*

"Luminously written ... [It] has the excitement that is one of the things we read fiction for: not for comedies of manners alone, but for an evocation of the unfamiliar or the barely imaginable."

—*The Times Literary Supplement* (London)

"*Life of Pi* is a terrific book. It's fresh, original, smart, devious, and crammed with absorbing lore."

—Margaret Atwood, *The Sunday Times* (London)

"Absurd, macabre, unreliable and sad, deeply sensual in its evoking of smells and sights, the whole trip and the narrator's insanely curious voice (which evokes an intellectual humming-bird compelled to sip deep from every possible blossom) suggests Joseph Conrad and Salman Rushdie hallucinating together over the meaning of *The Old Man and the Sea* and *Gulliver's Travels*." —*Financial Times* (London)

"This is a novel, says the jacket blurb, that will make you believe in God. I am not sure about that. But it is a story so magical, so playful, so harrowing and astonishing that it will make you believe imagination might be the first step." —*The Times of London*

LIFE OF PI

YANN MARTEL

life of pi

A NOVEL

MARINER BOOKS
HOUGHTON MIFFLIN HARCOURT
BOSTON • NEW YORK

Copyright © 2001 by Yann Martel

All rights reserved

For information about permission to reproduce selections from this book,
write to Permissions, Houghton Mifflin Harcourt Publishing Company,
215 Park Avenue South, New York, New York 10003.

www.hmhbooks.com

Originally published in Canada by Random House of Canada
First Harvest edition 2003

Library of Congress Cataloging-in-Publication Data
Martel, Yann.
Life of Pi: a novel / Yann Martel. — 1st ed.
p.   cm.
ISBN 978-0-15-100811-7
ISBN 978-0-15-602732-8 (pbk.)
1. Survival after airplane accidents, shipwrecks, etc. — Fiction.
2. Human-animal relationships — Fiction. 3. Pacific Ocean — Fiction.
4. Storytelling — Fiction. 5. Teenage boys — Fiction. 6. Ocean travel — Fiction.
7. Zoo animals — Fiction. 8. Orphans — Fiction. 9. Tigers — Fiction. I. Title.
PR9199.3.M3855 L54 2002
813'.54 — DC21   2001039737

Text design: C. S. Richardson
Text set in ACaslon

Printed in the United States of America
DOC 60 59 58 57

à mes parents et à mon frère

This book was born as I was hungry. Let me explain. In the spring of 1996, my second book, a novel, came out in Canada. It didn't fare well. Reviewers were puzzled, or damned it with faint praise. Then readers ignored it. Despite my best efforts at playing the clown or the trapeze artist, the media circus made no difference. The book did not move. Books lined the shelves of bookstores like kids standing in a row to play baseball or soccer, and mine was the gangly, unathletic kid that no one wanted on their team. It vanished quickly and quietly.

The fiasco did not affect me too much. I had already moved on to another story, a novel set in Portugal in 1939. Only I was feeling restless. And I had a little money.

So I flew to Bombay. This is not so illogical if you realize three things: that a stint in India will beat the restlessness out of any living creature; that a little money can go a long way there; and that a novel set in Portugal in 1939 may have very little to do with Portugal in 1939.

I had been to India before, in the north, for five months. On that first trip I had come to the subcontinent completely unprepared. Actually, I had a preparation of one word. When I told a friend who knew the country well of my travel plans, he said casually, "They speak a funny English in India. They like words like bamboozle." *I remembered his words as my plane started its descent towards Delhi, so the word* bamboozle *was my one preparation for the rich, noisy, functioning madness of India. I used the word on occasion, and truth be told, it served me well. To a clerk at a train* station I said, "I didn't think the fare would be so expensive. You're not try-ing to bamboozle me, are you?" He smiled and chanted, "No sir! There is no bamboozlement here. I have quoted you the correct fare."

This second time to India I knew better what to expect and I knew what I wanted: I would settle in a hill station and write my novel. I had visions of myself sitting at a table on a large veranda, my notes spread out in front of me next to a steaming cup of tea. Green hills heavy with mists would lie at my feet and the shrill cries of monkeys would fill my ears. The weather would be just right, requiring a light sweater mornings and evenings, and something short-sleeved midday. Thus set up, pen in hand, for the sake of greater truth, I would turn Portugal into a fiction. That's what fiction is about, isn't it, the selective transforming of reality? The twisting of it to bring out its essence? What need did I have to go to Portugal?

The lady who ran the place would tell me stories about the struggle to boot the British out. We would agree on what I was to have for lunch and supper the next day. After my writing day was over, I would go for walks in the rolling hills of the tea estates.

Unfortunately, the novel sputtered, coughed and died. It happened in Matheran, not far from Bombay, a small hill station with some monkeys but no tea estates. It's a misery peculiar to would-be writers. Your theme is good, as are your sentences. Your characters are so ruddy with life they prac-tically need birth certificates. The plot you've mapped out for them is grand, simple and gripping. You've done your research, gathering the facts—historical, social, climatic, culinary—that will give your story its feel of authenticity. The dialogue zips along, crackling with tension. The descrip-tions burst with colour, contrast and telling detail. Really, your story can only be great. But it all adds up to nothing. In spite of the obvious, shining promise of it, there comes a moment when you realize that the whisper that has been pestering you all along from the back of your mind is speaking the flat, awful truth: it won't work. An element is missing, that spark that brings to life a real story, regardless of whether the history or the food is right. Your story is emotionally dead, that's the crux of it. The discovery is something soul-destroying, I tell you. It leaves you with an aching hunger.

From Matheran I mailed the notes of my failed novel. I mailed them to a fictitious address in Siberia, with a return address, equally fictitious, in Bolivia. After the clerk had stamped the envelope and thrown it into a sorting bin, I sat down, glum and disheartened. "What now, Tolstoy? What other bright ideas do you have for your life?" I asked myself.

Well, I still had a little money and I was still feeling restless. I got up and walked out of the post office to explore the south of India.

I would have liked to say, "I'm a doctor," to those who asked me what I did, doctors being the current purveyors of magic and miracle. But I'm sure we would have had a bus accident around the next bend, and with all eyes fixed on me I would have to explain, amidst the crying and moaning of victims, that I meant in law; then, to their appeal to help them sue the government over the mishap, I would have to confess that as a matter of fact it was a Bachelor's in philosophy; next, to the shouts of what meaning such a bloody tragedy could have, I would have to admit that I had hardly touched Kierkegaard; and so on. I stuck to the humble, bruised truth.

Along the way, here and there, I got the response, "A writer? Is that so? I have a story for you." Most times the stories were little more than anecdotes, short of breath and short of life.

I arrived in the town of Pondicherry, a tiny self-governing Union Territory south of Madras, on the coast of Tamil Nadu. In population and size it is an inconsequent part of India—by comparison, Prince Edward Island is a giant within Canada—but history has set it apart. For Pondicherry was once the capital of that most modest of colonial empires, French India. The French would have liked to rival the British, very much so, but the only Raj they managed to get was a handful of small ports. They clung to these for nearly three hundred years. They left Pondicherry in 1954, leaving behind nice white buildings, broad streets at right angles to each other, street names such as rue de la Marine and rue Saint-Louis, and képis, *caps*, for the policemen.

I was at the Indian Coffee House, on Nehru Street. It's one big room with green walls and a high ceiling. Fans whirl above you to keep the warm, humid air moving. The place is furnished to capacity with identical square tables, each with its complement of four chairs. You sit where you can, with whoever is at a table. The coffee is good and they serve French toast. Conversation is easy to come by. And so, a spry, bright-eyed elderly man with great shocks of pure white hair was talking to me. I confirmed to him that Canada was cold and that French was indeed spoken in parts of it and that I liked India and so on and so forth—the usual light talk between friendly, curious Indians and foreign backpackers. He took in my line of work with a widening of the eyes and a nodding of the head. It was time to go. I had my hand up, trying to catch my waiter's eye to get the bill.

Then the elderly man said, "I have a story that will make you believe in God."

I stopped waving my hand. But I was suspicious. Was this a Jehovah's Witness knocking at my door? "Does your story take place two thousand years ago in a remote corner of the Roman Empire?" I asked.

"No."

Was he some sort of Muslim evangelist? "Does it take place in seventh-century Arabia?"

"No, no. It starts right here in Pondicherry just a few years back, and it ends, I am delighted to tell you, in the very country you come from."

"And it will make me believe in God?"

"Yes."

"That's a tall order."

"Not so tall that you can't reach."

My waiter appeared. I hesitated for a moment. I ordered two coffees. We introduced ourselves. His name was Francis Adirubasamy. "Please tell me your story," I said.

"You must pay proper attention," he replied.

"I will." I brought out pen and notepad.

"Tell me, have you been to the botanical garden?" he asked.

"I went yesterday."

"Did you notice the toy train tracks?"

"Yes, I did."

"A train still runs on Sundays for the amusement of the children. But it used to run twice an hour every day. Did you take note of the names of the stations?"

"One is called Roseville. It's right next to the rose garden."

"That's right. And the other?"

"I don't remember."

"The sign was taken down. The other station was once called Zootown. The toy train had two stops: Roseville and Zootown. Once upon a time there was a zoo in the Pondicherry Botanical Garden."

He went on. I took notes, the elements of the story. "You must talk to him," he said, of the main character. "I knew him very, very well. He's a grown man now. You must ask him all the questions you want."

Later, in Toronto, among nine columns of Patels in the phone book, I found him, the main character. My heart pounded as I dialed his phone number. The voice that answered had an Indian lilt to its Canadian accent, light but unmistakable, like a trace of incense in the air. "That was a very long time ago," he said. Yet he agreed to meet. We met many times. He showed me the diary he kept during the events. He showed me the yellowed newspaper clippings that made him briefly, obscurely famous. He told me his story. All the while I took notes. Nearly a year later, after considerable difficulties, I received a tape and a report from the Japanese Ministry of Transport. It was as I listened to that tape that I agreed with Mr. Adirubasamy that this was, indeed, a story to make you believe in God.

It seemed natural that Mr. Patel's story should be told mostly in the first person—in his voice and through his eyes. But any inaccuracies or mistakes are mine.

I have a few people to thank. I am most obviously indebted to Mr. Patel. My gratitude to him is as boundless as the Pacific Ocean and I hope that my telling of his tale does not disappoint him. For getting me started on the story, I have Mr. Adirubasamy to thank. For helping me complete it, I am grateful to three officials of exemplary professionalism: Mr. Kazuhiko Oda, lately of the Japanese Embassy in Ottawa; Mr. Hiroshi Watanabe, of Oika Shipping Company; and, especially, Mr. Tomohiro Okamoto, of the Japanese Ministry of Transport, now retired. Also, I am indebted to Mr. Moacyr Scliar, for the spark of life. Lastly, I would like to express my sincere gratitude to that great institution, the Canada Council for the Arts, without whose grant I could not have brought together this story that has nothing to do with Portugal in 1939. If we, citizens, do not support our artists, then we sacrifice our imagination on the altar of crude reality and we end up believing in nothing and having worthless dreams.

PART ONE

Toronto and Pondicherry

CHAPTER 1

My suffering left me sad and gloomy.

Academic study and the steady, mindful practice of religion slowly brought me back to life. I have kept up what some people would consider my strange religious practices. After one year of high school, I attended the University of Toronto and took a double-major Bachelor's degree. My majors were religious studies and zoology. My fourth-year thesis for religious studies concerned certain aspects of the cosmogony theory of Isaac Luria, the great sixteenth-century Kabbalist from Safed. My zoology thesis was a functional analysis of the thyroid gland of the three-toed sloth. I chose the sloth because its demeanour—calm, quiet and introspective—did something to soothe my shattered self.

There are two-toed sloths and there are three-toed sloths, the case being determined by the forepaws of the animals, since all sloths have three claws on their hind paws. I had the great luck one summer of studying the three-toed sloth *in situ* in the equatorial jungles of Brazil. It is a highly intriguing creature. Its only real habit is indolence. It sleeps or rests on average twenty hours a day. Our team tested the sleep habits of five wild three-toed sloths by placing on their heads, in the early evening after they had fallen asleep, bright red plastic dishes filled with water. We found them still in place late the next morning, the water of the dishes swarming with insects. The sloth is at its busiest at sunset, using the word *busy* here in the most relaxed sense. It moves along the bough of a tree in its characteristic upside-down position at the speed of roughly 400 metres an hour. On the ground, it crawls to its next tree at the rate of 250 metres an hour, when motivated, which is 440 times slower than a motivated cheetah. Unmotivated, it covers four to five metres in an hour.

The three-toed sloth is not well informed about the outside world. On a scale of 2 to 10, where 2 represents unusual dullness and 10 extreme acuity, Beebe (1926) gave the sloth's senses of taste, touch, sight and hearing a rating of 2, and its sense of smell a rating of 3. If you come upon a sleeping three-toed sloth in the wild, two or three nudges should suffice to awaken it; it will then look sleepily in every direction but yours. Why it should look about is uncertain since the sloth sees everything in a Magoo-like blur. As for hearing, the sloth is not so much deaf as uninterested in sound. Beebe reported that firing guns next to sleeping or feeding sloths elicited little reaction. And the sloth's slightly better sense of smell should not be overestimated. They are said to be able to sniff and avoid decayed branches, but Bullock (1968) reported that sloths fall to the ground clinging to decayed branches "often".

How does it survive, you might ask.

Precisely by being so slow. Sleepiness and slothfulness keep it out of harm's way, away from the notice of jaguars, ocelots, harpy eagles and anacondas. A sloth's hairs shelter an algae that is brown during the dry season and green during the wet season, so the animal blends in with the surrounding moss and foliage and looks like a nest of white ants or of squirrels, or like nothing at all but part of a tree.

The three-toed sloth lives a peaceful, vegetarian life in perfect harmony with its environment. "A good-natured smile is forever on its lips," reported Tirler (1966). I have seen that smile with my own eyes. I am not one given to projecting human traits and emotions onto animals, but many a time during that month in Brazil, looking up at sloths in repose, I felt I was in the presence of upside-down yogis deep in meditation or hermits deep in prayer, wise beings whose intense imaginative lives were beyond the reach of my scientific probing.

Sometimes I got my majors mixed up. A number of my fellow religious-studies students—muddled agnostics who didn't know which way was up, who were in the thrall of reason, that fool's gold for the bright—reminded me of the three-toed sloth; and the three-toed sloth, such a beautiful example of the miracle of life, reminded me of God.

I never had problems with my fellow scientists. Scientists are a friendly, atheistic, hard-working, beer-drinking lot whose minds are preoccupied with sex, chess and baseball when they are not preoccupied with science.

I was a very good student, if I may say so myself. I was tops at St. Michael's College four years in a row. I got every possible student award from the Department of Zoology. If I got none from the Department of Religious Studies, it is simply because there are no student awards in this department (the rewards of religious study are not in mortal hands, we all know that). I would have received the Governor General's Academic Medal, the University of Toronto's highest undergraduate award, of which no small number of illustrious Canadians have been recipients, were it not for a beef-eating pink boy with a neck like a tree trunk and a temperament of unbearable good cheer.

I still smart a little at the slight. When you've suffered a great deal in life, each additional pain is both unbearable and trifling. My life is like a memento mori painting from European art: there is always a grinning skull at my side to remind me of the folly of human ambition. I mock this skull. I look at it and I say, "You've got the wrong fellow. You may not believe in life, but I don't believe in death. Move on!" The skull snickers and moves ever closer, but that doesn't surprise me.

The reason death sticks so closely to life isn't biological necessity—it's envy. Life is so beautiful that death has fallen in love with it, a jealous, possessive love that grabs at what it can. But life leaps over oblivion lightly, losing only a thing or two of no importance, and gloom is but the passing shadow of a cloud. The pink boy also got the nod from the Rhodes Scholarship committee. I love him and I hope his time at Oxford was a rich experience. If Lakshmi, goddess of wealth, one day favours me bountifully, Oxford is fifth on the list of cities I would like to visit before I pass on, after Mecca, Varanasi, Jerusalem and Paris.

I have nothing to say of my working life, only that a tie is a noose, and inverted though it is, it will hang a man nonetheless if he's not careful.

I love Canada. I miss the heat of India, the food, the house lizards on the walls, the musicals on the silver screen, the cows wandering the streets, the crows cawing, even the talk of cricket matches, but I love Canada. It is a great country much too cold for good sense, inhabited by compassionate, intelligent people with bad hairdos. Anyway, I have nothing to go home to in Pondicherry.

Richard Parker has stayed with me. I've never forgotten him. Dare I say I miss him? I do. I miss him. I still see him in my dreams. They are nightmares mostly, but nightmares tinged with love. Such is the strangeness of the human heart. I still cannot understand how he could abandon me so unceremoniously, without any sort of goodbye, without looking back even once. That pain is like an axe that chops at my heart.

The doctors and nurses at the hospital in Mexico were incredibly kind to me. And the patients, too. Victims of cancer or car accidents, once they heard my story, they hobbled and wheeled over to see me, they and their families, though none of them spoke English and I spoke no Spanish. They smiled at me, shook my hand, patted me on the head, left gifts of food and clothing on my bed. They moved me to uncontrollable fits of laughing and crying.

Within a couple of days I could stand, even make two, three steps, despite nausea, dizziness and general weakness. Blood tests revealed that I was anemic, and that my level of sodium was very high and my potassium low. My body retained fluids and my legs swelled up tremendously. I looked as if I had been grafted with a pair of elephant legs. My urine was a deep, dark yellow going on to brown. After a week or so, I could walk just about normally and I could wear shoes if I didn't lace them up. My skin healed, though I still have scars on my shoulders and back.

The first time I turned a tap on, its noisy, wasteful, superabundant gush was such a shock that I became incoherent and my legs collapsed beneath me and I fainted in the arms of a nurse.

The first time I went to an Indian restaurant in Canada I used my fingers. The waiter looked at me critically and said, "Fresh off the boat, are you?" I blanched. My fingers, which a second before had been taste buds savouring the food a little ahead of my mouth, became dirty under his gaze. They froze like criminals caught in the act. I didn't dare lick them. I wiped them guiltily on my napkin. He had no idea how deeply those words wounded me. They were like nails being driven into my flesh. I picked up the knife and fork. I had hardly ever used such instruments. My hands trembled. My sambar lost its taste.

CHAPTER 2

He lives in Scarborough. He's a small, slim man—no more than five foot five. Dark hair, dark eyes. Hair greying at the temples. Can't be older than forty. Pleasing coffee-coloured complexion. Mild fall weather, yet puts on a big winter parka with fur-lined hood for the walk to the diner. Expressive face. Speaks quickly, hands flitting about. No small talk. He launches forth.

CHAPTER 3

I was named after a swimming pool. Quite peculiar considering my parents never took to water. One of my father's earliest business contacts was Francis Adirubasamy. He became a good friend of the family. I called him Mamaji, *mama* being the Tamil word for *uncle* and *ji* being a suffix used in India to indicate respect and affection. When he was a young man, long before I was born, Mamaji was a champion competitive swimmer, the champion of all South India. He looked the part his whole life. My brother Ravi once told me that when Mamaji was born he didn't want to give up on breathing water and so the doctor, to save his life, had to take him by the feet and swing him above his head round and round.

"It did the trick!" said Ravi, wildly spinning his hand above his head. "He coughed out water and started breathing air, but it forced all his flesh and blood to his upper body. That's why his chest is so thick and his legs are so skinny."

I believed him. (Ravi was a merciless teaser. The first time he called Mamaji "Mr. Fish" to my face I left a banana peel in his bed.) Even in his sixties, when he was a little stooped and a lifetime of counter-obstetric gravity had begun to nudge his flesh downwards, Mamaji swam thirty lengths every morning at the pool of the Aurobindo Ashram.

He tried to teach my parents to swim, but he never got them to go beyond wading up to their knees at the beach and making ludicrous round motions with their arms, which, if they were practising the breaststroke, made them look as if they were walking through a jungle, spreading the tall grass ahead of them, or, if it was the front crawl, as if they were running down a hill and flailing their arms so as not to fall. Ravi was just as unenthusiastic.

Mamaji had to wait until I came into the picture to find a willing disciple. The day I came of swimming age, which, to Mother's distress, Mamaji claimed was seven, he brought me down to the beach, spread his arms seaward and said, "This is my gift to you."

"And then he nearly drowned you," claimed Mother.

I remained faithful to my aquatic guru. Under his watchful eye I lay on the beach and fluttered my legs and scratched away at the sand with my hands, turning my head at every stroke to breathe. I must have looked like a child throwing a peculiar, slow-motion tantrum. In the water, as he held me at the surface, I tried my best to swim. It was much more difficult than on land. But Mamaji was patient and encouraging.

When he felt that I had progressed sufficiently, we turned our backs on the laughing and the shouting, the running and the splashing, the blue-green waves and the bubbly surf, and headed for the proper rectangularity and the formal flatness (and the paying admission) of the ashram swimming pool.

I went there with him three times a week throughout my childhood, a Monday, Wednesday, Friday early morning ritual with the clockwork regularity of a good front-crawl stroke. I have vivid memories of this dignified old man stripping down to nakedness next to me, his body slowly emerging as he neatly disposed of each item of clothing, decency being salvaged at the very end by a slight turning away and a magnificent pair of imported athletic bathing trunks. He stood straight and he was ready. It had an epic simplicity. Swimming instruction, which in time became swimming practice, was gruelling, but there was the deep pleasure of doing a stroke with increasing ease and speed, over and over, till hypnosis practically, the water turning from molten lead to liquid light.

It was on my own, a guilty pleasure, that I returned to the sea, beckoned by the mighty waves that crashed down and reached for me in humble tidal ripples, gentle lassos that caught their willing Indian boy.

My gift to Mamaji one birthday, I must have been thirteen or so, was two full lengths of credible butterfly. I finished so spent I could hardly wave to him.

Beyond the activity of swimming, there was the talk of it. It was the talk that Father loved. The more vigorously he resisted actually swimming, the more he fancied it. Swim lore was his vacation talk from the workaday talk of running a zoo. Water without a hippopotamus was so much more manageable than water with one.

Mamaji studied in Paris for two years, thanks to the colonial administration. He had the time of his life. This was in the early 1930s, when the French were still trying to make Pondicherry as Gallic as the British were trying to make the rest of India Britannic. I don't recall exactly what Mamaji studied. Something commercial, I suppose. He was a great storyteller, but forget about his studies or the Eiffel Tower or the Louvre or the cafés of the Champs-Elysées. All his stories had to do with swimming pools and swimming competitions. For example, there was the Piscine Deligny, the city's oldest pool, dating back to 1796, an open-air barge moored to the Quai d'Orsay and the venue for the swimming events of the 1900 Olympics. But none of the times were recognized by the International Swimming Federation because the pool was six metres too long. The water in the pool came straight from the Seine, unfiltered and unheated. "It was cold and dirty," said Mamaji. "The water, having crossed all of Paris, came in foul enough. Then people at the pool made it utterly disgusting." In conspiratorial whispers, with shocking details to back up his claim, he assured us that the French had very low standards of personal hygiene. "Deligny was bad enough. Bain Royal, another latrine on the Seine, was worse. At least at Deligny they scooped out the dead fish." Nevertheless, an Olympic pool is an Olympic pool, touched by immortal glory. Though it was a cesspool, Mamaji spoke of Deligny with a fond smile.

One was better off at the Piscines Château-Landon, Rouvet or du boulevard de la Gare. They were indoor pools with roofs, on land and open year-round. Their water was supplied by the condensation from steam engines from nearby factories and so was cleaner and warmer. But these pools were still a bit dingy and tended to be crowded. "There was so much gob and spit floating in the water, I thought I was swimming through jellyfish," chuckled Mamaji.

The Piscines Hébert, Ledru-Rollin and Butte-aux-Cailles were bright, modern, spacious pools fed by artesian wells. They set the standard for excellence in municipal swimming pools. There was the Piscine des Tourelles, of course, the city's other great Olympic pool, inaugurated during the second Paris games, of 1924. And there were still others, many of them.

But no swimming pool in Mamaji's eyes matched the glory of the Piscine Molitor. It was the crowning aquatic glory of Paris, indeed, of the entire civilized world.

"It was a pool the gods would have delighted to swim in. Molitor had the best competitive swimming club in Paris. There were two pools, an indoor and an outdoor. Both were as big as small oceans. The indoor pool always had two lanes reserved for swimmers who wanted to do lengths. The water was so clean and clear you could have used it to make your morning coffee. Wooden changing cabins, blue and white, surrounded the pool on two floors. You could look down and see everyone and everything. The porters who marked your cabin door with chalk to show that it was occupied were limping old men, friendly in an ill-tempered way. No amount of shouting and tomfoolery ever ruffled them. The showers gushed hot, soothing water. There was a steam room and an exercise room. The outside pool became a skating rink in winter. There was a bar, a cafeteria, a large sunning deck, even two small beaches with real sand. Every bit of tile, brass and wood gleamed. It was—it was . . ."

It was the only pool that made Mamaji fall silent, his memory making too many lengths to mention.

Mamaji remembered, Father dreamed.

That is how I got my name when I entered this world, a last, welcome addition to my family, three years after Ravi: Piscine Molitor Patel.

CHAPTER 4

Our good old nation was just seven years old as a republic when it became bigger by a small territory. Pondicherry entered the Union of India on November 1, 1954. One civic achievement called for another. A portion of the grounds of the Pondicherry Botanical Garden was made available rent-free for an exciting business opportunity and—lo and behold—India had a brand new zoo, designed and run according to the most modern, biologically sound principles.

It was a huge zoo, spread over numberless acres, big enough to require a train to explore it, though it seemed to get smaller as I grew older, train included. Now it's so small it fits in my head. You must imagine a hot and humid place, bathed in sunshine and bright colours. The riot of flowers is incessant. There are trees, shrubs and climbing plants in profusion—peepuls, gulmohurs, flames of the forest, red silk cottons, jacarandas, mangoes, jackfruits and many others that would remain unknown to you if they didn't have neat labels at their feet. There are benches. On these benches you see men sleeping, stretched out, or couples sitting, young couples, who steal glances at each other shyly and whose hands flutter in the air, happening to touch. Suddenly, amidst the tall and slim trees up ahead, you notice two giraffes quietly observing you. The sight is not the last of your surprises. The next moment you are startled by a furious outburst coming from a great troupe of monkeys, only outdone in volume by the shrill cries of strange birds. You come to a turnstile. You distractedly pay a small sum of money. You move on. You see a low wall. What can you expect beyond a low wall? Certainly not a shallow pit with two mighty Indian rhinoceros. But that is what you find. And when you turn your head you see the elephant that was there all along, so big you didn't notice it. And in the pond you realize those are hippopotamuses floating in the water. The more you look, the more you see. You are in Zootown!

Before moving to Pondicherry, Father ran a large hotel in Madras. An abiding interest in animals led him to the zoo business. A natural transition, you might think, from hotelkeeping to zookeeping. Not so. In many ways, running a zoo is a hotelkeeper's worst nightmare. Consider: the guests never leave their rooms; they expect not only lodging but full board; they receive a constant flow of visitors, some of whom are noisy and unruly. One has to wait until they saunter to their balconies, so to speak, before one can clean their rooms, and then one has to wait until they tire of the view and return to their rooms before one can clean their balconies; and there is much cleaning to do, for the guests are as unhygienic as alcoholics. Each guest is very particular about his or her diet, constantly complains about the slowness of the service, and never, ever tips. To speak frankly, many are sexual deviants, either terribly repressed and subject to explosions of frenzied lasciviousness or openly depraved, in either case regularly affronting management with gross outrages of free sex and incest. Are these the sorts of guests you would want to welcome to your inn? The Pondicherry Zoo was the source of some pleasure and many headaches for Mr. Santosh Patel, founder, owner, director, head of a staff of fifty-three, and my father.

To me, it was paradise on earth. I have nothing but the fondest memories of growing up in a zoo. I lived the life of a prince. What maharaja's son had such vast, luxuriant grounds to play about? What palace had such a menagerie? My alarm clock during my childhood was a pride of lions. They were no Swiss clocks, but the lions could be counted upon to roar their heads off between five-thirty and six every morning. Breakfast was punctuated by the shrieks and cries of howler monkeys, hill mynahs and Moluccan cockatoos. I left for school under the benevolent gaze not only of Mother but also of bright-eyed otters and burly American bison and stretching and yawning orang-utans. I looked up as I ran under some trees, other-wise peafowl might excrete on me. Better to go by the trees that sheltered the large colonies of fruit bats; the only assault there at that early hour was the bats' discordant concerts of squeaking and chattering. On my way out I might stop by the terraria to look at some shiny frogs glazed bright, bright green, or yellow and deep blue, or brown and pale green. Or it might be birds that caught my attention: pink flamingoes or black swans or one-wattled cassowaries, or something smaller, silver diamond doves, Cape glossy starlings, peach-faced lovebirds, Nanday conures, orange-fronted parakeets. Not likely that the elephants, the seals, the big cats or the bears would be up and doing, but the baboons, the macaques, the mangabeys, the gibbons, the deer, the tapirs, the llamas, the giraffes, the mongooses were early risers. Every morning before I was out the main gate I had one last impression that was both ordinary and unforgettable: a pyramid of turtles; the iridescent snout of a mandrill; the stately silence of a giraffe; the obese, yellow open mouth of a hippo; the beak-and-claw climbing of a macaw parrot up a wire fence; the greeting claps of a shoebill's bill; the senile, lecherous expression of a camel. And all these riches were had quickly, as I hurried to school. It was after school that I discovered in a leisurely way what it's like to have an elephant search your clothes in the friendly hope of finding a hidden nut, or an orang-utan pick through your hair for tick snacks, its wheeze of disappointment at what an empty pantry your head is. I wish I could convey the perfection of a seal slipping into water or a spider monkey swinging from point to point or a lion merely turning its head. But language founders in such seas. Better to picture it in your head if you want to feel it.

In zoos, as in nature, the best times to visit are sunrise and sunset. That is when most animals come to life. They stir and leave their shelter and tiptoe to the water's edge. They show their raiments. They sing their songs. They turn to each other and perform their rites. The reward for the watching eye and the listening ear is great. I spent more hours than I can count a quiet witness to the highly mannered, manifold expressions of life that grace our planet. It is something so bright, loud, weird and delicate as to stupefy the senses.

I have heard nearly as much nonsense about zoos as I have about God and religion. Well-meaning but misinformed people think animals in the wild are "happy" because they are "free". These people usually have a large, handsome predator in mind, a lion or a cheetah (the life of a gnu or of an aardvark is rarely exalted). They imagine this wild animal roaming about the savannah on digestive walks after eating a prey that accepted its lot piously, or going for callisthenic runs to stay slim after overindulging. They imagine this animal overseeing its offspring proudly and tenderly, the whole family watching the setting of the sun from the limbs of trees with sighs of pleasure. The life of the wild animal is simple, noble and meaningful, they imagine. Then it is captured by wicked men and thrown into tiny jails. Its "happiness" is dashed. It yearns mightily for "freedom" and does all it can to escape. Being denied its "freedom" for too long, the animal becomes a shadow of itself, its spirit broken. So some people imagine.

This is not the way it is.

Animals in the wild lead lives of compulsion and necessity within an unforgiving social hierarchy in an environment where the supply of fear is high and the supply of food low and where territory must constantly be defended and parasites forever endured. What is the meaning of freedom in such a context? Animals in the wild are, in practice, free neither in space nor in time, nor in their personal relations. In theory—that is, as a simple physical possibility—an animal could pick up and go, flaunting all the social conventions and boundaries proper to its species. But such an event is less likely to happen than for a member of our own species, say a shopkeeper with all the usual ties—to family, to friends, to society—to drop everything and walk away from his life with only the spare change in his pockets and the clothes on his frame. If a man, boldest and most intelligent of creatures, won't wander from place to place, a stranger to all, beholden to none, why would an animal, which is by temperament far more conservative? For that is what animals are, conservative, one might even say reactionary. The smallest changes can upset them. They want things to be just so, day after day, month after month. Surprises are highly disagreeable to them. You see this in their spatial relations. An animal inhabits its space, whether in a zoo or in the wild, in the same way chess pieces move about a chessboard—significantly. There is no more happenstance, no more "freedom", involved in the whereabouts of a lizard or a bear or a deer than in the location of a knight on a chessboard. Both speak of pattern and purpose. In the wild, animals stick to the same paths for the same pressing reasons, season after season. In a zoo, if an animal is not in its normal place in its regular posture at the usual hour, it means something. It may be the reflection of nothing more than a minor change in the environment. A coiled hose left out by a keeper has made a menacing impression. A puddle has formed that bothers the animal. A ladder is making a shadow. But it could mean something more. At its worst, it could be that most dreaded thing to a zoo director: a *symptom*, a herald of trouble to come, a reason to inspect the dung, to cross-examine the keeper, to summon the vet. All this because a stork is not standing where it usually stands!

But let me pursue for a moment only one aspect of the question.

If you went to a home, kicked down the front door, chased the people who lived there out into the street and said, "Go! You are free! Free as a bird! Go! Go!"—do you think they would shout and dance for joy? They wouldn't. Birds are not free. The people you've just evicted would sputter, "With what right do you throw us out? This is our home. We own it. We have lived here for years. We're calling the police, you scoundrel."

Don't we say, "There's no place like home"? That's certainly what animals feel. Animals are territorial. That is the key to their minds. Only a familiar territory will allow them to fulfill the two relentless imperatives of the wild: the avoidance of enemies and the getting of food and water. A biologically sound zoo enclosure—whether cage, pit, moated island, corral, terrarium, aviary or aquarium—is just another territory, peculiar only in its size and in its proximity to human territory. That it is so much smaller than what it would be in nature stands to reason. Territories in the wild are large not as a matter of taste but of necessity. In a zoo, we do for animals what we have done for ourselves with houses: we bring together in a small space what in the wild is spread out. Whereas before for us the cave was here, the river over there, the hunting grounds a mile that way, the lookout next to it, the berries somewhere else—all of them infested with lions, snakes, ants, leeches and poison ivy—now the river flows through taps at hand's reach and we can wash next to where we sleep, we can eat where we have cooked, and we can surround the whole with a protective wall and keep it clean and warm. A house is a compressed territory where our basic needs can be fulfilled close by and safely. A sound zoo enclosure is the equivalent for an animal (with the noteworthy absence of a fireplace or the like, present in every human habitation). Finding within it all the places it needs—a lookout, a place for resting, for eating and drinking, for bathing, for grooming, etc.—and finding that there is no need to go hunting, food appearing six days a week, an animal will take possession of its zoo space in the same way it would lay claim to a new space in the wild, exploring it and marking it out in the normal ways of its species, with sprays of urine perhaps. Once this moving-in ritual is done and the animal has settled, it will not feel like a nervous tenant, and even less like a prisoner, but rather like a landholder, and it will behave in the same way within its enclosure as it would in its territory in the wild, including defending it tooth and nail should it be invaded. Such an enclosure is subjectively neither better nor worse for an animal than its condition in the wild; so long as it fulfills the animal's needs, a territory, natural or constructed, simply *is*, without judgment, a given, like the spots on a leopard. One might even argue that if an animal could choose with intelligence, it would opt for living in a zoo, since the major difference between a zoo and the wild is the absence of parasites and enemies and the abundance of food in the first, and their respective abundance and scarcity in the second. Think about it yourself. Would you rather be put up at the Ritz with free room service and unlimited access to a doctor or be homeless without a soul to care for you? But animals are incapable of such discernment. Within the limits of their nature, they make do with what they have.

A good zoo is a place of carefully worked-out coincidence: exactly where an animal says to us, "Stay out!" with its urine or other secretion, we say to it, "Stay in!" with our barriers. Under such conditions of diplomatic peace, all animals are content and we can relax and have a look at each other.

In the literature can be found legions of examples of animals that could escape but did not, or did and returned. There is the case of the chimpanzee whose cage door was left unlocked and had swung open. Increasingly anxious, the chimp began to shriek and to slam the door shut repeatedly—with a deafening clang each time—until the keeper, notified by a visitor, hurried over to remedy the situation. A herd of roe-deer in a European zoo stepped out of their corral when the gate was left open. Frightened by visitors, the deer bolted for the nearby forest, which had its own herd of wild roe-deer and could support more. Nonetheless, the zoo roe-deer quickly returned to their corral. In another zoo a worker was walking to his work site at an early hour, carrying planks of wood, when, to his horror, a bear emerged from the morning mist, heading straight for him at a confident pace. The man dropped the planks and ran for his life. The zoo staff immediately started searching for the escaped bear. They found it back in its enclosure, having climbed down into its pit the way it had climbed out, by way of a tree that had fallen over. It was thought that the noise of the planks of wood falling to the ground had frightened it.

But I don't insist. I don't mean to defend zoos. Close them all down if you want (and let us hope that what wildlife remains can survive in what is left of the natural world). I know zoos are no longer in people's good graces. Religion faces the same problem. Certain illusions about freedom plague them both.

The Pondicherry Zoo doesn't exist any more. Its pits are filled in, the cages torn down. I explore it now in the only place left for it, my memory.

CHAPTER 5

My name isn't the end of the story about my name. When your name is Bob no one asks you, "How do you spell that?" Not so with Piscine Molitor Patel.

Some thought it was P. Singh and that I was a Sikh, and they wondered why I wasn't wearing a turban.

In my university days I visited Montreal once with some friends. It fell to me to order pizzas one night. I couldn't bear to have yet another French speaker guffawing at my name, so when the man on the phone asked, "Can I 'ave your name?" I said, "I am who I am." Half an hour later two pizzas arrived for "Ian Hoolihan".

It is true that those we meet can change us, sometimes so profoundly that we are not the same afterwards, even unto our names. Witness Simon who is called Peter, Matthew also known as Levi, Nathaniel who is also Bartholomew, Judas, not Iscariot, who took the name Thaddeus, Simeon who went by Niger, Saul who became Paul.

My Roman soldier stood in the schoolyard one morning when I was twelve. I had just arrived. He saw me and a flash of evil genius lit up his dull mind. He raised his arm, pointed at me and shouted, "It's *Pissing* Patel!"

In a second everyone was laughing. It fell away as we filed into the class. I walked in last, wearing my crown of thorns.

The cruelty of children comes as news to no one. The words would waft across the yard to my ears, unprovoked, uncalled for: "Where's Pissing? I've got to go." Or: "You're facing the wall. Are you Pissing?" Or something of the sort. I would freeze or, the contrary, pursue my activity, pretending not to have heard. The sound would disappear, but the hurt would linger, like the smell of piss long after it has evaporated.

Teachers started doing it too. It was the heat. As the day wore on, the geography lesson, which in the morning had been as compact as an oasis, started to stretch out like the Thar Desert; the history lesson, so alive when the day was young, became parched and dusty; the mathematics lesson, so precise at first, became muddled. In their afternoon fatigue, as they wiped their foreheads and the backs of their necks with their handkerchiefs, without meaning to offend or get a laugh, even teachers forgot the fresh aquatic promise of my name and distorted it in a shameful way. By nearly imperceptible modulations I could hear the change. It was as if their tongues were charioteers driving wild horses. They could manage well enough the first syllable, the *Pea*, but eventually the heat was too much and they lost control of their frothy-mouthed steeds and could no longer rein them in for the climb to the second syllable, the *seen*. Instead they plunged hell-bent into *sing*, and next time round, all was lost. My hand would be up to give an answer, and I would be acknowledged with a "Yes, Pissing." Often the teacher wouldn't realize what he had just called me. He would look at me wearily after a moment, wondering why I wasn't coming out with the answer. And sometimes the class, as beaten down by the heat as he was, wouldn't react either. Not a snicker or a smile. But I always heard the slur.

I spent my last year at St. Joseph's School feeling like the persecuted prophet Muhammad in Mecca, peace be upon him. But just as he planned his flight to Medina, the Hejira that would mark the beginning of Muslim time, I planned my escape and the beginning of a new time for me.

After St. Joseph's, I went to Petit Séminaire, the best private English-medium secondary school in Pondicherry. Ravi was already there, and like all younger brothers, I would suffer from following in the footsteps of a popular older sibling. He was the athlete of his generation at Petit Séminaire, a fearsome bowler and a powerful batter, the captain of the town's best cricket team, our very own Kapil Dev.

That I was a swimmer made no waves; it seems to be a law of human nature that those who live by the sea are suspicious of swimmers, just as those who live in the mountains are suspicious of mountain climbers. But following in someone's shadow wasn't my escape, though I would have taken any name over "Pissing", even "Ravi's brother". I had a better plan than that.

I put it to execution on the very first day of school, in the very first class. Around me were other alumni of St. Joseph's. The class started the way all new classes start, with the stating of names. We called them out from our desks in the order in which we happened to be sitting.

"Ganapathy Kumar," said Ganapathy Kumar.

"Vipin Nath," said Vipin Nath.

"Shamshool Hudha," said Shamshool Hudha.

"Peter Dharmaraj," said Peter Dharmaraj.

Each name elicited a tick on a list and a brief mnemonic stare from the teacher. I was terribly nervous.

"Ajith Giadson," said Ajith Giadson, four desks away . . .

"Sampath Saroja," said Sampath Saroja, three away . . .

"Stanley Kumar," said Stanley Kumar, two away . . .

"Sylvester Naveen," said Sylvester Naveen, right in front of me.

It was my turn. Time to put down Satan. Medina, here I come.

I got up from my desk and hurried to the blackboard. Before the teacher could say a word, I picked up a piece of chalk and said as I wrote:

My name is

Piscine Molitor Patel,

known to all as

—I double underlined the first two letters of my given name—

For good measure I added

$$\pi = 3.14$$

and I drew a large circle, which I then sliced in two with a diameter, to evoke that basic lesson of geometry.

There was silence. The teacher was staring at the board. I was holding my breath. Then he said, "Very well, Pi. Sit down. Next time you will ask permission before leaving your desk."

"Yes, sir."

He ticked my name off. And looked at the next boy.

"Mansoor Ahamad," said Mansoor Ahamad.

I was saved.

"Gautham Selvaraj," said Gautham Selvaraj.

I could breathe.

"Arun Annaji," said Arun Annaji.

A new beginning.

I repeated the stunt with every teacher. Repetition is important in the training not only of animals but also of humans. Between one commonly named boy and the next, I rushed forward and emblazoned, sometimes with a terrible screech, the details of my rebirth. It got to be that after a few times the boys sang along with me, a crescendo that climaxed, after a quick intake of air while I underlined the proper note, with such a rousing rendition of my new name that it would have been the delight of any choirmaster. A few boys followed up with a whispered, urgent "Three! Point! One! Four!" as I wrote as fast as I could, and I ended the concert by slicing the circle with such vigour that bits of chalk went flying.

When I put my hand up that day, which I did every chance I had, teachers granted me the right to speak with a single syllable that was music to my ears. Students followed suit. Even the St. Joseph's devils. In fact, the name caught on. Truly we are a nation of aspiring engineers: shortly after, there was a boy named Omprakash who was calling himself Omega, and another who was passing himself off as Upsilon, and for a while there was a Gamma, a Lambda and a Delta. But I was the first and the most enduring of the Greeks at Petit Séminaire. Even my brother, the captain of the cricket team, that local god, approved. He took me aside the next week.

"What's this I hear about a nickname you have?" he said.

I kept silent. Because whatever mocking was to come, it was to come. There was no avoiding it.

"I didn't realize you liked the colour yellow so much."

The colour yellow? I looked around. No one must hear what he was about to say, especially not one of his lackeys. "Ravi, what do you mean?" I whispered.

"It's all right with me, brother. Anything's better than 'Pissing'. Even 'Lemon Pie'."

As he sauntered away he smiled and said, "You look a bit red in the face."

But he held his peace.

And so, in that Greek letter that looks like a shack with a corrugated tin roof, in that elusive, irrational number with which scientists try to understand the universe, I found refuge.

CHAPTER 6

He's an excellent cook. His overheated house is always smelling of something delicious. His spice rack looks like an apothecary's shop. When he opens his refrigerator or his cupboards, there are many brand names I don't rec-

ognize; in fact, I can't even tell what language they're in. We are in India. But he handles Western dishes equally well. He makes me the most zesty yet subtle macaroni and cheese I've ever had. And his vegetarian tacos would be the envy of all Mexico.

I notice something else: his cupboards are jam-packed. Behind every door, on every shelf, stand mountains of neatly stacked cans and packages. A reserve of food to last the siege of Leningrad.

CHAPTER 7

It was my luck to have a few good teachers in my youth, men and women who came into my dark head and lit a match. One of these was Mr. Satish Kumar, my biology teacher at Petit Séminaire and an active Communist who was always hoping Tamil Nadu would stop electing movie stars and go the way of Kerala. He had a most peculiar appearance. The top of his head was bald and pointy, yet he had the most impressive jowls I have ever seen, and his narrow shoulders gave way to a massive stomach that looked like the base of a mountain, except that the mountain stood in thin air, for it stopped abruptly and disappeared horizontally into his pants. It's a mystery to me how his stick-like legs supported the weight above them, but they did, though they moved in surprising ways at times, as if his knees could bend in any direction. His construction was geometric: he looked like two triangles, a small one and a larger one, balanced on two parallel lines. But organic, quite warty actually, and with sprigs of black hair sticking out of his ears. And friendly. His smile seemed to take up the whole base of his triangular head.

Mr. Kumar was the first avowed atheist I ever met. I discovered this not in the classroom but at the zoo. He was a regular visitor who read the labels and descriptive notices in their entirety and approved of every animal he saw. Each to him was a triumph of logic and mechanics, and nature as a whole was an exceptionally fine illustration of science. To his ears, when an animal felt the urge to mate, it said "Gregor Mendel", recalling the father of genetics, and when it was time to show its mettle, "Charles Darwin", the father of natural selection, and what we took to be bleating, grunting, hissing, snorting, roaring, growling, howling, chirping and screeching were but the thick accents of foreigners. When Mr. Kumar visited the zoo, it was to take the pulse of the universe, and his stethoscopic mind always confirmed to him that everything was in order, that everything *was* order. He left the zoo feeling scientifically refreshed.

The first time I saw his triangular form teetering and tottering about the zoo, I was shy to approach him. As much as I liked him as a teacher, he was a figure of authority, and I, a subject. I was a little afraid of him. I observed him at a distance. He had just come to the rhinoceros pit. The two Indian rhinos were great attractions at the zoo because of the goats. Rhinos are social animals, and when we got Peak, a young wild male, he was showing signs of suffering from isolation and he was eating less and less. As a stopgap measure, while he searched for a female, Father thought of seeing if Peak couldn't be accustomed to living with goats. If it worked, it would save a valuable animal. If it didn't, it would only cost a few goats. It worked marvellously. Peak and the herd of goats became inseparable, even when Summit arrived. Now, when the rhinos bathed, the goats stood around the muddy pool, and when the goats ate in their corner, Peak and Summit stood next to them like guards. The living arrangement was very popular with the public.

Mr. Kumar looked up and saw me. He smiled and, one hand holding onto the railing, the other waving, signalled me to come over.

"Hello, Pi," he said.

"Hello, sir. It's good of you to come to the zoo."

"I come here all the time. One might say it's my temple. This is interesting . . ." He was indicating the pit. "If we had politicians like these goats and rhinos we'd have fewer problems in our country. Unfortunately we have a prime minister who has the armour plating of a rhinoceros without any of its good sense."

I didn't know much about politics. Father and Mother complained regularly about Mrs. Gandhi, but it meant little to me. She lived far away in the north, not at the zoo and not in Pondicherry. But I felt I had to say something.

"Religion will save us," I said. Since when I could remember, religion had been very close to my heart.

"Religion?" Mr. Kumar grinned broadly. "I don't believe in religion. Religion is darkness."

Darkness? I was puzzled. I thought, Darkness is the last thing that religion is. Religion is light. Was he testing me? Was he saying, "Religion is darkness," the way he sometimes said in class things like "Mammals lay eggs," to see if someone would correct him? ("Only platypuses, sir.")

"There are no grounds for going beyond a scientific explanation of reality and no sound reason for believing anything but our sense experience. A clear intellect, close attention to detail and a little scientific knowledge will expose religion as superstitious bosh. God does not exist."

Did he say that? Or am I remembering the lines of later atheists? At any rate, it was something of the sort. I had never heard such words.

"Why tolerate darkness? Everything is here and clear, if only we look carefully."

He was pointing at Peak. Now though I had great admiration for Peak, I had never thought of a rhinoceros as a light bulb.

He spoke again. "Some people say God died during the Partition in 1947. He may have died in 1971 during the war. Or he may have died yesterday here in Pondicherry in an orphanage. That's what some people say, Pi. When I was your age, I lived in bed, racked with polio. I asked myself every day, 'Where is God? Where is God? Where is God?' God never came. It wasn't God who saved me—it was medicine. Reason is my prophet and it tells me that as a watch stops, so we die. It's the end. If the watch doesn't work properly, it must be fixed here and now by us. One day we will take hold of the means of production and there will be justice on earth."

This was all a bit much for me. The tone was right—loving and brave—but the details seemed bleak. I said nothing. It wasn't for fear of angering Mr. Kumar. I was more afraid that in a few words thrown out he might destroy something that I loved. What if his words had the effect of polio on me? What a terrible disease that must be if it could kill God in a man.

He walked off, pitching and rolling in the wild sea that was the steady ground. "Don't forget the test on Tuesday. Study hard, 3.14!"

"Yes, Mr. Kumar."

He became my favourite teacher at Petit Séminaire and the reason I studied zoology at the University of Toronto. I felt a kinship with him. It was my first clue that atheists are my brothers and sisters of a different faith, and every word they speak speaks of faith. Like me, they go as far as the legs of reason will carry them—and then they leap.

I'll be honest about it. It is not atheists who get stuck in my craw, but agnostics. Doubt is useful for a while. We must all pass through the garden of Gethsemane. If Christ played with doubt, so must we. If Christ spent an anguished night in prayer, if He burst out from the Cross, "My God, my God, why have you forsaken me?" then surely we are also permitted doubt. But we must move on. To choose doubt as a philosophy of life is akin to choosing immobility as a means of transportation.

CHAPTER 8

We commonly say in the trade that the most dangerous animal in a zoo is Man. In a general way we mean how our species' excessive predatoriness has made the entire planet our prey. More specifically, we have in mind the people who feed fishhooks to the otters, razors to the bears, apples with small nails in them to the elephants and hardware variations on the theme: ballpoint pens, paper clips, safety pins, rubber bands, combs, coffee spoons, horseshoes, pieces of broken glass, rings, brooches and other jewellery (and not just cheap plastic bangles: gold wedding bands, too), drinking straws, plastic cutlery, ping-pong balls, tennis balls and so on. The obituary of zoo animals that have died from being fed foreign bodies would include gorillas, bison, storks, rheas, ostriches, seals, sea lions, big cats, bears, camels, elephants, monkeys, and most every variety of deer, ruminant and songbird. Among zookeepers, Goliath's death is famous; he was a bull elephant seal, a great big venerable beast of two tons, star of his European zoo, loved by all visitors. He died of internal bleeding after someone fed him a broken beer bottle.

The cruelty is often more active and direct. The literature contains reports on the many torments inflicted upon zoo animals: a shoebill dying of shock after having its beak smashed with a hammer; a moose stag losing its beard, along with a strip of flesh the size of an index finger, to a visitor's knife (this same moose was poisoned six months later); a monkey's arm broken after reaching out for proffered nuts; a deer's antlers attacked with a hacksaw; a zebra stabbed with a sword; and other assaults on other animals, with walking sticks, umbrellas, hairpins, knitting needles, scissors and whatnot, often with an aim to taking an eye out or to injuring sexual parts. Animals are also poisoned. And there are indecencies even more bizarre: onanists breaking a sweat on monkeys, ponies, birds; a religious freak who cut a snake's head off; a deranged man who took to urinating in an elk's mouth.

At Pondicherry we were relatively fortunate. We were spared the sadists who plied European and American zoos. Nonetheless, our golden agouti vanished, stolen by someone who ate it, Father suspected. Various birds—pheasants, peacocks, macaws—lost feathers to people greedy for their beauty. We caught a man with a knife climbing into the pen for mouse deer; he said he was going to punish evil Ravana (who in the Ramayana took the form of a deer when he kidnapped Sita, Rama's consort). Another man was nabbed in the process of stealing a cobra. He was a snake charmer whose own snake had died. Both were saved: the cobra from a life of servitude and bad music, and the man from a possible death bite. We had to deal on occasion with stone throwers, who found the animals too placid and wanted a reaction. And we had the lady whose sari was caught by a lion. She spun like a yo-yo, choosing mortal embarrassment over mortal end. The thing was, it wasn't even an accident. She had leaned over, thrust her hand in the cage and waved the end of her sari in the lion's face, with what intent we never figured out. She was not injured; there were many fascinated men who came to her assistance. Her flustered explanation to Father was, "Whoever heard of a lion eating a cotton sari? I thought lions were carnivores." Our worst troublemakers were the visitors who gave food to the animals. Despite our vigilance, Dr. Atal, the zoo veterinarian, could tell by the number of animals with digestive disturbances which had been the busy days at the zoo. He called "tidbit-itis" the cases of enteritis or gastritis due to too many carbohydrates, especially sugar. Sometimes we wished people had stuck to sweets. People have a notion that animals can eat anything without the least consequence to their health. Not so. One of our sloth bears became seriously ill with severe hemorrhagic enteritis after being given fish that had gone putrid by a man who was convinced he was doing a good deed.

Just beyond the ticket booth Father had had painted on a wall in bright red letters the question: DO YOU KNOW WHICH IS THE MOST DANGEROUS ANIMAL IN THE ZOO? An arrow pointed to a small curtain. There were so many eager, curious hands that pulled at the curtain that we had to replace it regularly. Behind it was a mirror.

But I learned at my expense that Father believed there was another animal even more dangerous than us, and one that was extremely common, too, found on every continent, in every habitat: the redoubtable species *Animalus anthropomorphicus*, the animal as seen through human eyes. We've all met one, perhaps even owned one. It is an animal that is "cute", "friendly", "loving", "devoted", "merry", "understanding". These animals lie in ambush in every toy store and children's zoo. Countless stories are told of them. They are the pendants of those "vicious", "bloodthirsty", "depraved" animals that inflame the ire of the maniacs I have just mentioned, who vent their spite on them with walking sticks and umbrellas. In both cases we look at an animal and see a mirror. The obsession with putting ourselves at the centre of everything is the bane not only of theologians but also of zoologists.

I learned the lesson that an animal is an animal, essentially and practically removed from us, twice: once with Father and once with Richard Parker.

It was on a Sunday morning. I was quietly playing on my own. Father called out.

"Children, come here."

Something was wrong. His tone of voice set off a small alarm bell in my head. I quickly reviewed my conscience. It was clear. Ravi must be in trouble again. I wondered what he had done this time. I walked into the living room. Mother was there. That was unusual. The disciplining of children, like the tending of animals, was generally left to Father. Ravi walked in last, guilt written all over his criminal face.

"Ravi, Piscine, I have a very important lesson for you today."

"Oh really, is this necessary?" interrupted Mother. Her face was flushed.

I swallowed. If Mother, normally so unruffled, so calm, was worried, even upset, it meant we were in *serious* trouble. I exchanged glances with Ravi.

"Yes, it is," said Father, annoyed. "It may very well save their lives."

Save our lives! It was no longer a small alarm bell that was ringing in my head—they were big bells now, like the ones we heard from Sacred Heart of Jesus Church, not far from the zoo.

"But Piscine? He's only eight," Mother insisted.

"He's the one who worries me the most."

"I'm innocent!" I burst out. "It's Ravi's fault, whatever it is. He did it!"

"What?" said Ravi. "I haven't done anything wrong." He gave me the evil eye.

"Shush!" said Father, raising his hand. He was looking at Mother. "Gita, you've seen Piscine. He's at that age when boys run around and poke their noses everywhere."

Me? A run-arounder? An everywhere-nose-poker? Not so, not so! Defend me, Mother, defend me, I implored in my heart. But she only sighed and nodded, a signal that the terrible business could proceed.

"Come with me," said Father.

We set out like prisoners off to their execution.

We left the house, went through the gate, entered the zoo. It was early and the zoo hadn't opened yet to the public. Animal keepers and groundskeepers were going about their work. I noticed Sitaram, who oversaw the orang-utans, my favourite keeper. He paused to watch us go by. We passed birds, bears, apes, monkeys, ungulates, the terrarium house, the rhinos, the elephants, the giraffes.

We came to the big cats, our tigers, lions and leopards. Babu, their keeper, was waiting for us. We went round and down the path, and he unlocked the door to the cat house, which was at the centre of a moated island. We entered. It was a vast and dim cement cavern, circular in shape, warm and humid, and smelling of cat urine. All around were great big cages divided up by thick, green, iron bars. A yellowish light filtered down from the skylights. Through the cage exits we could see the vegetation of the surrounding island, flooded with sunlight. The cages were empty—save one: Mahisha, our Bengal tiger patriarch, a lanky, hulking beast of 550 pounds, had been detained. As soon as we stepped in, he loped up to the bars of his cage and set off a full-throated snarl, ears flat against his skull and round eyes fixed on Babu. The sound was so loud and fierce it seemed to shake the whole cat house. My knees started quaking. I got close to Mother. She was trembling, too. Even Father seemed to pause and steady himself. Only Babu was indifferent to the outburst and to the searing stare that bored into him like a drill. He had a tested trust in iron bars. Mahisha started pacing to and fro against the limits of his cage.

Father turned to us. "What animal is this?" he bellowed above Mahisha's snarling.

"It's a tiger," Ravi and I answered in unison, obediently pointing out the blindingly obvious.

"Are tigers dangerous?"

"Yes, Father, tigers are dangerous."

"Tigers are *very* dangerous," Father shouted. "I want you to understand that you are never—under *any* circumstances—to touch a tiger, to pet a tiger, to put your hands through the bars of a cage, even to get close to a cage. Is that clear? Ravi?"

Ravi nodded vigorously.

"Piscine?"

I nodded even more vigorously.

He kept his eyes on me.

I nodded so hard I'm surprised my neck didn't snap and my head fall to the floor.

I would like to say in my own defence that though I may have anthropomorphized the animals till they spoke fluent English, the pheasants complaining in uppity British accents of their tea being cold and the baboons planning their bank robbery getaway in the flat, menacing tones of American gangsters, the fancy was always conscious. I quite deliberately dressed wild animals in tame costumes of my imagination. But I never deluded myself as to the real nature of my playmates. My poking nose had more sense than that. I don't know where Father got the idea that his youngest son was itching to step into a cage with a ferocious carnivore. But wherever the strange worry came from—and Father *was* a worrier—he was clearly determined to rid himself of it that very morning.

"I'm going to show you how dangerous tigers are," he continued. "I want you to remember this lesson for the rest of your lives."

He turned to Babu and nodded. Babu left. Mahisha's eyes followed him and did not move from the door he disappeared through. He returned a few seconds later carrying a goat with its legs tied. Mother gripped me from behind. Mahisha's snarl turned into a growl deep in the throat.

Babu unlocked, opened, entered, closed and locked a cage next to the tiger's cage. Bars and a trapdoor separated the two. Immediately

Mahisha was up against the dividing bars, pawing them. To his growling he now added explosive, arrested *woofs*. Babu placed the goat on the floor; its flanks were heaving violently, its tongue hung from its mouth, and its eyes were spinning orbs. He untied its legs. The goat got to its feet. Babu exited the cage in the same careful way he had entered it. The cage had two floors, one level with us, the other at the back, higher by about three feet, that led outside to the island. The goat scrambled to this second level. Mahisha, now unconcerned with Babu, paralleled the move in his cage in a fluid, effortless motion. He crouched and lay still, his slowly moving tail the only sign of tension.

Babu stepped up to the trapdoor between the cages and started pulling it open. In anticipation of satisfaction, Mahisha fell silent. I heard two things at that moment: Father saying "Never forget this lesson" as he looked on grimly; and the bleating of the goat. It must have been bleating all along, only we couldn't hear it before.

I could feel Mother's hand pressed against my pounding heart.

The trapdoor resisted with sharp cries. Mahisha was beside himself—he looked as if he were about to burst through the bars. He seemed to hesitate between staying where he was, at the place where his prey was closest but most certainly out of reach, and moving to the ground level, further away but where the trapdoor was located. He raised himself and started snarling again.

The goat started to jump. It jumped to amazing heights. I had no idea a goat could jump so high. But the back of the cage was a high and smooth cement wall.

With sudden ease the trapdoor slid open. Silence fell again, except for bleating and the *click-click* of the goat's hooves against the floor.

A streak of black and orange flowed from one cage to the next.

Normally the big cats were not given food one day a week, to simulate conditions in the wild. We found out later that Father had ordered that Mahisha not be fed for three days.

I don't know if I saw blood before turning into Mother's arms or if I daubed it on later, in my memory, with a big brush. But I heard. It was enough to scare the living vegetarian daylights out of me. Mother bundled us out. We were in hysterics. She was incensed.

"How could you, Santosh? They're children! They'll be scarred for the rest of their lives."

Her voice was hot and tremulous. I could see she had tears in her eyes. I felt better.

"Gita, my bird, it's for their sake. What if Piscine had stuck his hand through the bars of the cage one day to touch the pretty orange fur? Better a goat than him, no?"

His voice was soft, nearly a whisper. He looked contrite. He never called her "my bird" in front of us.

We were huddled around her. He joined us. But the lesson was not over, though it was gentler after that.

Father led us to the lions and leopards.

"Once there was a madman in Australia who was a black belt in karate. He wanted to prove himself against the lions. He lost. Badly. The keepers found only half his body in the morning."

"Yes, Father."

The Himalayan bears and the sloth bears.

"One strike of the claws from these cuddly creatures and your innards will be scooped out and splattered all over the ground."

"Yes, Father."

The hippos.

"With those soft, flabby mouths of theirs they'll crush your body to a bloody pulp. On land they can outrun you."

"Yes, Father."

The hyenas.

"The strongest jaws in nature. Don't think that they're cowardly or that they only eat carrion. They're not and they don't! They'll start eating you while you're still alive."

"Yes, Father."

The orang-utans.

"As strong as ten men. They'll break your bones as if they were twigs. I know some of them were once pets and you played with them when they were small. But now they're grown-up and wild and un-predictable."

"Yes, Father."

The ostrich.

"Looks flustered and silly, doesn't it? Listen up: it's one of the most dangerous animals in a zoo. Just one kick and your back is bro-ken or your torso is crushed."

"Yes, Father."

The spotted deer.

"So pretty, aren't they? If the male feels he has to, he'll charge you and those short little antlers will pierce you like daggers."

"Yes, Father."

The Arabian camel.

"One slobbering bite and you've lost a chunk of flesh."

"Yes, Father."

The black swans.

"With their beaks they'll crack your skull. With their wings they'll break your arms."

"Yes, Father."

The smaller birds.

"They'll cut through your fingers with their beaks as if they were butter."

"Yes, Father."

The elephants.

"The most dangerous animal of all. More keepers and visitors are killed by elephants than by any other animal in a zoo. A young elephant will most likely dismember you and trample your body parts flat. That's what happened to one poor lost soul in a European zoo who got into the elephant house through a window. An older, more patient animal will squeeze you against a wall or sit on you. Sounds funny—but think about it!"

"Yes, Father."

"There are animals we haven't stopped by. Don't think they're harmless. Life will defend itself no matter how small it is. Every animal is ferocious and dangerous. It may not kill you, but it will certainly injure you. It will scratch you and bite you, and you can look forward to a swollen, pus-filled infection, a high fever and a ten-day stay in the hospital."

"Yes, Father."

We came to the guinea pigs, the only other animals besides Mahisha to have been starved at Father's orders, having been denied their previous evening's meal. Father unlocked the cage. He brought out a bag of feed from his pocket and emptied it on the floor.

"You see these guinea pigs?"

"Yes, Father."

The creatures were trembling with weakness as they frantically nibbled their kernels of corn.

"Well . . ." He leaned down and scooped one up. "They're not dangerous." The other guinea pigs scattered instantly.

Father laughed. He handed me the squealing guinea pig. He meant to end on a light note.

The guinea pig rested in my arms tensely. It was a young one. I went to the cage and carefully lowered it to the floor. It rushed to its mother's side. The only reason these guinea pigs weren't dangerous—didn't draw blood with their teeth and claws—was that they were practically domesticated. Otherwise, to grab a wild guinea pig with your bare hands would be like taking hold of a knife by the blade.

The lesson was over. Ravi and I sulked and gave Father the cold shoulder for a week. Mother ignored him too. When I went by the rhinoceros pit I fancied the rhinos' heads were hung low with sadness over the loss of one of their dear companions.

But what can you do when you love your father? Life goes on and you don't touch tigers. Except that now, for having accused Ravi of an unspecified crime he hadn't committed, I was as good as dead. In years subsequent, when he was in the mood to terrorize me, he would whisper to me, "Just wait till we're alone. *You're the next goat!*"

CHAPTER 9

Getting animals used to the presence of humans is at the heart of the art and science of zookeeping. The key aim is to diminish an animal's flight distance, which is the minimum distance at which an animal wants to keep a perceived enemy. A flamingo in the wild won't mind you if you stay more than three hundred yards away. Cross that limit and it becomes tense. Get even closer and you trigger a flight reaction from which the bird will not cease until the three-hundred-yard limit is set again, or until heart and lungs fail. Different animals have different flight distances and they gauge them in different ways. Cats look, deer listen, bears smell. Giraffes will allow you to come to within thirty yards of them if you are in a motor car, but will run if you are 150 yards away on foot. Fiddler crabs scurry when you're ten yards away; howler monkeys stir in their branches when you're at twenty; African buffaloes react at seventy-five.

Our tools for diminishing flight distance are the knowledge we have of an animal, the food and shelter we provide, the protection we afford. When it works, the result is an emotionally stable, stress-free wild animal that not only stays put, but is healthy, lives a very long time, eats without fuss, behaves and socializes in natural ways and—the best sign—reproduces. I won't say that our zoo compared to the zoos of San Diego or Toronto or Berlin or Singapore, but you can't keep a good zookeeper down. Father was a natural. He made up for a lack of formal training with an intuitive gift and a keen eye. He had a knack for looking at an animal and guessing what was on its mind. He was attentive to his charges, and they, in return, multiplied, some to excess.

CHAPTER 10

Yet there will always be animals that seek to escape from zoos. Animals that are kept in unsuitable enclosures are the most obvious example. Every animal has particular habitat needs that must be met. If its enclosure is too sunny or too wet or too empty, if its perch is too high or too exposed, if the ground is too sandy, if there are too few branches to make a nest, if the food trough is too low, if there is not enough mud to wallow in—and so many other ifs—then the animal will not be at peace. It is not so much a question of constructing an imitation of conditions in the wild as of getting to the *essence* of these conditions. Everything in an enclosure must be just right—in other words, within the limits of the animal's capacity to adapt. A plague upon bad zoos with bad enclosures! They bring all zoos into disrepute.

Wild animals that are captured when they are fully mature are another example of escape-prone animals; often they are too set in their ways to reconstruct their subjective worlds and adapt to a new environment.

But even animals that were bred in zoos and have never known the wild, that are perfectly adapted to their enclosures and feel no tension in the presence of humans, will have moments of excitement that push them to seek to escape. All living things contain a measure of madness that moves them in strange, sometimes inexplicable ways. This madness can be saving; it is part and parcel of the ability to adapt. Without it, no species would survive.

Whatever the reason for wanting to escape, sane or insane, zoo detractors should realize that animals don't escape *to somewhere* but *from something*. Something within their territory has frightened them—the intrusion of an enemy, the assault of a dominant animal, a startling noise—and set off a flight reaction. The animal flees, or tries to. I was surprised to read at the Toronto Zoo—a very fine zoo, I might add—that leopards can jump eighteen feet straight up. Our leopard enclosure in Pondicherry had a wall *sixteen* feet high at the back; I surmise that Rosie and Copycat never jumped out not because of constitutional weakness but simply because they had no reason to. Animals that escape go from the known into the unknown—and if there is one thing an animal hates above all else, it is the unknown. Escaping animals usually hide in the very first place they find that gives them a sense of security, and they are dangerous only to those who happen to get between them and their reckoned safe spot.

CHAPTER 11

Consider the case of the female black leopard that escaped from the Zurich Zoo in the winter of 1933. She was new to the zoo and seemed to get along with the male leopard. But various paw injuries hinted at matrimonial strife. Before any decision could be taken about what to do, she squeezed through a break in the roof bars of her cage and vanished in the night. The discovery that a wild carnivore was free in their midst created an uproar among the citizens of Zurich. Traps were set and hunting dogs were let loose. They only rid the canton of its few half-wild dogs. Not a trace of the leopard was found for *ten weeks*. Finally, a casual labourer came upon it under a barn twenty-five miles away and shot it. Remains of roe-deer were found nearby. That a big, black, tropical cat managed to survive for more than two months in a Swiss winter without being seen by anyone, let alone attacking anyone, speaks plainly to the fact that escaped zoo animals are not dangerous absconding criminals but simply wild creatures seeking to fit in.

And this case is just one among many. If you took the city of Tokyo and turned it upside down and shook it, you would be amazed at the animals that would fall out. It would pour more than cats and dogs, I tell you. Boa constrictors, Komodo dragons, crocodiles, piranhas, ostriches, wolves, lynx, wallabies, manatees, porcupines, orang-utans, wild boar—that's the sort of rainfall you could expect on your umbrella. And they expected to find—ha! In the middle of a Mexican tropical jungle, imagine! Ha! Ha! It's laughable, simply laughable. What were they thinking?

CHAPTER 12

At times he gets agitated. It's nothing I say (I say very little). It's his own story that does it. Memory is an ocean and he bobs on its surface. I worry that he'll want to stop. But he wants to tell me his story. He goes on. After all these years, Richard Parker still preys on his mind.

He's a sweet man. Every time I visit he prepares a South Indian vegetarian feast. I told him I like spicy food. I don't know why I said such a stupid thing. It's a complete lie. I add dollop of yogurt after dollop of yogurt. Nothing doing. Each time it's the same: my taste buds shrivel up and die, my skin goes beet red, my eyes well up with tears, my head feels like a house on fire, and my digestive tract starts to twist and groan in agony like a boa constrictor that has swallowed a lawn mower.

CHAPTER 13

So you see, if you fall into a lion's pit, the reason the lion will tear you to pieces is not because it's hungry—be assured, zoo animals are amply fed—or because it's bloodthirsty, but because you've invaded its territory.

As an aside, that is why a circus trainer must always enter the lion ring first, and in full sight of the lions. In doing so, he establishes that the ring is *his* territory, not theirs, a notion that he reinforces by shouting, by stomping about, by snapping his whip. The lions are impressed. Their disadvantage weighs heavily on them. Notice how they come in: mighty predators though they are, "kings of beasts", they crawl in with their tails low and they keep to the edges of the ring, which is always round so that they have nowhere to hide. They are in the presence of a strongly dominant male, a super-alpha male, and they must submit to his dominance rituals. So they open their jaws wide, they sit up, they jump through paper-covered hoops, they crawl through tubes, they walk backwards, they roll over. "He's a queer one," they think dimly. "Never seen a top lion like him. But he runs a good pride. The larder's always full and—let's be honest, mates—his antics keep us busy. Napping all the time does get a bit boring. At least we're not riding bicycles like the brown bears or catching flying plates like the chimps."

Only the trainer better make sure he always remains super alpha. He will pay dearly if he unwittingly slips to beta. Much hostile and aggressive behaviour among animals is the expression of social insecurity. The animal in front of you must know where it stands, whether above you or below you. Social rank is central to how it leads its life. Rank determines whom it can associate with and how; where and when it can eat; where it can rest; where it can drink; and so on. Until it knows its rank for certain, the animal lives a life of unbearable anarchy. It remains nervous, jumpy, dangerous. Luckily for the circus trainer, decisions about social rank among higher animals are not always based on brute force. Hediger (1950) says, "When two creatures meet, the one that is able to intimidate its opponent is recognized as socially superior, so that a social decision does not always depend on a fight; an encounter in some circumstances may be enough." Words of a wise animal man. Mr. Hediger was for many years a zoo director, first of the Basel Zoo and then of the Zurich Zoo. He was a man well versed in the ways of animals.

It's a question of brain over brawn. The nature of the circus trainer's ascendancy is psychological. Foreign surroundings, the trainer's erect posture, calm demeanour, steady gaze, fearless step forward, strange roar (for example, the snapping of a whip or the blowing of a whistle)— these are so many factors that will fill the animal's mind with doubt and fear, and make clear to it where it stands, the very thing it wants to know. Satisfied, Number Two will back down and Number One can turn to the audience and shout, "Let the show go on! And now, ladies and gentlemen, through hoops of *real* fire . . ."

CHAPTER 14

It is interesting to note that the lion that is the most amenable to the circus trainer's tricks is the one with the lowest social standing in the pride, the omega animal. It has the most to gain from a close relationship with the super-alpha trainer. It is not only a matter of extra treats.

A close relationship will also mean protection from the other members of the pride. It is this compliant animal, to the public no different from the others in size and apparent ferocity, that will be the star of the show, while the trainer leaves the beta and gamma lions, more cantankerous subordinates, sitting on their colourful barrels on the edge of the ring.

The same is true of other circus animals and is also seen in zoos. Socially inferior animals are the ones that make the most strenuous, resourceful efforts to get to know their keepers. They prove to be the ones most faithful to them, most in need of their company, least likely to challenge them or be difficult. The phenomenon has been observed with big cats, bison, deer, wild sheep, monkeys and many other animals. It is a fact commonly known in the trade.

CHAPTER 15

His house is a temple. In the entrance hall hangs a framed picture of Ganesha, he of the elephant head. He sits facing out—rosy-coloured, pot-bellied, crowned and smiling—three hands holding various objects, the fourth held palm out in blessing and in greeting. He is the lord overcomer of obstacles, the god of good luck, the god of wisdom, the patron of learning. Simpatico in the highest. He brings a smile to my lips. At his feet is an attentive rat. His vehicle. Because when Lord Ganesha travels, he travels atop a rat. On the wall opposite the picture is a plain wooden Cross.

In the living room, on a table next to the sofa, there is a small framed picture of the Virgin Mary of Guadalupe, flowers tumbling from her open mantle. Next to it is a framed photo of the black-robed Kaaba, holiest sanctum of Islam, surrounded by a ten-thousandfold swirl of the faithful. On the television set is a brass statue of Shiva as Nataraja, the cosmic lord of the dance, who controls the motions of the universe and the flow of time. He dances on the demon of ignorance, his four arms held out in choreographic gesture, one foot on the demon's back, the other lifted in the air. When Nataraja brings this foot down, they say time will stop.

There is a shrine in the kitchen. It is set in a cupboard whose door he has replaced with a fretwork arch. The arch partly hides the yellow light bulb that in the evenings lights up the shrine. Two pictures rest behind a small altar: to the side, Ganesha again, and in the centre, in a larger frame, smiling and blue-skinned, Krishna playing the flute. Both have smears of red and yellow powder on the glass over their foreheads. In a copper dish on the altar are three silver murtis, representations. He identifies them for me with a pointed finger: Lakshmi; Shakti, the mother goddess, in the form of Parvati; and Krishna, this time as a playful baby crawling on all fours. In between the goddesses is a stone Shiva yoni linga, which looks like half an avocado with a phallic stump rising from its centre, a Hindu symbol representing the male and female energies of the universe. To one side of the dish is a small conch shell set on a pedestal; to the other, a small silver handbell. Grains of rice lie about, as well as a flower just beginning to wilt. Many of these items are anointed with dabs of yellow and red.

On the shelf below are various articles of devotion: a beaker full of water; a copper spoon; a lamp with a wick coiled in oil; sticks of incense; and small bowls full of red powder, yellow powder, grains of rice and lumps of sugar.

There is another Virgin Mary in the dining room.

Upstairs in his office there is a brass Ganesha sitting cross-legged next to the computer, a wooden Christ on the Cross from Brazil on a wall, and a green prayer rug in a corner. The Christ is expressive—He suffers. The prayer rug lies in its own clear space. Next to it, on a low bookstand, is a book covered by a cloth. At the centre of the cloth is a single Arabic word, intricately woven, four letters: an alif, two lams and a ha. The word God in Arabic.

The book on the bedside table is a Bible.

CHAPTER 16

We are all born like Catholics, aren't we—in limbo, without religion, until some figure introduces us to God? After that meeting the matter ends for most of us. If there is a change, it is usually for the lesser rather than the greater; many people seem to lose God along life's way. That was not my case. The figure in question for me was an older sister of Mother's, of a more traditional mind, who brought me to a temple when I was a small baby. Auntie Rohini was delighted to meet her newborn nephew and she thought she would include Mother Goddess in the delight. "It will be his symbolic first outing," she said. "It's a samskara!" Symbolic indeed. We were in Madurai; I was the fresh veteran of a seven-hour train journey. No matter. Off we went on this Hindu rite of passage, Mother carrying me, Auntie propelling her. I have no conscious memory of this first go-around in a temple, but some smell of incense, some play of light and shadow, some flame, some burst of colour, something of the sultriness and mystery of the place must have stayed with me. A germ of religious exaltation, no bigger than a mustard seed, was sown in me and left to germinate. It has never stopped growing since that day.

I am a Hindu because of sculptured cones of red kumkum powder and baskets of yellow turmeric nuggets, because of garlands of flowers and pieces of broken coconut, because of the clanging of bells to announce one's arrival to God, because of the whine of the reedy nadaswaram and the beating of drums, because of the patter of bare feet against stone floors down dark corridors pierced by shafts of sunlight, because of the fragrance of incense, because of flames of arati lamps circling in the darkness, because of bhajans being sweetly sung, because of elephants standing around to bless, because of colourful murals telling colourful stories, because of foreheads carrying, variously signified, the same word—*faith*. I became loyal to these sense

47

impressions even before I knew what they meant or what they were for. It is my heart that commands me so. I feel at home in a Hindu temple. I am aware of Presence, not personal the way we usually feel presence, but something larger. My heart still skips a beat when I catch sight of the murti, of God Residing, in the inner sanctum of a temple. Truly I am in a sacred cosmic womb, a place where everything is born, and it is my sweet luck to behold its living core. My hands naturally come together in reverent worship. I hunger for prasad, that sugary offering to God that comes back to us as a sanctified treat. My palms need to feel the heat of a hallowed flame whose blessing I bring to my eyes and forehead.

But religion is more than rite and ritual. There is what the rite and ritual stand for. Here too I am a Hindu. The universe makes sense to me through Hindu eyes. There is Brahman, the world soul, the sustaining frame upon which is woven, warp and weft, the cloth of being, with all its decorative elements of space and time. There is Brahman nirguna, without qualities, which lies beyond understanding, beyond description, beyond approach; with our poor words we sew a suit for it—One, Truth, Unity, Absolute, Ultimate Reality, Ground of Being—and try to make it fit, but Brahman nirguna always bursts the seams. We are left speechless. But there is also Brahman saguna, with qualities, where the suit fits. Now we call it Shiva, Krishna, Shakti, Ganesha; we can approach it with some understanding; we can discern certain attributes—loving, merciful, frightening—and we feel the gentle pull of relationship. Brahman saguna is Brahman made manifest to our limited senses, Brahman expressed not only in gods but in humans, animals, trees, in a handful of earth, for everything has a trace of the divine in it. The truth of life is that Brahman is no different from atman, the spiritual force within us, what you might call the soul. The individual soul touches upon the world soul like a well reaches for the water table. That which sustains the universe beyond thought and language, and that which is at the core of us and struggles for expression, is the same thing. The finite within the infinite, the infinite within the finite. If you ask me how Brahman and atman relate precisely, I would say in the same way the Father, the Son and the Holy Spirit relate: mysteriously. But one thing is clear: atman seeks to realize Brahman, to be united with the Absolute, and it travels in this life on a pilgrimage where it is born and dies, and is born again and dies again, and again, and again, until it manages to shed the sheaths that imprison it here below. The paths to liberation are numerous, but the bank along the way is always the same, the Bank of Karma, where the liberation account of each of us is credited or debited depending on our actions.

This, in a holy nutshell, is Hinduism, and I have been a Hindu all my life. With its notions in mind I see my place in the universe.

But we should not cling! A plague upon fundamentalists and literalists! I am reminded of a story of Lord Krishna when he was a cowherd. Every night he invites the milkmaids to dance with him in the forest. They come and they dance. The night is dark, the fire in their midst roars and crackles, the beat of the music gets ever faster—the girls dance and dance and dance with their sweet lord, who has made himself so abundant as to be in the arms of each and every girl. But the moment the girls become possessive, the moment each one imagines that Krishna is her partner alone, he vanishes. So it is that we should not be jealous with God.

I know a woman here in Toronto who is very dear to my heart. She was my foster mother. I call her Auntieji and she likes that. She is Québécoise. Though she has lived in Toronto for over thirty years, her French-speaking mind still slips on occasion on the understanding of English sounds. And so, when she first heard of Hare Krishnas, she didn't hear right. She heard "Hairless Christians", and that is what they were to her for many years. When I corrected her, I told her that in fact she was not so wrong; that Hindus, in their capacity for love, are indeed hairless Christians, just as Muslims, in the way they see God in everything, are bearded Hindus, and Christians, in their devotion to God, are hat-wearing Muslims.

CHAPTER 17

First wonder goes deepest; wonder after that fits in the impression made by the first. I owe to Hinduism the original landscape of my religious imagination, those towns and rivers, battlefields and forests, holy mountains and deep seas where gods, saints, villains and ordinary people rub shoulders, and, in doing so, define who and why we are. I first heard of the tremendous, cosmic might of loving kindness in this Hindu land. It was Lord Krishna speaking. I heard him, and I followed him. And in his wisdom and perfect love, Lord Krishna led me to meet one man.

I was fourteen years old—and a well-content Hindu on a holiday—when I met Jesus Christ.

It was not often that Father took time off from the zoo, but one of the times he did we went to Munnar, just over in Kerala. Munnar is a small hill station surrounded by some of the highest tea estates in the world. It was early May and the monsoon hadn't come yet. The plains of Tamil Nadu were beastly hot. We made it to Munnar after a winding, five-hour car ride from Madurai. The coolness was as pleasing as having mint in your mouth. We did the tourist thing. We visited a Tata tea factory. We enjoyed a boat ride on a lake. We toured a cattle-breeding centre. We fed salt to some Nilgiri tahrs—a species of wild goat—in a national park. ("We have some in our zoo. You should come to Pondicherry," said Father to some Swiss tourists.) Ravi and I went for walks in the tea estates near town. It was all an excuse to keep our lethargy a little busy. By late afternoon Father and Mother were as settled in the tea room of our comfortable hotel as two cats sunning themselves at a window. Mother read while Father chatted with fellow guests.

There are three hills within Munnar. They don't bear comparison with the tall hills—mountains, you might call them—that surround the town, but I noticed the first morning, as we were having breakfast, that they did stand out in one way: on each stood a Godhouse. The hill on the right, across the river from the hotel, had a Hindu temple high on its side; the hill in the middle, further away, held up a mosque; while the hill on the left was crowned with a Christian church.

On our fourth day in Munnar, as the afternoon was coming to an end, I stood on the hill on the left. Despite attending a nominally Christian school, I had not yet been inside a church—and I wasn't about to dare the deed now. I knew very little about the religion. It had a reputation for few gods and great violence. But good schools. I walked around the church. It was a building unremittingly unrevealing of what it held inside, with thick, featureless walls pale blue in colour and high, narrow windows impossible to look in through. A fortress.

I came upon the rectory. The door was open. I hid around a corner to look upon the scene. To the left of the door was a small board with the words *Parish Priest* and *Assistant Priest* on it. Next to each was a small sliding block. Both the priest and his assistant were IN, the board informed me in gold letters, which I could plainly see. One priest was working in his office, his back turned to the bay windows, while the other was seated on a bench at a round table in the large vestibule that evidently functioned as a room for receiving visitors. He sat facing the door and the windows, a book in his hands, a Bible I presumed. He read a little, looked up, read a little more, looked up again. It was done in a way that was leisurely, yet alert and composed. After some minutes, he closed the book and put it aside. He folded his hands together on the table and sat there, his expression serene, showing neither expectation nor resignation.

The vestibule had clean, white walls; the table and benches were of dark wood; and the priest was dressed in a white cassock—it was all neat, plain, simple. I was filled with a sense of peace. But more than the setting, what arrested me was my intuitive understanding that he was there—open, patient—in case someone, anyone, should want to talk to him; a problem of the soul, a heaviness of the heart, a darkness of the conscience, he would listen with love. He was a man whose profession it was to love, and he would offer comfort and guidance to the best of his ability.

I was moved. What I had before my eyes stole into my heart and thrilled me.

He got up. I thought he might slide his block over, but he didn't. He retreated further into the rectory, that's all, leaving the door between the vestibule and the next room as open as the outside door. I noted this, how both doors were wide open. Clearly, he and his colleague were still available.

I walked away and I dared. I entered the church. My stomach was in knots. I was terrified I would meet a Christian who would shout at me, "What are you doing here? How dare you enter this sacred place, you defiler? Get out, right now!"

There was no one. And little to be understood. I advanced and observed the inner sanctum. There was a painting. Was this the murti? Something about a human sacrifice. An angry god who had to be appeased with blood. Dazed women staring up in the air and fat babies with tiny wings flying about. A charismatic bird. Which one was the god? To the side of the sanctum was a painted wooden sculpture. The victim again, bruised and bleeding in bold colours. I stared at his knees. They were badly scraped. The pink skin was peeled back and looked like the petals of a flower, revealing kneecaps that were fire-engine red. It was hard to connect this torture scene with the priest in the rectory.

The next day, at around the same time, I let myself IN.

Catholics have a reputation for severity, for judgment that comes down heavily. My experience with Father Martin was not at all like that. He was very kind. He served me tea and biscuits in a tea set that tinkled and rattled at every touch; he treated me like a grown-up; and he told me a story. Or rather, since Christians are so fond of capital letters, a Story.

And what a story. The first thing that drew me in was disbelief. What? Humanity sins but it's God's Son who pays the price? I tried to imagine Father saying to me, "Piscine, a lion slipped into the llama pen today and killed two llamas. Yesterday another one killed a black buck. Last week two of them ate the camel. The week before it was painted storks and grey herons. And who's to say for sure who snacked on our golden agouti? The situation has become intolerable. Something must be done. I have decided that the only way the lions can atone for their sins is if I feed you to them."

"Yes, Father, that would be the right and logical thing to do. Give me a moment to wash up."

"Hallelujah, my son."

"Hallelujah, Father."

What a downright weird story. What peculiar psychology.

I asked for another story, one that I might find more satisfying. Surely this religion had more than one story in its bag—religions abound with stories. But Father Martin made me understand that the stories that came before it—and there were many—were simply prologue to the Christians. Their religion had one Story, and to it they came back again and again, over and over. It was story enough for them.

I was quiet that evening at the hotel.

That a god should put up with adversity, I could understand. The gods of Hinduism face their fair share of thieves, bullies, kidnappers and usurpers. What is the Ramayana but the account of one long, bad day for Rama? Adversity, yes. Reversals of fortune, yes. Treachery, yes. But *humiliation? Death?* I couldn't imagine Lord Krishna consenting to be stripped naked, whipped, mocked, dragged through the streets and, to top it off, crucified—and at the hands of mere humans, to boot. I'd never heard of a Hindu god dying. Brahman Revealed did not go for death. Devils and monsters did, as did mortals, by the thousands and millions—that's what they were there for. Matter, too, fell away. But divinity should not be blighted by death. It's wrong. The world soul cannot die, even in one contained part of it. It was wrong of this Christian God to let His avatar die. That is tantamount to letting a part of Himself die. For if the Son is to die, it cannot be fake. If God on the Cross is God shamming a human tragedy, it turns the Passion of Christ into the Farce of Christ. The death of the Son must be real. Father Martin assured me that it was. But once a dead God, always a dead God, even resurrected. The Son must have the taste of death forever in His mouth. The Trinity must be tainted by it; there must be a certain stench at the right hand of God the Father. The horror must be real. Why would God wish that upon Himself? Why not leave death to the mortals? Why make dirty what is beautiful, spoil what is perfect?

Love. That was Father Martin's answer.

And what about this Son's deportment? There is the story of baby Krishna, wrongly accused by his friends of eating a bit of dirt. His foster mother, Yashoda, comes up to him with a wagging finger. "You shouldn't eat dirt, you naughty boy," she scolds him. "But I haven't," says the unchallenged lord of all and everything, in sport disguised as a frightened human child. "Tut! Tut! Open your mouth," orders Yashoda. Krishna does as he is told. He opens his mouth. Yashoda gasps. She sees in Krishna's mouth the whole complete entire timeless universe, all the stars and planets of space and the distance between them, all the lands and seas of the earth and the life in them; she sees all the days of yesterday and all the days of tomorrow; she sees all ideas and all emotions, all pity and all hope, and the three strands of matter; not a pebble, candle, creature, village or galaxy is missing, including herself and every bit of dirt in its truthful place. "My Lord, you can close your mouth," she says reverently.

There is the story of Vishnu incarnated as Vamana the dwarf. He asks of demon king Bali only as much land as he can cover in three strides. Bali laughs at this runt of a suitor and his puny request. He consents. Immediately Vishnu takes on his full cosmic size. With one stride he covers the earth, with the second the heavens, and with the third he boots Bali into the netherworld.

Even Rama, that most human of avatars, who had to be reminded of his divinity when he grew long-faced over the struggle to get Sita, his wife, back from Ravana, evil king of Lanka, was no slouch. No spindly cross would have kept him down. When push came to shove, he transcended his limited human frame with strength no man could have and weapons no man could handle.

That is God as God should be. With shine and power and might. Such as can rescue and save and put down evil.

This Son, on the other hand, who goes hungry, who suffers from thirst, who gets tired, who is sad, who is anxious, who is heckled and harassed, who has to put up with followers who don't get it and opponents who don't respect Him—what kind of a god is that? It's a god on too human a scale, that's what. There are miracles, yes, mostly of a medical nature, a few to satisfy hungry stomachs; at best a storm is tempered, water is briefly walked upon. If that is magic, it is minor magic, on the order of card tricks. Any Hindu god can do a hundred times better. This Son is a god who spent most of His time telling stories, *talking*. This Son is a god who walked, a pedestrian god—and in a hot place, at that—with a stride like any human stride, the sandal reaching just above the rocks along the way; and when He splurged on transportation, it was a regular donkey. This Son is a god who died in three hours, with moans, gasps and laments. What kind of a god is that? What is there to inspire in this Son?

Love, said Father Martin.

And this Son appears only once, long ago, far away? Among an obscure tribe in a backwater of West Asia on the confines of a long-vanished empire? Is done away with before He has a single grey hair on His head? Leaves not a single descendant, only scattered, partial testimony, His complete works doodles in the dirt? Wait a minute. This is more than Brahman with a serious case of stage fright. This is Brahman selfish. This is Brahman ungenerous and unfair. This is Brahman practically unmanifest. If Brahman is to have only one son, He must be as abundant as Krishna with the milkmaids, no? What could justify such divine stinginess?

Love, repeated Father Martin.

I'll stick to my Krishna, thank you very much. I find his divinity utterly compelling. You can keep your sweaty, chatty Son to yourself.

That was how I met that troublesome rabbi of long ago: with disbelief and annoyance.

I had tea with Father Martin three days in a row. Each time, as teacup rattled against saucer, as spoon tinkled against edge of cup, I asked questions.

The answer was always the same.

He bothered me, this Son. Every day I burned with greater indignation against Him, found more flaws to Him.

He's *petulant!* It's morning in Bethany and God is hungry; God wants His breakfast. He comes to a fig tree. It's not the season for figs, so the tree has no figs. God is peeved. The Son mutters, "May you never bear fruit again," and instantly the fig tree withers. So says Matthew, backed up by Mark.

I ask you, is it the fig tree's fault that it's not the season for figs? What kind of a thing is that to do to an innocent fig tree, wither it instantly?

I couldn't get Him out of my head. Still can't. I spent three solid days thinking about Him. The more He bothered me, the less I could forget Him. And the more I learned about Him, the less I wanted to leave Him.

On our last day, a few hours before we were to leave Munnar, I hurried up the hill on the left. It strikes me now as a typically Christian scene. Christianity is a religion in a rush. Look at the world created in seven days. Even on a symbolic level, that's creation in a frenzy. To one born in a religion where the battle for a single soul can be a relay race run over many centuries, with innumerable generations passing along the baton, the quick resolution of Christianity has a dizzying effect. If Hinduism flows placidly like the Ganges, then Christianity bustles like Toronto at rush hour. It is a religion as swift as a swallow, as urgent as an ambulance. It turns on a dime, expresses itself in the instant. In a moment you are lost or saved. Christianity stretches back through the ages, but in essence it exists only at one time: right now.

I booted up that hill. Though Father Martin was not IN—alas, his block was slid over—thank God he was in.

Short of breath I said, "Father, I would like to be a Christian, please."

He smiled. "You already are, Piscine—in your heart. Whoever meets Christ in good faith is a Christian. Here in Munnar you met Christ."

He patted me on the head. It was more of a thump, actually. His hand went BOOM BOOM BOOM on my head.

I thought I would explode with joy.

"When you come back, we'll have tea again, my son."

"Yes, Father."

It was a good smile he gave me. The smile of Christ.

I entered the church, without fear this time, for it was now my house too. I offered prayers to Christ, who is alive. Then I raced down the hill on the left and raced up the hill on the right—to offer thanks to Lord Krishna for having put Jesus of Nazareth, whose humanity I found so compelling, in my way.

CHAPTER 18

Islam followed right behind, hardly a year later. I was fifteen years old and I was exploring my hometown. The Muslim quarter wasn't far from the zoo. A small, quiet neighbourhood with Arabic writing and crescent moons inscribed on the façades of the houses.

I came to Mullah Street. I had a peek at the Jamia Masjid, the Great Mosque, being careful to stay on the outside, of course. Islam had a reputation worse than Christianity's—fewer gods, greater violence, and I had never heard anyone say good things about Muslim schools—so I wasn't about to step in, empty though the place was. The building, clean and white except for various edges painted green, was an open construction unfolding around an empty central room. Long straw mats covered the floor everywhere. Above, two slim, fluted minarets rose in the air before a background of soaring coconut trees. There was nothing evidently religious or, for that matter, interesting about the place, but it was pleasant and quiet.

I moved on. Just beyond the mosque was a series of attached single-storey dwellings with small shaded porches. They were rundown and poor, their stucco walls a faded green. One of the dwellings was a small shop. I noticed a rack of dusty bottles of Thums Up and four transparent plastic jars half-full of candies. But the main ware was something else, something flat, roundish and white. I got close. It seemed to be some sort of unleavened bread. I poked at one. It flipped up stiffly. They looked like three-day-old nans. Who would eat these, I wondered. I picked one up and wagged it to see if it would break.

A voice said, "Would you like to taste one?"

I nearly jumped out of my skin. It's happened to all of us: there's sunlight and shade, spots and patterns of colour, your mind is elsewhere—so you don't make out what is right in front of you.

Not four feet away, sitting cross-legged before his breads, was a man. I was so startled my hands flew up and the bread went sailing halfway across the street. It landed on a pat of fresh cow dung.

"I'm so sorry, sir. I didn't see you!" I burst out. I was just about ready to run away.

"Don't worry," he said calmly. "It will feed a cow. Have another one."

He tore one in two. We ate it together. It was tough and rubbery, real work for the teeth, but filling. I calmed down.

"So you make these," I said, to make conversation.

"Yes. Here, let me show you how." He got off his platform and waved me into his house.

It was a two-room hovel. The larger room, dominated by an oven, was the bakery, and the other, separated by a flimsy curtain, was his bedroom. The bottom of the oven was covered with smooth pebbles. He was explaining to me how the bread baked on these heated pebbles when the nasal call of the muezzin wafted through the air from the mosque. I knew it was the call to prayer, but I didn't know what it entailed. I imagined it beckoned the Muslim faithful to the mosque, much like bells summoned us Christians to church. Not so. The baker interrupted himself mid-sentence and said, "Excuse me." He ducked into the next room for a minute and returned with a rolled-up carpet, which he unfurled on the floor of his bakery, throwing up a small storm of flour. And right there before me, in the midst of his workplace, he prayed. It was incongruous, but it was I who felt out of place. Luckily, he prayed with his eyes closed.

He stood straight. He muttered in Arabic. He brought his hands next to his ears, thumbs touching the lobes, looking as if he were straining to hear Allah replying. He bent forward. He stood straight again. He fell to his knees and brought his hands and forehead to the floor. He sat up. He fell forward again. He stood. He started the whole thing again.

Why, Islam is nothing but an easy sort of exercise, I thought. Hot-weather yoga for the Bedouins. Asanas without sweat, heaven without strain.

He went through the cycle four times, muttering throughout. When he had finished—with a right-left turning of the head and a short bout of meditation—he opened his eyes, smiled, stepped off his carpet and rolled it up with a flick of the hand that spoke of old habit. He returned it to its spot in the next room. He came back to me. "What was I saying?" he asked.

So it went the first time I saw a Muslim pray—quick, necessary, physical, muttered, striking. Next time I was praying in church—on my knees, immobile, silent before Christ on the Cross—the image of this callisthenic communion with God in the middle of bags of flour kept coming to my mind.

CHAPTER 19

I went to see him again.

"What's your religion about?" I asked.

His eyes lit up. "It is about the Beloved," he replied.

I challenge anyone to understand Islam, its spirit, and not to love it. It is a beautiful religion of brotherhood and devotion.

The mosque was truly an open construction, to God and to breeze. We sat cross-legged listening to the imam until the time came to pray. Then the random pattern of sitters disappeared as we stood and arranged ourselves shoulder to shoulder in rows, every space ahead being filled by someone from behind until every line was solid and we were row after row of worshippers. It felt good to bring my forehead to the ground. Immediately it felt like a deeply religious contact.

CHAPTER 20

He was a Sufi, a Muslim mystic. He sought fana, union with God, and his relationship with God was personal and loving. "If you take two steps towards God," he used to tell me, "God runs to you!"

He was a very plain-featured man, with nothing in his looks or in his dress that made memory cry hark. I'm not surprised I didn't see him the first time we met. Even when I knew him very well, encounter after encounter, I had difficulty recognizing him. His name was Satish Kumar. These are common names in Tamil Nadu, so the coincidence is not so remarkable. Still, it pleased me that this pious baker, as plain as a shadow and of solid health, and the Communist biology teacher and science devotee, the walking mountain on stilts, sadly afflicted with polio in his childhood, carried the same name. Mr. and Mr. Kumar taught me biology and Islam. Mr. and Mr. Kumar led me to study zoology and religious studies at the University of Toronto. Mr. and Mr. Kumar were the prophets of my Indian youth.

We prayed together and we practised dhikr, the recitation of the ninety-nine revealed names of God. He was a hafiz, one who knows the Qur'an by heart, and he sang it in a slow, simple chant. My Arabic was never very good, but I loved its sound. The guttural eruptions and long flowing vowels rolled just beneath my comprehension like a beautiful brook. I gazed into this brook for long spells of time. It was not wide, just one man's voice, but it was as deep as the universe.

I described Mr. Kumar's place as a hovel. Yet no mosque, church or temple ever felt so sacred to me. I sometimes came out of that bakery feeling heavy with glory. I would climb onto my bicycle and pedal that glory through the air.

One such time I left town and on my way back, at a point where the land was high and I could see the sea to my left and down the road a long ways, I suddenly felt I was in heaven. The spot was in fact no different from when I had passed it not long before, but my way of seeing it had changed. The feeling, a paradoxical mix of pulsing energy and profound peace, was intense and blissful. Whereas before the road, the sea, the trees, the air, the sun all spoke differently to me, now they spoke one language of unity. Tree took account of road, which was aware of air, which was mindful of sea, which shared things with sun. Every element lived in harmonious relation with its neighbour, and all was kith and kin. I knelt a mortal; I rose an immortal. I felt like the centre of a small circle coinciding with the centre of a much larger one. Atman met Allah.

One other time I felt God come so close to me. It was in Canada, much later. I was visiting friends in the country. It was winter. I was out alone on a walk on their large property and returning to the house. It was a clear, sunny day after a night of snowfall. All nature was blanketed in white. As I was coming up to the house, I turned my head. There was a wood and in that wood, a small clearing. A breeze, or perhaps it was an animal, had shaken a branch. Fine snow was falling through the air, glittering in the sunlight. In that falling golden dust in that sun-splashed clearing, I saw the Virgin Mary. Why her, I don't know. My devotion to Mary was secondary. But it was her. Her skin was pale. She was wearing a white dress and a blue cloak; I remember being struck by their pleats and folds. When I say I *saw* her, I don't quite mean it literally, though she did have body and colour. I *felt* I saw her, a vision beyond vision. I stopped and squinted. She looked beautiful and supremely regal. She was smiling at me with loving kindness. After some seconds she left me. My heart beat with fear and joy.

The presence of God is the finest of rewards.

CHAPTER 21

I am sitting in a downtown café, after, thinking. I have just spent most of an afternoon with him. Our encounters always leave me weary of the glum contentment that characterizes my life. What were those words he used that struck me? Ah, yes: "dry, yeastless factuality", "the better story". I take pen and paper out and write:

> *Words of divine consciousness: moral exaltation; lasting feelings of elevation, elation, joy; a quickening of the moral sense, which strikes one as more important than an intellectual understanding of things; an alignment of the universe along moral lines, not intellectual ones; a realization that the founding principle of existence is what we call love, which works itself out sometimes not clearly, not cleanly, not immediately, nonetheless ineluctably.*

I pause. What of God's silence? I think it over. I add:

> *An intellect confounded yet a trusting sense of presence and of ultimate purpose.*

CHAPTER 22

I can well imagine an atheist's last words: "White, white! L-L-Love! My God!"—and the deathbed leap of faith. Whereas the agnostic, if he stays true to his reasonable self, if he stays beholden to dry, yeast-less factuality, might try to explain the warm light bathing him by saying, "Possibly a f-f-failing oxygenation of the b-b-brain," and, to the very end, lack imagination and miss the better story.

CHAPTER 23

Alas, the sense of community that a common faith brings to a people spelled trouble for me. In time, my religious doings went from the notice of those to whom it didn't matter and only amused, to that of those to whom it did matter—and they were not amused.

"What is your son doing going to temple?" asked the priest.

"Your son was seen in church crossing himself," said the imam.

"Your son has gone Muslim," said the pandit.

Yes, it was all forcefully brought to the attention of my bemused parents. You see, they didn't know. They didn't know that I was a practising Hindu, Christian and Muslim. Teenagers always hide a few things from their parents, isn't that so? All sixteen-year-olds have secrets, don't they? But fate decided that my parents and I and the three wise men, as I shall call them, should meet one day on the Goubert Salai seaside esplanade and that my secret should be outed. It was a lovely, breezy, hot Sunday afternoon and the Bay of Bengal glittered under a blue sky. Townspeople were out for a stroll. Children screamed and laughed. Coloured balloons floated in the air. Ice cream sales were brisk. Why think of business on such a day, I ask? Why couldn't they have just walked by with a nod and a smile? It was not to be. We were to meet not just one wise man but all three, and not one after another but at the same time, and each would decide upon seeing us that right then was the golden occasion to meet that Pondicherry notable, the zoo director, he of the model devout son. When I saw the first, I smiled; by the time I had laid eyes on the third, my smile had frozen into a mask of horror. When it was clear that all three were converging on us, my heart jumped before sinking very low.

The wise men seemed annoyed when they realized that all three of them were approaching the same people. Each must have assumed that the others were there for some business other than pastoral and had rudely chosen that moment to deal with it. Glances of displeasure were exchanged.

My parents looked puzzled to have their way gently blocked by three broadly smiling religious strangers. I should explain that my family was anything but orthodox. Father saw himself as part of the New India—rich, modern and as secular as ice cream. He didn't have a religious bone in his body. He was a businessman, pronounced *busy*nessman in his case, a hardworking, earthbound professional, more concerned with inbreeding among the lions than any over-arching moral or existential scheme. It's true that he had all new animals blessed by a priest and there were two small shrines at the zoo, one to Lord Ganesha and one to Hanuman, gods likely to please a zoo director, what with the first having the head of an elephant and the second being a monkey, but Father's calculation was that this was good for business, not good for his soul, a matter of public relations rather than personal salvation. Spiritual worry was alien to him; it was financial worry that rocked his being. "One epidemic in the collection," he used to say, "and we'll end up in a road crew breaking up stones." Mother was mum, bored and neutral on the subject. A Hindu upbringing and a Baptist education had precisely cancelled each other out as far as religion was concerned and had left her serenely impious. I suspect she suspected that I had a different take on the matter, but she never said anything when as a child I devoured the comic books of the Ramayana and the Mahabharata and an illustrated children's Bible and other stories of the gods. She herself was a big reader. She was pleased to see me with my nose buried in a book, any book, so long as it wasn't naughty. As for Ravi, if Lord Krishna had held a cricket bat rather than a flute, if Christ had appeared more plainly to him as an umpire, if the prophet Muhammad, peace be upon him, had shown some notions of bowling, he might have lifted a religious eyelid, but they didn't, and so he slumbered.

After the "Hellos" and the "Good days", there was an awkward silence. The priest broke it when he said, with pride in his voice, "Piscine is a good Christian boy. I hope to see him join our choir soon."

My parents, the pandit and the imam looked surprised.

"You must be mistaken. He's a good Muslim boy. He comes without fail to Friday prayer, and his knowledge of the Holy Qur'an is coming along nicely." So said the imam.

My parents, the priest and the pandit looked incredulous.

The pandit spoke. "You're both wrong. He's a good Hindu boy. I see him all the time at the temple coming for darshan and performing puja."

My parents, the imam and the priest looked astounded.

"There is no mistake," said the priest. "I know this boy. He is Piscine Molitor Patel and he's a Christian."

"I know him too, and I tell you he's a Muslim," asserted the imam.

"Nonsense!" cried the pandit. "Piscine was born a Hindu, lives a Hindu and will die a Hindu!"

The three wise men stared at each other, breathless and disbelieving.

Lord, avert their eyes from me, I whispered in my soul.

All eyes fell upon me.

"Piscine, can this be true?" asked the imam earnestly. "Hindus and Christians are idolaters. They have many gods."

"And Muslims have many wives," responded the pandit.

The priest looked askance at both of them. "Piscine," he nearly whispered, "there is salvation only in Jesus."

"Balderdash! Christians know nothing about religion," said the pandit.

"They strayed long ago from God's path," said the imam.

"Where's God in your religion?" snapped the priest. "You don't have a single miracle to show for it. What kind of religion is that, without miracles?"

"It isn't a circus with dead people jumping out of tombs all the time, that's what! We Muslims stick to the essential miracle of existence. Birds flying, rain falling, crops growing—these are miracles enough for us."

"Feathers and rain are all very nice, but we like to know that God is truly with us."

"Is that so? Well, a whole lot of good it did God to be with you—you tried to kill him! You banged him to a cross with great big nails. Is that a civilized way to treat a prophet? The prophet Muhammad—peace be upon him—brought us the word of God without any undignified nonsense and died at a ripe old age."

"The word of God? To that illiterate merchant of yours in the middle of the desert? Those were drooling epileptic fits brought on by the swaying of his camel, not divine revelation. That, or the sun frying his brains!"

"If the Prophet—p.b.u.h.—were alive, he would have choice words for you," replied the imam, with narrowed eyes.

"Well, he's not! Christ is alive, while your old 'p.b.u.h.' is dead, dead, dead!"

The pandit interrupted them quietly. In Tamil he said, "The real question is, why is Piscine dallying with these *foreign* religions?"

The eyes of the priest and the imam properly popped out of their heads. They were both native Tamils.

"God is universal," spluttered the priest.

The imam nodded strong approval. "There is only one God."

"And with their one god Muslims are always causing troubles and provoking riots. The proof of how bad Islam is, is how uncivilized Muslims are," pronounced the pandit.

"Says the slave-driver of the caste system," huffed the imam. "Hindus enslave people and worship dressed-up dolls."

"They are golden calf lovers. They kneel before cows," the priest chimed in.

"While Christians kneel before a white man! They are the flunkies of a foreign god. They are the nightmare of all non-white people."

"And they eat pigs and are cannibals," added the imam for good measure.

"What it comes down to," the priest put out with cool rage, "is whether Piscine wants *real* religion—or myths from a cartoon strip."

"God—or idols," intoned the imam gravely.

"Our gods—or colonial gods," hissed the pandit.

It was hard to tell whose face was more inflamed. It looked as if they might come to blows.

Father raised his hands. "Gentlemen, gentlemen, please!" he interjected. "I would like to remind you there is freedom of practice in this country."

Three apoplectic faces turned to him.

"Yes! Prac*tice*—singular!" the wise men screamed in unison. Three index fingers, like punctuation marks, jumped to attention in the air to emphasize their point.

They were not pleased at the unintended choral effect or the spontaneous unity of their gestures. Their fingers came down quickly, and they sighed and groaned each on his own. Father and Mother stared on, at a loss for words.

The pandit spoke first. "Mr. Patel, Piscine's piety is admirable. In these troubled times it's good to see a boy so keen on God. We all agree on that." The imam and the priest nodded. "But he can't be a Hindu, a Christian *and* a Muslim. It's impossible. He must choose."

"I don't think it's a crime, but I suppose you're right," Father replied.

The three murmured agreement and looked heavenward, as did Father, whence they felt the decision must come. Mother looked at me.

A silence fell heavily on my shoulders.

"Hmmm, Piscine?" Mother nudged me. "How do you feel about the question?"

"Bapu Gandhi said, 'All religions are true.' I just want to love God," I blurted out, and looked down, red in the face.

My embarrassment was contagious. No one said anything. It happened that we were not far from the statue of Gandhi on the esplanade. Stick in hand, an impish smile on his lips, a twinkle in his eyes, the Mahatma walked. I fancy that he heard our conversation, but that he paid even greater attention to my heart. Father cleared his throat and said in a half-voice, "I suppose that's what we're all trying to do—love God."

I thought it very funny that he should say that, he who hadn't stepped into a temple with a serious intent since I had had the faculty of memory. But it seemed to do the trick. You can't reprimand a boy for wanting to love God. The three wise men pulled away with stiff, grudging smiles on their faces.

Father looked at me for a second, as if to speak, then thought better, said, "Ice cream, anyone?" and headed for the closest ice-cream wallah before we could answer. Mother gazed at me a little longer, with an expression that was both tender and perplexed.

That was my introduction to interfaith dialogue. Father bought three ice cream sandwiches. We ate them in unusual silence as we continued on our Sunday walk.

CHAPTER 24

Ravi had a field day of it when he found out.

"So, Swami Jesus, will you go on the hajj this year?" he said, bringing the palms of his hands together in front of his face in a reverent namaskar. "Does Mecca beckon?" He crossed himself. "Or will it be to Rome for your coronation as the next Pope Pius?" He drew in the air a Greek letter, making clear the spelling of his mockery. "Have you found time yet to get the end of your pecker cut off and become a Jew? At the rate you're going, if you go to temple on Thursday, mosque on Friday, synagogue on Saturday and church on Sunday, you only need to convert to three more religions to be on holiday for the rest of your life."

And other lampoonery of such kind.

CHAPTER 25

And that wasn't the end of it. There are always those who take it upon themselves to defend God, as if Ultimate Reality, as if the sustaining frame of existence, were something weak and helpless. These people walk by a widow deformed by leprosy begging for a few paise, walk by children dressed in rags living in the street, and they think, "Business as usual." But if they perceive a slight against God, it is a different story. Their faces go red, their chests heave mightily, they sputter angry words. The degree of their indignation is astonishing. Their resolve is frightening.

These people fail to realize that it is on the inside that God must be defended, not on the outside. They should direct their anger at themselves. For evil in the open is but evil from within that has been let out. The main battlefield for good is not the open ground of the public arena but the small clearing of each heart. Meanwhile, the lot of widows and homeless children is very hard, and it is to their defence, not God's, that the self-righteous should rush.

Once an oaf chased me away from the Great Mosque. When I went to church the priest glared at me so that I could not feel the peace of Christ. A Brahmin sometimes shooed me away from darshan. My religious doings were reported to my parents in the hushed, urgent tones of treason revealed.

As if this small-mindedness did God any good.

To me, religion is about our dignity, not our depravity.

I stopped attending Mass at Our Lady of Immaculate Conception and went instead to Our Lady of Angels. I no longer lingered after Friday prayer among my brethren. I went to temple at crowded times when the Brahmins were too distracted to come between God and me.

CHAPTER 26

A few days after the meeting on the esplanade, I took my courage into my hands and went to see Father at his office.

"Father?"

"Yes, Piscine."

"I would like to be baptized and I would like a prayer rug."

My words intruded slowly. He looked up from his papers after some seconds.

"A what? What?"

"I would like to pray outside without getting my pants dirty. And I'm attending a Christian school without having received the proper baptism of Christ."

"Why do you want to pray outside? In fact, why do you want to pray at all?"

"Because I love God."

"Aha." He seemed taken aback by my answer, nearly embarrassed by it. There was a pause. I thought he was going to offer me ice cream again. "Well, Petit Séminaire is Christian only in name. There are many Hindu boys there who aren't Christians. You'll get just as good an education without being baptized. Praying to Allah won't make any difference, either."

"But I want to pray to Allah. I want to be a Christian."

"You can't be both. You must be either one or the other."

"Why can't I be both?"

"They're separate religions! They have nothing in common."

"That's not what they say! They both claim Abraham as theirs. Muslims say the God of the Hebrews and Christians is the same as the God of the Muslims. They recognize David, Moses and Jesus as prophets."

"What does this have to do with us, Piscine? We're *Indians!*"

"There have been Christians and Muslims in India for centuries! Some people say Jesus is buried in Kashmir."

He said nothing, only looked at me, his brow furrowed. Suddenly business called.

"Talk to Mother about it."

She was reading.

"Mother?"

"Yes, darling."

"I would like to be baptized and I would like a prayer rug."

"Talk to Father about it."

"I did. He told me to talk to you about it."

"Did he?" She laid her book down. She looked out in the direction of the zoo. At that moment I'm sure Father felt a blow of chill air against the back of his neck. She turned to the bookshelf. "I have a book here that you'll like." She already had her arm out, reaching for a volume. It was Robert Louis Stevenson. This was her usual tactic.

"I've already read that, Mother. Three times."

"Oh." Her arm hovered to the left.

"The same with Conan Doyle," I said.

Her arm swung to the right. "R. K. Narayan? You can't possibly have read all of Narayan?"

"These matters are important to me, Mother."

"*Robinson Crusoe!*"

"Mother!"

"But Piscine!" she said. She settled back into her chair, a path-of-least-resistance look on her face, which meant I had to put up a stiff fight in precisely the right spots. She adjusted a cushion. "Father and I find your religious zeal a bit of a mystery."

"It is a Mystery."

"Hmmm. I don't mean it that way. Listen, my darling, if you're going to be religious, you must be either a Hindu, a Christian or a Muslim. You heard what they said on the esplanade."

"I don't see why I can't be all three. Mamaji has two passports. He's Indian and French. Why can't I be a Hindu, a Christian and a Muslim?"

"That's different. France and India are nations on earth."

"How many nations are there in the sky?"

She thought for a second. "One. That's the point. One nation, one passport."

"One nation in the sky?"

"Yes. Or none. There's that option too, you know. These are terribly old-fashioned things you've taken to."

"If there's only one nation in the sky, shouldn't all passports be valid for it?"

A cloud of uncertainty came over her face.

"Bapu Gandhi said—"

"Yes, I know what Bapu Gandhi said." She brought a hand to her forehead. She had a weary look, Mother did. "Good grief," she said.

CHAPTER 27

Later that evening I overheard my parents speaking.

"You said yes?" said Father.

"I believe he asked you too. You referred him to me," replied Mother.

"Did I?"

"You did."

"I had a very busy day . . ."

"You're not busy now. You're quite comfortably unemployed by the looks of it. If you want to march into his room and pull the prayer rug from under his feet and discuss the question of Christian baptism with him, please go ahead. I won't object."

"No, no." I could tell from his voice that Father was settling deeper into his chair. There was a pause.

"He seems to be attracting religions the way a dog attracts fleas," he pursued. "I don't understand it. We're a modern Indian family; we live in a modern way; India is on the cusp of becoming a truly modern and advanced nation—and here we've produced a son who thinks he's the reincarnation of Sri Ramakrishna."

"If Mrs. Gandhi is what being modern and advanced is about, I'm not sure I like it," Mother said.

"Mrs. Gandhi will pass! Progress is unstoppable. It is a drumbeat to which we must all march. Technology helps and good ideas spread—these are two laws of nature. If you don't let technology help you, if you resist good ideas, you condemn yourself to dinosaurhood! I am utterly convinced of this. Mrs. Gandhi and her foolishness will pass. The New India will come."

(Indeed she would pass. And the New India, or one family of it, would decide to move to Canada.)

Father went on: "Did you hear when he said, 'Bapu Gandhi said, "All religions are true"'?"

"Yes."

"*Bapu* Gandhi? The boy is getting to be on affectionate terms with Gandhi? After Daddy Gandhi, what next? Uncle Jesus? And what's this nonsense—has he really become a *Muslim*?"

"It seems so."

"A Muslim! A devout Hindu, all right, I can understand. A Christian in addition, it's getting to be a bit strange, but I can stretch my mind. The Christians have been here for a long time—Saint Thomas, Saint Francis Xavier, the missionaries and so on. We owe them good schools."

"Yes."

"So all that I can sort of accept. But *Muslim*? It's totally foreign to our tradition. They're outsiders."

"They've been here a very long time too. They're a hundred times more numerous than the Christians."

"That makes no difference. They're outsiders."

"Perhaps Piscine is marching to a different drumbeat of progress."

"You're defending the boy? You don't mind it that he's fancying himself a Muslim?"

"What can we do, Santosh? He's taken it to heart, and it's not doing anyone any harm. Maybe it's just a phase. It too may pass—like Mrs. Gandhi."

"Why can't he have the normal interests of a boy his age? Look at Ravi. All he can think about is cricket, movies and music."

"You think that's better?"

"No, no. Oh, I don't know what to think. It's been a long day." He sighed. "I wonder how far he'll go with these interests."

Mother chuckled. "Last week he finished a book called *The Imitation of Christ*."

"*The* Imitation *of Christ!* I say again, I wonder how far he'll go with these interests!" cried Father.

They laughed.

CHAPTER 28

I loved my prayer rug. Ordinary in quality though it was, it glowed with beauty in my eyes. I'm sorry I lost it. Wherever I laid it I felt special affection for the patch of ground beneath it and the immediate surroundings, which to me is a clear indication that it was a good prayer rug because it helped me remember that the earth is the creation of God and sacred the same all over. The pattern, in gold lines upon a background of red, was plain: a narrow rectangle with a triangular peak at one extremity to indicate the qibla, the direction of prayer, and little curlicues floating around it, like wisps of smoke or accents from a strange language. The pile was soft. When I prayed, the short, unknotted tassels were inches from the tip of my forehead at one end of the carpet and inches from the tip of my toes at the other, a cozy size to make you feel at home anywhere upon this vast earth.

I prayed outside because I liked it. Most often I unrolled my prayer rug in a corner of the yard behind the house. It was a secluded spot in the shade of a coral tree, next to a wall that was covered with bougainvillea. Along the length of the wall was a row of potted poinsettias. The bougainvillea had also crept through the tree. The contrast between its purple bracts and the red flowers of the tree was very pretty. And when that tree was in bloom, it was a regular aviary of crows, mynahs, babblers, rosy pastors, sunbirds and parakeets. The wall was to my right, at a wide angle. Ahead of me and to my left, beyond the milky, mottled shade of the tree, lay the sun-drenched open space of the yard. The appearance of things changed, of course, depending on the weather, the time of day, the time of year. But it's all very clear in my memory, as if it never changed. I faced Mecca with the help of a line I scratched into the pale yellow ground and carefully kept up.

Sometimes, upon finishing my prayers, I would turn and catch sight of Father or Mother or Ravi observing me, until they got used to the sight.

My baptism was a slightly awkward affair. Mother played along nicely, Father looked on stonily, and Ravi was mercifully absent because of a cricket match, which did not prevent him from commenting at great length on the event. The water trickled down my face and down my neck; though just a beaker's worth, it had the refreshing effect of a monsoon rain.

CHAPTER 29

Why do people move? What makes them uproot and leave everything they've known for a great unknown beyond the horizon? Why climb this Mount Everest of formalities that makes you feel like a beggar? Why enter this jungle of foreignness where everything is new, strange and difficult?

The answer is the same the world over: people move in the hope of a better life.

The mid-1970s were troubled times in India. I gathered that from the deep furrows that appeared on Father's forehead when he read the papers. Or from snippets of conversation that I caught between him and Mother and Mamaji and others. It's not that I didn't understand the drift of what they said—it's that I wasn't interested. The orang-utans were as eager for chapattis as ever; the monkeys never asked after the news from Delhi; the rhinos and goats continued to live in peace; the birds twittered; the clouds carried rain; the sun was hot; the earth breathed; God was—there was no Emergency in my world.

Mrs. Gandhi finally got the best of Father. In February 1976, the Tamil Nadu government was brought down by Delhi. It had been one of Mrs. Gandhi's most vocal critics. The takeover was smoothly enforced—Chief Minister Karunanidhi's ministry vanished quietly into "resignation" or house arrest—and what does the fall of one local government matter when the whole country's Constitution has been suspended these last eight months? But it was to Father the crowning touch in Mrs. Gandhi's dictatorial takeover of the nation. The camel at the zoo was unfazed, but that straw broke Father's back.

He shouted, "Soon she'll come down to our zoo and tell us that her jails are full, she needs more space. Could we put Desai with the lions?"

Morarji Desai was an opposition politician. No friend of Mrs. Gandhi's. It makes me sad, my father's ceaseless worrying. Mrs. Gandhi could have personally bombed the zoo, it would have been fine with me if Father had been gay about it. I wish he hadn't fretted so much. It's hard on a son to see his father sick with worry.

But worry he did. Any business is risky business, and none more so than small *b* business, the one that risks the shirt on its back. A zoo is a cultural institution. Like a public library, like a museum, it is at the service of popular education and science. And by this token, not much of a money-making venture, for the Greater Good and the Greater Profit are not compatible aims, much to Father's chagrin.

The truth was, we were not a rich family, certainly not by Canadian standards. We were a poor family that happened to own a lot of animals, though not the roof above their heads (or above ours, for that matter). The life of a zoo, like the life of its inhabitants in the wild, is precarious. It is neither big enough a business to be above the law nor small enough to survive on its margins. To prosper, a zoo needs parliamentary government, democratic elections, freedom of speech, freedom of the press, freedom of association, rule of law and everything else enshrined in India's Constitution. Impossible to enjoy the animals otherwise. Long-term, bad politics is bad for business.

People move because of the wear and tear of anxiety. Because of the gnawing feeling that no matter how hard they work their efforts will yield nothing, that what they build up in one year will be torn down in one day by others. Because of the impression that the future is blocked up, that *they* might do all right but not their children. Because of the feeling that nothing will change, that happiness and prosperity are possible only somewhere else.

The New India split to pieces and collapsed in Father's mind. Mother assented. We would bolt.

It was announced to us one evening during dinner. Ravi and I were thunderstruck. *Canada!* If Andhra Pradesh, just north of us, was alien, if Sri Lanka, a monkey's hop across a strait, was the dark side of the moon, imagine what Canada was. Canada meant absolutely nothing to us. It was like Timbuktu, by definition a place permanently far away.

CHAPTER 30

He's married. I am bent down, taking my shoes off, when I hear him say, "I would like you to meet my wife." I look up and there beside him is . . . Mrs.

Patel. "Hello," she says, extending her hand and smiling. "Piscine has been telling me lots about you." I can't say the same of her. I had no idea. She's on her way out, so we talk only a few minutes. She's also Indian but has a more typically Canadian accent. She must be second generation. She's a little younger than him, skin slightly darker, long black hair woven in a tress. Bright dark eyes and lovely white teeth. She has in her arms a dry-cleaned white lab coat in a protective plastic film. She's a pharmacist. When I say, "Nice meeting you, Mrs. Patel," she replies, "Please, make it Meena." After a quick kiss between husband and wife, she's off on a working Saturday.

This house is more than a box full of icons. I start noticing small signs of conjugal existence. They were there all along, but I hadn't seen them because I wasn't looking for them.

He's a shy man. Life has taught him not to show off what is most precious to him.

Is she the nemesis of my digestive tract?

"I've made a special chutney for you," he says. He's smiling.

No, he is.

CHAPTER 31

They met once, Mr. and Mr. Kumar, the baker and the teacher. The first Mr. Kumar had expressed the wish to see the zoo. "All these years and I've never seen it. It's so close by, too. Will you show it to me?" he asked.

"Yes, of course," I replied. "It would be an honour."

We agreed to meet at the main gate the next day after school.

I worried all that day. I scolded myself, "You fool! Why did you say the main gate? At any time there will be a crowd of people there. Have you forgotten how plain he looks? You'll never recognize him!" If I walked by him without seeing him he would be hurt. He would think

I had changed my mind and didn't want to be seen with a poor Muslim baker. He would leave without saying a word. He wouldn't be angry—he would accept my claims that it was the sun in my eyes—but he wouldn't want to come to the zoo any more. I could see it happening that way. I *had* to recognize him. I would hide and wait until I was certain it was him, that's what I would do. But I had noticed before that it was when I tried my hardest to recognize him that I was least able to pick him out. The very effort seemed to blind me.

At the appointed hour I stood squarely before the main gate of the zoo and started rubbing my eyes with both hands.

"What are you doing?"

It was Raj, a friend.

"I'm busy."

"You're busy rubbing your eyes?"

"Go away."

"Let's go to Beach Road."

"I'm waiting for someone."

"Well, you'll miss him if you keep rubbing your eyes like that."

"Thank you for the information. Have fun on Beach Road."

"How about Government Park?"

"I can't, I tell you."

"Come on."

"Please, Raj, move on!"

He left. I went back to rubbing my eyes.

"Will you help me with my math homework, Pi?"

It was Ajith, another friend.

"Later. Go away."

"Hello, Piscine."

It was Mrs. Radhakrishna, a friend of Mother's. In a few more words I eased her on her way.

"Excuse me. Where's Laporte Street?"

A stranger.

"That way."

"How much is admission to the zoo?"

Another stranger.

"Five rupees. The ticket booth is right there."

"Has the chlorine got to your eyes?"

It was Mamaji.

"Hello, Mamaji. No, it hasn't."

"Is your father around?"

"I think so."

"See you tomorrow morning."

"Yes, Mamaji."

"I am here, Piscine."

My hands froze over my eyes. That voice. Strange in a familiar way, familiar in a strange way. I felt a smile welling up in me.

"*Salaam alaykum*, Mr. Kumar! How good to see you."

"*Wa alaykum as-salaam.* Is something wrong with your eyes?"

"No, nothing. Just a bit of dust."

"They look quite red."

"It's nothing."

He headed for the ticket booth but I called him back.

"No, no. Not for you, master."

It was with pride that I waved the ticket collector's hand away and showed Mr. Kumar into the zoo.

He marvelled at everything, at how to tall trees came tall giraffes, how carnivores were supplied with herbivores and herbivores with grass, how some creatures crowded the day and others the night, how some that needed sharp beaks had sharp beaks and others that needed limber limbs had limber limbs. It made me happy that he was so impressed.

He quoted from the Holy Qur'an: "In all this there are messages indeed for a people who use their reason."

We came to the zebras. Mr. Kumar had never heard of such creatures, let alone seen one. He was dumbfounded.

"They're called zebras," I said.

"Have they been painted with a brush?"

"No, no. They look like that naturally."

"What happens when it rains?"

"Nothing."

"The stripes don't melt?"

"No."

I had brought some carrots. There was one left, a large and sturdy specimen. I took it out of the bag. At that moment I heard a slight scraping of gravel to my right. It was Mr. Kumar, coming up to the railing in his usual limping and rolling gait.

"Hello, sir."

"Hello, Pi."

The baker, a shy but dignified man, nodded at the teacher, who nodded back.

An alert zebra had noticed my carrot and had come up to the low fence. It twitched its ears and stamped the ground softly. I broke the carrot in two and gave one half to Mr. Kumar and one half to Mr. Kumar. "Thank you, Piscine," said one; "Thank you, Pi," said the other. Mr. Kumar went first, dipping his hand over the fence. The zebra's thick, strong, black lips grasped the carrot eagerly. Mr. Kumar wouldn't let go. The zebra sank its teeth into the carrot and snapped it in two. It crunched loudly on the treat for a few seconds, then reached for the remaining piece, lips flowing over Mr. Kumar's fingertips. He released the carrot and touched the zebra's soft nose.

It was Mr. Kumar's turn. He wasn't so demanding of the zebra. Once it had his half of the carrot between its lips, he let go. The lips hurriedly moved the carrot into the mouth.

Mr. and Mr. Kumar looked delighted.

"A *zebra*, you say?" said Mr. Kumar.

"That's right," I replied. "It belongs to the same family as the ass and the horse."

"The Rolls-Royce of equids," said Mr. Kumar.

"What a wondrous creature," said Mr. Kumar.

"This one's a Grant's zebra," I said.

Mr. Kumar said, "*Equus burchelli boehmi.*"

Mr. Kumar said, "*Allahu akbar.*"

I said, "It's very pretty."

We looked on.

CHAPTER 32

There are many examples of animals coming to surprising living arrangements. All are instances of that animal equivalent of anthropomorphism: zoomorphism, where an animal takes a human being, or another animal, to be one of its kind.

The most famous case is also the most common: the pet dog, which has so assimilated humans into the realm of doghood as to want to mate with them, a fact that any dog owner who has had to pull an amorous dog from the leg of a mortified visitor will confirm.

Our golden agouti and spotted paca got along very well, contentedly huddling together and sleeping against each other until the first was stolen.

I have already mentioned our rhinoceros-and-goat herd, and the case of circus lions.

There are confirmed stories of drowning sailors being pushed up to the surface of the water and held there by dolphins, a characteristic way in which these marine mammals help each other.

A case is mentioned in the literature of a stoat and a rat living in a companion relationship, while other rats presented to the stoat were devoured by it in the typical way of stoats.

We had our own case of the freak suspension of the predator-prey relationship. We had a mouse that lived for several *weeks* with the vipers. While other mice dropped in the terrarium disappeared within two days, this little brown Methuselah built itself a nest, stored the grains we gave it in various hideaways and scampered about in plain sight of the snakes. We were amazed. We put up a sign to bring the mouse to the public's attention. It finally met its end in a curious way: a young viper bit it. Was the viper unaware of the mouse's special status? Unsocialized to it, perhaps? Whatever the case, the mouse was bitten by a young viper but devoured—and immediately—by an adult. If there was a spell, it was broken by the young one. Things returned to normal after that. All mice disappeared down the vipers' gullets at the usual rate.

In the trade, dogs are sometimes used as foster mothers for lion cubs. Though the cubs grow to become larger than their caregiver, and far more dangerous, they never give their mother trouble and she never loses her placid behaviour or her sense of authority over her litter. Signs have to be put up to explain to the public that the dog is not live food left for the lions (just as we had to put up a sign pointing out that rhinoceros are herbivores and do not eat goats).

What could be the explanation for zoomorphism? Can't a rhinoceros distinguish big from small, tough hide from soft fur? Isn't it plain to a dolphin what a dolphin is like? I believe the answer lies in something I mentioned earlier, that measure of madness that moves life in strange but saving ways. The golden agouti, like the rhinoceros, was in need of companionship. The circus lions don't care to know that their leader is a weakling human; the fiction guarantees their social well-being and staves off violent anarchy. As for the lion cubs, they would positively keel over with fright if they knew their mother was a dog, for that would mean they were motherless, the absolute worst condition imaginable for any young, warm-blooded life. I'm sure even the adult viper, as it swallowed the mouse, must have felt somewhere in its undeveloped mind a twinge of regret, a feeling that something greater was just missed, an imaginative leap away from the lonely, crude reality of a reptile.

CHAPTER 33

He shows me family memorabilia. Wedding photos first. A Hindu wedding with Canada prominently on the edges. A younger him, a younger her. They went to Niagara Falls for their honeymoon. Had a lovely time. Smiles to prove it. We move back in time. Photos from his student days at U of T: with friends; in front of St. Mike's; in his room; during Diwali on Gerrard Street; reading at St. Basil's Church dressed in a white gown; wearing another kind of white gown in a lab of the zoology department; on graduation day. A smile every time, but his eyes tell another story.

Photos from Brazil, with plenty of three-toed sloths in situ.

With a turn of a page we jump over the Pacific—and there is next to nothing. He tells me that the camera did click regularly—on all the usual important occasions—but everything was lost. What little there is consists of what was assembled by Mamaji and mailed over after the events.

There is a photo taken at the zoo during the visit of a V.I.P. In black and white another world is revealed to me. The photo is crowded with people. A Union cabinet minister is the focus of attention. There's a giraffe in the background. Near the edge of the group, I recognize a younger Mr. Adirubasamy.

"Mamaji?" I ask, pointing.

"Yes," he says.

There's a man next to the minister, with horn-rimmed glasses and hair very cleanly combed. He looks like a plausible Mr. Patel, face rounder than his son's.

"Is this your father?" I ask.

He shakes his head. "I don't know who that is."

There's a pause of a few seconds. He says, "It's my father who took the picture."

On the same page there's another group shot, mostly of schoolchildren. He taps the photo.

"That's Richard Parker," he says.

I'm amazed. I look closely, trying to extract personality from appearance. Unfortunately, it's black and white again and a little out of focus. A photo taken in better days, casually. Richard Parker is looking away. He doesn't even realize that his picture is being taken.

The opposing page is entirely taken up by a colour photo of the swimming pool of the Aurobindo Ashram. It's a nice big outdoor pool with clear, sparkling water, a clean blue bottom and an attached diving pool.

The next page features a photo of the front gate of Petit Séminaire school. An arch has the school's motto painted on it: Nil magnum nisi bonum. No greatness without goodness.

And that's it. An entire childhood memorialized in four nearly irrelevant photographs.

He grows sombre.

"The worst of it," he says, "is that I can hardly remember what my mother looks like any more. I can see her in my mind, but it's fleeting. As soon as I try to have a good look at her, she fades. It's the same with her voice. If I saw her again in the street, it would all come back. But that's not likely to happen. It's very sad not to remember what your mother looks like."

He closes the book.

CHAPTER 34

Father said, "We'll sail like Columbus!"

"He was hoping to find India," I pointed out sullenly.

We sold the zoo, lock, stock and barrel. To a new country, a new life. Besides assuring our collection of a happy future, the transaction would pay for our immigration and leave us with a good sum to make a fresh start in Canada (though now, when I think of it, the sum is laughable—how blinded we are by money). We could have sold our animals to zoos in India, but American zoos were willing to pay higher prices. CITES, the Convention on International Trade in Endangered Species, had just come into effect, and the window on the trading of captured wild animals had slammed shut. The future of zoos would now lie with other zoos. The Pondicherry Zoo closed shop at just the right time. There was a scramble to buy our animals. The final buyers were a number of zoos, mainly the Lincoln Park Zoo in Chicago and the soon-to-open Minnesota Zoo, but odd animals were going to Los Angeles, Louisville, Oklahoma City and Cincinnati.

And two animals were being shipped to the Canada Zoo. That's how Ravi and I felt. We did not want to go. We did not want to live in a country of gale-force winds and minus-two-hundred-degree winters. Canada was not on the cricket map. Departure was made easier—as far as getting us used to the idea—by the time it took for all the pre-departure preparations. It took well over a year. I don't mean for us. I mean for the animals. Considering that animals dispense with clothes, footwear, linen, furniture, kitchenware, toiletries; that nationality means nothing to them; that they care not a jot for passports, money, employment prospects, schools, cost of housing, healthcare facilities—considering, in short, their lightness of being, it's amazing how hard it is to move them. Moving a zoo is like moving a city.

The paperwork was colossal. Litres of water used up in the wetting of stamps. *Dear Mr. So-and-so* written hundreds of times. Offers made. Sighs heard. Doubts expressed. Haggling gone through. Decisions sent higher up for approval. Prices agreed upon. Deals clinched. Dotted lines signed. Congratulations given. Certificates of origin sought. Certificates of health sought. Export permits sought. Import permits sought. Quarantine regulations clarified. Transportation organized. A fortune spent on telephone calls. It's a joke in the zoo business, a weary joke, that the paperwork involved in trading a shrew weighs more than an elephant, that the paperwork involved in trading an elephant weighs more than a whale, and that you must never try to trade a whale, never. There seemed to be a single file of nit-picking bureaucrats from Pondicherry to Minneapolis via Delhi and Washington, each with his form, his problem, his hesitation. Shipping the animals to the moon couldn't possibly have been more complicated. Father pulled nearly every hair off his head and came close to giving up on a number of occasions.

There were surprises. Most of our birds and reptiles, and our lemurs, rhinos, orang-utans, mandrills, lion-tailed macaques, giraffes, anteaters, tigers, leopards, cheetahs, hyenas, zebras, Himalayan and sloth bears, Indian elephants and Nilgiri tahrs, among others, were in demand, but others, Elfie for example, were met with silence. "A cataract operation!" Father shouted, waving the letter. "They'll take her if we do a cataract operation on her right eye. On a hippopotamus! What next? Nose jobs on the rhinos?" Some of our other animals were considered "too common", the lions and baboons, for example. Father judiciously traded these for an extra orang-utan from the Mysore Zoo and a chimpanzee from the Manila Zoo. (As for Elfie, she lived out the rest of her days at the Trivandrum Zoo.) One zoo asked for "an authentic Brahmin cow" for their children's zoo. Father walked out into the urban jungle of Pondicherry and bought a cow with dark wet eyes, a nice fat hump and horns so straight and at such right angles to its head that it looked as if it had licked an electrical outlet. Father had its horns painted bright orange and little plastic bells fitted to the tips, for added authenticity.

A deputation of three Americans came. I was very curious. I had never seen real live Americans. They were pink, fat, friendly, very competent and sweated profusely. They examined our animals. They put most of them to sleep and then applied stethoscopes to hearts, examined urine and feces as if horoscopes, drew blood in syringes and analyzed it, fondled humps and bumps, tapped teeth, blinded eyes with flashlights, pinched skins, stroked and pulled hairs. Poor animals. They must have thought they were being drafted into the U.S. Army. We got big smiles from the Americans and bone-crushing handshakes.

The result was that the animals, like us, got their working papers. They were future Yankees, and we, future Canucks.

CHAPTER 35

We left Madras on June 21st, 1977, on the Panamanian-registered Japanese cargo ship *Tsimtsum*. Her officers were Japanese, her crew was Taiwanese, and she was large and impressive. On our last day in Pondicherry I said goodbye to Mamaji, to Mr. and Mr. Kumar, to all my friends and even to many strangers. Mother was apparelled in her finest sari. Her long tress, artfully folded back and attached to the back of her head, was adorned with a garland of fresh jasmine flowers. She looked beautiful. And sad. For she was leaving India, India of the heat and monsoons, of rice fields and the Cauvery River, of coastlines and stone temples, of bullock carts and colourful trucks, of friends and known shopkeepers, of Nehru Street and Goubert Salai, of this and that, India so familiar to her and loved by her. While her men—I fancied myself one already, though I was only sixteen—were in a hurry to get going, were Winnipeggers at heart already, she lingered.

The day before our departure she pointed at a cigarette wallah and earnestly asked, "Should we get a pack or two?"

Father replied, "They have tobacco in Canada. And why do you want to buy cigarettes? We don't smoke."

Yes, they have tobacco in Canada—but do they have Gold Flake cigarettes? Do they have Arun ice cream? Are the bicycles Heroes? Are the televisions Onidas? Are the cars Ambassadors? Are the bookshops Higginbothams'? Such, I suspect, were the questions that swirled in Mother's mind as she contemplated buying cigarettes.

Animals were sedated, cages were loaded and secured, feed was stored, bunks were assigned, lines were tossed, and whistles were blown. As the ship was worked out of the dock and piloted out to sea, I wildly waved goodbye to India. The sun was shining, the breeze was steady, and seagulls shrieked in the air above us. I was terribly excited.

Things didn't turn out the way they were supposed to, but what can you do? You must take life the way it comes at you and make the best of it.

CHAPTER 36

The cities are large and memorably crowded in India, but when you leave them you travel through vast stretches of country where hardly a soul is to be seen. I remember wondering where 950 million Indians could be hiding.

I could say the same of his house.

I'm a little early. I've just set foot on the cement steps of the front porch when a teenager bursts out the front door. He's wearing a baseball uniform and carrying baseball equipment, and he's in a hurry. When he sees me he stops dead in his tracks, startled. He turns around and hollers into the house, "Dad! The writer's here." To me he says, "Hi," and rushes off.

His father comes to the front door. "Hello," he says.

"That was your son?" I ask, incredulous.

"Yes." To acknowledge the fact brings a smile to his lips. "I'm sorry you didn't meet properly. He's late for practice. His name is Nikhil. He goes by Nick."

I'm in the entrance hall. "I didn't know you had a son," I say. There's a barking. A small mongrel mutt, black and brown, races up to me, panting and sniffing. He jumps up against my legs. "Or a dog," I add.

"He's friendly. Tata, down!"

Tata ignores him. I hear "Hello." Only this greeting is not short and forceful like Nick's. It's a long, nasal and softly whining Helloooooooooo, with the ooooooooo reaching for me like a tap on the shoulder or a gentle tug at my pants.

I turn. Leaning against the sofa in the living room, looking up at me bashfully, is a little brown girl, pretty in pink, very much at home. She's holding an orange cat in her arms. Two front legs sticking straight up and a deeply sunk head are all that is visible of it above her crossed arms. The rest of the cat is hanging all the way down to the floor. The animal seems quite relaxed about being stretched on the rack in this manner.

"And this is your daughter," I say.

"Yes. Usha. Usha darling, are you sure Moccasin is comfortable like that?"

Usha drops Moccasin. He flops to the floor unperturbed.

"Hello, Usha," I say.

She comes up to her father and peeks at me from behind his leg.

"What are you doing, little one?" he says. "Why are you hiding?"

She doesn't reply, only looks at me with a smile and hides her face.

"How old are you, Usha?" I ask.

She doesn't reply.

Then Piscine Molitor Patel, known to all as Pi Patel, bends down and picks up his daughter.

"You know the answer to that question. Hmmm? You're four years old. One, two, three, four."

At each number he softly presses the tip of her nose with his index finger. She finds this terribly funny. She giggles and buries her face in the crook of his neck.

This story has a happy ending.

PART TWO

The Pacific Ocean

The ship sank. It made a sound like a monstrous metallic burp. Things bubbled at the surface and then vanished. Everything was screaming: the sea, the wind, my heart. From the lifeboat I saw something in the water.

I cried, "Richard Parker, is that you? It's so hard to see. Oh, that this rain would stop! Richard Parker? Richard Parker? Yes, it is you!"

I could see his head. He was struggling to stay at the surface of the water.

"Jesus, Mary, Muhammad and Vishnu, how good to see you, Richard Parker! Don't give up, please. Come to the lifeboat. Do you hear this whistle? *TREEEEEE! TREEEEEE! TREEEEEE!* You heard right. Swim, swim! You're a strong swimmer. It's not a hundred feet."

He had seen me. He looked panic-stricken. He started swimming my way. The water about him was shifting wildly. He looked small and helpless.

"Richard Parker, can you believe what has happened to us? Tell me it's a bad dream. Tell me it's not real. Tell me I'm still in my bunk on the *Tsimtsum* and I'm tossing and turning and soon I'll wake up from this nightmare. Tell me I'm still happy. Mother, my tender guardian angel of wisdom, where are you? And you, Father, my loving worrywart? And you, Ravi, dazzling hero of my childhood?

Vishnu preserve me, Allah protect me, Christ save me, I can't bear it! *TREEEEEE! TREEEEEE! TREEEEEE!*"

I was not wounded in any part of my body, but I had never experienced such intense pain, such a ripping of the nerves, such an ache of the heart.

He would not make it. He would drown. He was hardly moving forward and his movements were weak. His nose and mouth kept dipping underwater. Only his eyes were steadily on me.

"What are you doing, Richard Parker? Don't you love life? Keep swimming then! *TREEEEEE! TREEEEEE! TREEEEEE!* Kick with your legs. Kick! Kick! Kick!"

He stirred in the water and made to swim.

"And what of my extended family—birds, beasts and reptiles? They too have drowned. Every single thing I value in life has been destroyed. And I am allowed no explanation? I am to suffer hell without any account from heaven? In that case, what is the purpose of reason, Richard Parker? Is it no more than to shine at practicalities—the getting of food, clothing and shelter? Why can't reason give greater answers? Why can we throw a question further than we can pull in an answer? Why such a vast net if there's so little fish to catch?"

His head was barely above water. He was looking up, taking in the sky one last time. There was a lifebuoy in the boat with a rope tied to it. I took hold of it and waved it in the air.

"Do you see this lifebuoy, Richard Parker? Do you see it? Catch hold of it! *HUMPF!* I'll try again. *HUMPF!*"

He was too far. But the sight of the lifebuoy flying his way gave him hope. He revived and started beating the water with vigorous, desperate strokes.

"That's right! One, two. One, two. One, two. Breathe when you can. Watch for the waves. *TREEEEEE! TREEEEEE! TREEEEEE!*"

My heart was chilled to ice. I felt ill with grief. But there was no time for frozen shock. It was shock in activity. Something in me did not want to give up on life, was unwilling to let go, wanted to fight to the very end. Where that part of me got the heart, I don't know.

"Isn't it ironic, Richard Parker? We're in hell yet still we're afraid of immortality. Look how close you are! *TREEEEEE! TREEEEEE! TREEEEEE!* Hurrah, hurrah! You've made it, Richard Parker, you've made it. Catch! *HUMPF!*"

I threw the lifebuoy mightily. It fell in the water right in front of him. With his last energies he stretched forward and took hold of it.

"Hold on tight, I'll pull you in. Don't let go. Pull with your eyes while I pull with my hands. In a few seconds you'll be aboard and we'll be together. Wait a second. Together? We'll be *together*? Have I gone mad?"

I woke up to what I was doing. I yanked on the rope.

"Let go of that lifebuoy, Richard Parker! Let go, I said. I don't want you here, do you understand? Go somewhere else. Leave me alone. Get lost. Drown! Drown!"

He was kicking vigorously with his legs. I grabbed an oar. I thrust it at him, meaning to push him away. I missed and lost hold of the oar.

I grabbed another oar. I dropped it in an oarlock and pulled as hard as I could, meaning to move the lifeboat away. All I accomplished was to turn the lifeboat a little, bringing one end closer to Richard Parker.

I would hit him on the head! I lifted the oar in the air.

He was too fast. He reached up and pulled himself aboard.

"Oh my God!"

Ravi was right. Truly I was to be the next goat. I had a wet, trembling, half-drowned, heaving and coughing three-year-old adult Bengal tiger in my lifeboat. Richard Parker rose unsteadily to his feet on the tarpaulin, eyes blazing as they met mine, ears laid tight to his head, all weapons drawn. His head was the size and colour of the lifebuoy, with teeth.

I turned around, stepped over the zebra and threw myself overboard.

CHAPTER 38

I don't understand. For days the ship had pushed on, bullishly indifferent to its surroundings. The sun shone, rain fell, winds blew, currents flowed, the sea built up hills, the sea dug up valleys—the *Tsimtsum* did not care. It moved with the slow, massive confidence of a continent.

I had bought a map of the world for the trip; I had set it up in our cabin against a cork billboard. Every morning I got our position from the control bridge and marked it on the map with an orange-tipped pin. We sailed from Madras across the Bay of Bengal, down through the Strait of Malacca, around Singapore and up to Manila. I loved every minute of it. It was a thrill to be on a ship. Taking care of the animals kept us very busy. Every night we fell into bed weary to our bones. We were in Manila for two days, a question of fresh feed, new cargo and, we were told, the performing of routine maintenance work on the engines. I paid attention only to the first two. The fresh feed included a ton of bananas, and the new cargo, a female Congo chimpanzee, part of Father's wheeling and dealing. A ton of bananas bristles with a good three, four pounds of big black spiders. A chimpanzee is like a smaller, leaner gorilla, but meaner-looking, with less of the melancholy gentleness of its larger cousin. A chimpanzee shudders and grimaces when it touches a big black spider, like you and I would do, before squashing it angrily with its knuckles, not something you and I would do. I thought bananas and a chimpanzee were more interesting than a loud, filthy mechanical contraption in the dark bowels of a ship. Ravi spent his days there, watching the men work. Something was wrong with the engines, he said. Did something go wrong with the fixing of them? I don't know. I don't think anyone will ever know. The answer is a mystery lying at the bottom of thousands of feet of water.

We left Manila and entered the Pacific. On our fourth day out, midway to Midway, we sank. The ship vanished into a pinprick hole on my map. A mountain collapsed before my eyes and disappeared beneath my feet. All around me was the vomit of a dyspeptic ship. I felt sick to my stomach. I felt shock. I felt a great emptiness within me, which then filled with silence. My chest hurt with pain and fear for days afterwards.

I think there was an explosion. But I can't be sure. It happened while I was sleeping. It woke me up. The ship was no luxury liner. It was a grimy, hardworking cargo ship not designed for paying passengers or for their comfort. There were all kinds of noises all the time. It was precisely because the level of noise was so uniform that we slept like babies. It was a form of silence that nothing disturbed, not Ravi's snoring nor my talking in my sleep. So the explosion, if there was one, was not a new noise. It was an irregular noise. I woke up with a start, as if Ravi had burst a balloon in my ears. I looked at my watch. It was just after four-thirty in the morning. I leaned over and looked down at the bunk below. Ravi was still sleeping.

I dressed and climbed down. Normally I'm a sound sleeper. Normally I would have gone back to sleep. I don't know why I got up that night. It was more the sort of thing Ravi would do. He liked the word *beckon*; he would have said, "Adventure beckons," and would have gone off to prowl around the ship. The level of noise was back to normal again, but with a different quality perhaps, muffled maybe.

I shook Ravi. I said, "Ravi! There was a funny noise. Let's go exploring."

He looked at me sleepily. He shook his head and turned over, pulling the sheet up to his cheek. Oh, Ravi!

I opened the cabin door.

I remember walking down the corridor. Day or night it looked the same. But I felt the night in me. I stopped at Father and Mother's door and considered knocking on it. I remember looking at my watch and deciding against it. Father liked his sleep. I decided I would climb to the main deck and catch the dawn. Maybe I would see a shooting star. I was thinking about that, about shooting stars, as I climbed the stairs. We were two levels below the main deck. I had already forgotten about the funny noise.

It was only when I had pushed open the heavy door leading onto the main deck that I realized what the weather was like. Did it qualify as a storm? It's true there was rain, but it wasn't so very hard. It certainly wasn't a driving rain, like you see during the monsoons. And there was wind. I suppose some of the gusts would have upset umbrellas. But I walked through it without much difficulty. As for the sea, it looked rough, but to a landlubber the sea is always impressive and forbidding, beautiful and dangerous. Waves were reaching up, and their white foam, caught by the wind, was being whipped against the side of the ship. But I'd seen that on other days and the ship hadn't sunk. A cargo ship is a huge and stable structure, a feat of engineering. It's designed to stay afloat under the most adverse conditions. Weather like this surely wouldn't sink a ship? Why, I only had to close a door and the storm was gone. I advanced onto the deck. I gripped the railing and faced the elements. This was adventure.

"Canada, here I come!" I shouted as I was soaked and chilled. I felt very brave. It was dark still, but there was enough light to see by. Light on pandemonium it was. Nature can put on a thrilling show. The stage is vast, the lighting is dramatic, the extras are innumerable, and the budget for special effects is absolutely unlimited. What I had before me was a spectacle of wind and water, an earthquake of the senses, that even Hollywood couldn't orchestrate. But the earthquake stopped at the ground beneath my feet. The ground beneath my feet was solid. I was a spectator safely ensconced in his seat.

It was when I looked up at a lifeboat on the bridge castle that I started to worry. The lifeboat wasn't hanging straight down. It was leaning in from its davits. I turned and looked at my hands. My knuckles were white. The thing was, I wasn't holding on so tightly because of the weather, but because otherwise I would fall in towards the ship. The ship was listing to port, to the other side. It wasn't a severe list, but enough to surprise me. When I looked overboard the drop wasn't sheer any more. I could see the ship's great black side.

A shiver of cold went through me. I decided it was a storm after all. Time to return to safety. I let go, hotfooted it to the wall, moved over and pulled open the door.

Inside the ship, there were noises. Deep structural groans. I stumbled and fell. No harm done. I got up. With the help of the handrails I went down the stairwell four steps at a time. I had gone down just one level when I saw water. Lots of water. It was blocking my way. It was surging from below like a riotous crowd, raging, frothing and boiling. Stairs vanished into watery darkness. I couldn't believe my eyes. What was this water doing here? Where had it come from? I stood nailed to the spot, frightened and incredulous and ignorant of what I should do next. Down there was where my family was.

I ran up the stairs. I got to the main deck. The weather wasn't entertaining any more. I was very afraid. Now it was plain and obvious: the ship was listing badly. And it wasn't level the other way either. There was a noticeable incline going from bow to stern. I looked overboard. The water didn't look to be eighty feet away. The ship was sinking. My mind could hardly conceive it. It was as unbelievable as the moon catching fire.

Where were the officers and the crew? What were they doing? Towards the bow I saw some men running in the gloom. I thought I saw some animals too, but I dismissed the sight as illusion crafted by rain and shadow. We had the hatch covers over their bay pulled open when the weather was good, but at all times the animals were kept confined to their cages. These were dangerous wild animals we were transporting, not farm livestock. Above me, on the bridge, I thought I heard some men shouting.

The ship shook and there was that sound, the monstrous metallic burp. What was it? Was it the collective scream of humans and animals protesting their oncoming death? Was it the ship itself giving up the ghost? I fell over. I got to my feet. I looked overboard again. The sea was rising. The waves were getting closer. We were sinking fast.

I clearly heard monkeys shrieking. Something was shaking the deck. A gaur—an Indian wild ox—exploded out of the rain and thundered by me, terrified, out of control, berserk. I looked at it, dumbstruck and amazed. Who in God's name had let it out?

I ran for the stairs to the bridge. Up there was where the officers were, the only people on the ship who spoke English, the masters of our destiny here, the ones who would right this wrong. They would explain everything. They would take care of my family and me. I climbed to the middle bridge. There was no one on the starboard side. I ran to the port side. I saw three men, crew members. I fell. I got up. They were looking overboard. I shouted. They turned. They looked at me and at each other. They spoke a few words. They came towards me quickly. I felt gratitude and relief welling up in me. I said, "Thank God I've found you. What is happening? I am very scared. There is water at the bottom of the ship. I am worried about my family. I can't get to the level where our cabins are. Is this normal? Do you think—"

One of the men interrupted me by thrusting a life jacket into my arms and shouting something in Chinese. I noticed an orange whistle dangling from the life jacket. The men were nodding vigorously at me. When they took hold of me and lifted me in their strong arms, I thought nothing of it. I thought they were helping me. I was so full of trust in them that I felt grateful as they carried me in the air. Only when they threw me overboard did I begin to have doubts.

CHAPTER 39

I landed with a trampoline-like bounce on the half-unrolled tarpaulin covering a lifeboat forty feet below. It was a miracle I didn't hurt myself. I lost the life jacket, except for the whistle, which stayed in my hand. The lifeboat had been lowered partway and left to hang. It was leaning out from its davits, swinging in the storm, some twenty feet above the water. I looked up. Two of the men were looking down at me, pointing wildly at the lifeboat and shouting. I didn't understand what they wanted me to do. I thought they were going to jump in after me. Instead they turned their heads, looked horrified, and this creature appeared in the air, leaping with the grace of a racehorse. The zebra missed the tarpaulin. It was a male Grant, weighing over five hundred pounds. It landed with a loud crash on the last bench, smashing it and shaking the whole lifeboat. The animal called out. I might have expected the braying of an ass or the neighing of a horse. It was nothing of the sort. It could only be called a burst of barking, a *kwa-ha-ha, kwa-ha-ha, kwa-ha-ha* put out at the highest pitch of distress. The creature's lips were widely parted, standing upright and quivering, revealing yellow teeth and dark pink gums. The lifeboat fell through the air and we hit the seething water.

CHAPTER 40

Richard Parker did not jump into the water after me. The oar I intended to use as a club floated. I held on to it as I reached for the lifebuoy, now vacant of its previous occupant. It was terrifying to be in the water. It was black and cold and in a rage. I felt as if I were at the bottom of a crumbling well. Water kept crashing down on me. It stung my eyes. It pulled me down. I could hardly breathe. If there hadn't been the lifebuoy I wouldn't have lasted a minute.

I saw a triangle slicing the water fifteen feet away. It was a shark's fin. An awful tingle, cold and liquid, went up and down my spine. I swam as fast as I could to one end of the lifeboat, the end still covered by the tarpaulin. I pushed myself up on the lifebuoy with my arms. I couldn't see Richard Parker. He wasn't on the tarpaulin or on a bench. He was at the bottom of the lifeboat. I pushed myself up again. All I could see, briefly, at the other end, was the zebra's head thrashing about. As I fell back into the water another shark's fin glided right before me.

The bright orange tarpaulin was held down by a strong nylon rope that wove its way between metal grommets in the tarpaulin and blunt hooks on the side of the boat. I happened to be treading water at the bow. The tarpaulin was not as securely fixed going over the stem—which had a very short prow, what in a face would be called a snub nose—as it was elsewhere around the boat. There was a little looseness in the tarpaulin as the rope went from one hook on one side of the stem to the next hook on the other side. I lifted the oar in the air and I shoved its handle into this looseness, into this lifesaving detail. I pushed the oar in as far as it would go. The lifeboat now had a prow projecting over the waves, if crookedly. I pulled myself up and wrapped my legs around the oar. The oar handle pushed up against the tarpaulin, but tarpaulin, rope and oar held. I was out of the water, if only by a fluctuating two, three feet. The crest of the larger waves kept striking me.

I was alone and orphaned, in the middle of the Pacific, hanging on to an oar, an adult tiger in front of me, sharks beneath me, a storm raging about me. Had I considered my prospects in the light of reason, I surely would have given up and let go of the oar, hoping that I might drown before being eaten. But I don't recall that I had a single thought during those first minutes of relative safety. I didn't even notice daybreak. I held on to the oar, I just held on, God only knows why.

After a while I made good use of the lifebuoy. I lifted it out of the water and put the oar through its hole. I worked it down until the ring was hugging me. Now it was only with my legs that I had to hold on. If Richard Parker appeared, it would be more awkward to drop from the oar, but one terror at a time, Pacific before tiger.

CHAPTER 41

The elements allowed me to go on living. The lifeboat did not sink. Richard Parker kept out of sight. The sharks prowled but did not lunge. The waves splashed me but did not pull me off.

I watched the ship as it disappeared with much burbling and belching. Lights flickered and went out. I looked about for my family, for survivors, for another lifeboat, for anything that might bring me hope. There was nothing. Only rain, marauding waves of black ocean and the flotsam of tragedy.

The darkness melted away from the sky. The rain stopped.

I could not stay in the position I was in forever. I was cold. My neck was sore from holding up my head and from all the craning I had been doing. My back hurt from leaning against the lifebuoy. And I needed to be higher up if I were to see other lifeboats.

I inched my way along the oar till my feet were against the bow of the boat. I had to proceed with extreme caution. My guess was that Richard Parker was on the floor of the lifeboat beneath the tarpaulin, his back to me, facing the zebra, which he had no doubt killed by now. Of the five senses, tigers rely the most on their sight. Their eyesight is very keen, especially in detecting motion. Their hearing is good. Their smell is average. I mean compared to other animals, of course. Next to Richard Parker, I was deaf, blind and nose-dead. But at the moment he could not see me, and in my wet condition could probably not smell me, and what with the whistling of the wind and the hissing of the sea as waves broke, if I were careful, he would not hear me. I had a chance so long as he did not sense me. If he did, he would kill me right away. Could he burst through the tarpaulin, I wondered.

Fear and reason fought over the answer. Fear said Yes. He was a fierce, 450-pound carnivore. Each of his claws was as sharp as a knife. Reason said No. The tarpaulin was sturdy canvas, not a Japanese paper wall. I had landed upon it from a height. Richard Parker could shred it with his claws with a little time and effort, but he couldn't pop through it like a jack-in-the-box. And he had not seen me. Since he had not seen me, he had no reason to claw his way through it.

I slid along the oar. I brought both my legs to one side of the oar and placed my feet on the gunnel. The gunnel is the top edge of a boat, the rim if you want. I moved a little more till my legs were on the boat. I kept my eyes fixed on the horizon of the tarpaulin. Any second I expected to see Richard Parker rising up and coming for me. Several times I had fits of fearful trembling. Precisely where I wanted to be most still—my legs—was where I trembled most. My legs drummed upon the tarpaulin. A more obvious rapping on Richard Parker's door couldn't be imagined. The trembling spread to my arms and it was all I could do to hold on. Each fit passed.

When enough of my body was on the boat I pulled myself up. I looked beyond the end of the tarpaulin. I was surprised to see that the zebra was still alive. It lay near the stern, where it had fallen, listless, but its stomach was still panting and its eyes were still moving, expressing terror. It was on its side, facing me, its head and neck awkwardly propped against the boat's side bench. It had badly broken a rear leg. The angle of it was completely unnatural. Bone protruded through skin and there was bleeding. Only its slim front legs had a semblance of normal position. They were bent and neatly tucked against its twisted torso. From time to time the zebra shook its head and barked and snorted. Otherwise it lay quietly.

It was a lovely animal. Its wet markings glowed brightly white and intensely black. I was so eaten up by anxiety that I couldn't dwell on it; still, in passing, as a faint afterthought, the queer, clean, artistic boldness of its design and the fineness of its head struck me. Of greater significance to me was the strange fact that Richard Parker had not killed it. In the normal course of things he should have killed the zebra. That's what predators do: they kill prey. In the present circumstances, where Richard Parker would be under tremendous mental strain, fear should have brought out an exceptional level of aggression. The zebra should have been properly butchered.

The reason behind its spared life was revealed shortly. It froze my blood—and then brought a slight measure of relief. A head appeared beyond the end of the tarpaulin. It looked at me in a direct, frightened way, ducked under, appeared again, ducked under again, appeared once more, disappeared a last time. It was the bear-like, balding-looking head of a spotted hyena. Our zoo had a clan of six, two dominant females and four subordinate males. They were supposed to be going to Minnesota. The one here was a male. I recognized it by its right ear, which was badly torn, its healed jagged edge testimony to old violence. Now I understood why Richard Parker had not killed the zebra: he was no longer aboard. There couldn't be both a hyena and a tiger in such a small space. He must have fallen off the tarpaulin and drowned.

I had to explain to myself how a hyena had come to be on the lifeboat. I doubted hyenas were capable of swimming in open seas. I concluded that it must have been on board all along, hiding under the tarpaulin, and that I hadn't noticed it when I landed with a bounce. I realized something else: the hyena was the reason those sailors had thrown me into the lifeboat. They weren't trying to save my life. That was the last of their concerns. They were using me as fodder. They were hoping that the hyena would attack me and that somehow I would get rid of it and make the boat safe for them, no matter if it cost me my life. Now I knew what they were pointing at so furiously just before the zebra appeared.

I never thought that finding myself confined in a small space with a spotted hyena would be good news, but there you go. In fact, the good news was double: if it weren't for this hyena, the sailors wouldn't have thrown me into the lifeboat and I would have stayed on the ship and I surely would have drowned; and if I had to share quarters with a wild animal, better the upfront ferocity of a dog than the power and stealth of a cat. I breathed the smallest sigh of relief. As a precautionary measure I moved onto the oar. I sat astride it, on the rounded edge of the speared lifebuoy, my left foot against the tip of the prow, my right foot on the gunnel. It was comfortable enough and I was facing the boat.

I looked about. Nothing but sea and sky. The same when we were at the top of a swell. The sea briefly imitated every land feature—every hill, every valley, every plain. Accelerated geotectonics. Around the world in eighty swells. But nowhere on it could I find my family. Things floated in the water but none that brought me hope. I could see no other lifeboats.

The weather was changing rapidly. The sea, so immense, so

breathtakingly immense, was settling into a smooth and steady motion, with the waves at heel; the wind was softening to a tuneful breeze; fluffy, radiantly white clouds were beginning to light up in a vast fathomless dome of delicate pale blue. It was the dawn of a beautiful day in the Pacific Ocean. My shirt was already beginning to dry. The night had vanished as quickly as the ship.

I began to wait. My thoughts swung wildly. I was either fixed on practical details of immediate survival or transfixed by pain, weeping silently, my mouth open and my hands at my head.

CHAPTER 42

She came floating on an island of bananas in a halo of light, as lovely as the Virgin Mary. The rising sun was behind her. Her flaming hair looked stunning.

I cried, "Oh blessed Great Mother, Pondicherry fertility goddess, provider of milk and love, wondrous arm spread of comfort, terror of ticks, picker-up of crying ones, are you to witness this tragedy too? It's not right that gentleness meet horror. Better that you had died right away. How bitterly glad I am to see you. You bring joy and pain in equal measure. Joy because you are with me, but pain because it won't be for long. What do you know about the sea? Nothing. What do I know about the sea? Nothing. Without a driver this bus is lost. Our lives are over. Come aboard if your destination is oblivion— it should be our next stop. We can sit together. You can have the window seat, if you want. But it's a sad view. Oh, enough of this dissembling. Let me say it plainly: I love you, I love you, I love you. I love you, I love you, I love you. Not the spiders, please."

It was Orange Juice—so called because she tended to drool—our prize Borneo orang-utan matriarch, zoo star and mother of two fine boys, surrounded by a mass of black spiders that crawled around her like malevolent worshippers. The bananas on which she floated were held together by the nylon net with which they had been lowered into the ship. When she stepped off the bananas into the boat, they bobbed up and rolled over. The net became loose. Without thinking about it, only because it was at hand's reach and about to sink, I took hold of the net and pulled it aboard, a casual gesture that would turn out to be a lifesaver in many ways; this net would become one of my most precious possessions.

The bananas came apart. The black spiders crawled as fast as they could, but their situation was hopeless. The island crumbled beneath them. They all drowned. The lifeboat briefly floated in a sea of fruit.

I had picked up what I thought was a useless net, but did I think of reaping from this banana manna? No. Not a single one. It was banana split in the wrong sense of the term: the sea dispersed them. This colossal waste would later weigh on me heavily. I would nearly go into convulsions of dismay at my stupidity.

Orange Juice was in a fog. Her gestures were slow and tentative and her eyes reflected deep mental confusion. She was in a state of profound shock. She lay flat on the tarpaulin for several minutes, quiet and still, before reaching over and falling into the lifeboat proper. I heard a hyena's scream.

CHAPTER 43

The last trace I saw of the ship was a patch of oil glimmering on the surface of the water.

I was certain I wasn't alone. It was inconceivable that the *Tsimtsum* should sink without eliciting a peep of concern. Right now in Tokyo, in Panama City, in Madras, in Honolulu, why, even in Winnipeg, red lights were blinking on consoles, alarm bells were ringing, eyes were opening wide in horror, mouths were gasping, "My God! The *Tsimtsum* has sunk!" and hands were reaching for phones. More red lights were starting to blink and more alarm bells were starting to ring. Pilots were running to their planes with their shoelaces still untied, such was their hurry. Ship officers were spinning their wheels till they were feeling dizzy. Even submarines were swerving underwater to join in the rescue effort. We would be rescued soon. A ship would appear on the horizon. A gun would be found to kill the hyena and put the zebra out of its misery. Perhaps Orange Juice could be saved. I would climb aboard and be greeted by my family. They would have been picked up in another lifeboat. I only had to ensure my survival for the next few hours until this rescue ship came.

I reached from my perch for the net. I rolled it up and tossed it midway on the tarpaulin to act as a barrier, however small. Orange Juice had seemed practically cataleptic. My guess was she was dying of shock. It was the hyena that worried me. I could hear it whining. I clung to the hope that a zebra, a familiar prey, and an orang-utan, an unfamiliar one, would distract it from thoughts of me.

I kept one eye on the horizon, one eye on the other end of the lifeboat. Other than the hyena's whining, I heard very little from the animals, no more than claws scuffing against a hard surface and occasional groans and arrested cries. No major fight seemed to be taking place.

Mid-morning the hyena appeared again. In the preceding minutes its whining had been rising in volume to a scream. It jumped over the zebra onto the stern, where the lifeboat's side benches came together to form a triangular bench. It was a fairly exposed position, the distance between bench and gunnel being about twelve inches. The animal nervously peered beyond the boat. Beholding a vast expanse of shifting water seemed to be the last thing it wanted to see, for it instantly brought its head down and dropped to the bottom of the boat behind the zebra. That was a cramped space; between the broad back of the zebra and the sides of the buoyancy tanks that went all round the boat beneath the benches, there wasn't much room left for a hyena. It thrashed about for a moment before climbing to the stern again and jumping back over the zebra to the middle of the boat, disappearing beneath the tarpaulin. This burst of activity lasted less than ten seconds. The hyena came to within fifteen feet of me. My only reaction was to freeze with fear. The zebra, by comparison, swiftly reared its head and barked.

I was hoping the hyena would stay under the tarpaulin. I was disappointed. Nearly immediately it leapt over the zebra and onto the stern bench again. There it turned on itself a few times, whimpering and hesitating. I wondered what it was going to do next. The answer came quickly: it brought its head low and ran around the zebra in a circle, transforming the stern bench, the side benches and the cross bench just beyond the tarpaulin into a twenty-five-foot indoor track. It did one lap—two—three—four—five—and onwards, non-stop, till I lost count. And the whole time, lap after lap, it went *yip yip yip yip yip* in a high-pitched way. My reaction, once again, was very slow. I was seized by fear and could only watch. The beast was going at a good clip, and it was no small animal; it was an adult male that looked to be about 140 pounds. The beating of its legs against the benches made the whole boat shake, and its claws were loudly clicking on their surface. Each time it came from the stern I tensed. It was hair-raising enough to see the thing racing my way; worse still was the fear that it would keep going straight. Clearly, Orange Juice, wherever she was, would not be an obstacle. And the rolled-up tarpaulin and the bulge of the net were even more pitiful defences. With the slightest of efforts the hyena could be at the bow right at my feet. It didn't seem intent on that course of action; every time it came to the cross bench, it took it, and I saw the upper half of its body moving rapidly along the edge of the tarpaulin. But in this state, the hyena's behaviour was highly unpredictable and it could decide to attack me without warning.

After a number of laps it stopped short at the stern bench and crouched, directing its gaze downwards, to the space below the tarpaulin. It lifted its eyes and rested them upon me. The look was nearly the typical look of a hyena—blank and frank, the curiosity apparent with nothing of the mental set revealed, jaw hanging open, big ears sticking up rigidly, eyes bright and black—were it not for the strain that exuded from every cell of its body, an anxiety that made the animal glow, as if with a fever. I prepared for my end. For nothing. It started running in circles again.

When an animal decides to do something, it can do it for a very long time. All morning the hyena ran in circles going *yip yip yip yip yip*. Once in a while it briefly stopped at the stern bench, but otherwise every lap was identical to the previous one, with no variations in movement, in speed, in the pitch or the volume of the yipping, in the counter-clockwise direction of travel. Its yipping was shrill and annoying in the extreme. It became so tedious and draining to watch that I eventually turned my head to the side, trying to keep guard with the corner of my eyes. Even the zebra, which at first snorted each time the hyena raced by its head, fell into a stupor.

Yet every time the hyena paused at the stern bench, my heart jumped. And as much as I wanted to direct my attention to the horizon, to where my salvation lay, it kept straying back to this maniacal beast.

I am not one to hold a prejudice against any animal, but it is a plain fact that the spotted hyena is not well served by its appearance. It is ugly beyond redemption. Its thick neck and high shoulders that slope to the hindquarters look as if they've come from a discarded prototype for the giraffe, and its shaggy, coarse coat seems to have been patched together from the leftovers of creation. The colour is a bungled mix of tan, black, yellow, grey, with the spots having none of the classy ostentation of a leopard's rosettes; they look rather like the symptoms of a skin disease, a virulent form of mange. The head is broad and too massive, with a high forehead, like that of a bear, but suffering from a receding hairline, and with ears that look ridiculously mouse-like, large and round, when they haven't been torn off in battle. The mouth is forever open and panting. The nostrils are too big. The tail is scraggly and unwagging. The gait is shambling. All the parts put together look doglike, but like no dog anyone would want as a pet.

But I had not forgotten Father's words. These were not cowardly carrion-eaters. If *National Geographic* portrayed them as such, it was because *National Geographic* filmed during the day. It is when the moon rises that the hyena's day starts, and it proves to be a devastating hunter. Hyenas attack in packs whatever animal can be run down, its flanks opened while still in full motion. They go for zebras, gnus and water buffaloes, and not only the old or the infirm in a herd—full-grown members too. They are hardy attackers, rising up from buttings and kickings immediately, never giving up for simple lack of will. And they are clever; anything that can be distracted from its mother is good. The ten-minute-old gnu is a favourite dish, but hyenas also eat young lions and young rhinoceros. They are diligent when their efforts are rewarded. In fifteen minutes flat, all that will be left of a zebra is the skull, which may yet be dragged away and gnawed down at leisure by young ones in the lair. Nothing goes to waste; even grass upon which blood has been spilt will be eaten. Hyenas' stomachs swell visibly as they swallow huge chunks of kill. If they are lucky, they become so full they have difficulty moving. Once they've digested their kill, they cough up dense hairballs, which they pick clean of edibles before rolling in them. Accidental cannibalism is a common occurrence during the excitement of a feeding; in reaching for a bite of zebra, a hyena will take in the ear or nostril of a clan member, no hard feelings intended. The hyena feels no disgust at this mistake. Its delights are too many to admit to disgust at anything.

In fact, a hyena's catholicity of taste is so indiscriminate it nearly forces admiration. A hyena will drink from water even as it is urinating in it. The animal has another original use for its urine: in hot, dry weather it will cool itself by relieving its bladder on the ground and stirring up a refreshing mud bath with its paws. Hyenas snack on the excrement of herbivores with clucks of pleasure. It's an open question as to what hyenas *won't* eat. They eat their own kind (the rest of those whose ears and noses they gobbled down as appetizers) once they're dead, after a period of aversion that lasts about one day. They will even attack motor vehicles—the headlights, the exhaust pipe, the side mirrors. It is not their gastric juices that limit hyenas, but the power of their jaws, which is formidable.

That was the animal I had racing around in circles before me. An animal to pain the eye and chill the heart.

Things ended in typical hyena fashion. It stopped at the stern and started producing deep groans interrupted by fits of heavy panting. I pushed myself away on the oar till only the tips of my feet were holding on to the boat. The animal hacked and coughed. Abruptly it vomited. A gush landed behind the zebra. The hyena dropped into what it had just produced. It stayed there, shaking and whining and turning around on itself, exploring the furthest confines of animal anguish. It did not move from the restricted space for the rest of the day. At times the zebra made noises about the predator just behind it, but mostly it lay in hopeless and sullen silence.

CHAPTER 44

The sun climbed through the sky, reached its zenith, began to come down. I spent the entire day perched on the oar, moving only as much as was necessary to stay balanced. My whole being tended towards the spot on the horizon that would appear and save me. It was a state of tense, breathless boredom. Those first hours are associated in my memory with one sound, not one you'd guess, not the yipping of the hyena or the hissing of the sea: it was the buzzing of flies. There were flies aboard the lifeboat. They emerged and flew about in the way of flies, in great, lazy orbits except when they came close to each other, when they spiralled together with dizzying speed and a burst of buzzing. Some were brave enough to venture out to where I was. They looped around me, sounding like sputtering, single-prop airplanes, before hurrying home. Whether they were native to the boat or had come with one of the animals, the hyena most likely, I can't say. But whatever their origin, they didn't last long; they all disappeared within two days. The hyena, from behind the zebra, snapped at them and ate a number. Others were probably swept out to sea by the wind. Perhaps a few lucky ones came to their life's term and died of old age.

As evening approached, my anxiety grew. Everything about the end of the day scared me. At night a ship would have difficulty seeing me. At night the hyena might become active again and maybe Orange Juice too.

Darkness came. There was no moon. Clouds hid the stars. The contours of things became hard to distinguish. Everything disappeared, the sea, the lifeboat, my own body. The sea was quiet and there was hardly any wind, so I couldn't even ground myself in sound. I seemed to be floating in pure, abstract blackness. I kept my eyes fixed on where I thought the horizon was, while my ears were on guard for any sign of the animals. I couldn't imagine lasting the night.

Sometime during the night the hyena began snarling and the zebra barking and squealing, and I heard a repeated knocking sound. I shook with fright and—I will hide nothing here—relieved myself in my pants. But these sounds came from the other end of the lifeboat. I couldn't feel any shaking that indicated movement. The hellish beast was apparently staying away from me. From nearer in the blackness I began hearing loud expirations and groans and grunts and various wet mouth sounds. The idea of Orange Juice stirring was too much for my nerves to bear, so I did not consider it. I simply ignored the thought. There were also noises coming from beneath me, from the water, sudden flapping sounds and swishing sounds that were over and done with in an instant. The battle for life was taking place there too.

The night passed, minute by slow minute.

CHAPTER 45

I was cold. It was a distracted observation, as if it didn't concern me. Daybreak came. It happened quickly, yet by imperceptible degrees. A corner of the sky changed colours. The air began filling with light. The calm sea opened up around me like a great book. Still it felt like night. Suddenly it was day.

Warmth came only when the sun, looking like an electrically lit orange, broke across the horizon, but I didn't need to wait that long to feel it. With the very first rays of light it came alive in me: hope. As things emerged in outline and filled with colour, hope increased until it was like a song in my heart. Oh, what it was to bask in it! Things would work out yet. The worst was over. I had survived the night. Today I would be rescued. To think that, to string those words together in my mind, was itself a source of hope. Hope fed on hope. As the horizon became a neat, sharp line, I scanned it eagerly. The day was clear again and visibility was perfect. I imagined Ravi would greet me first and with a tease. "What's this?" he would say. "You find yourself a great big lifeboat and you fill it with animals? You think you're Noah or something?" Father would be unshaven and dishevelled. Mother would look to the sky and take me in her arms. I went through a dozen versions of what it was going to be like on the rescue ship, variations on the theme of sweet reunion. That morning the horizon might curve one way, my lips resolutely curved the other, in a smile.

Strange as it might sound, it was only after a long time that I looked to see what was happening in the lifeboat. The hyena had attacked the zebra. Its mouth was bright red and it was chewing on a piece of hide. My eyes automatically searched for the wound, for the area under attack. I gasped with horror.

The zebra's broken leg was missing. The hyena had bitten it off and dragged it to the stern, behind the zebra. A flap of skin hung limply over the raw stump. Blood was still dripping. The victim bore its suffering patiently, without showy remonstrations. A slow and constant grinding of its teeth was the only visible sign of distress. Shock, revulsion and anger surged through me. I felt intense hatred for the hyena. I thought of doing something to kill it. But I did nothing. And my outrage was short-lived. I must be honest about that. I didn't have pity to spare for long for the zebra. When your own life is threatened, your sense of empathy is blunted by a terrible, selfish hunger for survival. It was sad that it was suffering so much—and being such a big, strapping creature it wasn't at the end of its ordeal—but there was nothing I could do about it. I felt pity and then I moved on. This is not something I am proud of. I am sorry I was so callous about the matter. I have not forgotten that poor zebra and what it went through. Not a prayer goes by that I don't think of it.

There was still no sign of Orange Juice. I turned my eyes to the horizon again.

That afternoon the wind picked up a little and I noticed something about the lifeboat: despite its weight, it floated lightly on the water, no doubt because it was carrying less than its capacity. We had plenty of freeboard, the distance between the water and the gunnel; it would take a mean sea to swamp us. But it also meant that whatever end of the boat was facing the wind tended to fall away, bringing us broadside to the waves. With small waves the result was a ceaseless, fist-like beating against the hull, while larger waves made for a tiresome rolling of the boat as it leaned from side to side. This jerky and incessant motion was making me feel queasy.

Perhaps I would feel better in a new position. I slid down the oar and shifted back onto the bow. I sat facing the waves, with the rest of the boat to my left. I was closer to the hyena, but it wasn't stirring.

It was as I was breathing deeply and concentrating on making my nausea go away that I saw Orange Juice. I had imagined her completely out of sight, near the bow beneath the tarpaulin, as far from the hyena as she could get. Not so. She was on the side bench, just beyond the edge of the hyena's indoor track and barely hidden from me by the bulge of rolled-up tarpaulin. She lifted her head only an inch or so and right away I saw her.

Curiosity got the best of me. I had to see her better. Despite the rolling of the boat I brought myself to a kneeling position. The hyena looked at me, but did not move. Orange Juice came into sight. She was deeply slouched and holding on to the gunnel with both her hands, her head sunk very low between her arms. Her mouth was open and her tongue was lolling about. She was visibly panting. Despite the tragedy afflicting me, despite not feeling well, I let out a laugh. Everything about Orange Juice at that moment spelled one word: *seasickness*. The image of a new species popped into my head: the rare seafaring *green* orang-utan. I returned to my sitting position. The poor dear looked so *humanly* sick! It is a particularly funny thing to read human traits in animals, especially in apes and monkeys, where it is so easy. Simians are the clearest mirrors we have in the animal world. That is why they are so popular in zoos. I laughed again. I brought my hands to my chest, surprised at how I felt. Oh my. This laughter was like a volcano of happiness erupting in me. And Orange Juice had not only cheered me up; she had also taken on both our feelings of seasickness. I was feeling fine now.

I returned to scrutinizing the horizon, my hopes high.

Besides being deathly seasick, there was something else about Orange Juice that was remarkable: she was uninjured. And she had her back turned to the hyena, as if she felt she could safely ignore it. The ecosystem on this lifeboat was decidedly baffling. Since there are no natural conditions in which a spotted hyena and an orang-utan can meet, there being none of the first in Borneo and none of the second in Africa, there is no way of knowing how they would relate. But it seemed to me highly improbable, if not totally incredible, that when brought together these frugivorous tree-dwellers and carnivorous savannah-dwellers would so radically carve out their niches as to pay no attention to each other. Surely an orang-utan would smell of prey to a hyena, albeit a strange one, one to be remembered afterwards for producing stupendous hairballs, nonetheless better-tasting than an exhaust pipe and well worth looking out for when near trees. And surely a hyena would smell of a predator to an orang-utan, a reason for being vigilant when a piece of durian has been dropped to the ground accidentally. But nature forever holds surprises. Perhaps it was not so. If goats could be brought to live amicably with rhinoceros, why not orang-utans with hyenas? That would be a big winner at a zoo. A sign would have to be put up. I could see it already: "Dear Public, Do not be afraid for the orang-utans! They are in the trees because that is where they live, not because they are afraid of the spotted hyenas. Come back at mealtime, or at sunset when they get thirsty, and you will see them climbing down from their trees and moving about the grounds, absolutely unmolested by the hyenas." Father would be fascinated.

Sometime that afternoon I saw the first specimen of what would become a dear, reliable friend of mine. There was a bumping and scraping sound against the hull of the lifeboat. A few seconds later, so close to the boat I could have leaned down and grabbed it, a large sea turtle appeared, a hawksbill, flippers lazily turning, head sticking out of the water. It was striking-looking in an ugly sort of way, with a rugged, yellowish brown shell about three feet long and spotted with patches of algae, and a dark green face with a sharp beak, no lips, two solid holes for nostrils, and black eyes that stared at me intently. The expression was haughty and severe, like that of an ill-tempered old man who has complaining on his mind. The queerest thing about the reptile was simply that it was. It looked incongruous, floating there in the water, so odd in its shape compared to the sleek, slippery design of fish. Yet it was plainly in its element and it was I who was the odd one out. It hovered by the boat for several minutes.

I said to it, "Go tell a ship I'm here. Go, go." It turned and sank out of sight, back flippers pushing water in alternate strokes.

CHAPTER 46

Clouds that gathered where ships were supposed to appear, and the passing of the day, slowly did the job of unbending my smile. It is pointless to say that this or that night was the worst of my life. I have so many bad nights to choose from that I've made none the champion. Still, that second night at sea stands in my memory as one of exceptional suffering, different from the frozen anxiety of the first night in being a more conventional sort of suffering, the broken-down kind consisting of weeping and sadness and spiritual pain, and different from later ones in that I still had the strength to appreciate fully what I felt. And that dreadful night was preceded by a dreadful evening.

I noticed the presence of sharks around the lifeboat. The sun was beginning to pull the curtains on the day. It was a placid explosion of orange and red, a great chromatic symphony, a colour canvas of supernatural proportions, truly a splendid Pacific sunset, quite wasted on me. The sharks were makos—swift, pointy-snouted predators with long, murderous teeth that protruded noticeably from their mouths. They were about six or seven feet long, one was larger still. I watched them anxiously. The largest one came at the boat quickly, as if to attack, its dorsal fin rising out of the water by several inches, but it dipped below just before reaching us and glided underfoot with fearsome grace. It returned, not coming so close this time, then disappeared. The other sharks paid a longer visit, coming and going at different depths, some in plain sight at hand's reach below the surface of the water, others deeper down. There were other fish too, big and small, colourful, differently shaped. I might have considered them more closely had my attention not been drawn elsewhere: Orange Juice's head came into sight.

She turned and brought her arm onto the tarpaulin in a motion that imitated exactly the way you or I would bring out an arm and place it on the back of the chair next to our own in a gesture of expansive relaxation. But such was clearly not her disposition. Bearing an expression profoundly sad and mournful, she began to look about, slowly turning her head from side to side. Instantly the likeness of apes lost its amusing character. She had given birth at the zoo to two young ones, strapping males five and eight years old that were her—and our—pride. It was unmistakably these she had on her mind as she searched over the water, unintentionally mimicking what I had been doing these last thirty-six hours. She noticed me and expressed nothing about it. I was just another animal that had lost everything and was vowed to death. My mood plummeted.

Then, with only a snarl for notice, the hyena went amok. It hadn't moved from its cramped quarters all day. It put its front legs on the zebra's side, reached over and gathered a fold of skin in its jaws. It pulled roughly. A strip of hide came off the zebra's belly like gift-wrap paper comes off a gift, in a smooth-edged swath, only silently, in the way of tearing skin, and with greater resistance. Immediately blood poured forth like a river. Barking, snorting and squealing, the zebra came to life to defend itself. It pushed on its front legs and reared its head in an attempt to bite the hyena, but the beast was out of reach. It shook its good hind leg, which did no more than explain the origin of the previous night's knocking: it was the hoof beating against the side of the boat. The zebra's attempts at self-preservation only whipped the hyena into a frenzy of snarling and biting. It made a gaping wound in the zebra's side. When it was no longer satisfied with the reach it had from behind the zebra, the hyena climbed onto its haunches. It started pulling out coils of intestines and other viscera. There was no order to what it was doing. It bit here, swallowed there, seemingly overwhelmed by the riches before it. After devouring half the liver, it started tugging on the whitish, balloon-like stomach bag. But it was heavy, and with the zebra's haunches being higher than its belly—and blood being slippery—the hyena started to slide into its victim. It plunged head and shoulders into the zebra's guts, up to the knees of its front legs. It pushed itself out, only to slide back down. It finally settled in this position, half in, half out. The zebra was being eaten alive from the inside.

It protested with diminishing vigour. Blood started coming out its nostrils. Once or twice it reared its head straight up, as if appealing to heaven—the abomination of the moment was perfectly expressed.

Orange Juice did not view these doings indifferently. She raised herself to her full height on her bench. With her incongruously small legs and massive torso, she looked like a refrigerator on crooked wheels. But with her giant arms lifted in the air, she looked impressive. Their span was greater than her height—one hand hung over the water, the other reached across the width of the lifeboat nearly to the opposite side. She pulled back her lips, showing off enormous canines, and began to *roar*. It was a deep, powerful, huffing roar, amazing for an animal normally as silent as a giraffe. The hyena was as startled as I was by the outburst. It cringed and retreated. But not for long. After an intense stare at Orange Juice, the hairs on its neck and shoulders stood up and its tail rose straight in the air. It climbed back onto the dying zebra. There, blood dripping from its mouth, it responded to Orange Juice in kind, with a higher-pitched roar. The two animals were three feet apart, wide-open jaws directly facing. They put all their energies into their cries, their bodies shaking with the effort. I could see deep down the hyena's throat. The Pacific air, which until a minute before had been carrying the whistling and whispering of the sea, a natural melody I would have called soothing had the circumstances been happier, was all at once filled with this appalling noise, like the fury of an all-out battle, with the ear-splitting firing of guns and cannons and the thunderous blasts of bombs. The hyena's roar filled the higher range of what my ears could hear, Orange Juice's bass roar filled the lower range, and somewhere in between I could hear the cries of the helpless zebra. My ears were full. Nothing more, not one more sound, could push into them and be registered.

I began to tremble uncontrollably. I was convinced the hyena was going to lunge at Orange Juice.

I could not imagine that matters could get worse, but they did. The zebra snorted some of its blood overboard. Seconds later there was a hard knock against the boat, followed by another. The water began to churn around us with sharks. They were searching for the source of the blood, for the food so close at hand. Their tail fins flashed out of the water, their heads swung out. The boat was hit repeatedly. I was not afraid we would capsize—I thought the sharks would actually punch through the metal hull and sink us.

With every bang the animals jumped and looked alarmed, but they were not to be distracted from their main business of roaring in each other's faces. I was certain the shouting match would turn physical. Instead it broke off abruptly after a few minutes. Orange Juice, with huffs and lip-smacking noises, turned away, and the hyena lowered its head and retreated behind the zebra's butchered body. The sharks, finding nothing, stopped knocking on the boat and eventually left. Silence fell at last.

A foul and pungent smell, an earthy mix of rust and excrement, hung in the air. There was blood everywhere, coagulating to a deep red crust. A single fly buzzed about, sounding to me like an alarm bell of insanity. No ship, nothing at all, had appeared on the horizon that day, and now the day was ending. When the sun slipped below the horizon, it was not only the day that died and the poor zebra, but my family as well. With that second sunset, disbelief gave way to pain and grief. They were dead; I could no longer deny it. What a thing to acknowledge in your heart! To lose a brother is to lose someone with whom you can share the experience of growing old, who is supposed to bring you a sister-in-law and nieces and nephews, creatures to people the tree of your life and give it new branches. To lose your father is to lose the one whose guidance and help you seek, who supports you like a tree trunk supports its branches. To lose your mother, well, that is like losing the sun above you.

It is like losing—I'm sorry, I would rather not go on. I lay down on the tarpaulin and spent the whole night weeping and grieving, my face buried in my arms. The hyena spent a good part of the night eating.

CHAPTER 47

The day broke, humid and overcast, with the wind warm and the sky a dense blanket of grey clouds that looked like bunched-up, dirty cotton sheets. The sea had not changed. It heaved the lifeboat up and down in a regular motion.

The zebra was still alive. I couldn't believe it. It had a two-foot-wide hole in its body, a fistula like a freshly erupted volcano, spewed half-eaten organs glistening in the light or giving off a dull, dry shine, yet, in its strictly essential parts, it continued to pump with life, if weakly. Movement was confined to a tremor in the rear leg and an occasional blinking of the eyes. I was horrified. I had no idea a living being could sustain so much injury and go on living.

The hyena was tense. It was not settling down to its night of rest despite the daylight. Perhaps it was a result of taking in so much food; its stomach was grossly dilated. Orange Juice was in a dangerous mood too. She was fidgeting and showing her teeth.

I stayed where I was, curled up near the prow. I was weak in body and in soul. I was afraid I would fall into the water if I tried to balance on the oar.

The zebra was dead by noon. It was glassy-eyed and had become perfectly indifferent to the hyena's occasional assaults.

Violence broke out in the afternoon. Tension had risen to an unbearable level. The hyena was yipping. Orange Juice was grunting and making loud lip-smacking noises. All of a sudden their complaining fused and shot up to top volume. The hyena jumped over the remains of the zebra and made for Orange Juice.

I believe I have made clear the menace of a hyena. It was certainly so clear in my mind that I gave up on Orange Juice's life before she even had a chance to defend it. I underestimated her. I underestimated her grit.

She thumped the beast on the head. It was something shocking. It made my heart melt with love and admiration and fear. Did I mention she was a former pet, callously discarded by her Indonesian owners? Her story was like that of every inappropriate pet. It goes something like this: The pet is bought when it is small and cute. It gives much amusement to its owners. Then it grows in size and in appetite. It reveals itself incapable of being house-trained. Its increasing strength makes it harder to handle. One day the maid pulls the sheet from its nest because she has decided to wash it, or the son jokingly pinches a morsel of food from its hands—over some such seemingly small matter, the pet flashes its teeth in anger and the family is frightened. The very next day the pet finds itself bouncing at the back of the family Jeep in the company of its human brothers and sisters. A jungle is entered. Everyone in the vehicle finds it a strange and formidable place. A clearing is come to. It is briefly explored. All of a sudden the Jeep roars to life and its wheels kick up dirt and the pet sees all the ones it has known and loved looking at it from the back window as the Jeep speeds away. It has been left behind. The pet does not understand. It is as unprepared for this jungle as its human siblings are. It waits around for their return, trying to quell the panic rising in it. They do not return. The sun sets. Quickly it becomes depressed and gives up on life. It dies of hunger and exposure in the next few days. Or is attacked by dogs.

Orange Juice could have been one of these forlorn pets. Instead she ended up at the Pondicherry Zoo. She remained gentle and un-aggressive her whole life. I have memories from when I was a child of her never-ending arms surrounding me, her fingers, each as long as my whole hand, picking at my hair. She was a young female practising her maternal skills. As she matured into her full wild self, I observed her at a distance. I thought I knew her so well that I could predict her every move. I thought I knew not only her habits but also her limits. This display of ferocity, of savage courage, made me realize that I was wrong. All my life I had known only a part of her.

She thumped the beast on the head. And what a thump it was. The beast's head hit the bench it had just reached, making such a sharp noise, besides splaying its front legs flat out, that I thought surely either the bench or its jaw or both must break. The hyena was up again in an instant, every hair on its body as erect as the hairs on my head, but its hostility wasn't quite so kinetic now. It withdrew. I exulted. Orange Juice's stirring defence brought a glow to my heart.

It didn't last long.

An adult female orang-utan cannot defeat an adult male spotted hyena. That is the plain empirical truth. Let it become known among zoologists. Had Orange Juice been a male, had she loomed as large on the scales as she did in my heart, it might have been another matter. But portly and overfed though she was from living in the comfort of a zoo, even so she tipped the scales at barely 110 pounds. Female orang-utans are half the size of males. But it is not simply a question of weight and brute strength. Orange Juice was far from defenceless. What it comes down to is attitude and knowledge. What does a fruit eater know about killing? Where would it learn where to bite, how hard, for how long? An orang-utan may be taller, may have very strong and agile arms and long canines, but if it does not know how to use these as weapons, they are of little use. The hyena, with only its jaws, will overcome the ape because it knows what it wants and how to get it.

The hyena came back. It jumped on the bench and caught Orange Juice at the wrist before she could strike. Orange Juice hit the hyena on the head with her other arm, but the blow only made the beast snarl viciously. She made to bite, but the hyena moved faster. Alas, Orange Juice's defence lacked precision and coherence. Her fear was something useless that only hampered her. The hyena let go of her wrist and expertly got to her throat.

Dumb with pain and horror, I watched as Orange Juice thumped the hyena ineffectually and pulled at its hair while her throat was being squeezed by its jaws. To the end she reminded me of us: her eyes expressed fear in such a humanlike way, as did her strained whimpers. She made an attempt to climb onto the tarpaulin. The hyena violently shook her. She fell off the bench to the bottom of the lifeboat, the hyena with her. I heard noises but no longer saw anything.

I was next. That much was clear to me. With some difficulty I stood up. I could hardly see through the tears in my eyes. I was no longer crying because of my family or because of my impending death. I was far too numb to consider either. I was crying because I was exceedingly tired and it was time to get rest.

I advanced over the tarpaulin. Though tautly stretched at the end of the boat, it sagged a little in the middle; it made for three or four toilsome, bouncy steps. And I had to reach over the net and the rolled-up tarpaulin. And these efforts in a lifeboat that was constantly rolling. In the condition I was in, it felt like a great trek. When I laid my foot on the middle cross bench, its hardness had an invigorating effect on me, as if I had just stepped on solid ground. I planted both my feet on the bench and enjoyed my firm stand. I was feeling dizzy, but since the capital moment of my life was coming up this dizziness only added to my sense of frightened sublimity. I raised my hands to the level of my chest—the weapons I had against the hyena. It looked up at me. Its mouth was red. Orange Juice lay next to it, against the dead zebra. Her arms were spread wide open and her short legs were folded together and slightly turned to one side. She looked like a simian Christ on the Cross. Except for her head. She was beheaded. The neck wound was still bleeding. It was a sight horrible to the eyes and killing to the spirit. Just before throwing myself upon the hyena, to collect myself before the final struggle, I looked down.

Between my feet, under the bench, I beheld Richard Parker's head. It was gigantic. It looked the size of the planet Jupiter to my dazed senses. His paws were like volumes of *Encyclopaedia Britannica*.

I made my way back to the bow and collapsed.

I spent the night in a state of delirium. I kept thinking I had slept and was awaking after dreaming of a tiger.

CHAPTER 48

Richard Parker was so named because of a clerical error. A panther was terrorizing the Khulna district of Bangladesh, just outside the Sundarbans. It had recently carried off a little girl. All that was found of her was a tiny hand with a henna pattern on the palm and a few plastic bangles. She was the seventh person killed in two months by the marauder. And it was growing bolder. The previous victim was a man who had been attacked in broad daylight in his field. The beast dragged him off into the forest, where it ate a good part of his head, the flesh off his right leg and all his innards. His corpse was found hanging in the fork of a tree. The villagers kept a watch nearby that night, hoping to surprise the panther and kill it, but it never appeared. The Forest Department hired a professional hunter. He set up a small, hidden platform in a tree near a river where two of the attacks had taken place. A goat was tied to a stake on the river's bank. The hunter waited several nights. He assumed the panther would be an old, wasted male with worn teeth, incapable of catching anything more difficult than a human. But it was a sleek tiger that stepped into the open one night. A female with a single cub. The goat bleated. Oddly, the cub, who looked to be about three months old, paid little attention to the goat. It raced to the water's edge, where it drank eagerly. Its mother followed suit. Of hunger and thirst, thirst is the greater imperative. Only once the tiger had quenched her thirst did she turn to the goat to satisfy her hunger. The hunter had two rifles with him: one with real bullets, the other with immobilizing darts. This animal was not the man-eater, but so close to human habitation she might pose a threat to the villagers, especially as she was with cub. He picked up the gun with the darts. He fired as the tiger was about to fell the goat. The tiger reared up and snarled and raced away. But immobilizing darts don't bring on sleep gently, like a good cup of tea; they knock out like a bottle of hard liquor straight up. A burst of activity on the animal's part makes it act all the faster. The hunter called his assistants on the radio. They found the tiger about two hundred yards from the river. She was still conscious. Her back legs had given way and her balance on her front legs was woozy. When the men got close, she tried to get away but could not manage it. She turned on them, lifting a paw that was meant to kill. It only made her lose her balance. She collapsed and the Pondicherry Zoo had two new tigers. The cub was found in a bush close by, meowing with fear. The hunter, whose name was Richard Parker, picked it up with his bare hands and, remembering how it had rushed to drink in the river, baptized it Thirsty. But the shipping clerk at the Howrah train station was evidently a man both befuddled and diligent. All the papers we received with the cub clearly stated that its name was Richard Parker, that the hunter's first name was Thirsty and that his family name was None Given. Father had had a good chuckle over the mix-up and Richard Parker's name had stuck.

I don't know if Thirsty None Given ever got the man-eating panther.

CHAPTER 49

In the morning I could not move. I was pinned by weakness to the tarpaulin. Even thinking was exhausting. I applied myself to thinking straight. At length, as slowly as a caravan of camels crossing a desert, some thoughts came together.

The day was like the previous one, warm and overcast, the clouds low, the breeze light. That was one thought. The boat was rocking gently, that was another.

I thought of sustenance for the first time. I had not had a drop to drink or a bite to eat or a minute of sleep in three days. Finding this obvious explanation for my weakness brought me a little strength.

Richard Parker was still on board. In fact, he was directly beneath me. Incredible that such a thing should need consent to be true, but it was only after much deliberation, upon assessing various mental items and points of view, that I concluded that it was not a dream or a delusion or a misplaced memory or a fancy or any other such falsity, but a solid, true thing witnessed while in a weakened, highly agitated state. The truth of it would be confirmed as soon as I felt well enough to investigate.

How I had failed to notice for two and a half days a 450-pound Bengal tiger in a lifeboat twenty-six feet long was a conundrum I would have to try to crack later, when I had more energy. The feat surely made Richard Parker the largest stowaway, proportionally speaking, in the history of navigation. From tip of nose to tip of tail he took up over a third of the length of the ship he was on.

You might think I lost all hope at that point. I did. And as a result I perked up and felt much better. We see that in sports all the time, don't we? The tennis challenger starts strong but soon loses confidence in his playing. The champion racks up the games. But in the final set, when the challenger has nothing left to lose, he becomes relaxed again, insouciant, daring. Suddenly he's playing like the devil and the champion must work hard to get those last points. So it was with me. To cope with a hyena seemed remotely possible, but I was so obviously outmatched by Richard Parker that it wasn't even worth worrying about. With a tiger aboard, my life was over. That being settled, why not do something about my parched throat?

I believe it was this that saved my life that morning, that I was quite literally dying of thirst. Now that the word had popped into my head I couldn't think of anything else, as if the word itself were salty and the more I thought of it, the worse the effect. I have heard that the hunger for air exceeds as a compelling sensation the thirst for water. Only for a few minutes, I say. After a few minutes you die and the discomfort of asphyxiation goes away. Whereas thirst is a drawn-out affair. Look: Christ on the Cross died of suffocation, but His only complaint was of thirst. If thirst can be so taxing that even God Incarnate complains about it, imagine the effect on a regular human. It was enough to make me go raving mad. I have never known a worse physical hell than this putrid taste and pasty feeling in the mouth, this unbearable pressure at the back of the throat, this sensation that my blood was turning to a thick syrup that barely flowed. Truly, by comparison, a tiger was nothing.

And so I pushed aside all thoughts of Richard Parker and fearlessly went exploring for fresh water.

The divining rod in my mind dipped sharply and a spring gushed water when I remembered that I was on a genuine, regulation lifeboat and that such a lifeboat was surely outfitted with supplies. That seemed like a perfectly reasonable proposition. What captain would fail in so elementary a way to ensure the safety of his crew? What ship chandler would not think of making a little extra money under the noble guise of saving lives? It was settled. There was water aboard. All I had to do was find it.

Which meant I had to move.

I made it to the middle of the boat, to the edge of the tarpaulin. It was a hard crawl. I felt I was climbing the side of a volcano and I was about to look over the rim into a boiling cauldron of orange lava. I lay flat. I carefully brought my head over. I did not look over any more than I had to. I did not see Richard Parker. The hyena was plainly visible, though. It was back behind what was left of the zebra. It was looking at me.

I was no longer afraid of it. It wasn't ten feet away, yet my heart didn't skip a beat. Richard Parker's presence had at least that useful aspect. To be afraid of this ridiculous dog when there was a tiger about was like being afraid of splinters when trees are falling down. I became very angry at the animal. "You ugly, foul creature," I muttered. The only reason I didn't stand up and beat it off the lifeboat with a stick was lack of strength and stick, not lack of heart.

Did the hyena sense something of my mastery? Did it say to itself, "Super alpha is watching me—I better not move"? I don't know. At any rate, it didn't move. In fact, in the way it ducked its head it seemed to want to hide from me. But it was no use hiding. It would get its just deserts soon enough.

Richard Parker also explained the animals' strange behaviour. Now it was clear why the hyena had confined itself to such an absurdly small space behind the zebra and why it had waited so long before killing it. It was fear of the greater beast and fear of touching the greater beast's food. The strained, temporary peace between Orange Juice and the hyena, and my reprieve, were no doubt due to the same reason: in the face of such a superior predator, all of us were prey, and normal ways of preying were affected. It seemed the presence of a tiger had saved me from a hyena—surely a textbook example of jumping from the frying pan into the fire.

But the great beast was not behaving like a great beast, to such an extent that the hyena had taken liberties. Richard Parker's passivity, and for three long days, needed explaining. Only in two ways could I account for it: sedation and seasickness. Father regularly sedated a number of the animals to lessen their stress. Might he have sedated Richard Parker shortly before the ship sank? Had the shock of the shipwreck—the noises, the falling into the sea, the terrible struggle to swim to the lifeboat—increased the effect of the sedative? Had seasickness taken over after that? These were the only plausible explanations I could come up with.

I lost interest in the question. Only water interested me.

I took stock of the lifeboat.

CHAPTER 50

It was three and a half feet deep, eight feet wide and twenty-six feet long, exactly. I know because it was printed on one of the side benches in black letters. It also said that the lifeboat was designed to accommodate a maximum of thirty-two people. Wouldn't that have been merry, sharing it with so many? Instead we were three and it was awfully crowded. The boat was symmetrically shaped, with rounded ends that were hard to tell apart. The stern was hinted at by a small fixed rudder, no more than a rearward extension of the keel, while the bow, except for my addition, featured a stem with the saddest, bluntest prow in boat-building history. The aluminum hull was studded with rivets and painted white.

That was the outside of the lifeboat. Inside, it was not as spacious as might be expected because of the side benches and the buoyancy tanks. The side benches ran the whole length of the boat, merging at the bow and stern to form end benches that were roughly triangular in shape. The benches were the top surfaces of the sealed buoyancy tanks. The side benches were one and a half feet wide and the end benches were three feet deep; the open space of the lifeboat was thus twenty feet long and five feet wide. That made a territory of one hundred square feet for Richard Parker. Spanning this space widthwise were three cross benches, including the one smashed by the zebra. These benches were two feet wide and were evenly spaced. They were two feet above the floor of the boat—the play Richard Parker had before he would knock his head against the ceiling, so to speak, if he were beneath a bench. Under the tarpaulin, he had another twelve inches of space, the distance between the gunnel, which supported the tarpaulin, and the benches, so three feet in all, barely enough for him to stand. The floor, consisting of narrow planks of treated wood, was flat and the vertical sides of the buoyancy tanks were at right angles to it. So, curiously, the boat had rounded ends and rounded sides, but the interior volume was rectangular.

It seems orange—such a nice Hindu colour—is the colour of survival because the whole inside of the boat and the tarpaulin and the life jackets and the lifebuoy and the oars and most every ther significant object aboard was orange. Even the plastic, beadless whistles were orange.

The words *Tsimtsum* and *Panama* were printed on each side of the bow in stark, black, roman capitals.

The tarpaulin was made of tough, treated canvas, rough on the skin after a while. It had been unrolled to just past the middle cross bench. So one cross bench was hidden beneath the tarpaulin, in Richard Parker's den; the middle cross bench was just beyond the edge of the tarpaulin, in the open; and the third cross bench lay broken beneath the dead zebra.

There were six oarlocks, U-shaped notches in the gunnel for holding an oar in place, and five oars, since I had lost one trying to push Richard Parker away. Three oars rested on one side bench, one rested on the other and one made up my life-saving prow. I doubted the usefulness of these oars as a means of propulsion. This lifeboat was no racing shell. It was a heavy, solid construction designed for stolid floating, not for navigating, though I suppose that if we had been thirty-two to row we could have made some headway.

I did not grasp all these details—and many more—right away. They came to my notice with time and as a result of necessity. I would be in the direst of dire straits, facing a bleak future, when some small thing, some detail, would transform itself and appear in my mind in a new light. It would no longer be the small thing it was before, but the most important thing in the world, the thing that would save my life. This happened time and again. How true it is that necessity is the mother of invention, how very true.

CHAPTER 51

But that first time I had a good look at the lifeboat I did not see the detail I wanted. The surface of the stern and side benches was continuous and unbroken, as were the sides of the buoyancy tanks. The floor lay flat against the hull; there could be no cache beneath it. It was certain: there was no locker or box or any other sort of container anywhere. Only smooth, uninterrupted orange surfaces.

My estimation of captains and ship chandlers wavered. My hopes for survival flickered. My thirst remained.

And what if the supplies were at the bow, beneath the tarpaulin? I turned and crawled back. I felt like a dried-out lizard. I pushed down on the tarpaulin. It was tautly stretched. If I unrolled it, I would give myself access to what supplies might be stored below. But that meant creating an opening onto Richard Parker's den.

There was no question. Thirst pushed me on. I eased the oar from under the tarpaulin. I placed the lifebuoy around my waist. I laid the oar across the bow. I leaned over the gunnel and with my thumbs pushed from under one of the hooks the rope that held down the tarpaulin. I had a difficult time of it. But after the first hook, it was easier with the second and the third. I did the same on the other side of the stem. The tarpaulin became slack beneath my elbows. I was lying flat on it, my legs pointed towards the stern.

I unrolled it a little. Immediately I was rewarded. The bow was like the stern; it had an end bench. And upon it, just a few inches from the stem, a hasp glittered like a diamond. There was the outline of a lid. My heart began to pound. I unrolled the tarpaulin further. I peeked under. The lid was shaped like a rounded-out triangle, three feet wide and two feet deep. At that moment I perceived an orange mass. I jerked my head back. But the orange wasn't moving and didn't look right. I looked again. It wasn't a tiger. It was a life jacket. There were a number of life jackets at the back of Richard Parker's den.

A shiver went through my body. Between the life jackets, partially, as if through some leaves, I had my first, unambiguous, clear-headed glimpse of Richard Parker. It was his haunches I could see, and part of his back. Tawny and striped and simply enormous. He was facing the stern, lying flat on his stomach. He was still except for the breathing motion of his sides. I blinked in disbelief at how close he was. He was right there, two feet beneath me. Stretching, I could have pinched his bottom. And between us there was nothing but a thin tarpaulin, easily got round.

"God preserve me!" No supplication was ever more passionate yet more gently carried by the breath. I lay absolutely motionless.

I had to have water. I brought my hand down and quietly undid the hasp. I pulled on the lid. It opened onto a locker.

I have just mentioned the notion of details that become lifesavers.

Here was one: the lid was hinged an inch or so from the edge of the bow bench—which meant that as the lid opened, it became a barrier that closed off the twelve inches of open space between tarpaulin and bench through which Richard Parker could get to me after pushing aside the life jackets. I opened the lid till it fell against the crosswise oar and the edge of the tarpaulin. I moved onto the stem, facing the boat, one foot on the edge of the open locker, the other against the lid. If Richard Parker decided to attack me from below, he would have to push on the lid. Such a push would both warn me and help me fall backwards into the water with the lifebuoy. If he came the other way, climbing atop the tarpaulin from astern, I was in the best position to see him early and, again, take to the water. I looked about the lifeboat. I couldn't see any sharks.

I looked down between my legs. I thought I would faint for joy. The open locker glistened with shiny new things. Oh, the delight of the manufactured good, the man-made device, the created thing! That moment of material revelation brought an intensity of pleasure—a heady mix of hope, surprise, disbelief, thrill, gratitude, all crushed into one—unequalled in my life by any Christmas, birthday, wedding, Diwali or other gift-giving occasion. I was positively giddy with happiness.

My eyes immediately fell upon what I was looking for. Whether in a bottle, a tin can or a carton, water is unmistakably packaged. On this lifeboat, the wine of life was served in pale golden cans that fit nicely in the hand. *Drinking Water* said the vintage label in black letters. *HP Foods Ltd.* were the vintners. *500 ml* were the contents. There were stacks of these cans, too many to count at a glance.

With a shaking hand I reached down and picked one up. It was cool to the touch and heavy. I shook it. The bubble of air inside made a dull *glub glub glub* sound. I was about to be delivered from my hellish thirst. My pulse raced at the thought. I only had to open the can.

I paused. How would I do that?

I had a can—surely I had a can opener? I looked in the locker. There was a great quantity of things. I rummaged about. I was losing patience. Aching expectation had run its fruitful course. I had to drink *now*—or I would die. I could not find the desired instrument. But there was no time for useless distress. Action was needed. Could I prise it open with my fingernails? I tried. I couldn't. My teeth? It wasn't worth trying. I looked over the gunnel. The tarpaulin hooks. Short, blunt, solid. I kneeled on the bench and leaned over. Holding the can with both my hands, I sharply brought it up against a hook. A good dint. I did it again. Another dint next to the first. By dint of dinting, I managed the trick. A pearl of water appeared. I licked it off. I turned the can and banged the opposite side of the top against the hook to make another hole. I worked like a fiend. I made a larger hole. I sat back on the gunnel. I held the can up to my face. I opened my mouth. I tilted the can.

My feelings can perhaps be imagined, but they can hardly be described. To the gurgling beat of my greedy throat, pure, delicious, beautiful, crystalline water flowed into my system. Liquid life, it was. I drained that golden cup to the very last drop, sucking at the hole to catch any remaining moisture. I went, "Ahhhhhh!", tossed the can overboard and got another one. I opened it the way I had the first and its contents vanished just as quickly. That can sailed overboard too, and I opened the next one. Which, shortly, also ended up in the ocean. Another can was dispatched. I drank four cans, two litres of that most exquisite of nectars, before I stopped. You might think such a rapid intake of water after prolonged thirst might upset my system. Nonsense! I never felt better in my life. Why, feel my brow! My forehead was wet with fresh, clean, refreshing perspiration. Everything in me, right down to the pores of my skin, was expressing joy.

A sense of well-being quickly overcame me. My mouth became moist and soft. I forgot about the back of my throat. My skin relaxed.

My joints moved with greater ease. My heart began to beat like a merry drum and blood started flowing through my veins like cars from a wedding party honking their way through town. Strength and suppleness came back to my muscles. My head became clearer. Truly, I was coming back to life from the dead. It was glorious, it was glorious. I tell you, to be drunk on alcohol is disgraceful, but to be drunk on water is noble and ecstatic. I basked in bliss and plenitude for several minutes.

A certain emptiness made itself felt. I touched my belly. It was a hard and hollow cavity. Food would be nice now. A masala dosai with a coconut chutney—hmmmmm! Even better: oothappam! HMM-MMM! Oh! I brought my hands to my mouth—IDLI! The mere thought of the word provoked a shot of pain behind my jaws and a deluge of saliva in my mouth. My right hand started twitching. It reached and nearly touched the delicious flattened balls of parboiled rice in my imagination. It sank its fingers into their steaming hot flesh . . . It formed a ball soaked with sauce . . . It brought it to my mouth . . . I chewed . . . Oh, it was exquisitely painful!

I looked into the locker for food. I found cartons of Seven Oceans Standard Emergency Ration, from faraway, exotic Bergen, Norway. The breakfast that was to make up for nine missed meals, not to mention odd tiffins that Mother had brought along, came in a half-kilo block, dense, solid and vacuum-packed in silver-coloured plastic that was covered with instructions in twelve languages. In English it said the ration consisted of eighteen fortified biscuits of baked wheat, *animal fat* and glucose, and that no more than six should be eaten in a twenty-four-hour period. Pity about the fat, but given the exceptional circumstances the vegetarian part of me would simply pinch its nose and bear it.

At the top of the block were the words *Tear here to open* and a black arrow pointing to the edge of the plastic. The edge gave way under my fingers. Nine wax-paper-wrapped rectangular bars tumbled out. I unwrapped one. It naturally broke into two. Two nearly square biscuits, pale in colour and fragrant in smell. I bit into one. Lord, who would have thought? I never suspected. It was a secret held from me: Norwegian cuisine was the best in the world! These biscuits were amazingly good. They were savoury and delicate to the palate, neither too sweet nor too salty. They broke up under the teeth with a delightful crunching sound. Mixed with saliva, they made a granular paste that was enchantment to the tongue and mouth. And when I swallowed, my stomach had only one thing to say: Hallelujah!

The whole package disappeared in a few minutes, wrapping paper flying away in the wind. I considered opening another carton, but I thought better. No harm in exercising a little restraint. Actually, with half a kilo of emergency ration in my stomach, I felt quite heavy.

I decided I should find out what exactly was in the treasure chest before me. It was a large locker, larger than its opening. The space extended right down to the hull and ran some little ways into the side benches. I lowered my feet into the locker and sat on its edge, my back against the stem. I counted the cartons of Seven Ocean. I had eaten one; there were thirty-one left. According to the instructions, each 500-gram carton was supposed to last one survivor three days. That meant I had food rations to last me—31 x 3—93 days! The instructions also suggested survivors restrict themselves to half a litre of water every twenty-four hours. I counted the cans of water. There were 124. Each contained half a litre. So I had water rations to last me 124 days. Never had simple arithmetic brought such a smile to my face.

What else did I have? I plunged my arm eagerly into the locker and brought up one marvellous object after another. Each one, no matter what it was, soothed me. I was so sorely in need of company and comfort that the attention brought to making each one of these mass-produced goods felt like a special attention paid to me. I repeatedly mumbled, "Thank you! Thank you! Thank you!"

CHAPTER 52

After a thorough investigation, I made a complete list:

- 192 tablets of anti-seasickness medicine
- 124 tin cans of fresh water, each containing 500 millilitres, so 62 litres in all
- 32 plastic vomit bags
- 31 cartons of emergency rations, 500 grams each, so 15.5 kilos in all
- 16 wool blankets
- 12 solar stills
- 10 or so orange life jackets, each with an orange, beadless whistle attached by a string
- 6 morphine ampoule syringes
- 6 hand flares
- 5 buoyant oars
- 4 rocket parachute flares
- 3 tough, transparent plastic bags, each with a capacity of about 50 litres
- 3 can openers
- 3 graduated glass beakers for drinking
- 2 boxes of waterproof matches
- 2 buoyant orange smoke signals
- 2 mid-size orange plastic buckets
- 2 buoyant orange plastic bailing cups
- 2 multi-purpose plastic containers with airtight lids
- 2 yellow rectangular sponges
- 2 buoyant synthetic ropes, each 50 metres long

- 2 non-buoyant synthetic ropes of unspecified length, but each at least 30 metres long
- 2 fishing kits with hooks, lines and sinkers
- 2 gaffs with very sharp barbed hooks
- 2 sea anchors
- 2 hatchets
- 2 rain catchers
- 2 black ink ballpoint pens
- 1 nylon cargo net
- 1 solid lifebuoy with an inner diameter of 40 centimetres and an outer diameter of 80 centimetres, and an attached rope
- 1 large hunting knife with a solid handle, a pointed end and one edge a sharp blade and the other a sawtoothed blade; attached by a long string to a ring in the locker
- 1 sewing kit with straight and curving needles and strong white thread
- 1 first-aid kit in a waterproof plastic case
- 1 signalling mirror
- 1 pack of filter-tipped Chinese cigarettes
- 1 large bar of dark chocolate
- 1 survival manual
- 1 compass
- 1 notebook with 98 lined pages
- 1 boy with a complete set of light clothing but for one lost shoe
- 1 spotted hyena
- 1 Bengal tiger
- 1 lifeboat
- 1 ocean
- 1 God

I ate a quarter of the large chocolate bar. I examined one of the rain catchers. It was a device that looked like an inverted umbrella with a good-sized catchment pouch and a connecting rubber tube.

I crossed my arms on the lifebuoy around my waist, brought my head down and fell soundly asleep.

CHAPTER 53

I slept all morning. I was roused by anxiety. That tide of food, water and rest that flowed through my weakened system, bringing me a new lease on life, also brought me the strength to see how desperate my situation was. I awoke to the reality of Richard Parker. There was a tiger in the lifeboat. I could hardly believe it, yet I knew I had to. And I had to save myself.

I considered jumping overboard and swimming away, but my body refused to move. I was hundreds of miles from landfall, if not over a thousand miles. I couldn't swim such a distance, even with a lifebuoy. What would I eat? What would I drink? How would I keep the sharks away? How would I keep warm? How would I know which way to go? There was not a shadow of doubt about the matter: to leave the lifeboat meant certain death. But what was staying aboard? He would come at me like a typical cat, without a sound. Before I knew it he would seize the back of my neck or my throat and I would be pierced by fang-holes. I wouldn't be able to speak. The lifeblood would flow out of me unmarked by a final utterance. Or he would kill me by clubbing me with one of his great paws, breaking my neck.

"I'm going to die," I blubbered through quivering lips.

Oncoming death is terrible enough, but worse still is oncoming death with time to spare, time in which all the happiness that was yours and all the happiness that might have been yours becomes clear to you. You see with utter lucidity all that you are losing. The sight brings on an oppressive sadness that no car about to hit you or water about to drown you can match. The feeling is truly unbearable. The words *Father, Mother, Ravi, India, Winnipeg* struck me with searing poignancy.

I was giving up. I would have given up—if a voice hadn't made itself heard in my heart. The voice said, "I will not die. I refuse it. I will make it through this nightmare. I will beat the odds, as great as they are. I have survived so far, miraculously. Now I will turn miracle into routine. The amazing will be seen every day. I will put in all the hard work necessary. Yes, so long as God is with me, I will not die. Amen."

My face set to a grim and determined expression. I speak in all modesty as I say this, but I discovered at that moment that I have a fierce will to live. It's not something evident, in my experience. Some of us give up on life with only a resigned sigh. Others fight a little, then lose hope. Still others—and I am one of those—never give up. We fight and fight and fight. We fight no matter the cost of battle, the losses we take, the improbability of success. We fight to the very end. It's not a question of courage. It's something constitutional, an inability to let go. It may be nothing more than life-hungry stupidity.

Richard Parker started growling that very instant, as if he had been waiting for me to become a worthy opponent. My chest became tight with fear.

"Quick, man, quick," I wheezed. I had to organize my survival. Not a second to waste. I needed shelter and right away. I thought of the prow I had made with an oar. But now the tarpaulin was unrolled at the bow; there was nothing to hold the oar in place. And I had no proof that hanging at the end of an oar provided real safety from Richard Parker. He might easily reach and nab me. I had to find something else. My mind worked fast.

I built a raft. The oars, if you remember, floated. And I had life jackets and a sturdy lifebuoy.

With bated breath I closed the locker and reached beneath the tarpaulin for the extra oars on the side benches. Richard Parker noticed. I could see him through the life jackets. As I dragged each oar out—you can imagine how carefully—he stirred in reaction. But he did not turn. I pulled out three oars. A fourth was already resting crosswise on the tarpaulin. I raised the locker lid to close the opening onto Richard Parker's den.

I had four buoyant oars. I set them on the tarpaulin around the lifebuoy. The lifebuoy was now squared by the oars. My raft looked like a game of tic-tac-toe with an O in the centre as the first move.

Now came the dangerous part. I needed the life jackets. Richard Parker's growling was now a deep rumble that shook the air. The hyena responded with a whine, a wavering, high-pitched whine, a sure sign that trouble was on the way.

I had no choice. I had to act. I lowered the lid again. The life jackets were at hand's reach. Some were right against Richard Parker. The hyena broke into a scream.

I reached for the closest life jacket. I had difficulty grasping it, my hand was trembling so much. I pulled the jacket out. Richard Parker did not seem to notice. I pulled another one out. And another. I was feeling faint with fear. I was having great difficulty breathing. If need be, I told myself, I could throw myself overboard with these life jackets. I pulled a last one out. I had four life jackets.

Pulling the oars in one after the next, I worked them through the armholes of the life jackets—in one armhole, out the other—so that the life jackets became secured to the four corners of the raft. I tied each one shut.

I found one of the buoyant ropes in the locker. With the knife, I cut four segments. I tightly lashed the four oars where they met. Ah, to have had a practical education in knots! At each corner I made ten knots and still I worried that the oars would come apart. I worked feverishly, all the while cursing my stupidity. A tiger aboard and I had waited three days and three nights to save my life!

I cut four more segments of the buoyant rope and tied the lifebuoy to each side of the square. I wove the lifebuoy's rope through the life jackets, around the oars, in and out of the lifebuoy—all round the raft—as yet another precaution against the raft breaking into pieces.

The hyena was now screaming at top pitch.

One last thing to do. "God, give me the time," I implored. I took the rest of the buoyant line. There was a hole that went through the stem of the boat, near the top. I brought the buoyant rope through it and hitched it. I only had to hitch the other end of the rope to the raft and I might be saved.

The hyena fell silent. My heart stopped and then beat triple speed. I turned.

"Jesus, Mary, Muhammad and Vishnu!"

I saw a sight that will stay with me for the rest of my days. Richard Parker had risen and emerged. He was not fifteen feet from me. Oh, the size of him! The hyena's end had come, and mine. I stood rooted to the spot, paralyzed, in thrall to the action before my eyes. My brief experience with the relations of unconfined wild animals in lifeboats had made me expect great noise and protest when the time came for bloodshed. But it happened practically in silence. The hyena died neither whining nor whimpering, and Richard Parker killed without a sound. The flame-coloured carnivore emerged from beneath the tarpaulin and made for the hyena. The hyena was leaning against the stern bench, behind the zebra's carcass, transfixed. It did not put up a fight. Instead it shrank to the floor, lifting a forepaw in a futile gesture of defence. The look on its face was of terror. A massive paw landed on its shoulders. Richard Parker's jaws closed on the side of the hyena's neck. Its glazed eyes widened. There was a noise of organic crunching as windpipe and spinal cord were crushed. The hyena shook. Its eyes went dull. It was over.

Richard Parker let go and growled. But a quiet growl, private and half-hearted, it seemed. He was panting, his tongue hanging from his mouth. He licked his chops. He shook his head. He sniffed the dead hyena. He raised his head high and smelled the air. He placed his forepaws on the stern bench and lifted himself. His feet were wide apart. The rolling of the boat, though gentle, was visibly not to his liking. He looked beyond the gunnel at the open seas. He put out a low, mean snarl. He smelled the air again. He slowly turned his head. It turned—turned—turned full round—till he was looking straight at me.

I wish I could describe what happened next, not as I saw it, which I might manage, but as I felt it. I beheld Richard Parker from the angle that showed him off to greatest effect: from the back, half-raised, with his head turned. The stance had something of a pose to it, as if it were an intentional, even affected, display of mighty art. And what art, what might. His presence was overwhelming, yet equally evident was the lithesome grace of it. He was incredibly muscular, yet his haunches were thin and his glossy coat hung loosely on his frame. His body, bright brownish orange streaked with black vertical stripes, was incomparably beautiful, matched with a tailor's eye for harmony by his pure white chest and underside and the black rings of his long tail. His head was large and round, displaying formidable sideburns, a stylish goatee and some of the finest whiskers of the cat world, thick, long and white. Atop the head were small, expressive ears shaped like perfect arches. His carrot orange face had a broad bridge and a pink nose, and it was made up with brazen flair. Wavy dabs of black circled the face in a pattern that was striking yet subtle, for it brought less attention to itself than it did to the one part of the face left untouched by it, the bridge, whose rufous lustre shone nearly with a radiance. The patches of white above the eyes, on the cheeks and around the mouth came off as finishing touches worthy of a Kathakali dancer. The result was a face that looked like the wings of a butterfly and bore an expression vaguely old and Chinese. But when Richard Parker's amber eyes met mine, the stare was intense, cold and unflinching, not flighty or friendly, and spoke of self-possession on the point of exploding with rage. His ears twitched and then swivelled right around. One of his lips began to rise and fall. The yellow canine thus coyly revealed was as long as my longest finger.

Every hair on me was standing up, shrieking with fear.

That's when the rat appeared. Out of nowhere, a scrawny brown rat materialized on the side bench, nervous and breathless. Richard Parker looked as astonished as I was. The rat leapt onto the tarpaulin and raced my way. At the sight, in shock and surprise, my legs gave way beneath me and I practically fell into the locker. Before my in-credulous eyes the rodent hopped over the various parts of the raft, jumped onto me and climbed to the top of my head, where I felt its little claws clamping down on my scalp, holding on for dear life.

Richard Parker's eyes had followed the rat. They were now fixed on my head.

He completed the turn of his head with a slow turn of his body, moving his forepaws sideways along the side bench. He dropped to the floor of the boat with ponderous ease. I could see the top of his head, his back and his long, curled tail. His ears lay flat against his skull. In three paces he was at the middle of the boat. Without effort the front half of his body rose in the air and his forepaws came to rest on the rolled-up edge of the tarpaulin.

He was less than ten feet away. His head, his chest, his paws—so big! so big! His teeth—an entire army battalion in a mouth. He was making to jump onto the tarpaulin. I was about to die.

But the tarpaulin's strange softness bothered him. He pressed at it tentatively. He looked up anxiously—the exposure to so much light and open space did not please him either. And the rolling motion of the boat continued to unsettle him. For a brief moment, Richard Parker was hesitating.

I grabbed the rat and threw it his way. I can still see it in my mind as it sailed through the air—its outstretched claws and erect tail, its tiny elongated scrotum and pinpoint anus. Richard Parker opened his maw and the squealing rat disappeared into it like a baseball into a catcher's mitt. Its hairless tail vanished like a spaghetti noodle sucked into a mouth.

He seemed satisfied with the offering. He backed down and returned beneath the tarpaulin. My legs instantly became functional again. I leapt up and raised the locker lid again to block the open space between bow bench and tarpaulin.

I heard loud sniffing and the noise of a body being dragged. His shifting weight made the boat rock a little. I began hearing the sound of a mouth eating. I peeked beneath the tarpaulin. He was in the middle of the boat. He was eating the hyena by great chunks, voraciously. This chance would not come again. I reached and retrieved the remaining life jackets—six in all—and the last oar. They would go to improving the raft. I noticed in passing a smell. It was not the sharp smell of cat piss. It was vomit. There was a patch of it on the floor of the boat. It must have come from Richard Parker. So he was indeed seasick.

I hitched the long rope to the raft. Lifeboat and raft were now tethered. Next I attached a life jacket to each side of the raft, on its underside. Another life jacket I strapped across the hole of the lifebuoy to act as a seat. I turned the last oar into a footrest, lashing it on one side of the raft, about two feet from the lifebuoy, and tying the remaining life jacket to it. My fingers trembled as I worked, and my breath was short and strained. I checked and rechecked all my knots.

I looked about the sea. Only great, gentle swells. No whitecaps. The wind was low and constant. I looked down. There were fish— big fish with protruding foreheads and very long dorsal fins, *dorados* they are called, and smaller fish, lean and long, unknown to me, and smaller ones still—and there were sharks.

I eased the raft off the lifeboat. If for some reason it did not float, I was as good as dead. It took to the water beautifully. In fact, the buoyancy of the life jackets was such that they pushed the oars and the lifebuoy right out of the water. But my heart sank. As soon as the raft touched the water, the fish scattered—except for the sharks. They remained. Three or four of them. One swam directly beneath the raft. Richard Parker growled.

I felt like a prisoner being pushed off a plank by pirates.

I brought the raft as close to the lifeboat as the protruding tips of the oars would allow. I leaned out and lay my hands on the lifebuoy. Through the "cracks" in the floor of the raft—yawning crevasses would be more accurate—I looked directly into the bottomless depths of the sea. I heard Richard Parker again. I flopped onto the raft on my stomach. I lay flat and spread-eagled and did not move a finger. I expected the raft to overturn at any moment. Or a shark to lunge and bite right through the life jackets and oars. Neither happened. The raft sank lower and pitched and rolled, the tips of the oars dipping underwater, but it floated robustly. Sharks came close, but did not touch.

I felt a gentle tug. The raft swung round. I raised my head. The lifeboat and the raft had already separated as far as the rope would go, about forty feet. The rope tensed and lifted out of the water and wavered in the air. It was a highly distressing sight. I had fled the lifeboat to save my life. Now I wanted to get back. This raft business was far too precarious. It only needed a shark to bite the rope, or a knot to become undone, or a large wave to crash upon me, and I would be lost.

Compared to the raft, the lifeboat now seemed a haven of comfort and security.

I gingerly turned over. I sat up. Stability was good, so far. My footrest worked well enough. But it was all too small. There was just enough space to sit on and no more. This toy raft, mini-raft, micro-raft, might do for a pond, but not for the Pacific Ocean. I took hold of the rope and pulled. The closer I got to the lifeboat, the slower I pulled. When I was next to the lifeboat, I heard Richard Parker. He was still eating.

I hesitated for long minutes.

I stayed on the raft. I didn't see what else I could do. My options were limited to perching above a tiger or hovering over sharks. I knew perfectly well how dangerous Richard Parker was. Sharks, on the other hand, had not yet proved to be dangerous. I checked the knots that held the rope to the lifeboat and to the raft. I let the rope out until I was thirty or so feet from the lifeboat, the distance that about rightly balanced my two fears: being too close to Richard Parker and being too far from the lifeboat. The extra rope, ten feet or so, I looped around the footrest oar. I could easily let out slack if the need arose.

The day was ending. It started to rain. It had been overcast and warm all day. Now the temperature dropped, and the downpour was steady and cold. All around me heavy drops of fresh water plopped loudly and wastefully into the sea, dimpling its surface. I pulled on the rope again. When I was at the bow I turned onto my knees and took hold of the stem. I pulled myself up and carefully peeped over the gunnel. He wasn't in sight.

I hurriedly reached down into the locker. I grabbed a rain catcher, a fifty-litre plastic bag, a blanket and the survival manual. I slammed the locker lid shut. I didn't mean to slam it—only to protect my precious goods from the rain—but the lid slipped from my wet hand. It was a bad mistake. In the very act of revealing myself to Richard Parker by bringing down what blocked his view, I made a great loud noise to attract his attention. He was crouched over the hyena. His head turned instantly. Many animals intensely dislike being disturbed while they are eating. Richard Parker snarled. His claws tensed. The tip of his tail twitched electrically. I fell back onto the raft, and I believe it was terror as much as wind and current that widened the distance between raft and lifeboat so swiftly. I let out all the rope. I expected Richard Parker to burst forth from the boat, sailing through the air, teeth and claws reaching for me. I kept my eyes on the boat. The longer I looked, the more unbearable was the expectation.

He did not appear.

By the time I had opened the rain catcher above my head and tucked my feet into the plastic bag, I was already soaked to the bones. And the blanket had got wet when I fell back onto the raft. I wrapped myself with it nonetheless.

Night crept up. My surroundings disappeared into pitch-black darkness. Only the regular tugging of the rope at the raft told me that I was still attached to the lifeboat. The sea, inches beneath me yet too far for my eyes, buffeted the raft. Fingers of water reached up furtively through the cracks and wet my bottom.

CHAPTER 54

It rained all night. I had a horrible, sleepless time of it. It was noisy. On the rain catcher the rain made a drumming sound, and around me, coming from the darkness beyond, it made a hissing sound, as if I were at the centre of a great nest of angry snakes. Shifts in the wind changed the direction of the rain so that parts of me that were beginning to feel warm were soaked anew. I shifted the rain catcher, only to be unpleasantly surprised a few minutes later when the wind changed once more. I tried to keep a small part of me dry and warm, around my chest, where I had placed the survival manual, but the wetness spread with perverse determination. I spent the whole night shivering with cold. I worried constantly that the raft would come apart, that the knots holding me to the lifeboat would become loose, that a shark would attack. With my hands I checked the knots and lashings incessantly, trying to read them the way a blind man would read Braille.

The rain grew stronger and the sea rougher as the night progressed. The rope to the lifeboat tautened with a jerk rather than with a tug, and the rocking of the raft became more pronounced and erratic. It continued to float, rising above every wave, but there was no freeboard and the surf of every breaking wave rode clear across it, washing around me like a river washing around a boulder. The sea was warmer than the rain, but it meant that not the smallest part of me stayed dry that night.

At least I drank. I wasn't really thirsty, but I forced myself to drink. The rain catcher looked like an inverted umbrella, an umbrella blown open by the wind. The rain flowed to its centre, where there was a hole. The hole was connected by a rubber tube to a catchment pouch made of thick, transparent plastic. At first the water had a rubbery taste, but quickly the rain rinsed the catcher and the water tasted fine.

During those long, cold, dark hours, as the pattering of the invisible rain got to be deafening, and the sea hissed and coiled and tossed me about, I held on to one thought: Richard Parker. I hatched several plans to get rid of him so that the lifeboat might be mine.

Plan Number One: Push Him off the Lifeboat. What good would that do? Even if I did manage to shove 450 pounds of living, fierce animal off the lifeboat, tigers are accomplished swimmers. In the

Sundarbans they have been known to swim five miles in open, choppy waters. If he found himself unexpectedly overboard, Richard Parker would simply tread water, climb back aboard and make me pay the price for my treachery.

Plan Number Two: Kill Him with the Six Morphine Syringes. But I had no idea what effect they would have on him. Would they be enough to kill him? And how exactly was I supposed to get the morphine into his system? I could remotely conceive surprising him once, for an instant, the way his mother had been when she was captured— but to surprise him long enough to give him *six consecutive injections*? Impossible. All I would do by pricking him with a needle would be to get a cuff in return that would take my head off.

Plan Number Three: Attack Him with All Available Weaponry. Ludicrous. I wasn't Tarzan. I was a puny, feeble, vegetarian life form. In India it took riding atop great big elephants and shooting with powerful rifles to kill tigers. What was I supposed to do here? Fire off a rocket flare in his face? Go at him with a hatchet in each hand and a knife between my teeth? Finish him off with straight and curving sewing needles? If I managed to *nick* him, it would be a feat. In return he would tear me apart limb by limb, organ by organ. For if there's one thing more dangerous than a healthy animal, it's an injured animal.

Plan Number Four: Choke Him. I had rope. If I stayed at the bow and got the rope to go around the stern and a noose to go around his neck, I could pull on the rope while he pulled to get at me. And so, in the very act of reaching for me, he would choke himself. A clever, suicidal plan.

Plan Number Five: Poison Him, Set Him on Fire, Electrocute Him. How? With what?

Plan Number Six: Wage a War of Attrition. All I had to do was let the unforgiving laws of nature run their course and I would be saved. Waiting for him to waste away and die would require no effort on my part. I had supplies for months to come. What did he have? Just a few dead animals that would soon go bad. What would he eat after that? Better still: where would he get water? He might last for weeks without food, but no animal, however mighty, can do without water for any extended period of time.

A modest glow of hope flickered to life within me, like a candle in the night. I had a plan and it was a good one. I only needed to survive to put it into effect.

CHAPTER 55

Dawn came and matters were worse for it. Because now, emerging from the darkness, I could see what before I had only felt, the great curtains of rain crashing down on me from towering heights and the waves that threw a path over me and trod me underfoot one after another.

Dull-eyed, shaking and numb, one hand gripping the rain catcher, the other clinging to the raft, I continued to wait.

Sometime later, with a suddenness emphasized by the silence that followed, the rain stopped. The sky cleared and the waves seemed to flee with the clouds. The change was as quick and radical as changing countries on land. I was now in a different ocean. Soon the sun was alone in the sky, and the ocean was a smooth skin reflecting the light with a million mirrors.

I was stiff, sore and exhausted, barely grateful to be still alive. The words "Plan Number Six, Plan Number Six, Plan Number Six" repeated themselves in my mind like a mantra and brought me a small measure of comfort, though I couldn't recall for the life of me what Plan Number Six was. Warmth started coming to my bones. I closed the rain catcher. I wrapped myself with the blanket and curled up on my side in such a way that no part of me touched the water. I fell asleep. I don't know how long I slept. It was mid-morning when I awoke, and hot. The blanket was nearly dry. It had been a brief bout of deep sleep. I lifted myself onto an elbow.

All about me was flatness and infinity, an endless panorama of blue. There was nothing to block my view. The vastness hit me like a punch in the stomach. I fell back, winded. This raft was a joke. It was nothing but a few sticks and a little cork held together by string. Water came through every crack. The depth beneath would make a bird dizzy. I caught sight of the lifeboat. It was no better than half a walnut shell. It held on to the surface of the water like fingers gripping the edge of a cliff. It was only a matter of time before gravity pulled it down.

My fellow castaway came into view. He raised himself onto the gunnel and looked my way. The sudden appearance of a tiger is arresting in any environment, but it was all the more so here. The weird contrast between the bright, striped, living orange of his coat and the inert white of the boat's hull was incredibly compelling. My overwrought senses screeched to a halt. Vast as the Pacific was around us, suddenly, between us, it seemed a very narrow moat, with no bars or walls.

"Plan Number Six, Plan Number Six, Plan Number Six," my mind whispered urgently. But what *was* Plan Number Six? Ah yes. The war of attrition. The waiting game. Passivity. Letting things happen. The unforgiving laws of nature. The relentless march of time and the hoarding of resources. That was Plan Number Six.

A thought rang in my mind like an angry shout: "You fool and idiot! You dimwit! You brainless baboon! *Plan Number Six is the worst plan of all!* Richard Parker is afraid of the sea right now. It was nearly his grave. But crazed with thirst and hunger he will surmount his fear, and he will do whatever is necessary to appease his need. He will turn this moat into a bridge. He will swim as far as he has to, to catch the drifting raft and the food upon it. As for water, have you forgotten that tigers from the Sundarbans are known to drink saline water? Do you really think you can outlast his kidneys? I tell you, if you wage a war of attrition, you will lose it! You will *die!* IS THAT CLEAR?"

CHAPTER 56

I must say a word about fear. It is life's only true opponent. Only fear can defeat life. It is a clever, treacherous adversary, how well I know. It has no decency, respects no law or convention, shows no mercy. It goes for your weakest spot, which it finds with unerring ease. It begins in your mind, always. One moment you are feeling calm, self-possessed, happy. Then fear, disguised in the garb of mild-mannered doubt, slips into your mind like a spy. Doubt meets disbelief and disbelief tries to push it out. But disbelief is a poorly armed foot soldier. Doubt does away with it with little trouble. You become anxious. Reason comes to do battle for you. You are reassured. Reason is fully equipped with the latest weapons technology. But, to your amazement, despite superior tactics and a number of undeniable victories, reason is laid low. You feel yourself weakening, wavering. Your anxiety becomes dread.

Fear next turns fully to your body, which is already aware that something terribly wrong is going on. Already your lungs have flown away like a bird and your guts have slithered away like a snake. Now your tongue drops dead like an opossum, while your jaw begins to gallop on the spot. Your ears go deaf. Your muscles begin to shiver as if they had malaria and your knees to shake as though they were dancing. Your heart strains too hard, while your sphincter relaxes too much. And so with the rest of your body. Every part of you, in the manner most suited to it, falls apart. Only your eyes work well. They always pay proper attention to fear.

Quickly you make rash decisions. You dismiss your last allies: hope and trust. There, you've defeated yourself. Fear, which is but an impression, has triumphed over you.

The matter is difficult to put into words. For fear, real fear, such as shakes you to your foundation, such as you feel when you are brought face to face with your mortal end, nestles in your memory like a gangrene: it seeks to rot everything, even the words with which to speak of it. So you must fight hard to express it. You must fight hard to shine the light of words upon it. Because if you don't, if your fear becomes a wordless darkness that you avoid, perhaps even manage to forget, you open yourself to further attacks of fear because you never truly fought the opponent who defeated you.

CHAPTER 57

It was Richard Parker who calmed me down. It is the irony of this story that the one who scared me witless to start with was the very same who brought me peace, purpose, I dare say even wholeness.

He was looking at me intently. After a time I recognized the gaze. I had grown up with it. It was the gaze of a contented animal looking out from its cage or pit the way you or I would look out from a restaurant table after a good meal, when the time has come for conversation and people-watching. Clearly, Richard Parker had eaten his fill of hyena and drunk all the rainwater he wanted. No lips were rising and falling, no teeth were showing, no growling or snarling was coming from him. He was simply taking me in, observing me, in a manner that was sober but not menacing. He kept twitching his ears and varying the sideways turn of his head. It was all so, well, *catlike*. He looked like a nice, big, fat domestic cat, a 450-pound tabby.

He made a sound, a snort from his nostrils. I pricked up my ears. He did it a second time. I was astonished. *Prusten*?

Tigers make a variety of sounds. They include a number of roars and growls, the loudest of these being most likely the full-throated *aaonh*, usually made during the mating season by males and oestrous females. It's a cry that travels far and wide, and is absolutely petrifying when heard close up. Tigers go *woof* when they are caught unawares, a short, sharp detonation of fury that would instantly make your legs jump up and run away if they weren't frozen to the spot. When they charge, tigers put out throaty, coughing roars. The growl they use for purposes of threatening has yet another guttural quality. And tigers hiss and snarl, which, depending on the emotion behind it, sounds either like autumn leaves rustling on the ground, but a little more resonant, or, when it's an infuriated snarl, like a giant door with rusty hinges slowly opening—in both cases, utterly spine-chilling. Tigers make other sounds too. They grunt and they moan. They purr, though not as melodiously or as frequently as small cats, and only as they breathe out. (Only small cats purr breathing both ways. It is one of the characteristics that distinguishes big cats from small cats. Another is that only big cats can roar. A good thing that is. I'm afraid the popularity of the domestic cat would drop very quickly if little kitty could roar its displeasure.) Tigers even go *meow*, with an inflection similar to that of domestic cats, but louder and in a deeper range, not as encouraging to one to bend down and pick them up. And tigers can be utterly, majestically silent, that too.

I had heard all these sounds growing up. Except for prusten. If I knew of it, it was because Father had told me about it. He had read descriptions of it in the literature. But he had heard it only once, while on a working visit to the Mysore Zoo, in their animal hospital, from a young male being treated for pneumonia. Prusten is the quietest of tiger calls, a puff through the nose to express friendliness and harmless intentions.

Richard Parker did it again, this time with a rolling of the head. He looked exactly as if he were asking me a question.

I looked at him, full of fearful wonder. There being no immediate threat, my breath slowed down, my heart stopped knocking about in my chest, and I began to regain my senses.

I had to tame him. It was at that moment that I realized this necessity. It was not a question of him or me, but of him *and* me. We were, literally and figuratively, in the same boat. We would live—or we would die—together. He might be killed in an accident, or he could die shortly of natural causes, but it would be foolish to count on such an eventuality. More likely the worst would happen: the simple passage of time, in which his animal toughness would easily outlast my human frailty. Only if I tamed him could I possibly trick him into dying first, if we had to come to that sorry business.

But there's more to it. I will come clean. I will tell you a secret: a part of me was glad about Richard Parker. A part of me did not want Richard Parker to die at all, because if he died I would be left alone with despair, a foe even more formidable than a tiger. If I still had the will to live, it was thanks to Richard Parker. He kept me from thinking too much about my family and my tragic circumstances. He pushed me to go on living. I hated him for it, yet at the same time I was grateful. I *am* grateful. It's the plain truth: without Richard Parker, I wouldn't be alive today to tell you my story.

I looked around at the horizon. Didn't I have here a perfect circus ring, inescapably round, without a single corner for him to hide in? I looked down at the sea. Wasn't this an ideal source of treats with which to condition him to obey? I noticed a whistle hanging from one of the life jackets. Wouldn't this make a good whip with which to keep him in line? What was missing here to tame Richard Parker? Time? It might be weeks before a ship sighted me. I had all the time in the world. Resolve? There's nothing like extreme need to give you resolve. Knowledge? Was I not a zookeeper's son? Reward? Was there any reward greater than life? Any punishment worse than death? I looked at Richard Parker. My panic was gone. My fear was dominated. Survival was at hand.

Let the trumpets blare. Let the drums roll. Let the show begin. I rose to my feet. Richard Parker noticed. The balance was not easy. I took a deep breath and shouted, "Ladies and gentlemen, boys and girls, hurry to your seats! Hurry, hurry. You don't want to be late. Sit down, open your eyes, open your hearts and prepare to be amazed. Here it is, for your enjoyment and instruction, for your gratification and edification, the show you've been waiting for all your life, THE GREATEST SHOW ON EARTH! Are you ready for the miracle of it? Yes? Well then: they are amazingly adaptable. You've seen them in freezing, snow-covered temperate forests. You've seen them in dense, tropical monsoon jungles. You've seen them in sparse, semi-arid scrublands. You've seen them in brackish mangrove swamps. Truly, they would fit anywhere. But you've never seen them where you are about to see them now! Ladies and gentlemen, boys and girls, without further ado, it is my pleasure and honour to present to you: THE PI PATEL, INDO-CANADIAN, TRANS-PACIFIC, FLOAT-ING CIRCUUUUUSSSSSSSSSSSSS!!! *TREEEEEE! TREEEEEE! TREEEEEE! TREEEEEE! TREEEEEE! TREEEEEE!*"

I had an effect on Richard Parker. At the very first blow of the whistle he cringed and he snarled. Ha! Let him jump into the water if he wanted to! Let him try!

"*TREEEEEE! TREEEEEE! TREEEEEE! TREEEEEE! TREEEEEE! TREEEEEE!*"

He roared and he clawed the air. But he did not jump. He might not be afraid of the sea when he was driven mad by hunger and thirst, but for the time being it was a fear I could rely on.

"TREEEEEE! TREEEEEE! TREEEEEE! TREEEEEE! TREEEEEE! TREEEEEE!"

He backed off and dropped to the bottom of the boat. The first training session was over. It was a resounding success. I stopped whistling and sat down heavily on the raft, out of breath and exhausted.

And so it came to be:

Plan Number Seven: Keep Him Alive.

CHAPTER 58

I pulled out the survival manual. Its pages were still wet. I turned them carefully. The manual was written by a British Royal Navy commander. It contained a wealth of practical information on surviving at sea after a shipwreck. It included survival tips such as:

- Always read instructions carefully.
- Do not drink urine. Or sea water. Or bird blood.
- Do not eat jellyfish. Or fish that are armed with spikes. Or that have parrot-like beaks. Or that puff up like balloons.
- Pressing the eyes of fish will paralyze them.
- The body can be a hero in battle. If a castaway is injured, beware of well-meaning but ill-founded medical treatment. Ignorance is the worst doctor, while rest and sleep are the best nurses.
- Put up your feet at least five minutes every hour.
- Unnecessary exertion should be avoided. But an idle mind tends to sink, so the mind should be kept occupied with whatever light distraction may suggest itself. Playing card

games, Twenty Questions and I Spy With My Little Eye are excellent forms of simple recreation. Community singing is another sure-fire way to lift the spirits. Yarn spinning is also highly recommended.

- Green water is shallower than blue water.
- Beware of far-off clouds that look like mountains. Look for green. Ultimately, a foot is the only good judge of land.
- Do not go swimming. It wastes energy. Besides, a survival craft may drift faster than you can swim. Not to mention the danger of sea life. If you are hot, wet your clothes instead.
- Do not urinate in your clothes. The momentary warmth is not worth the nappy rash.
- Shelter yourself. Exposure can kill faster than thirst or hunger.
- So long as no excessive water is lost through perspiration, the body can survive up to fourteen days without water. If you feel thirsty, suck a button.
- Turtles are an easy catch and make for excellent meals. Their blood is a good, nutritious, salt-free drink; their flesh is tasty and filling; their fat has many uses; and the castaway will find turtle eggs a real treat. Mind the beak and the claws.
- Don't let your morale flag. Be daunted, but not defeated. Remember: the spirit, above all else, counts. If you have the will to live, you will. Good luck!

There were also a few highly cryptic lines distilling the art and science of navigation. I learned that the horizon, as seen from a height of five feet on a calm day, was two and a half miles away.

The injunction not to drink urine was quite unnecessary. No one called "Pissing" in his childhood would be caught dead with a cup of pee at his lips, even alone in a lifeboat in the middle of the Pacific. And the gastronomic suggestions only confirmed to my mind that the English didn't know the meaning of the word *food*. Otherwise, the manual was a fascinating pamphlet on how to avoid being pickled in brine. Only one important topic was not addressed: the establishing of alpha-omega relationships with major lifeboat pests.

I had to devise a training program for Richard Parker. I had to make him understand that I was the top tiger and that his territory was limited to the floor of the boat, the stern bench and the side benches as far as the middle cross bench. I had to fix in his mind that the top of the tarpaulin and the bow of the boat, bordered by the neutral territory of the middle bench, was *my* territory and utterly forbidden to him.

I had to start fishing very soon. It would not take long for Richard Parker to finish the animal carcasses. At the zoo the adult lions and tigers ate on average ten pounds of meat a day.

There were many other things I had to do. I had to find a means of sheltering myself. If Richard Parker stayed under the tarpaulin all the time, it was for a good reason. To be continuously outside, exposed to sun, wind, rain and sea, was exhausting, and not only to the body but also to the mind. Hadn't I just read that exposure could inflict a quick death? I had to devise some sort of canopy.

I had to tie the raft to the lifeboat with a second rope, in case the first should break or become loose.

I had to improve the raft. At present it was seaworthy, but hardly habitable. I would have to make it fit for living in until I could move to my permanent quarters on the lifeboat. For example, I had to find a way to stay dry on it. My skin was wrinkled and swollen all over from being constantly wet. That had to change. And I had to find a way to store things on the raft.

I had to stop hoping so much that a ship would rescue me. I should not count on outside help. Survival had to start with me. In my experience, a castaway's worst mistake is to hope too much and do too little. Survival starts by paying attention to what is close at hand

and immediate. To look out with idle hope is tantamount to dreaming one's life away.

There was much I had to do.

I looked out at the empty horizon. There was so much water. And I was all alone. All alone.

I burst into hot tears. I buried my face in my crossed arms and sobbed. My situation was patently hopeless.

CHAPTER 59

Alone or not, lost or not, I was thirsty and hungry. I pulled on the rope. There was a slight tension. As soon as I lessened my grip on it, it slid out, and the distance between the lifeboat and the raft increased. So the lifeboat drifted faster than the raft, pulling it along. I noted the fact without thinking anything of it. My mind was more focused on the doings of Richard Parker.

By the looks of it, he was under the tarpaulin.

I pulled the rope till I was right next to the bow. I reached up to the gunnel. As I was crouched, preparing myself for a quick raid on the locker, a series of waves got me thinking. I noticed that with the raft next to it, the lifeboat had changed directions. It was no longer perpendicular to the waves but broadside to them and was beginning to roll from side to side, that rolling that was so unsettling for the stomach. The reason for this change became clear to me: the raft, when let out, was acting as a sea anchor, as a drag that pulled on the lifeboat and turned its bow to face the waves. You see, waves and steady winds are usually perpendicular to each other. So, if a boat is pushed by a wind but held back by a sea anchor, it will turn until it offers the least resistance to the wind—that is, until it is in line with it and at right angles to the waves, which makes for a front-to-back pitching that is much more comfortable than a side-to-side rolling. With the raft next to the boat, the dragging effect was gone, and there was nothing to steer the boat head into the wind. Therefore it turned broadside and rolled.

What may seem like a detail to you was something which would save my life and which Richard Parker would come to regret.

As if to confirm my fresh insight, I heard him growl. It was a disconsolate growl, with something indefinably green and queasy in its tone. He was maybe a good swimmer, but he was not much of a sailor.

I had a chance yet.

Lest I got cocky about my abilities to manipulate him, I received at that moment a quiet but sinister warning about what I was up against. It seemed Richard Parker was such a magnetic pole of life, so charismatic in his vitality, that other expressions of life found it intolerable. I was on the point of raising myself over the bow when I heard a gentle thrashing buzz. I saw something small land in the water next to me.

It was a cockroach. It floated for a second or two before being swallowed by an underwater mouth. Another cockroach landed in the water. In the next minute, ten or so cockroaches plopped into the water on either side of the bow. Each was claimed by a fish.

The last of the foreign life forms was abandoning ship.

I carefully brought my eyes over the gunnel. The first thing I saw, lying in a fold of the tarpaulin above the bow bench, was a large cockroach, perhaps the patriarch of the clan. I watched it, strangely interested. When it decided it was time, it deployed its wings, rose in the air with a minute clattering, hovered above the lifeboat momentarily, as if making sure no one had been left behind, and then veered overboard to its death.

Now we were two. In five days the populations of orang-utans, zebras, hyenas, rats, flies and cockroaches had been wiped out. Except for the bacteria and worms that might still be alive in the remains of the animals, there was no other life left on the lifeboat but Richard Parker and me.

It was not a comforting thought.

I lifted myself and breathlessly opened the locker lid. I deliberately did not look under the tarpaulin for fear that looking would be like shouting and would attract Richard Parker's attention. Only once the lid was leaning against the tarpaulin did I dare let my senses consider what was beyond it.

A smell came to my nose, a musky smell of urine, quite sharp, what every cat cage in a zoo smells of. Tigers are highly territorial, and it is with their urine that they mark the boundaries of their territory. Here was good news wearing a foul dress: the odour was coming exclusively from below the tarpaulin. Richard Parker's territorial claims seemed to be limited to the floor of the boat. This held promise. If I could make the tarpaulin mine, we might get along.

I held my breath, lowered my head and cocked it to the side to see beyond the edge of the lid. There was rainwater, about four inches of it, sloshing about the floor of the lifeboat—Richard Parker's own freshwater pond. He was doing exactly what I would be doing in his place: cooling off in the shade. The day was getting beastly hot. He was flat on the floor of the boat, facing away from me, his hind legs sticking straight back and splayed out, back paws facing up, and stomach and inner thighs lying directly against the floor. The position looked silly but was no doubt very pleasant.

I returned to the business of survival. I opened a carton of emergency ration and ate my fill, about one-third of the package. It was remarkable how little it took to make my stomach feel full. I was about to drink from the rain-catcher pouch slung across my shoulder when my eyes fell upon the graduated drinking beakers. If I couldn't go for a dip, could I at least have a sip? My own supplies of water would not last forever. I took hold of one of the beakers, leaned over, lowered the lid just as much as I needed to and tremulously dipped the beaker into Parker's Pond, four feet from his back paws. His up-turned pads with their wet fur looked like little desert islands sur-rounded by seaweed.

I brought back a good 500 millilitres. It was a little discoloured. Specks were floating in it. Did I worry about ingesting some horrid bacteria? I didn't even think about it. All I had on my mind was my thirst. I drained that beaker to the dregs with great satisfaction.

Nature is preoccupied with balance, so it did not surprise me that nearly right away I felt the urge to urinate. I relieved myself in the beaker. I produced so exactly the amount I had just downed that it was as if a minute hadn't passed and I were still considering Richard Parker's rainwater. I hesitated. I felt the urge to tilt the beaker into my mouth once more. I resisted the temptation. But it was hard. Mock-ery be damned, my urine looked delicious! I was not suffering yet from dehydration, so the liquid was pale in colour. It glowed in the sunlight, looking like a glass of apple juice. And it was guaranteed fresh, which certainly couldn't be said of the canned water that was my staple. But I heeded my better judgment. I splashed my urine on the tarpaulin and over the locker lid to stake my claim.

I stole another two beakers of water from Richard Parker, with-out urinating this time. I felt as freshly watered as a potted plant.

Now it was time to improve my situation. I turned to the contents of the locker and the many promises they held.

I brought out a second rope and tethered the raft to the lifeboat with it.

I discovered what a solar still is. A solar still is a device to produce fresh water from salt water. It consists of an inflatable transparent cone set upon a round lifebuoy-like buoyancy chamber that has a surface of black rubberized canvas stretched across its centre. The still operates on the principle of distillation: sea water lying beneath the sealed cone on the black canvas is heated by the sun and evaporates, gathering on the inside surface of the cone. This salt-free water trickles down and collects in a gully on the perimeter of the cone, from which it drains into a pouch. The lifeboat came equipped with twelve solar stills. I read the instructions carefully, as the survival manual told me to. I inflated all twelve cones with air and I filled each buoyancy chamber with the requisite ten litres of sea water. I strung the stills together, tying one end of the flotilla to the lifeboat and the other to the raft, which meant that not only would I not lose any stills should one of my knots become loose, but also that I had, in effect, a second emergency rope to keep me tethered to the lifeboat. The stills looked pretty and very technological as they floated on the water, but they also looked flimsy, and I was doubtful of their capacity to produce fresh water.

I directed my attention to improving the raft. I examined every knot that held it together, making sure each was tight and secure. After some thought, I decided to transform the fifth oar, the footrest oar, into a mast of sorts. I undid the oar. With the sawtoothed edge of the hunting knife I painstakingly cut a notch into it, about halfway down, and with the knife's point I drilled three holes through its flat part. Work was slow but satisfying. It kept my mind busy. When I had finished I lashed the oar in a vertical position to the inside of one of the corners of the raft, flat part, the masthead, rising in the air, handle disappearing underwater. I ran the rope tightly into the notch, to prevent the oar from slipping down. Next, to ensure that the mast would stand straight, and to give myself lines from which to hang a canopy and supplies, I threaded ropes through the holes I had drilled in the masthead and tied them to the tips of the horizontal oars. I strapped the life jacket that had been attached to the footrest oar to the base of the mast. It would play a double role: it would provide extra flotation to compensate for the vertical weight of the mast, and it would make for a slightly raised seat for me.

I threw a blanket over the lines. It slid down. The angle of the lines was too steep. I folded the lengthwise edge of the blanket over once, cut two holes midway down, about a foot apart, and linked the holes with a piece of string, which I made by unweaving a length of rope. I threw the blanket over the lines again, with the new girdle string going around the masthead. I now had a canopy.

It took me a good part of the day to fix up the raft. There were so many details to look after. The constant motion of the sea, though gentle, didn't make my work any easier. And I had to keep an eye on Richard Parker. The result was no galleon. The mast, so called, ended hardly a few inches above my head. As for the deck, it was just big enough to sit on cross-legged or to lie on in a tight, nearly-to-term fetal position. But I wasn't complaining. It was seaworthy and it would save me from Richard Parker.

By the time I had finished my work, the afternoon was nearing its end. I gathered a can of water, a can opener, four biscuits of survival ration and four blankets. I closed the locker (very softly this time), sat down on the raft and let out the rope. The lifeboat drifted away. The main rope tensed, while the security rope, which I had deliberately measured out longer, hung limply. I laid two blankets beneath me, carefully folding them so that they didn't touch the water. I wrapped the other two around my shoulders and rested my back against the mast. I enjoyed the slight elevation I gained from sitting on the extra life jacket. I was hardly higher up from the water than one would be from a floor sitting on a thick cushion; still, I hoped not to get wet so much.

I enjoyed my meal as I watched the sun's descent in a cloudless sky. It was a relaxing moment. The vault of the world was magnificently tinted. The stars were eager to participate; hardly had the blanket of colour been pulled a little than they started to shine through the deep blue. The wind blew with a faint, warm breeze and the sea moved about kindly, the water peaking and troughing like people dancing in a circle who come together and raise their hands and move apart and come together again, over and over.

Richard Parker sat up. Only his head and a little of his shoulders showed above the gunnel. He looked out. I shouted, "Hello, Richard Parker!" and I waved. He looked at me. He snorted or sneezed, neither word quite captures it. Prusten again. What a stunning creature. Such a noble mien. How apt that in full it is a *Royal* Bengal tiger. I counted myself lucky in a way. What if I had ended up with a creature that looked silly or ugly, a tapir or an ostrich or a flock of turkeys? That would have been a more trying companionship in some ways.

I heard a splash. I looked down at the water. I gasped. I thought I was alone. The stillness in the air, the glory of the light, the feeling of comparative safety—all had made me think so. There is commonly an element of silence and solitude to peace, isn't there? It's hard to imagine being at peace in a busy subway station, isn't it? So what was all this commotion?

With just one glance I discovered that the sea is a city. Just below me, all around, unsuspected by me, were highways, boulevards, streets and roundabouts bustling with submarine traffic. In water that was dense, glassy and flecked by millions of lit-up specks of plankton, fish like trucks and buses and cars and bicycles and pedestrians were madly racing about, no doubt honking and hollering at each other. The predominant colour was green. At multiple depths, as far as I could see, there were evanescent trails of phosphorescent green bubbles, the wake of speeding fish. As soon as one trail faded, another appeared. These trails came from all directions and disappeared in all directions. They were like those time-exposure photographs you see of cities at night, with the long red streaks made by the tail lights of cars. Except that here the cars were driving above and under each other as if they were on interchanges that were stacked ten storeys high. And here the cars were of the craziest colours. The dorados—there must have been over fifty patrolling beneath the raft—showed off their bright gold, blue and green as they whisked by. Other fish that I could not identify were yellow, brown, silver, blue, red, pink, green, white, in all kinds of combinations, solid, streaked and speckled. Only the sharks stubbornly refused to be colourful. But whatever the size or colour of a vehicle, one thing was constant: the furious driving. There were many collisions—all involving fatalities, I'm afraid—and a number of cars spun wildly out of control and collided against barriers, bursting above the surface of the water and splashing down in showers of luminescence. I gazed upon this urban hurly-burly like someone observing a city from a hot-air balloon. It was a spectacle wondrous and awe-inspiring. This is surely what Tokyo must look like at rush hour.

I looked on until the lights went out in the city.

From the *Tsimtsum* all I had seen were dolphins. I had assumed that the Pacific, but for passing schools of fish, was a sparsely inhabited waste of water. I have learned since that cargo ships travel too quickly for fish. You are as likely to see sea life from a ship as you are to see wildlife in a forest from a car on a highway. Dolphins, very fast swimmers, play about boats and ships much like dogs chase cars: they race along until they can no longer keep up. If you want to see wildlife, it is on foot, and quietly, that you must explore a forest. It is the same with the sea. You must stroll through the Pacific at a walking pace, so to speak, to see the wealth and abundance that it holds.

I settled on my side. For the first time in five days I felt a measure of calm. A little bit of hope—hard earned, well deserved, reasonable—glowed in me. I fell asleep.

CHAPTER 60

I awoke once during the night. I pushed the canopy aside and looked out. The moon was a sharply defined crescent and the sky was perfectly clear. The stars shone with such fierce, contained brilliance that it seemed absurd to call the night dark. The sea lay quietly, bathed in a shy, light-footed light, a dancing play of black and silver that extended without limits all about me. The volume of things was confounding—the volume of air above me, the volume of water around and beneath me. I was half-moved, half-terrified. I felt like the sage Markandeya, who fell out of Vishnu's mouth while Vishnu was sleeping and so beheld the entire universe, everything that there is. Before the sage could die of fright, Vishnu awoke and took him back into his mouth. For the first time I noticed—as I would notice repeatedly during my ordeal, between one throe of agony and the next—that my suffering was taking place in a grand setting. I saw my suffering for what it was, finite and insignificant, and I was still. My suffering did not fit anywhere, I realized. And I could accept this. It was all right. (It was daylight that brought my protest: "No! No! No! My suffering *does* matter. I want to live! I can't help but mix my life with that of the universe. Life is a peephole, a single tiny entry onto a vastness—how can I not dwell on this brief, cramped view I have of things? This peephole is all I've got!") I mumbled words of Muslim prayer and went back to sleep.

CHAPTER 61

The next morning I was not too wet and I was feeling strong. I thought this was remarkable considering the strain I was under and how little I had eaten in the last several days.

It was a fine day. I decided to try my hand at fishing, for the first time in my life. After a breakfast of three biscuits and one can of water, I read what the survival manual had to say on the subject. The first problem arose: bait. I thought about it. There were the dead animals, but stealing food from under a tiger's nose was a proposition I was not up to. He would not realize that it was an investment that would bring him an excellent return. I decided to use my leather shoe. I had only one left. The other I had lost when the ship sank.

I crept up to the lifeboat and I gathered from the locker one of the fishing kits, the knife and a bucket for my catch. Richard Parker was lying on his side. His tail jumped to life when I was at the bow but his head did not lift. I let the raft out.

I attached a hook to a wire leader, which I tied to a line. I added some lead weights. I picked three that had an intriguing torpedo shape. I removed my shoe and cut it into pieces. It was hard work; the leather was tough. I carefully worked the hook into a flat piece of hide, not through it but into it, so that the point of the hook was hidden. I let the line down deep. There had been so many fish the previous evening that I expected easy success.

I had none. The whole shoe disappeared bit by bit, slight tug on the line by slight tug on the line, happy freeloading fish by happy freeloading fish, bare hook by bare hook, until I was left with only the rubber sole and the shoelace. When the shoelace proved an unconvincing earthworm, out of sheer exasperation I tried the sole, all of it. It was not a good idea. I felt a slight, promising tug and then the line was unexpectedly light. All I pulled in was line. I had lost the whole tackle.

This loss did not strike me as a terrible blow. There were other hooks, leader wires and weights in the kit, besides a whole other kit. And I wasn't even fishing for myself. I had plenty of food in store.

Still, a part of my mind—the one that says what we don't want to hear—rebuked me. "Stupidity has a price. You should show more care and wisdom next time."

Later that morning a second turtle appeared. It came right up to the raft. It could have reached up and bit my bottom if it had wanted to. When it turned I reached for its hind flipper, but as soon as I touched it I recoiled in horror. The turtle swam away.

The same part of my mind that had rebuked me over my fishing fiasco scolded me again. "What exactly do you intend to feed that tiger of yours? How much longer do you think he'll last on three dead animals? Do I need to remind you that tigers are not carrion eaters? Granted, when he's on his last legs he probably won't lift his nose at much. But don't you think that before he submits to eating puffy, putrefied zebra he'll try the fresh, juicy Indian boy just a short dip away? And how are we doing with the water situation? You know how tigers get impatient with thirst. Have you smelled his breath recently? It's pretty awful. That's a bad sign. Perhaps you're hoping that he'll lap up the Pacific and in quenching his thirst allow you to walk to America? Quite amazing, this limited capacity to excrete salt that Sundarbans tigers have developed. Comes from living in a tidal mangrove forest, I suppose. But it *is* a limited capacity. Don't they say that drinking too much saline water makes a man-eater of a tiger? Oh, look. Speak of the devil. There he is. He's yawning. My, my, what an enormous pink cave. Look at those long yellow stalactites and stalagmites. Maybe today you'll get a chance to visit."

Richard Parker's tongue, the size and colour of a rubber hot-water bottle, retreated and his mouth closed. He swallowed.

I spent the rest of the day worrying myself sick. I stayed away from the lifeboat. Despite my own dire predictions, Richard Parker passed the time calmly enough. He still had water from the rainfall and he didn't seem too concerned with hunger. But he did make various tiger noises—growls and moans and the like—that did nothing to put me at ease. The riddle seemed irresolvable: to fish I needed bait, but I would have bait only once I had fish. What was I supposed to do? Use one of my toes? Cut off one of my ears?

A solution appeared in the late afternoon in a most unexpected way. I had pulled myself up to the lifeboat. More than that: I had climbed aboard and was rummaging through the locker, feverishly looking for an idea that would save my life. I had tied the raft so that it was about six feet from the boat. I fancied that with a jump and a pull at a loose knot I could save myself from Richard Parker. Desperation had pushed me to take such a risk.

Finding nothing, no bait and no new idea, I sat up—only to discover that I was dead centre in the focus of his stare. He was at the other end of the lifeboat, where the zebra used to be, turned my way and sitting up, looking as if he'd been patiently waiting for me to notice him. How was it that I hadn't heard him stir? What delusion was I under that I thought I could outwit him? Suddenly I was hit hard across the face. I cried out and closed my eyes. With feline speed he had leapt across the lifeboat and struck me. I was to have my face clawed off—this was the gruesome way I was to die. The pain was so severe I felt nothing. Blessed be shock. Blessed be that part of us that protects us from too much pain and sorrow. At the heart of life is a fuse box. I whimpered, "Go ahead, Richard Parker, finish me off. But please, what you must do, do it quickly. A blown fuse should not be overtested."

He was taking his time. He was at my feet, making noises. No doubt he had discovered the locker and its riches. I fearfully opened an eye.

It was a fish. There was a fish in the locker. It was flopping about like a fish out of water. It was about fifteen inches long and it had wings. A flying fish. Slim and dark grey-blue, with dry, featherless wings and round, unblinking, yellowish eyes. It was this flying fish that had struck me across the face, not Richard Parker. He was still fifteen feet away, no doubt wondering what I was going on about. But he had seen the fish. I could read a keen curiosity on his face. He seemed about ready to investigate.

I bent down, picked up the fish and threw it towards him. This was the way to tame him! Where a rat had gone, a flying fish would follow. Unfortunately, the flying fish flew. In mid-air, just ahead of Richard Parker's open mouth, the fish swerved and dropped into the water. It happened with lightning speed. Richard Parker turned his head and snapped his mouth, jowls flapping, but the fish was too quick for him. He looked astonished and displeased. He turned to me again. "Where's my treat?" his face seemed to inquire. Fear and sadness gripped me. I turned with the half-hearted, half-abandoned hope that I could jump onto the raft before he could jump onto me.

At that precise instant there was a vibration in the air and we were struck by a school of flying fish. They came like a swarm of locusts. It was not only their numbers; there was also something insect-like about the clicking, whirring sound of their wings. They burst out of the water, dozens of them at a time, some of them flick-flacking over a hundred yards through the air. Many dived into the water just before the boat. A number sailed clear over it. Some crashed into its side, sounding like firecrackers going off. Several lucky ones returned to the water after a bounce on the tarpaulin. Others, less fortunate, fell directly into the boat, where they started a racket of flapping and flailing and splashing. And still others flew right into us. Standing unprotected as I was, I felt I was living the martyrdom of Saint Sebastian. Every fish that hit me was like an arrow entering my flesh. I clutched at a blanket to protect myself while also trying to catch some of the fish. I received cuts and bruises all over my body.

The reason for this onslaught became evident immediately: dorados were leaping out of the water in hot pursuit of them. The much larger dorados couldn't match their flying, but they were faster swimmers and their short lunges were very powerful. They could overtake flying fish if they were just behind them and lunging from the water at the same time and in the same direction. There were sharks too; they also leapt out of the water, not so cleanly but with devastating consequence for some dorados. This aquatic mayhem didn't last long, but while it did, the sea bubbled and boiled, fish jumped and jaws worked hard.

Richard Parker was tougher than I was in the face of these fish, and far more efficient. He raised himself and went about blocking, swiping and biting all the fish he could. Many were eaten live and whole, struggling wings beating in his mouth. It was a dazzling display of might and speed. Actually, it was not so much the speed that was impressive as the pure animal confidence, the total absorption in the moment. Such a mix of ease and concentration, such a being-in-the-present, would be the envy of the highest yogis.

When it was over, the result, besides a very sore body for me, was six flying fish in the locker and a much greater number in the lifeboat. I hurriedly wrapped a fish in a blanket, gathered a hatchet and made for the raft.

I proceeded with great deliberation. The loss of my tackle that morning had had a sobering effect on me. I couldn't allow myself another mistake. I unwrapped the fish carefully, keeping a hand pressed down on it, fully aware that it would try to jump away to save itself. The closer the fish was to appearing, the more afraid and disgusted I became. Its head came into sight. The way I was holding it, it looked like a scoop of loathsome fish ice cream sticking out of a wool blanket cone. The thing was gasping for water, its mouth and gills opening and closing slowly. I could feel it pushing with its wings against my hand. I turned the bucket over and brought its head against the bottom. I took hold of the hatchet. I raised it in the air.

Several times I started bringing the hatchet down, but I couldn't complete the action. Such sentimentalism may seem ridiculous considering what I had witnessed in the last days, but those were the deeds of others, of predatory animals. I suppose I was partly responsible for the rat's death, but I'd only thrown it; it was Richard Parker who had killed it. A lifetime of peaceful vegetarianism stood between me and the willful beheading of a fish.

I covered the fish's head with the blanket and turned the hatchet around. Again my hand wavered in the air. The idea of beating a soft, living head with a hammer was simply too much.

I put the hatchet down. I would break its neck, sight unseen, I decided. I wrapped the fish tightly in the blanket. With both hands I started bending it. The more I pressed, the more the fish struggled. I imagined what it would feel like if I were wrapped in a blanket and someone were trying to break my neck. I was appalled. I gave up a number of times. Yet I knew it had to be done, and the longer I waited, the longer the fish's suffering would go on.

Tears flowing down my cheeks, I egged myself on until I heard a cracking sound and I no longer felt any life fighting in my hands. I pulled back the folds of the blanket. The flying fish was dead. It was split open and bloody on one side of its head, at the level of the gills.

I wept heartily over this poor little deceased soul. It was the first sentient being I had ever killed. I was now a killer. I was now as guilty as Cain. I was sixteen years old, a harmless boy, bookish and religious, and now I had blood on my hands. It's a terrible burden to carry. All sentient life is sacred. I never forget to include this fish in my prayers.

After that it was easier. Now that it was dead, the flying fish looked like fish I had seen in the markets of Pondicherry. It was something else, something outside the essential scheme of creation. I chopped it up into pieces with the hatchet and put it in the bucket.

In the dying hours of the day I tried fishing again. At first I had no better luck than I'd had in the morning. But success seemed less elusive. The fish nibbled at the hook with fervour. Their interest was evident. I realized that these were small fish, too small for the hook. So I cast my line further out and let it sink deeper, beyond the reach of the small fish that concentrated around the raft and lifeboat.

It was when I used the flying fish's head as bait, and with only one sinker, casting my line out and pulling it in quickly, making the head skim over the surface of the water, that I finally had my first strike. A dorado surged forth and lunged for the fish head. I let out a little slack, to make sure it had properly swallowed the bait, before giving the line a good yank. The dorado exploded out of the water, tugging on the line so hard I thought it was going to pull me off the raft. I braced myself. The line became very taut. It was good line; it would not break. I started bringing the dorado in. It struggled with all its might, jumping and diving and splashing. The line cut into my hands. I wrapped my hands in the blanket. My heart was pounding. The fish was as strong as an ox. I was not sure I would be able to pull it in.

I noticed all the other fish had vanished from around the raft and boat. No doubt they had sensed the dorado's distress. I hurried. Its struggling would attract sharks. But it fought like a devil. My arms were aching. Every time I got it close to the raft, it beat about with such frenzy that I was cowed into letting out some line.

At last I managed to haul it aboard. It was over three feet long. The bucket was useless. It would fit the dorado like a hat. I held the fish down by kneeling on it and using my hands. It was a writhing mass of pure muscle, so big its tail stuck out from beneath me, pounding hard against the raft. It was giving me a ride like I imagine a bucking bronco would give a cowboy. I was in a wild and triumphant mood. A dorado is a magnificent-looking fish, large, fleshy and sleek, with a bulging forehead that speaks of a forceful personality, a very long dorsal fin as proud as a cock's comb, and a coat of scales that is smooth and bright. I felt I was dealing fate a serious blow by engaging such a handsome adversary. With this fish I was retaliating against the sea, against the wind, against the sinking of ships, against all circumstances that were working against me. "Thank you, Lord Vishnu, thank you!" I shouted. "Once you saved the world by taking the form of a fish. Now you have saved *me* by taking the form of a fish. Thank you, thank you!"

Killing it was no problem. I would have spared myself the trouble—after all, it was for Richard Parker and he would have dispatched it with expert ease—but for the hook that was embedded in its mouth. I exulted at having a dorado at the end of my line—I would be less keen if it were a tiger. I went about the job in a direct way. I took the hatchet in both my hands and vigorously beat the fish on the head with the hammerhead (I still didn't have the stomach to use the sharp edge). The dorado did a most extraordinary thing as it died: it began to flash all kinds of colours in rapid succession. Blue, green, red, gold and violet flickered and shimmered neon-like on its surface as it struggled. I felt I was beating a rainbow to death. (I found out later that the dorado is famed for its death-knell iridescence.) At last it lay still and dull-coloured, and I could remove the hook. I even managed to retrieve a part of my bait.

You may be astonished that in such a short period of time I could go from weeping over the muffled killing of a flying fish to gleefully bludgeoning to death a dorado. I could explain it by arguing that profiting from a pitiful flying fish's navigational mistake made me shy and sorrowful, while the excitement of actively capturing a great dorado made me sanguinary and self-assured. But in point of fact the explanation lies elsewhere. It is simple and brutal: a person can get used to anything, even to killing.

It was with a hunter's pride that I pulled the raft up to the lifeboat. I brought it along the side, keeping very low. I swung my arm and dropped the dorado into the boat. It landed with a heavy thud and pro-voked a gruff expression of surprise from Richard Parker. After a sniff or two, I heard the wet mashing sound of a mouth at work. I pushed my-self off, not forgetting to blow the whistle hard several times, to remind Richard Parker of who had so graciously provided him with fresh food. I stopped to pick up some biscuits and a can of water. The five remaining flying fish in the locker were dead. I pulled their wings off, throwing them away, and wrapped the fish in the now-consecrated fish blanket.

By the time I had rinsed myself of blood, cleaned up my fishing gear, put things away and had my supper, night had come on. A thin layer of clouds masked the stars and the moon, and it was very dark. I was tired, but still excited by the events of the last hours. The feel-ing of busyness was profoundly satisfying; I hadn't thought at all about my plight or myself. Fishing was surely a better way of passing the time than yarn-spinning or playing I Spy. I determined to start again the next day as soon as there was light.

I fell asleep, my mind lit up by the chameleon-like flickering of the dying dorado.

CHAPTER 62

I slept in fits that night. Shortly before sunrise I gave up trying to fall asleep again and lifted myself on an elbow. I spied with my little eye a tiger. Richard Parker was restless. He was moaning and growling and pacing about the lifeboat. It was impressive. I assessed the situa-tion. He couldn't be hungry. Or at least not dangerously hungry. Was he thirsty? His tongue hung from his mouth, but only on occasion, and he was not panting. And his stomach and paws were still wet. But they were not dripping wet. There probably wasn't much water left in the boat. Soon he would be thirsty.

I looked up at the sky. The cloud cover had vanished. But for a few wisps on the horizon, the sky was clear. It would be another hot, rainless day. The sea moved in a lethargic way, as if already exhausted by the oncoming heat.

I sat against the mast and thought over our problem. The biscuits and the fishing gear assured us of the solid part of our diet. It was the liquid part that was the rub. It all came down to what was so abundant around us but marred by salt. I could perhaps mix some sea water with his fresh water, but I had to procure more fresh water to start with. The cans would not last long between the two of us—in fact, I was loath to share even one with Richard Parker—and it would be foolish to rely on rainwater.

The solar stills were the only other possible source of drinkable water. I looked at them doubtfully. They had been out two days now. I noticed that one of them had lost a little air. I pulled on the rope to tend to it. I topped off its cone with air. Without any real expectation I reached underwater for the distillate pouch that was clipped to the round buoyancy chamber. My fingers took hold of a bag that was unexpectedly fat. A shiver of thrill went through me. I controlled myself. As likely as not, salt water had leaked in. I unhooked the pouch and, following the instructions, lowered it and tilted the still so that any more water from beneath the cone might flow into it. I closed the two small taps that led to the pouch, detached it and pulled it out of the water. It was rectangular in shape and made of thick, soft, yellow plastic, with calibration marks on one side. I tasted the water. I tasted it again. It was salt-free.

"My sweet sea cow!" I exclaimed to the solar still. "You've produced, and how! What a delicious milk. Mind you, a little rubbery, but I'm not complaining. Why, look at me drink!"

I finished the bag. It had a capacity of one litre and was nearly full. After a moment of sigh-producing, shut-eyed satisfaction, I reattached the pouch. I checked the other stills. Each one had an udder similarly heavy. I collected the fresh milk, over eight litres of it, in the fish bucket. Instantly these technological contraptions became as precious to me as cattle are to a farmer. Indeed, as they floated placidly in an arc, they looked almost like cows grazing in a field. I ministered to their needs, making sure that there was enough sea water inside each and that the cones and chambers were inflated to just the right pressure.

After adding a little sea water to the bucket's contents, I placed it on the side bench just beyond the tarpaulin. With the end of the morning coolness, Richard Parker seemed safely settled below. I tied the bucket in place using rope and the tarpaulin hooks on the side of the boat. I carefully peeked over the gunnel. He was lying on his side. His den was a foul sight. The dead mammals were heaped together, a grotesque pile of decayed animal parts. I recognized a leg or two, various patches of hide, parts of a head, a great number of bones. Flying-fish wings were scattered about.

I cut up a flying fish and tossed a piece onto the side bench. After I had gathered what I needed for the day from the locker and was ready to go, I tossed another piece over the tarpaulin in front of Richard Parker. It had the intended effect. As I drifted away I saw him come out into the open to fetch the morsel of fish. His head turned and he noticed the other morsel and the new object next to it. He lifted himself. He hung his huge head over the bucket. I was afraid he would tip it over. He didn't. His face disappeared into it, barely fitting, and he started to lap up the water. In very little time the bucket started shaking and rattling emptily with each strike of his tongue. When he looked up, I stared him aggressively in the eyes and I blew on the whistle a few times. He disappeared under the tarpaulin.

It occurred to me that with every passing day the lifeboat was resembling a zoo enclosure more and more: Richard Parker had his sheltered area for sleeping and resting, his food stash, his lookout and now his water hole.

The temperature climbed. The heat became stifling. I spent the rest of the day in the shade of the canopy, fishing. It seems I had had beginner's luck with that first dorado. I caught nothing the whole day, not even in the late afternoon, when marine life appeared in abundance. A turtle turned up, a different kind this time, a green sea turtle, bulkier and smoother-shelled, but curious in the same fixed way as a hawksbill. I did nothing about it, but I started thinking that I should.

The only good thing about the day being so hot was the sight the solar stills presented. Every cone was covered on the inside with drops and rivulets of condensation.

The day ended. I calculated that the next morning would make it a week since the *Tsimtsum* had sunk.

CHAPTER 63

The Robertson family survived thirty-eight days at sea. Captain Bligh of the celebrated mutinous *Bounty* and his fellow castaways survived forty-seven days. Steven Callahan survived seventy-six. Owen Chase, whose account of the sinking of the whaling ship *Essex* by a whale inspired Herman Melville, survived eighty-three days at sea with two mates, interrupted by a one-week stay on an inhospitable island. The Bailey family survived 118 days. I have heard of a Korean merchant sailor named Poon, I believe, who survived the Pacific for 173 days in the 1950s.

I survived 227 days. That's how long my trial lasted, over seven months.

I kept myself busy. That was one key to my survival. On a lifeboat, even on a raft, there's always something that needs doing. An average day for me, if such a notion can be applied to a castaway, went like this:

Sunrise to mid-morning:
  wake up
  prayers
  breakfast for Richard Parker
  general inspection of raft and lifeboat, with particular at-
      tention paid to all knots and ropes
  tending of solar stills (wiping, inflating, topping off with water)
  breakfast and inspection of food stores
  fishing and preparing of fish if any caught (gutting, clean-
      ing, hanging of strips of flesh on lines to cure in the sun)
Mid-morning to late afternoon:
  prayers
  light lunch
  rest and restful activities (writing in diary, examining of
      scabs and sores, upkeeping of equipment, puttering
      about locker, observation and study of Richard Parker,
      picking at of turtle bones, etc.)

Late afternoon to early evening:
  prayers
  fishing and preparing of fish
  tending of curing strips of flesh (turning over, cutting away
      of putrid parts)
  dinner preparations
  dinner for self and Richard Parker

Sunset:
  general inspection of raft and lifeboat (knots and ropes again)
  collecting and safekeeping of distillate from solar stills
  storing of all foods and equipment

> arrangements for night (making of bed, safe storage on raft of
>   flare, in case of ship, and rain catcher, in case of rain)
> prayers

Night:
>   fitful sleeping
>   prayers

Mornings were usually better than late afternoons, when the emptiness of time tended to make itself felt.

Any number of events affected this routine. Rainfall, at any time of the day or night, stopped all other business; for as long as it fell, I held up the rain catchers and was feverishly occupied storing their catch. A turtle's visit was another major disruption. And Richard Parker, of course, was a regular disturbance. Accommodating him was a priority I could not neglect for an instant. He didn't have much of a routine beyond eating, drinking and sleeping, but there were times when he stirred from his lethargy and rambled about his territory, making noises and being cranky. Thankfully, every time, the sun and the sea quickly tired him and he returned to beneath the tarpaulin, to lying on his side again, or flat on his stomach, his head on top of his crossed front legs.

But there was more to my dealings with him than strict necessity. I also spent hours observing him because it was a distraction. A tiger is a fascinating animal at any time, and all the more so when it is your sole companion.

At first, looking out for a ship was something I did all the time, compulsively. But after a few weeks, five or six, I stopped doing it nearly entirely.

And I survived because I made a point of forgetting. My story started on a calendar day—July 2nd, 1977—and ended on a calendar day—February 14th, 1978—but in between there was no calendar.

I did not count the days or the weeks or the months. Time is an illusion that only makes us pant. I survived because I forgot even the very notion of time.

What I remember are events and encounters and routines, markers that emerged here and there from the ocean of time and imprinted themselves on my memory. The smell of spent hand-flare shells, and prayers at dawn, and the killing of turtles, and the biology of algae, for example. And many more. But I don't know if I can put them in order for you. My memories come in a jumble.

CHAPTER 64

My clothes disintegrated, victims of the sun and the salt. First they became gauze-thin. Then they tore until only the seams were left. Lastly, the seams broke. For months I lived stark naked except for the whistle that dangled from my neck by a string.

Salt-water boils—red, angry, disfiguring—were a leprosy of the high seas, transmitted by the water that soaked me. Where they burst, my skin was exceptionally sensitive; accidentally rubbing an open sore was so painful I would gasp and cry out. Naturally, these boils developed on the parts of my body that got the most wet and the most wear on the raft; that is, my backside. There were days when I could hardly find a position in which I could rest. Time and sunshine healed a sore, but the process was slow, and new boils appeared if I didn't stay dry.

CHAPTER 65

I spent hours trying to decipher the lines in the survival manual on navigation. Plain and simple explanations on living off the sea were given in abundance, but a basic knowledge of seafaring was assumed by the author of the manual. The castaway was to his mind an experienced sailor who, compass, chart and sextant in hand, knew how he found his way into trouble, if not how he would get out of it. The result was advice such as "Remember, time is distance. Don't forget to wind your watch," or "Latitude can be measured with the fingers, if need be." I had a watch, but it was now at the bottom of the Pacific. I lost it when the *Tsimtsum* sank. As for latitude and longitude, my marine knowledge was strictly limited to what lived *in* the sea and did not extend to what cruised on top of it. Winds and currents were a mystery to me. The stars meant nothing to me. I couldn't name a single constellation. My family lived by one star alone: the sun. We were early to bed and early to rise. I had in my life looked at a number of beautiful starry nights, where with just two colours and the simplest of styles nature draws the grandest of pictures, and I felt the feelings of wonder and smallness that we all feel, and I got a clear sense of direction from the spectacle, most definitely, but I mean that in a spiritual sense, not in a geographic one. I hadn't the faintest idea how the night sky might serve as a road map. How could the stars, sparkle as they might, help me find my way if they kept moving?

I gave up trying to find out. Any knowledge I might gain was useless. I had no means of controlling where I was going—no rudder, no sails, no motor, some oars but insufficient brawn. What was the point of plotting a course if I could not act on it? And even if I could, how should I know where to go? West, back to where we came from? East, to America? North, to Asia? South, to where the shipping lanes were? Each seemed a good and bad course in equal measure.

So I drifted. Winds and currents decided where I went. Time became distance for me in the way it is for all mortals—I travelled down the road of life—and I did other things with my fingers than try to measure latitude. I found out later that I travelled a narrow road, the Pacific equatorial counter-current.

CHAPTER 66

I fished with a variety of hooks at a variety of depths for a variety of fish, from deep-sea fishing with large hooks and many sinkers to surface fishing with smaller hooks and only one or two sinkers. Success was slow to come, and when it did, it was much appreciated, but the effort seemed out of proportion to the reward. The hours were long, the fish were small, and Richard Parker was forever hungry.

It was the gaffs that finally proved to be my most valuable fishing equipment. They came in three screw-in pieces: two tubular sections that formed the shaft—one with a moulded plastic handle at its end and a ring for securing the gaff with a rope—and a head that consisted of a hook measuring about two inches across its curve and ending in a needle-sharp, barbed point. Assembled, each gaff was about five feet long and felt as light and sturdy as a sword.

At first I fished in open water. I would sink the gaff to a depth of four feet or so, sometimes with a fish speared on the hook as bait, and I would wait. I would wait for hours, my body tense till it ached. When a fish was in just the right spot, I jerked the gaff up with all the might and speed I could muster. It was a split-second decision. Experience taught me that it was better to strike when I felt I had a good chance of success than to strike wildly, for a fish learns from experience too, and rarely falls for the same trap twice.

When I was lucky, a fish was properly snagged on the hook, impaled, and I could confidently bring it aboard. But if I gaffed a large fish in the stomach or tail, it would often get away with a twist and a

forward spurt of speed. Injured, it would be easy prey for another predator, a gift I had not meant to make. So with large fish I aimed for the
ventral area beneath their gills and their lateral fins, for a fish's instinctive reaction when struck there was to swim *up*, away from the
hook, in the very direction I was pulling. Thus it would happen: sometimes more pricked than actually gaffed, a fish would burst out of the
water in my face. I quickly lost my revulsion at touching sea life. None
of this prissy fish blanket business any more. A fish jumping out of
water was confronted by a famished boy with a hands-on, no-holds-
barred approach to capturing it. If I felt the gaff's hold was uncertain,
I would let go of it—I had not forgotten to secure it with a rope to the
raft—and I would clutch at the fish with my hands. Fingers, though
blunt, were far more nimble than a hook. The struggle would be fast
and furious. Those fish were slippery and desperate, and I was just
plain desperate. If only I had had as many arms as the goddess
Durga—two to hold the gaffs, four to grasp the fish and two to wield
the hatchets. But I had to make do with two. I stuck fingers into eyes,
jammed hands into gills, crushed soft stomachs with knees, bit tails
with my teeth—I did whatever was necessary to hold a fish down until
I could reach for the hatchet and chop its head off.

With time and experience I became a better hunter. I grew bolder
and more agile. I developed an instinct, a feel, for what to do.

My success improved greatly when I started using part of the
cargo net. As a fishing net it was useless—too stiff and heavy and
with a weave that wasn't tight enough. But it was perfect as a lure.
Trailing freely in the water, it proved irresistibly attractive to fish, and
even more so when seaweed started growing on it. Fish that were
local in their ambit made the net their neighbourhood, and the quick
ones, the ones that tended to streak by, the dorados, slowed down to
visit the new development. Neither the residents nor the travellers
ever suspected that a hook was hidden in the weave. There were some

days—too few unfortunately—when I could have all the fish I cared to gaff. At such times I hunted far beyond the needs of my hunger or my capacity to cure; there simply wasn't enough space on the lifeboat, or lines on the raft, to dry so many strips of dorado, flying fish, jacks, groupers and mackerels, let alone space in my stomach to eat them. I kept what I could and gave the rest to Richard Parker. During those days of plenty, I laid hands on so many fish that my body began to glitter from all the fish scales that became stuck to it. I wore these spots of shine and silver like tilaks, the marks of colour that we Hindus wear on our foreheads as symbols of the divine. If sailors had come upon me then, I'm sure they would have thought I was a fish god standing atop his kingdom and they wouldn't have stopped. Those were the good days. They were rare.

Turtles were an easy catch indeed, as the survival manual said they were. Under the "hunting and gathering" heading, they would go under "gathering". Solid in build though they were, like tanks, they were neither fast nor powerful swimmers; with just one hand gripped around a back flipper, it was possible to hold on to a turtle. But the survival manual failed to mention that a turtle caught was not a turtle had. It still needed to be brought aboard. And hauling a struggling 130-pound turtle aboard a lifeboat was anything but easy. It was a labour that demanded feats of strength worthy of Hanuman. I did it by bringing the victim alongside the bow of the boat, carapace against hull, and tying a rope to its neck, a front flipper and a back flipper. Then I pulled until I thought my arms would come apart and my head would explode. I ran the ropes around the tarpaulin hooks on the opposite side of the bow; every time a rope yielded a little, I secured my gain before the rope slipped back. Inch by inch, a turtle was heaved out of the water. It took time. I remember one green sea turtle that hung from the side of the lifeboat for two days, the whole while thrashing about madly, free flippers beating in the air. Luckily, at the last stage, on the lip of the gunnel, it would often happen that a turtle would help me without meaning to. In an attempt to free its painfully twisted flippers, it would pull on them; if I pulled at the same moment, our conflicting efforts sometimes came together and suddenly it would happen, easily: in the most dramatic fashion imaginable, a turtle would surge over the gunnel and slide onto the tarpaulin. I would fall back, exhausted but jubilant.

Green sea turtles gave more meat than hawksbills, and their belly shells were thinner. But they tended to be bigger than hawksbills, often too big to lift out of the water for the weakened castaway that I became.

Lord, to think that I'm a strict vegetarian. To think that when I was a child I always shuddered when I snapped open a banana because it sounded to me like the breaking of an animal's neck. I descended to a level of savagery I never imagined possible.

CHAPTER 67

The underside of the raft became host to a multitude of sea life, like the net but smaller in form. It started with a soft green algae that clung to the life jackets. Stiffer algae of a darker kind joined it. They did well and became thick. Animal life appeared. The first that I saw were tiny, translucent shrimp, hardly half an inch long. They were followed by fish no bigger that looked like they were permanently under X-ray; their internal organs showed through their transparent skins. After that I noticed the black worms with the white spines, the green gelatinous slugs with the primitive limbs, the inch-long, motley-coloured fish with the potbellies, and lastly the crabs, half to three-quarters of an inch across and brown in colour. I tried everything but the worms, including the algae. Only the crabs didn't have an unpalatably bitter or salty taste. Every time they appeared, I popped them one after another into my mouth like candy until there were none left. I couldn't control myself. It was always a long wait between fresh crops of crabs.

The hull of the lifeboat invited life too, in the form of small gooseneck barnacles. I sucked their fluid. Their flesh made for good fishing bait.

I became attached to these oceanic hitchhikers, though they weighed the raft down a little. They provided distraction, like Richard Parker. I spent many hours doing nothing but lying on my side, a life jacket pushed out of place a few inches, like a curtain from a window, so that I might have a clear view. What I saw was an upside-down town, small, quiet and peaceable, whose citizens went about with the sweet civility of angels. The sight was a welcome relief for my frayed nerves.

CHAPTER 68

My sleep pattern changed. Though I rested all the time, I rarely slept longer than an hour or so at a stretch, even at night. It was not the ceaseless motion of the sea that disturbed me, nor the wind; you get used to those the way you get used to lumps in a mattress. It was apprehension and anxiety that roused me. It was remarkable how little sleep I got by on.

Unlike Richard Parker. He became a champion napper. Most of the time he rested beneath the tarpaulin. But on calm days when the sun was not too harsh and on calm nights, he came out. One of his favourite positions in the open was lying on the stern bench on his side, stomach overhanging the edge of it, front and back legs extending down the side benches. It was a lot of tiger to squeeze onto a fairly narrow ledge, but he managed it by making his back very round. When he was truly sleeping, he laid his head on his front legs, but when his mood was slightly more active, when he might choose to open his eyes and look about, he turned his head and lay his chin on the gunnel.

Another favourite position of his was sitting with his back to me, his rear half resting on the floor of the boat and his front half on the bench, his face buried into the stern, paws right next to his head, looking as if we were playing hide-and-seek and he were the one counting. In this position he tended to lie very still, with only the occasional twitching of his ears to indicate that he was not necessarily sleeping.

CHAPTER 69

On many nights I was convinced I saw a light in the distance. Each time I set off a flare. When I had used up the rocket flares, I expended the hand flares. Were they ships that failed to see me? The light of rising or setting stars bouncing off the ocean? Breaking waves that moonlight and forlorn hope fashioned into illusion? Whatever the case, every time it was for nothing. Never a result. Always the bitter emotion of hope raised and dashed. In time I gave up entirely on being saved by a ship. If the horizon was two and a half miles away at an altitude of five feet, how far away was it when I was sitting against the mast of my raft, my eyes not even three feet above the water? What chance was there that a ship crossing the whole great big Pacific would cut into such a tiny circle? Not only that: that it would cut into such a tiny circle *and see me*—what chance was there of that? No, humanity and its unreliable ways could not be counted upon. It was land I had to reach, hard, firm, certain land.

I remember the smell of the spent hand-flare shells. By some freak of chemistry they smelled exactly like cumin. It was intoxicating. I sniffed the plastic shells and immediately Pondicherry came to life in my mind, a marvellous relief from the disappointment of calling for help and not being heard. The experience was very strong, nearly a hallucination. From a single smell a whole town arose. (Now, when I smell cumin, I see the Pacific Ocean.)

Richard Parker always froze when a hand flare hissed to life. His eyes, round pupils the size of pinpricks, fixed on the light steadily. It was too bright for me, a blinding white centre with a pinkish red aureole. I had to turn away. I held the flare in the air at arm's length and waved it slowly. For about a minute heat showered down upon my forearm and everything was weirdly lit. Water around the raft, until a moment before opaquely black, showed itself to be crowded with fish.

CHAPTER 70

Butchering a turtle was hard work. My first one was a small hawksbill. It was its blood that tempted me, the "good, nutritious, salt-free drink" promised by the survival manual. My thirst was that bad. I took hold of the turtle's shell and grappled with one of its back flippers. When I had a good grip, I turned it over in the water and attempted to pull it onto the raft. The thing was thrashing violently. I would never be able to deal with it on the raft. Either I let it go—or I tried my luck on the lifeboat. I looked up. It was a hot and cloudless day. Richard Parker seemed to tolerate my presence at the bow on such days, when the air was like the inside of an oven and he did not move from under the tarpaulin until sunset.

I held on to one of the turtle's back flippers with one hand and I pulled on the rope to the lifeboat with the other. It was not easy climbing aboard. When I had managed it, I jerked the turtle in the air and brought it onto its back on the tarpaulin. As I had hoped,

Richard Parker did no more than growl once or twice. He was not up to exerting himself in such heat.

My determination was grim and blind. I felt I had no time to waste. I turned to the survival manual as to a cookbook. It said to lay the turtle on its back. Done. It advised that a knife should be "inserted into the neck" to sever the arteries and veins running through it. I looked at the turtle. There was no neck. The turtle had retracted into its shell; all that showed of its head was its eyes and its beak, surrounded by circles of skin. It was looking at me upside down with a stern expression. I took hold of the knife and, hoping to goad it, poked a front flipper. It only shrank further into its shell. I decided on a more direct approach. As confidently as if I had done it a thousand times, I jammed the knife just to the right of the turtle's head, at an angle. I pushed the blade deep into the folds of skin and twisted it. The turtle retreated even further, favouring the side where the blade was, and suddenly shot its head forward, beak snapping at me viciously. I jumped back. All four flippers came out and the creature tried to make its getaway. It rocked on its back, flippers beating wildly and head shaking from side to side. I took hold of a hatchet and brought it down on the turtle's neck, gashing it. Bright red blood shot out. I grabbed the beaker and collected about three hundred millilitres, a pop can's worth. I might have got much more, a litre I would guess, but the turtle's beak was sharp and its front flippers were long and powerful, with two claws on each. The blood I managed to collect gave off no particular smell. I took a sip. It tasted warm and animal, if my memory is right. It's hard to remember first impressions. I drank the blood to the last drop.

I thought I would use the hatchet to remove the tough belly shell, but it proved easier with the sawtoothed edge of the knife. I set one foot at the centre of the shell, the other clear of the flailing flippers. The leathery skin at the head end of the shell was easy cutting, except around the flippers. Sawing away at the rim, however, where shell met shell, was very hard work, especially as the turtle wouldn't stop moving. By the time I had gone all the way around I was bathed in sweat and exhausted. I pulled on the belly shell. It lifted reluctantly, with a wet sucking sound. Inner life was revealed, twitching and jerking—muscles, fat, blood, guts and bones. And still the turtle thrashed about. I slashed its neck to the vertebrae. It made no difference. Flippers continued to beat. With two blows of the hatchet I cut its head right off. The flippers did not stop. Worse, the separated head went on gulping for air and blinking its eyes. I pushed it into the sea. The living rest of the turtle I lifted and dropped into Richard Parker's territory. He was making noises and sounded as if he were about to stir. He had probably smelled the turtle's blood. I fled to the raft.

I watched sullenly as he loudly appreciated my gift and made a joyous mess of himself. I was utterly spent. The effort of butchering the turtle had hardly seemed worth the cup of blood.

I started thinking seriously about how I was going to deal with Richard Parker. This forbearance on his part on hot, cloudless days, if that is what it was and not simple laziness, was not good enough. I couldn't always be running away from him. I needed safe access to the locker and the top of the tarpaulin, no matter the time of day or the weather, no matter his mood. It was rights I needed, the sort of rights that come with might.

It was time to impose myself and carve out my territory.

CHAPTER 71

To those who should ever find themselves in a predicament such as I was in, I would recommend tl following program:

1. Choose a day when the waves are small but regular. You want a sea that will put on a good show when your lifeboat is broadside to it, though without capsizing your boat.

2. Stream your sea anchor full out to make your lifeboat as stable and comfortable as possible. Prepare your safe haven from the lifeboat in case you should need it (you most likely will). If you can, devise some means of bodily protection. Almost anything can make a shield. Wrapping clothes or blankets around your limbs will make for a minimal form of armour.

3. Now comes the difficult part: you must provoke the animal that is afflicting you. Tiger, rhinoceros, ostrich, wild boar, brown bear—no matter the beast, you must get its goat. The best way to do this will most likely be to go to the edge of your territory and noisily intrude into the neutral zone. I did just that: I went to the edge of the tarpaulin and stamped upon the middle bench as I mildly blew into the whistle. It is important that you make a consistent, recognizable noise to signal your aggression. But you must be careful. You want to provoke your animal, but only so much. You don't want it to attack you outright. If it does, God be with you. You will be torn to pieces, trampled flat, disembowelled, very likely eaten. You don't want that. You want an animal that is piqued, peeved, vexed, bothered, irked, annoyed—but not homicidal. Under no circumstances should you step into your animal's territory. Contain your aggression to staring into its eyes and hurling toots and taunts.

4. When your animal has been roused, work in all bad faith to provoke a border intrusion. A good way of bringing this about in my experience is to back off slowly as you are making your noises. BE SURE NOT TO BREAK EYE CONTACT! As soon as the animal has laid a paw in your territory, or even made a determined advance into the neutral territory,

you have achieved your goal. Don't be picky or legalistic as to where its paw actually landed. Be quick to be affronted. Don't wait to construe—misconstrue as fast as you can. The point here is to make your animal understand that its upstairs neighbour is exceptionally persnickety about territory.

5. Once your animal has trespassed upon your territory, be unflagging in your outrage. Whether you have fled to your safe haven off the lifeboat or retreated to the back of your territory on the lifeboat, START BLOWING YOUR WHISTLE AT FULL BLAST and IMMEDIATELY TRIP THE SEA ANCHOR. These two actions are of pivotal importance. You must not delay putting them into effect. If you can help your lifeboat get broadside to the waves by other means, with an oar for example, apply yourself right away. The faster your lifeboat broaches to the waves, the better.

6. Blowing a whistle continuously is exhausting for the weakened castaway, but you must not falter. Your alarmed animal must associate its increasing nausea with the shrill cries of the whistle. You can help things move along by standing at the end of your boat, feet on opposing gunnels, and swaying in rhythm to the motion imparted by the sea. However slight you are, however large your lifeboat, you will be amazed at the difference this will make. I assure you, in no time you'll have your lifeboat rocking and rolling like Elvis Presley. Just don't forget to be blowing your whistle all the while, and mind you don't make your lifeboat capsize.

7. You want to keep going until the animal that is your burden—your tiger, your rhinoceros, whatever—is properly green about the gills with seasickness. You want to hear it heaving and dry retching. You want to see it lying at the bottom of the lifeboat, limbs trembling, eyes rolled back, a deathly rattle coming from its gaping mouth. And all the

while you must be shattering the animal's ears with the piercing blows of your whistle. If you become sick yourself, don't waste your vomit by sending it overboard. Vomit makes an excellent border guard. Puke on the edges of your territory.

8. When your animal appears good and sick, you can stop. Seasickness comes on quickly, but it takes a long while to go away. You don't want to overstate your case. No one dies of nausea, but it can seriously sap the will to live. When enough is enough, stream the sea anchor, try to give shade to your animal if it has collapsed in direct sunlight, and make sure it has water available when it recovers, with anti-seasickness tablets dissolved in it, if you have any. Dehydration is a serious danger at this point. Otherwise, retreat to your territory and leave your animal in peace. Water, rest and relaxation, besides a stable lifeboat, will bring it back to life. The animal should be allowed to recover fully before going through steps 1 to 8 again.

9. Treatment should be repeated until the association in the animal's mind between the sound of the whistle and the feeling of intense, incapacitating nausea is fixed and totally unambiguous. Thereafter, the whistle alone will deal with trespassing or any other untoward behaviour. Just one shrill blow and you will see your animal shudder with malaise and repair at top speed to the safest, furthest part of its territory. Once this level of training is reached, use of the whistle should be sparing.

CHAPTER 72

In my case, to protect myself from Richard Parker while I trained him, I made a shield with a turtle shell. I cut a notch on each side of the shell and connected them with a length of rope. The shield was heavier than I would have liked, but do soldiers ever get to choose their ordnance?

The first time I tried, Richard Parker bared his teeth, rotated his ears full round, vomited a short guttural roar and charged. A great, full-clawed paw rose in the air and cuffed my shield. The blow sent me flying off the boat. I hit the water and instantly let go of the shield. It sank without a trace after hitting me in the shin. I was beside myself with terror—of Richard Parker, but also of being in the water. In my mind a shark was at that very second shooting up for me. I swam for the raft in frantic strokes, precisely the sort of wild thrashing that sharks find so deliciously inviting. Luckily there were no sharks. I reached the raft, let out all the rope and sat with my arms wrapped around my knees and my head down, trying to put out the fire of fear that was blazing within me. It was a long time before the trembling of my body stopped completely. I stayed on the raft for the rest of that day and the whole night. I did not eat or drink.

I was at it again next time I caught a turtle. Its shell was smaller, lighter, and made for a better shield. Once more I advanced and started stamping on the middle bench with my foot.

I wonder if those who hear this story will understand that my behaviour was not an act of insanity or a covert suicide attempt, but a simple necessity. Either I tamed him, made him see who was Number One and who was Number Two—or I died the day I wanted to climb aboard the lifeboat during rough weather and he objected.

If I survived my apprenticeship as a high seas animal trainer, it was because Richard Parker did not really want to attack me. Tigers, indeed all animals, do not favour violence as a means of settling scores. When animals fight, it is with the intent to kill and with the understanding that they may be killed. A clash is costly. And so animals have a full system of cautionary signals designed to avoid a showdown, and they are quick to back down when they feel they can.

Rarely will a tiger attack a fellow predator without warning. Typically a head-on rush for the adversary will be made, with much snarling and growling. But just before it is too late, the tiger will freeze, the menace rumbling deep in its throat. It will appraise the situation. If it decides that there is no threat, it will turn away, feeling that its point has been made.

Richard Parker made his point with me four times. Four times he struck at me with his right paw and sent me overboard, and four times I lost my shield. I was terrified before, during and after each attack, and I spent a long time shivering with fear on the raft. Eventually I learned to read the signals he was sending me. I found that with his ears, his eyes, his whiskers, his teeth, his tail and his throat, he spoke a simple, forcefully punctuated language that told me what his next move might be. I learned to back down before he lifted his paw in the air.

Then I made *my* point, feet on the gunnel, boat rolling, my single-note language blasting from the whistle, and Richard Parker moaning and gasping at the bottom of the boat.

My fifth shield lasted me the rest of his training.

CHAPTER 73

My greatest wish—other than salvation—was to have a book. A long book with a never-ending story. One I could read again and again, with new eyes and a fresh understanding each time. Alas, there was no scripture in the lifeboat. I was a disconsolate Arjuna in a battered chariot without the benefit of Krishna's words. The first time I came upon a Bible in the bedside table of a hotel room in Canada, I burst into tears. I sent a contribution to the Gideons the very next day, with a note urging them to spread the range of their activity to all places where worn and weary travellers might lay down their heads, not just to hotel rooms, and that they should leave not only Bibles, but other sacred writings as well. I cannot think of a better way to spread the faith. No thundering from a pulpit, no condemnation from bad churches, no peer pressure, just a book of scripture quietly waiting to say hello, as gentle and powerful as a little girl's kiss on your cheek.

At the very least, if I had had a good novel! But there was only the survival manual, which I must have read ten thousand times over the course of my ordeal.

I kept a diary. It's hard to read. I wrote as small as I could. I was afraid I would run out of paper. There's not much to it. Words scratched on a page trying to capture a reality that overwhelmed me. I started it a week or so after the sinking of the *Tsimtsum*. Before that I was too busy and scattered. The entries are not dated or numbered. What strikes me now is how time is captured. Several days, several weeks, all on one page. I talked about what you might expect: about things that happened and how I felt, about what I caught and what I didn't, about seas and weather, about problems and solutions, about Richard Parker. All very practical stuff.

CHAPTER 74

I practised religious rituals that I adapted to the circumstances—solitary Masses without priests or consecrated Communion hosts, darshans without murtis, and pujas with turtle meat for prasad, acts of devotion to Allah not knowing where Mecca was and getting my Arabic wrong. They brought me comfort, that is certain. But it was hard, oh, it was hard. Faith in God is an opening up, a letting go, a deep trust, a free act of love—but sometimes it was so hard to love.

Sometimes my heart was sinking so fast with anger, desolation and weariness, I was afraid it would sink to the very bottom of the Pacific and I would not be able to lift it back up.

At such moments I tried to elevate myself. I would touch the turban I had made with the remnants of my shirt and I would say aloud, "THIS IS GOD'S HAT!"

I would pat my pants and say aloud, "THIS IS GOD'S ATTIRE!"

I would point to Richard Parker and say aloud, "THIS IS GOD'S CAT!"

I would point to the lifeboat and say aloud, "THIS IS GOD'S ARK!"

I would spread my hands wide and say aloud, "THESE ARE GOD'S WIDE ACRES!"

I would point at the sky and say aloud, "THIS IS GOD'S EAR!"

And in this way I would remind myself of creation and of my place in it.

But God's hat was always unravelling. God's pants were falling apart. God's cat was a constant danger. God's ark was a jail. God's wide acres were slowly killing me. God's ear didn't seem to be listening.

Despair was a heavy blackness that let no light in or out. It was a hell beyond expression. I thank God it always passed. A school of fish appeared around the net or a knot cried out to be reknotted. Or I thought of my family, of how they were spared this terrible agony. The blackness would stir and eventually go away, and God would remain, a shining point of light in my heart. I would go on loving.

CHAPTER 75

On the day when I estimated it was Mother's birthday, I sang "Happy Birthday" to her out loud.

CHAPTER 76

I got into the habit of cleaning up after Richard Parker. As soon as I became aware that he had had a bowel movement, I went about getting to it, a risky operation involving nudging his feces my way with the gaff and reaching for them from the tarpaulin. Feces can be infected with parasites. This does not matter with animals in the wild since they rarely spend any time next to their feces and mostly have a neutral relationship to them; tree dwellers hardly see them at all and land animals normally excrete and move on. In the compact territory of a zoo, however, the case is quite different, and to leave feces in an animal's enclosure is to invite reinfection by encouraging the animal to eat them, animals being gluttons for anything that remotely resembles food. That is why enclosures are cleaned, out of concern for the intestinal health of animals, not to spare the eyes and noses of visitors. But upholding the Patel family's reputation for high standards in zookeeping was not my concern in the case at hand. In a matter of weeks Richard Parker became constipated and his bowel movements came no more than once a month, so my dangerous janitoring was hardly worth it from a sanitary point of view. It was for another reason that I did it: it was because the first time Richard Parker relieved himself in the lifeboat, I noticed that he tried to hide the result. The significance of this was not lost on me. To display his feces openly, to flaunt the smell of them, would have been a sign of social dominance. Conversely, to hide them, or try to, was a sign of deference—of deference to *me*.

I could tell that it made him nervous. He stayed low, his head cocked back and his ears flat to the sides, a quiet, sustained growl coming from him. I proceeded with exceptional alertness and deliberation, not only to preserve my life but also to give him the right signal. The right signal was that when I had his feces in my hand, I rolled them about for some seconds, brought them close to my nose and sniffed them loudly, and swung my gaze his way a few times in a showy manner, glaring at him wide-eyed (with fear, if only he knew) long enough to give him the willies, but not so long as to provoke him. And with each swing of my gaze, I blew in a low, menacing way in the whistle. By doing this, by badgering him with my eyes (for, of course, with all animals, including us, to stare is an aggressive act) and by sounding that whistle cry that had such ominous associations in his mind, I made clear to Richard Parker that it was my right, my lordly right, to fondle and sniff his feces if I wanted to. So you see, it was not good zookeeping I was up to, but psychological bullying. And it worked. Richard Parker never stared back; his gaze always floated in mid-air, neither on me nor off me. It was something I could feel as much as I felt his balls of excrement in my hand: mastery in the making. The exercise always left me utterly drained from the tension, yet exhilarated.

Since we are on the subject, I became as constipated as Richard Parker. It was the result of our diet, too little water and too much protein. For me, relieving myself, also a monthly act, was hardly that. It was a long-drawn, arduous and painful event that left me bathing in sweat and helpless with exhaustion, a trial worse than a high fever.

CHAPTER 77

As the cartons of survival rations diminished, I reduced my intake till I was following instructions exactly, holding myself to only two biscuits every eight hours. I was continuously hungry. I thought about food obsessively. The less I had to eat, the larger became the portions I dreamed of. My fantasy meals grew to be the size of India.

A Ganges of dhal soup. Hot chapattis the size of Rajasthan. Bowls of rice as big as Uttar Pradesh. Sambars to flood all of Tamil Nadu. Ice cream heaped as high as the Himalayas. My dreaming became quite expert: all ingredients for my dishes were always in fresh and plentiful supply; the oven or frying pan was always at just the right temperature; the proportion of things was always bang on; nothing was ever burnt or undercooked, nothing too hot or too cold. Every meal was simply perfect—only just beyond the reach of my hands.

By degrees the range of my appetite increased. Whereas at first I gutted fish and peeled their skin fastidiously, soon I no more than rinsed off their slimy slipperiness before biting into them, delighted to have such a treat between my teeth. I recall flying fish as being quite tasty, their flesh rosy white and tender. Dorado had a firmer texture and a stronger taste. I began to pick at fish heads rather than toss them to Richard Parker or use them as bait. It was a great discovery when I found that a fresh-tasting fluid could be sucked out not only from the eyes of larger fish but also from their vertebrae. Turtles—which previously I had roughly opened up with the knife and tossed onto the floor of the boat for Richard Parker, like a bowl of hot soup—became my favourite dish.

It seems impossible to imagine that there was a time when I looked upon a live sea turtle as a ten-course meal of great delicacy, a blessed respite from fish. Yet so it was. In the veins of turtles coursed a sweet lassi that had to be drunk as soon as it spurted from their necks, because it coagulated in less than a minute. The best poriyals and kootus in the land could not rival turtle flesh, either cured brown or fresh deep red. No cardamom payasam I ever tasted was as sweet or as rich as creamy turtle eggs or cured turtle fat. A chopped-up mixture of heart, lungs, liver, flesh and cleaned-out intestines sprinkled with fish parts, the whole soaked in a yolk-and-serum gravy, made an unsurpassable, finger-licking thali. By the end of my journey I was eating everything a turtle had to offer. In the algae that covered the shells of some hawksbills I sometimes found small crabs and barnacles. Whatever I found in a turtle's stomach became my turn to eat. I whiled away many a pleasant hour gnawing at a flipper joint or splitting open bones and licking out their marrow. And my fingers were forever picking away at bits of dry fat and dry flesh that clung to the inner sides of shells, rummaging for food in the automatic way of monkeys.

Turtle shells were very handy. I couldn't have done without them. They served not only as shields, but as cutting boards for fish and as bowls for mixing food. And when the elements had destroyed the blankets beyond repair, I used the shells to protect myself from the sun by propping them against each other and lying beneath them.

It was frightening, the extent to which a full belly made for a good mood. The one would follow the other measure for measure: so much food and water, so much good mood. It was such a terribly fickle existence. I was at the mercy of turtle meat for smiles.

By the time the last of the biscuits had disappeared, anything was good to eat, no matter the taste. I could put anything in my mouth, chew it and swallow it—delicious, foul or plain—so long as it wasn't salty. My body developed a revulsion for salt that I still experience to this day.

I tried once to eat Richard Parker's feces. It happened early on, when my system hadn't learned yet to live with hunger and my imagination was still wildly searching for solutions. I had delivered fresh solar-still water to his bucket not long before. After draining it in one go, he had disappeared below the tarpaulin and I had returned to attending to some small matter in the locker. As I always did in those early days, I glanced below the tarpaulin every so often to make sure he wasn't up to something. Well, this one time, lo, he was. He was crouched, his back was rounded and his rear legs were spread. His tail was raised, pushing up against the tarpaulin. The position was tell-tale. Right away I had food in mind, not animal hygiene. I decided there was little danger. He was turned the other way and his head was out of sight. If I respected his peace and quiet, he might not even notice me. I grabbed a bailing cup and stretched my arm forward. My cup arrived in the nick of time. At the second it was in position at the base of his tail, Richard Parker's anus distended, and out of it, like a bubble-gum balloon, came a black sphere of excrement. It fell into my cup with a clink, and no doubt I will be considered to have abandoned the last vestiges of humanness by those who do not understand the degree of my suffering when I say that it sounded to my ears like the music of a five-rupee coin dropped into a beggar's cup. A smile cracked my lips and made them bleed. I felt deep gratitude towards Richard Parker. I pulled back the cup. I took the turd in my fingers. It was very warm, but the smell was not strong. In size it was like a big ball of gulab jamun, but with none of the softness. In fact, it was as hard as a rock. Load a musket with it and you could have shot a rhino.

I returned the ball to the cup and added a little water. I covered it and set it aside. My mouth watered as I waited. When I couldn't stand the wait any longer, I popped the ball into my mouth. I couldn't eat it. The taste was acrid, but it wasn't that. It was rather my mouth's conclusion, immediate and obvious: there's nothing to be had here. It was truly waste matter, with no nutrients in it. I spat it out and was bitter at the loss of precious water. I took the gaff and went about collecting the rest of Richard Parker's feces. They went straight to the fish.

After just a few weeks my body began to deteriorate. My feet and ankles started to swell and I was finding it very tiring to stand.

CHAPTER 78

There were many skies. The sky was invaded by great white clouds, flat on the bottom but round and billowy on top. The sky was completely cloudless, of a blue quite shattering to the senses. The sky was a heavy, suffocating blanket of grey cloud, but without promise of rain. The sky was thinly overcast. The sky was dappled with small, white, fleecy clouds. The sky was streaked with high, thin clouds that looked like a cotton ball stretched apart. The sky was a featureless milky haze. The sky was a density of dark and blustery rain clouds that passed by without delivering rain. The sky was painted with a small number of flat clouds that looked like sandbars. The sky was a mere block to allow a visual effect on the horizon: sunlight flooding the ocean, the vertical edges between light and shadow perfectly distinct. The sky was a distant black curtain of falling rain. The sky was many clouds at many levels, some thick and opaque, others looking like smoke. The sky was black and spitting rain on my smiling face. The sky was nothing but falling water, a ceaseless deluge that wrinkled and bloated my skin and froze me stiff.

There were many seas. The sea roared like a tiger. The sea whispered in your ear like a friend telling you secrets. The sea clinked like small change in a pocket. The sea thundered like avalanches. The sea hissed like sandpaper working on wood. The sea sounded like someone vomiting. The sea was dead silent.

And in between the two, in between the sky and the sea, were all the winds.

And there were all the nights and all the moons.

To be a castaway is to be a point perpetually at the centre of a circle. However much things may appear to change—the sea may shift from whisper to rage, the sky might go from fresh blue to blinding white to darkest black—the geometry never changes. Your gaze is always a radius. The circumference is ever great. In fact, the circles multiply. To be a castaway is to be caught in a harrowing ballet of circles. You are at the centre of one circle, while above you two opposing circles spin about. The sun distresses you like a crowd, a noisy, invasive crowd that makes you cup your ears, that makes you close your eyes, that makes you want to hide. The moon distresses you by silently reminding you of your solitude; you open your eyes wide to escape your loneliness. When you look up, you sometimes wonder if at the centre of a solar storm, if in the middle of the Sea of Tranquillity, there isn't another one like you also looking up, also trapped by geometry, also struggling with fear, rage, madness, hopelessness, apathy.

Otherwise, to be a castaway is to be caught up in grim and exhausting opposites. When it is light, the openness of the sea is blinding and frightening. When it is dark, the darkness is claustrophobic. When it is day, you are hot and wish to be cool and dream of ice cream and pour sea water on yourself. When it is night, you are cold and wish to be warm and dream of hot curries and wrap yourself in blankets. When it is hot, you are parched and wish to be wet. When it rains, you are nearly drowned and wish to be dry. When there is food, there is too much of it and you must feast. When there is none, there is truly none and you starve. When the sea is flat and motionless, you wish it would stir. When it rises up and the circle that imprisons you is broken by hills of water, you suffer that peculiarity of the high seas, suffocation in open spaces, and you wish the sea would be flat again. The opposites often take place at the same moment, so that when the sun is scorching you till you are stricken down, you are also aware that it is drying the strips of fish and meat that are hanging from your lines and that it is a blessing for your solar stills. Conversely, when a rain squall is replenishing your fresh-water supplies, you also know that the humidity will affect your cured provisions and that some will probably go bad, turning pasty and green. When rough weather abates, and it becomes clear that you have survived the sky's attack and the sea's treachery, your jubilation is tempered by the rage that so much fresh water should fall directly into the sea and by the worry that it is the last rain you will ever see, that you will die of thirst before the next drops fall.

The worst pair of opposites is boredom and terror. Sometimes your life is a pendulum swing from one to the other. The sea is without a wrinkle. There is not a whisper of wind. The hours last forever. You are so bored you sink into a state of apathy close to a coma. Then the sea becomes rough and your emotions are whipped into a frenzy. Yet even these two opposites do not remain distinct. In your boredom there are elements of terror: you break down into tears; you are filled with dread; you scream; you deliberately hurt yourself. And in the grip of terror—the worst storm—you yet feel boredom, a deep weariness with it all.

Only death consistently excites your emotions, whether contemplating it when life is safe and stale, or fleeing it when life is threatened and precious.

Life on a lifeboat isn't much of a life. It is like an end game in chess, a game with few pieces. The elements couldn't be more simple, nor the stakes higher. Physically it is extraordinarily arduous, and morally it is killing. You must make adjustments if you want to survive. Much becomes expendable. You get your happiness where you can. You reach a point where you're at the bottom of hell, yet you have your arms crossed and a smile on your face, and you feel you're the luckiest person on earth. Why? Because at your feet you have a tiny dead fish.

CHAPTER 79

There were sharks every day, mainly makos and blue sharks, but also oceanic whitetips, and once a tiger shark straight from the blackest of nightmares. Dawn and dusk were their favourite times. They never seriously troubled us. On occasion one knocked the hull of the lifeboat with its tail. I don't think it was accidental (other marine life did it too, turtles and even dorados). I believe it was part of a shark's way of determining the nature of the lifeboat. A good whack on the offender's nose with a hatchet sent it vanishing post-haste into the deep. The main nuisance of sharks was that they made being in the water risky, like trespassing on a property where there's a sign saying Beware of Dog. Otherwise, I grew quite fond of sharks. They were like curmudgeonly old friends who would never admit that they liked me yet came round to see me all the time. The blue sharks were smaller, usually no more than four or five feet long, and the most attractive, sleek and slender, with small mouths and discreet gill slits. Their backs were a rich ultramarine and their stomachs snow white, colours that vanished to grey or black when they were at any depth, but which close to the surface sparkled with surprising brilliance. The makos were larger and had mouths bursting with frightening teeth, but they too were nicely coloured, an indigo blue that shimmered beautifully in the sun. The oceanic whitetips were often shorter than the makos—some of which stretched to twelve feet—but they were much stockier and had enormous dorsal fins that they sailed high above the surface of the water, like a war banner, a rapidly moving sight that was always nerve-racking to behold. Besides, they were a dull colour, a sort of greyish brown, and the mottled white tips of their fins held no special attraction.

I caught a number of small sharks, blue sharks for the most part, but some makos too. Each time it was just after sunset, in the dying light of the day, and I caught them with my bare hands as they came close to the lifeboat.

The first one was my largest, a mako over four feet long. It had come and gone near the bow several times. As it was passing by yet again, I impulsively dropped my hand into the water and grabbed it just ahead of the tail, where its body was thinnest. Its harsh skin afforded such a marvellously good grip that without thinking about what I was doing, I pulled. As I pulled, it jumped, giving my arm a terrific shake. To my horror and delight the thing vaulted in the air in an explosion of water and spray. For the merest fraction of a second I didn't know what to do next. The thing was smaller than I—but wasn't I being a foolhardy Goliath here? Shouldn't I let go? I turned and swung, and falling on the tarpaulin, I threw the mako towards the stern. The fish fell from the sky into Richard Parker's territory. It landed with a crash and started thwacking about with such thunder that I was afraid it would demolish the boat. Richard Parker was startled. He attacked immediately.

An epic battle began. Of interest to zoologists I can report the following: a tiger will not at first attack a shark out of water with its jaws but will rather strike at it with its forepaws. Richard Parker started clubbing the shark. I shuddered at every blow. They were simply terrible. Just one delivered to a human would break every bone, would turn any piece of furniture into splinters, would reduce an entire house into a pile of rubble. That the mako was not enjoying the treatment was evident from the way it was twisting and turning and beating its tail and reaching with its mouth.

Perhaps it was because Richard Parker was not familiar with sharks, had never encountered a predatory fish—whatever the case, it happened: an accident, one of those few times when I was reminded that Richard Parker was not perfect, that despite his honed instincts he too could bumble. He put his left paw into the mako's mouth. The mako closed its jaws. Immediately Richard Parker reared onto his back legs. The shark was jerked up, but it wouldn't let go. Richard Parker fell back down, opened his mouth wide and full-out roared. I felt a blast of hot air against my body. The air visibly shook, like the heat coming off a road on a hot day. I can well imagine that somewhere far off, 150 miles away, a ship's watch looked up, startled, and later reported the oddest thing, that he thought he heard a cat's meow coming from three o'clock. Days later that roar was still ringing in my guts. But a shark is deaf, conventionally speaking. So while I, who wouldn't think of pinching a tiger's paw, let alone of trying to swallow one, received a volcanic roar full in the face and quaked and trembled and turned liquid with fear and collapsed, the shark perceived only a dull vibration.

Richard Parker turned and started clawing the shark's head with his free front paw and biting it with his jaws, while his rear legs began tearing at its stomach and back. The shark held on to his paw, its only line of defence and attack, and thrashed its tail. Tiger and shark twisted and tumbled about. With great effort I managed to gain enough control of my body to get onto the raft and release it. The lifeboat drifted away. I saw flashes of orange and deep blue, of fur and skin, as the lifeboat rocked from side to side. Richard Parker's snarling was simply terrifying.

At last the boat stopped moving. After several minutes Richard Parker sat up, licking his left paw.

In the following days he spent much time tending his four paws. A shark's skin is covered with minute tubercles that make it as rough as sandpaper. He had no doubt cut himself while repeatedly raking the shark. His left paw was injured, but the damage did not seem permanent; no toes or claws were missing. As for the mako, except for the tips of the tail and the mouth area, incongruously untouched, it was a half-eaten, butchered mess. Chunks of reddish grey flesh and clumps of internal organs were strewn about.

I managed to gaff some of the shark's remains, but to my disappointment the vertebrae of sharks do not hold fluid. At least the flesh was tasty and unfishy, and the crunchiness of cartilage was a welcome respite from so much soft food.

Subsequently I went for smaller sharks, pups really, and I killed them myself. I found that stabbing them through the eyes with the knife was a faster, less tiresome way of killing them than hacking at the tops of their heads with the hatchet.

CHAPTER 80

Of all the dorados, I remember one in particular, a special dorado. It was early morning on a cloudy day, and we were in the midst of a storm of flying fish. Richard Parker was actively swatting at them. I was huddled behind a turtle shell, shielding myself from the flying fish. I had a gaff with a piece of net hanging from it extended into the open. I was hoping to catch fish in this way. I wasn't having much luck. A flying fish whizzed by. The dorado that was chasing it burst out of the water. It was a bad calculation. The anxious flying fish got away, just missing my net, but the dorado hit the gunnel like a cannonball. The thud it made shook the whole boat. A spurt of blood sprayed the tarpaulin. I reacted quickly. I dropped beneath the hail of flying fish and reached for the dorado just ahead of a shark. I pulled it aboard. It was dead, or nearly there, and turning all kinds of colours. What a catch! What a catch! I thought excitedly. Thanks be to you, Jesus-Matsya. The fish was fat and fleshy. It must have weighed a good forty pounds. It would feed a horde. Its eyes and spine would irrigate a desert.

Alas, Richard Parker's great head had turned my way. I sensed it from the corner of my eyes. The flying fish were still coming, but he was no longer interested in them; it was the fish in my hands that was now the focus of his attention. He was eight feet away. His mouth was half open, a fish wing dangling from it. His back became rounder. His rump wriggled. His tail twitched. It was clear: he was in a crouch and he was making to attack me. It was too late to get away, too late even to blow my whistle. My time had come.

But enough was enough. I had suffered so much. I was so hungry. There are only so many days you can go without eating.

And so, in a moment of insanity brought on by hunger—because I was more set on eating than I was on staying alive—without any means of defence, naked in every sense of the term, I looked Richard Parker dead in the eyes. Suddenly his brute strength meant only moral weakness. It was nothing compared to the strength in my mind. I stared into his eyes, wide-eyed and defiant, and we faced off. Any zookeeper will tell you that a tiger, indeed any cat, will not attack in the face of a direct stare but will wait until the deer or antelope or wild ox has turned its eyes. But to know that and to apply it are two very different things (and it's a useless bit of knowledge if you're hoping to stare down a gregarious cat. While you hold one lion in the thrall of your gaze, another will come up to you from behind). For two, perhaps three seconds, a terrific battle of minds for status and authority was waged between a boy and a tiger. He needed to make only the shortest of lunges to be on top of me. But I held my stare.

Richard Parker licked his nose, groaned and turned away. He angrily batted a flying fish. I had won. I gasped with disbelief, heaved the dorado into my hands and hurried away to the raft. Shortly thereafter, I delivered to Richard Parker a fair chunk of the fish.

From that day onwards I felt my mastery was no longer in question, and I began to spend progressively more time on the lifeboat, first at the bow, then, as I gained confidence, on the more comfortable tarpaulin. I was still scared of Richard Parker, but only when it was necessary. His simple presence no longer strained me. You can get used to anything—haven't I already said that? Isn't that what all survivors say?

Initially I lay on the tarpaulin with my head against its rolled-up bow edge. It was raised a little—since the ends of the lifeboat were higher than its middle—and so I could keep an eye on Richard Parker.

Later on I turned the other way, with my head resting just above the middle bench, my back to Richard Parker and his territory. In this position I was further away from the edges of the boat and less exposed to wind and spray.

CHAPTER 81

I know my survival is hard to believe. When I think back, I can hardly believe it myself.

My crude exploitation of Richard Parker's weak sea legs is not the only explanation. There is another: I was the source of food and water. Richard Parker had been a zoo animal as long as he could remember, and he was used to sustenance coming to him without his lifting a paw. True, when it rained and the whole boat became a rain catcher, he understood where the water came from. And when we were hit by a school of flying fish, there too my role was not apparent. But these events did not change the reality of things, which was that when he looked beyond the gunnel, he saw no jungle that he could hunt in and no river from which he could drink freely. Yet I brought him food and I brought him fresh water. My agency was pure and miraculous. It conferred power upon me. Proof: I remained alive day after day, week after week. Proof: he did not attack me, even when I was asleep on the tarpaulin. Proof: I am here to tell you this story.

CHAPTER 82

I kept rainwater and the water I collected from the solar stills in the locker, out of Richard Parker's sight, in the three 50-litre plastic bags. I sealed them with string. Those plastic bags wouldn't have been more precious to me had they contained gold, sapphires, rubies and diamonds. I worried incessantly about them. My worst nightmare was that I would open the locker one morning and find that all three had spilled or, worse still, had split. To forestall such a tragedy, I wrapped them in blankets to keep them from rubbing against the metal hull of the lifeboat, and I moved them as little as possible to reduce wear and tear. But I fretted over the necks of the bags. Would the string not wear them thin? How would I seal the bags if their necks were torn?

When the going was good, when the rain was torrential, when the bags had as much water as I thought they could take, I filled the bailing cups, the two plastic buckets, the two multi-purpose plastic containers, the three beakers and the empty cans of water (which I now preciously kept). Next I filled all the plastic vomit bags, sealing them by twisting them shut and making a knot. After that, if the rain was still coming down, I used myself as a container. I stuck the end of the rain-catcher tube in my mouth and I drank and I drank and I drank.

I always added a little sea water to Richard Parker's fresh water, in a greater proportion in the days following a rainfall, in a lesser during periods of drought. On occasion, in the early days, he dipped his head overboard, sniffed the sea and took a few sips, but quickly he stopped doing it.

Still, we barely got by. The scarcity of fresh water was the single most constant source of anxiety and suffering throughout our journey.

Of whatever food I caught, Richard Parker took the lion's share, so to speak. I had little choice in the matter. He was immediately aware when I landed a turtle or a dorado or a shark, and I had to give quickly and generously. I think I set world records for sawing open the belly shells of turtles. As for fish, they were hewn to pieces practically while they were still flopping about. If I got to be so indiscriminate about what I ate, it was not simply because of appalling hunger; it was also plain rush. Sometimes I just didn't have the time to consider what was before me. It either went into my mouth that instant or was lost to Richard Parker, who was pawing and stamping the ground and huffing impatiently on the edge of his territory. It came as an unmistakable indication to me of how low I had sunk the day I noticed, with a pinching of the heart, that I ate like an animal, that this noisy, frantic, unchewing wolfing-down of mine was exactly the way Richard Parker ate.

CHAPTER 83

The storm came on slowly one afternoon. The clouds looked as if they were stumbling along before the wind, frightened. The sea took its cue. It started rising and falling in a manner that made my heart sink. I took in the solar stills and the net. Oh, you should have seen that landscape! What I had seen up till now were mere hillocks of water. These swells were truly mountains. The valleys we found ourselves in were so deep they were gloomy. Their sides were so steep the lifeboat started sliding down them, nearly surfing. The raft was getting exceptionally rough treatment, being pulled out of the water and dragged along bouncing every which way. I deployed both sea anchors fully, at different lengths so that they would not interfere with each other.

Climbing the giant swells, the boat clung to the sea anchors like a mountain climber to a rope. We would rush up until we reached a snow-white crest in a burst of light and foam and a tipping forward of the lifeboat. The view would be clear for miles around. But the mountain would shift, and the ground beneath us would start sinking in a most stomach-sickening way. In no time we would be sitting once again at the bottom of a dark valley, different from the last but the same, with thousands of tons of water hovering above us and with only our flimsy lightness to save us. The land would move once more, the sea-anchor ropes would snap to tautness, and the roller coaster would start again.

The sea anchors did their job well—in fact, nearly too well. Every swell at its crest wanted to take us for a tumble, but the anchors, beyond the crest, heaved mightily and pulled us through, but at the expense of pulling the front of the boat down. The result was an explosion of foam and spray at the bow. I was soaked through and through each time.

Then a swell came up that was particularly intent on taking us along. This time the bow vanished underwater. I was shocked and chilled and scared witless. I barely managed to hold on. The boat was swamped. I heard Richard Parker roar. I felt death was upon us. The only choice left to me was death by water or death by animal. I chose death by animal.

While we sank down the back of the swell, I jumped onto the tarpaulin and unrolled it towards the stern, closing in Richard Parker. If he protested, I did not hear him. Faster than a sewing machine working a piece of cloth, I hooked down the tarpaulin on both sides of the boat. We were climbing again. The boat was lurching upwards steadily. It was hard to keep my balance. The lifeboat was now covered and the tarpaulin battened down, except at my end. I squeezed in between the side bench and the tarpaulin and pulled the remaining tarpaulin over my head. I did not have much space. Between bench and gunnel there was twelve inches, and the side benches were only one and a half feet wide. But I was not so foolhardy, even in the face of death, as to move onto the floor of the boat. There were four hooks left to catch. I slipped a hand through the opening and worked the rope. With each hook done, it was getting harder to get the next. I managed two. Two hooks left. The boat was rushing upwards in a smooth and unceasing motion. The incline was over thirty degrees. I could feel myself being pulled down towards the stern. Twisting my hand frantically I succeeded in catching one more hook with the rope. It was the best I could do. This was not a job meant to be done from the inside of the lifeboat but from the outside. I pulled hard on the rope, something made easier by the fact that holding on to it was preventing me from sliding down the length of the boat. The boat swiftly passed a forty-five-degree incline.

We must have been at a sixty-degree incline when we reached the summit of the swell and broke through its crest onto the other side. The smallest portion of the swell's supply of water crashed down on us. I felt as if I were being pummelled by a great fist. The lifeboat abruptly tilted forward and everything was reversed: I was now at the lower end of the lifeboat, and the water that had swamped it, with a tiger soaking in it, came my way. I did not feel the tiger—I had no precise idea of where Richard Parker was; it was pitch-black beneath the tarpaulin—but before we reached the next valley I was half-drowned.

For the rest of that day and into the night, we went up and down, up and down, up and down, until terror became monotonous and was replaced by numbness and a complete giving-up. I held on to the tarpaulin rope with one hand and the edge of the bow bench with the other, while my body lay flat against the side bench. In this position—water pouring in, water pouring out—the tarpaulin beat me to a pulp, I was soaked and chilled, and I was bruised and cut by bones and turtle shells. The noise of the storm was constant, as was Richard Parker's snarling.

Sometime during the night my mind noted that the storm was over. We were bobbing on the sea in a normal way. Through a tear in the tarpaulin I glimpsed the night sky. Starry and cloudless. I undid the tarpaulin and lay on top of it.

I noticed the loss of the raft at dawn. All that was left of it were two tied oars and the life jacket between them. They had the same effect on me as the last standing beam of a burnt-down house would have on a householder. I turned and scrutinized every quarter of the horizon. Nothing. My little marine town had vanished. That the sea anchors, miraculously, were not lost—they continued to tug at the lifeboat faithfully—was a consolation that had no effect. The loss of the raft was perhaps not fatal to my body, but it felt fatal to my spirits.

The boat was in a sorry state. The tarpaulin was torn in several places, some tears evidently the work of Richard Parker's claws. Much of our food was gone, either lost overboard or destroyed by the water that had come in. I was sore all over and had a bad cut on my thigh; the wound was swollen and white. I was nearly too afraid to check the contents of the locker. Thank God none of the water bags had split. The net and the solar stills, which I had not entirely deflated, had filled the empty space and prevented the bags from moving too much.

I felt exhausted and depressed. I unhooked the tarpaulin at the stern. Richard Parker was so silent I wondered whether he had drowned. He hadn't. As I rolled back the tarpaulin to the middle bench and daylight came to him, he stirred and growled. He climbed out of the water and set himself on the stern bench. I took out needle and thread and went about mending the tears in the tarpaulin.

Later I tied one of the buckets to a rope and bailed the boat. Richard Parker watched me distractedly. He seemed to find nearly everything I did boring. The day was hot and I proceeded slowly. One haul brought me something I had lost. I considered it. Cradled in the palm of my hand was all that remained between me and death: the last of the orange whistles.

CHAPTER 84

I was on the tarpaulin, wrapped in a blanket, sleeping and dreaming and awakening and daydreaming and generally passing the time. There was a steady breeze. From time to time spray was blown off the crest of a wave and wet the boat. Richard Parker had disappeared under the tarpaulin. He liked neither getting wet nor the ups and downs of the boat. But the sky was blue, the air was warm, and the sea was regular in its motion. I awoke because there was a blast. I opened my eyes and saw water in the sky. It crashed down on me. I looked up again. Cloudless blue sky. There was another blast, to my left, not as powerful as the first. Richard Parker growled fiercely. More water crashed against me. It had an unpleasant smell.

I looked over the edge of the boat. The first thing I saw was a large black object floating in the water. It took me a few seconds to understand what it was. An arching wrinkle around its edge was my clue. It was an eye. It was a whale. Its eye, the size of my head, was looking directly at me.

Richard Parker came up from beneath the tarpaulin. He hissed. I sensed from a slight change in the glint of the whale's eye that it was now looking at Richard Parker. It gazed for thirty seconds or so before gently sinking under. I worried that it might strike us with its tail, but it went straight down and vanished in the dark blue. Its tail was a huge, fading, round bracket.

I believe it was a whale looking for a mate. It must have decided that my size wouldn't do, and besides, I already seemed to have a mate.

We saw a number of whales but none so close up as that first one. I would be alerted to their presence by their spouting. They would emerge a short distance away, sometimes three or four of them, a short-lived archipelago of volcanic islands. These gentle behemoths always lifted my spirits. I was convinced that they understood my condition, that at the sight of me one of them exclaimed, "Oh! It's that castaway with the pussy cat Bamphoo was telling me about. Poor boy. Hope he has enough plankton. I must tell Mumphoo and Tomphoo and Stim-phoo about him. I wonder if there isn't a ship around I could alert. His mother would be very happy to see him again. Goodbye, my boy. I'll try to help. My name's Pimphoo." And so, through the grapevine, every whale of the Pacific knew of me, and I would have been saved long ago if Pimphoo hadn't sought help from a Japanese ship whose dastardly crew harpooned her, the same fate as befell Lamphoo at the hands of a Norwegian ship. The hunting of whales is a heinous crime.

Dolphins were fairly regular visitors. One group stayed with us a whole day and night. They were very gay. Their plunging and turning and racing just beneath the hull seemed to have no purpose other than sporting fun. I tried to catch one. But none came close to the gaff. And even if one had, they were too fast and too big. I gave up and just watched them.

I saw six birds in all. I took each one to be an angel announcing nearby land. But these were seafaring birds that could span the Pacific with hardly a flutter of the wings. I watched them with awe and envy and self-pity.

Twice I saw an albatross. Each flew by high in the air without taking any notice of us. I stared with my mouth open. They were something supernatural and incomprehensible.

Another time, a short distance from the boat, two Wilson's petrels skimmed by, feet skipping on the water. They, too, took no notice of us, and left me similarly amazed.

We at last attracted the attention of a short-tailed shearwater. It circled above us, eventually dropping down. It kicked out its legs, turned its wings and alighted in the water, floating as lightly as a cork. It eyed me with curiosity. I quickly baited a hook with a bit of flying fish and threw the line its way. I put no weights on the line and had difficulty getting it close to the bird. On my third try the bird paddled up to the sinking bait and plunged its head underwater to get at it. My heart pounded with excitement. I did not pull on the line for some seconds. When I did, the bird merely squawked and regurgitated what it had just swallowed. Before I could try again, it unfolded its wings and pulled itself up into the air. Within two, three beatings of its wings it was on its way.

I had better luck with a masked booby. It appeared out of nowhere, gliding towards us, wings spanning over three feet. It landed on the gunnel within hand's reach of me. Its round eyes took me in, the expression puzzled and serious. It was a large bird with a pure snowy white body and wings that were jet-black at their tips and rear edges. Its big, bulbous head had a very pointed orange-yellow beak and the red eyes behind the black mask made it look like a thief who had had a very long night. Only the oversized, brown webbed feet left something to be desired in their design. The bird was fearless. It spent several minutes tweaking its feathers with its beak, exposing soft down. When it was finished, it looked up and everything fell into place, and it showed itself for what it was: a smooth, beautiful, aerodynamic airship. When I offered it a bit of dorado, it pecked it out of my hand, jabbing the palm.

I broke its neck by leveraging its head backwards, one hand pushing up the beak, the other holding the neck. The feathers were so well attached that when I started pulling them out, skin came off—I was not plucking the bird; I was tearing it apart. It was light enough as it was, a volume with no weight. I took the knife and skinned it instead.

For its size there was a disappointing amount of flesh, only a little on its chest. It had a more chewy texture than dorado flesh, but I didn't find there was much of a difference in taste. In its stomach, besides the morsel of dorado I had just given it, I found three small fish. After rinsing them of digestive juices, I ate them. I ate the bird's heart, liver and lungs. I swallowed its eyes and tongue with a gulp of water. I crushed its head and picked out its small brain. I ate the webbings of its feet. The rest of the bird was skin, bone and feathers. I dropped it beyond the edge of the tarpaulin for Richard Parker, who hadn't seen the bird arrive. An orange paw reached out.

Days later feathers and down were still floating up from his den and being blown out to sea. Those that landed in the water were swallowed by fish.

None of the birds ever announced land.

CHAPTER 85

Once there was lightning. The sky was so black, day looked like night. The downpour was heavy. I heard thunder far away. I thought it would stay at that. But a wind came up, throwing the rain this way and that. Right after, a white splinter came crashing down from the sky, puncturing the water. It was some distance from the lifeboat, but the effect was perfectly visible. The water was shot through with what looked like white roots; briefly, a great celestial tree stood in the ocean. I had never imagined such a thing possible, lightning striking the sea. The clap of thunder was tremendous. The flash of light was incredibly vivid.

I turned to Richard Parker and said, "Look, Richard Parker, a bolt of lightning." I saw how he felt about it. He was flat on the floor of the boat, limbs splayed and visibly trembling.

The effect on me was completely the opposite. It was something to pull me out of my limited mortal ways and thrust me into a state of exalted wonder.

Suddenly a bolt struck much closer. Perhaps it was meant for us: we had just fallen off the crest of a swell and were sinking down its back when its top was hit. There was an explosion of hot air and hot water. For two, perhaps three seconds, a gigantic, blinding white shard of glass from a broken cosmic window danced in the sky, insubstantial yet overwhelmingly powerful. Ten thousand trumpets and twenty thousand drums could not have made as much noise as that bolt of lightning; it was positively deafening. The sea turned white and all colour disappeared. Everything was either pure white light or pure black shadow. The light did not seem to illuminate so much as to penetrate. As quickly as it had appeared, the bolt vanished—the spray of hot water had not finished landing upon us and already it was gone. The punished swell returned to black and rolled on indifferently.

I was dazed, thunderstruck—nearly in the true sense of the word. But not afraid.

"Praise be to Allah, Lord of All Worlds, the Compassionate, the Merciful, Ruler of Judgment Day!" I muttered. To Richard Parker I shouted, "Stop your trembling! This is miracle. This is an outbreak of divinity. This is . . . this is . . ." I could not find what it was, this thing so vast and fantastic. I was breathless and wordless. I lay back on the tarpaulin, arms and legs spread wide. The rain chilled me to the bone. But I was smiling. I remember that close encounter with electrocution and third-degree burns as one of the few times during my ordeal when I felt genuine happiness.

At moments of wonder, it is easy to avoid small thinking, to entertain thoughts that span the universe, that capture both thunder and tinkle, thick and thin, the near and the far.

CHAPTER 86

"Richard Parker, a ship!"

I had the pleasure of shouting that once. I was overwhelmed with happiness. All hurt and frustration fell away and I positively blazed with joy.

"We've made it! We're saved! Do you understand, Richard Parker? WE'RE SAVED! Ha, ha, ha, ha!"

I tried to control my excitement. What if the ship passed too far away to see us? Should I launch a rocket flare? Nonsense!

"It's coming right towards us, Richard Parker! Oh, I thank you, Lord Ganesha! Blessed be you in all your manifestations, Allah-Brahman!"

It couldn't miss us. Can there be any happiness greater than the happiness of salvation? The answer—believe me—is No. I got to my feet, the first time in a long time I had made such an effort.

"Can you believe it, Richard Parker? People, food, a bed. Life is ours once again. Oh, what bliss!"

The ship came closer still. It looked like an oil tanker. The shape of its bow was becoming distinct. Salvation wore a robe of black metal with white trim.

"And what if . . . ?"

I did not dare say the words. But might there not be a chance that Father and Mother and Ravi were still alive? The *Tsimtsum* had had a number of lifeboats. Perhaps they had reached Canada weeks ago and were anxiously waiting for news from me. Perhaps I was the only person from the wreck unaccounted for.

"My God, oil tankers are big!"

It was a mountain creeping up on us.

"Perhaps they're already in Winnipeg. I wonder what our house looks like. Do you suppose, Richard Parker, that Canadian houses have inner courtyards in the traditional Tamil style? Probably not. I suppose they would fill up with snow in winter. Pity. There's no peace like the peace of an inner courtyard on a sunny day. I wonder what spices grow in Manitoba?"

The ship was very close. The crew better be stopping short or turning sharply soon.

"Yes, what spices . . . ? Oh my God!"

I realized with horror that the tanker was not simply coming our way—it was in fact bearing down on us. The bow was a vast wall of metal that was getting wider every second. A huge wave girdling it was advancing towards us relentlessly. Richard Parker finally sensed the looming juggernaut. He turned and went "Woof! Woof!" but not doglike—it was tigerlike: powerful, scary and utterly suited to the situation.

"Richard Parker, it's going to run us over! What are we going to do? Quick, quick, a flare! No! Must row. Oar in oarlock . . . there! *HUMPF! HUMPF! HUMPF! HUMPF! HUMPF! HUM—*"

The bow wave pushed us up. Richard Parker crouched, and the hairs on him stood up. The lifeboat slid off the bow wave and missed the tanker by less than two feet.

The ship slid by for what seemed like a mile, a mile of high, black canyon wall, a mile of castle fortification with not a single sentinel to notice us languishing in the moat. I fired off a rocket flare, but I aimed it poorly. Instead of surging over the bulwarks and exploding in the captain's face, it ricocheted off the ship's side and went straight into the Pacific, where it died with a hiss. I blew on my whistle with all my might. I shouted at the top of my lungs. All to no avail.

Its engines rumbling loudly and its propellers chopping explosively underwater, the ship churned past us and left us bouncing and bobbing in its frothy wake. After so many weeks of natural sounds, these mechanical noises were strange and awesome and stunned me into silence.

In less than twenty minutes a ship of three hundred thousand tons became a speck on the horizon. When I turned away, Richard Parker was still looking in its direction. After a few seconds he turned away too and our gazes briefly met. My eyes expressed longing, hurt, anguish, loneliness. All he was aware of was that something stressful and momentous had happened, something beyond the outer limits of his understanding. He did not see that it was salvation barely missed. He only saw that the alpha here, this odd, unpredictable tiger, had been very excited. He settled down to another nap. His sole comment on the event was a cranky meow.

"I love you!" The words burst out pure and unfettered, infinite. The feeling flooded my chest. "Truly I do. I love you, Richard Parker. If I didn't have you now, I don't know what I would do. I don't think I would make it. No, I wouldn't. I would die of hopelessness. Don't give up, Richard Parker, don't give up. I'll get you to land, I promise, I promise!"

CHAPTER 87

One of my favourite methods of escape was what amounts to gentle asphyxiation. I used a piece of cloth that I cut from the remnants of a blanket. I called it my dream rag. I wet it with sea water so that it was soaked but not dripping. I lay comfortably on the tarpaulin and I placed the dream rag on my face, fitting it to my features. I would fall into a daze, not difficult for someone in such an advanced state of lethargy to begin with. But the dream rag gave a special quality to my daze. It must have been the way it restricted my air intake. I would be visited by the most extraordinary dreams, trances, visions, thoughts, sensations, remembrances. And time would be gobbled up. When a twitch or a gasp disturbed me and the rag fell away, I'd come to full consciousness, delighted to find that time had slipped by. The dryness of the rag was part proof. But more than that was the feeling that things were different, that the present moment was different from the previous present moment.

CHAPTER 88

One day we came upon trash. First the water glistened with patches of oil. Coming up soon after was the domestic and industrial waste: mainly plastic refuse in a variety of forms and colours, but also pieces of lumber, beer cans, wine bottles, tatters of cloth, bits of rope and, surrounding it all, yellow foam. We advanced into it. I looked to see if there was anything that might be of use to us. I picked out an empty corked wine bottle. The lifeboat bumped into a refrigerator that had lost its motor. It floated with its door to the sky. I reached out, grabbed the handle and lifted the door open. A smell leapt out so pungent and disgusting that it seemed to colour the air. Hand to my mouth, I looked in. There were stains, dark juices, a quantity of completely rotten vegetables, milk so curdled and infected it was a greenish jelly, and the quartered remains of a dead animal in such an advanced state of black putrefaction that I couldn't identify it. Judging by its size I think that it was lamb. In the closed, humid confines of the refrigerator, the smell had had the time to develop, to ferment, to grow bitter and angry. It assaulted my senses with a pent-up rage that made my head reel, my stomach churn and my legs wobble. Luckily, the sea quickly filled the horrid hole and the thing sank beneath the surface. The space left vacant by the departed refrigerator was filled by other trash.

We left the trash behind. For a long time, when the wind came from that direction, I could still smell it. It took the sea a day to wash off the oily smears from the sides of the lifeboat.

I put a message in the bottle: "Japanese-owned cargo ship *Tsimt-sum*, flying Panamanian flag, sank July 2nd, 1977, in Pacific, four days out of Manila. Am in lifeboat. Pi Patel my name. Have some food, some water, but Bengal tiger a serious problem. Please advise family in Winnipeg, Canada. Any help very much appreciated. Thank you." I corked the bottle and covered the cork with a piece of plastic. I tied the plastic to the neck of the bottle with nylon string, knotting it tightly. I launched the bottle into the water.

CHAPTER 89

Everything suffered. Everything became sun-bleached and weather-beaten. The lifeboat, the raft until it was lost, the tarpaulin, the stills, the rain catchers, the plastic bags, the lines, the blankets, the net—all became worn, stretched, slack, cracked, dried, rotted, torn, discoloured. What was orange became whitish orange. What was smooth became rough. What was rough became smooth. What was sharp became blunt. What was whole became tattered. Rubbing fish skins and turtle fat on things, as I did, greasing them a little, made no difference. The salt went on eating everything with its million hungry mouths. As for the sun, it roasted everything. It kept Richard Parker in partial subjugation. It picked skeletons clean and fired them to a gleaming white. It burned off my clothes and would have burned off my skin, dark though it was, had I not protected it beneath blankets and propped-up turtle shells. When the heat was unbearable I took a bucket and poured sea water on myself; some-times the water was so varm it felt like syrup. The sun also took care of all smells. I don't remember any smells. Or only the smell of the spent hand-flare shells. They smelled like cumin, did I mention that? I don't even remember what Richard Parker smelled like.

We perished away. It happened slowly, so that I didn't notice it all the time. But I noticed it regularly. We were two emaciated mammals, parched and starving. Richard Parker's fur lost its lustre, and some of it even fell away from his shoulders and haunches. He lost a lot of weight, became a skeleton in an oversized bag of faded fur. I, too, withered away, the moistness sucked out of me, my bones showing plainly through my thin flesh.

I began to imitate Richard Parker in sleeping an incredible number of hours. It wasn't proper sleep, but a state of semi-consciousness in which daydreams and reality were nearly indistinguishable. I made much use of my dream rag.

These are the last pages of my diary:

Today saw a shark bigger than any I've seen till now. A primeval monster twenty feet long. Striped. A tiger shark—very dangerous. Circled us. Feared it would attack. Have survived one tiger; thought I would die at the hands of another. Did not attack. Floated away. Cloudy weather, but nothing.

No rain. Only morning greyness. Dolphins. Tried to gaff one. Found I could not stand. R. P. weak and ill-tempered. Am so weak, if he attacks I won't be able to defend myself. Simply do not have the energy to blow whistle.

Calm and burning hot day. Sun beating without mercy. Feel my brains are boiling inside my head. Feel horrid.

Prostrate body and soul. Will die soon. R.P. breathing but not moving. Will die too. Will not kill me.

Salvation. An hour of heavy, delicious, beautiful rain. Filled mouth, filled bags and cans, filled body till it could not take another drop. Let myself be soaked to rinse off salt. Crawled over to see R. P. Not reacting. Body curled, tail flat. Coat clumpy with wetness. Smaller when wet. Bony. Touched him for first time ever. To see if dead. Not. Body still warm. Amazing to touch him. Even in this condition, firm, muscular, alive. Touched him and fur shuddered as if I were a gnat. At length, head half in water stirred. Better to drink than to drown. Better sign still: tail jumped. Threw piece of turtle meat in front of nose. Nothing. At last half rose—to drink. Drank and drank. Ate. Did not rise fully. Spent a good hour licking himself all over. Slept.

It's no use. Today I die.

I will die today.

I die.

This was my last entry. I went on from there, endured, but without noting it. Do you see these invisible spirals on the margins of the page? I thought I would run out of paper. It was the pens that ran out.

CHAPTER 90

I said, "Richard Parker, is something wrong? Have you gone blind?" as I waved my hand in his face.

For a day or two he had been rubbing his eyes and meowing disconsolately, but I thought nothing of it. Aches and pains were the only part of our diet that was abundant. I caught a dorado. We hadn't eaten anything in three days. A turtle had come up to the lifeboat the day before, but I had been too weak to pull it aboard. I cut the fish in two halves. Richard Parker was looking my way. I threw him his share. I expected him to catch it in his mouth smartly. It crashed into his blank face. He bent down. After sniffing left and right, he found the fish and began eating it. We were slow eaters now.

I peered into his eyes. They looked no different from any other day. Perhaps there was a little more discharge in the inner corners, but it was nothing dramatic, certainly not as dramatic as his overall appearance. The ordeal had reduced us to skin and bones.

I realized that I had my answer in the very act of looking. I was staring into his eyes as if I were an eye doctor, while he was looking back vacantly. Only a blind wild cat would fail to react to such a stare.

I felt pity for Richard Parker. Our end was approaching.

The next day I started feeling a stinging in my eyes. I rubbed and rubbed, but the itch wouldn't go away. The very opposite: it got worse, and unlike Richard Parker, my eyes started to ooze pus. Then darkness came, blink as I might. At first it was right in front of me, a black spot at the centre of everything. It spread into a blotch that reached to the edges of my vision. All I saw of the sun the next morning was a crack of light at the top of my left eye, like a small window too high up. By noon, everything was pitch-black.

I clung to life. I was weakly frantic. The heat was infernal. I had so little strength I could no longer stand. My lips were hard and cracked. My mouth was dry and pasty, coated with a glutinous saliva as foul to taste as it was to smell. My skin was burnt. My shrivelled muscles ached. My limbs, especially my feet, were swollen and a constant source of pain. I was hungry and once again there was no food. As for water, Richard Parker was taking so much that I was down to five spoonfuls a day. But this physical suffering was nothing compared to the moral torture I was about to endure. I would rate the day I went blind as the day my extreme suffering began. I could not tell you when exactly in the journey it happened. Time, as I said before, became irrelevant. It must have been sometime between the hundredth and the two-hundredth day. I was certain I would not last another one.

By the next morning I had lost all fear of death, and I resolved to die.

I came to the sad conclusion that I could no longer take care of Richard Parker. I had failed as a zookeeper. I was more affected by his imminent demise than I was by my own. But truly, broken down and wasted away as I was, I could do no more for him.

Nature was sinking fast. I could feel a fatal weakness creeping up on me. I would be dead by the afternoon. To make my going more comfortable I decided to put off a little the intolerable thirst I had been living with for so long. I gulped down as much water as I could take. If only I could have had a last bite to eat. But it seemed that was not to be. I set myself against the rolled-up edge of the tarpaulin in the middle of the boat. I closed my eyes and waited for my breath to leave my body. I muttered, "Goodbye, Richard Parker. I'm sorry for having failed you. I did my best. Farewell. Dear Father, dear Mother, dear Ravi, greetings. Your loving son and brother is coming to meet you. Not an hour has gone by that I haven't thought of you. The moment I see you will be the happiest of my life. And now I leave matters in the hands of God, who is love and whom I love."

I heard the words, "Is someone there?"

It's astonishing what you hear when you're alone in the blackness of your dying mind. A sound without shape or colour sounds strange. To be blind is to hear otherwise.

The words came again, "Is someone there?"

I concluded that I had gone mad. Sad but true. Misery loves company, and madness calls it forth.

"Is someone there?" came the voice again, insistent.

The clarity of my insanity was astonishing. The voice had its very own timbre, with a heavy, weary rasp. I decided to play along.

"Of course someone's there," I replied. "There's always some *one* there. Who would be asking the question otherwise?"

"I was hoping there would be someone *else*."

"What do you mean, someone *else*? Do you realize where you are?

If you're not happy with this figment of your fancy, pick another one. There are plenty of fancies to pick from."

Hmmm. Figment. *Fig*-ment. Wouldn't a fig be good?

"So there's no one, is there?"

"Shush . . . I'm dreaming of figs."

"Figs! Do you have a fig? Please can I have a piece? I beg you. Only a little piece. I'm starving."

"I don't have just one fig. I have a whole figment."

"A whole figment of figs! Oh please, can I have some? I . . ."

The voice, or whatever effect of wind and waves it was, faded.

"They're plump and heavy and fragrant," I continued. "The branches of the tree are bent over, they are so weighed down with figs. There must be over three hundred figs in that tree."

Silence.

The voice came back again. "Let's talk about food . . ."

"What a good idea."

"What would you have to eat if you could have anything you wanted?"

"Excellent question. I would have a magnificent buffet. I would start with rice and sambar. There would be black gram dhal rice and curd rice and—"

"I would have—"

"I'm not finished. And with my rice I would have spicy tamarind sambar and small onion sambar and—"

"Anything else?"

"I'm getting there. I'd also have mixed vegetable sagu and vegetable korma and potato masala and cabbage vadai and masala dosai and spicy lentil rasam and—"

"I see."

"Wait. And stuffed eggplant poriyal and coconut yam kootu and rice idli and curd vadai and vegetable bajji and—"

"It sounds very—"

"Have I mentioned the chutneys yet? Coconut chutney and mint chutney and green chilli pickle and gooseberry pickle, all served with the usual nans, popadoms, parathas and puris, of course."

"Sounds—"

"The salads! Mango curd salad and okra curd salad and plain fresh cucumber salad. And for dessert, almond payasam and milk payasam and jaggery pancake and peanut toffee and coconut burfi and vanilla ice cream with hot, thick chocolate sauce."

"Is that it?"

"I'd finish this snack with a ten-litre glass of fresh, clean, cool, chilled water and a coffee."

"It sounds very good."

"It does."

"Tell me, what is coconut yam kootu?"

"Nothing short of heaven, that's what. To make it you need yams, grated coconut, green plantains, chilli powder, ground black pepper, ground turmeric, cumin seeds, brown mustard seeds and some coconut oil. You sauté the coconut until it's golden brown—"

"May I make a suggestion?"

"What?"

"Instead of coconut yam kootu, why not boiled beef tongue with a mustard sauce?"

"That sounds non-veg."

"It is. And then tripe."

"Tripe? You've eaten the poor animal's tongue and now you want to eat its *stomach*?"

"Yes! I dream of *tripes à la mode de Caen*—warm—with sweetbread."

"Sweetbread? That sounds better. What is sweetbread?"

"Sweetbread is made from the pancreas of a calf."

"The pancreas!"

"Braised and with a mushroom sauce, it's simply delicious."

Where were these disgusting, sacrilegious recipes coming from? Was I so far gone that I was contemplating setting upon *a cow and her young*? What horrible crosswind was I caught in? Had the lifeboat drifted back into that floating trash?

"What will be the next affront?"

"Calf's brains in a brown butter sauce!"

"Back to the head, are we?"

"Brain soufflé!"

"I'm feeling sick. Is there anything you *won't* eat?"

"What I would give for oxtail soup. For roast suckling pig stuffed with rice, sausages, apricots and raisins. For veal kidney in a butter, mustard and parsley sauce. For a marinated rabbit stewed in red wine. For chicken liver sausages. For pork and liver pâté with veal. For frogs. Ah, give me frogs, give me frogs!"

"I'm barely holding on."

The voice faded. I was trembling with nausea. Madness in the mind was one thing, but it was not fair that it should go to the stomach.

Understanding suddenly dawned on me.

"Would you eat bleeding raw beef?" I asked.

"Of course! I love tartar steak."

"Would you eat the congealed blood of a dead pig?"

"Every day, with apple sauce!"

"Would you eat *anything* from an animal, the last remains?"

"Scrapple and sausage! I'd have a heaping plate!"

"How about a carrot? Would you eat a plain, raw carrot?"

There was no answer.

"Did you not hear me? Would you eat a carrot?"

"I heard you. To be honest, if I had the choice, I wouldn't. I don't have much of a stomach for that kind of food. I find it quite distasteful."

I laughed. I knew it. I wasn't hearing voices. I hadn't gone mad. It was Richard Parker who was speaking to me! The carnivorous rascal. All this time together and he had chosen an hour before we were to die to pipe up. I was elated to be on speaking terms with a tiger. Immediately I was filled with a vulgar curiosity, the sort that movie stars suffer from at the hands of their fans.

"I'm curious, tell me—have you ever killed a man?"

I doubted it. Man-eaters among animals are as rare as murderers among men, and Richard Parker was caught while still a cub. But who's to say that his mother, before she was nabbed by Thirsty, hadn't caught a human being?

"What a question," replied Richard Parker.

"Seems reasonable."

"It does?"

"Yes."

"Why?"

"You have the reputation that you have."

"I do?"

"Of course. Are you blind to that fact?"

"I am."

"Well, let me make clear what you evidently can't see: you have that reputation. So, have you ever killed a man?"

Silence.

"Well? Answer me."

"Yes."

"Oh! It sends shivers down my spine. How many?"

"Two."

"You've killed two men?"

246

"No. A man and a woman."

"At the same time?"

"No. The man first, the woman second."

"You monster! I bet you thought it was great fun. You must have found their cries and their struggles quite entertaining."

"Not really."

"Were they good?"

"Were they *good*?"

"Yes. Don't be so obtuse. Did they *taste* good?"

"No, they didn't taste good."

"I thought so. I've heard it's an acquired taste in animals. So why did you kill them?"

"Need."

"The need of a monster. Any regrets?"

"It was them or me."

"That is need expressed in all its amoral simplicity. But any regrets now?"

"It was the doing of a moment. It was circumstance."

"Instinct, it's called instinct. Still, answer the question, any regrets now?"

"I don't think about it."

"The very definition of an animal. That's all you are."

"And what are you?"

"A human being, I'll have you know."

"What boastful pride."

"It's the plain truth."

"So, you would throw the first stone, would you?"

"Have you ever had oothappam?"

"No, I haven't. But tell me about it. What is oothappam?"

"It is *so* good."

"Sounds delicious. Tell me more."

"Oothappam is often made with leftover batter, but rarely has a culinary afterthought been so memorable."

"I can already taste it."

I fell asleep. Or, rather, into a state of dying delirium.

But something was niggling at me. I couldn't say what. Whatever it was, it was disturbing my dying.

I came to. I knew what it was that was bothering me.

"Excuse me?"

"Yes?" came Richard Parker's voice faintly.

"Why do you have an accent?"

"I don't. It is you who has an accent."

"No, I don't. You pronounce *the* 'ze'."

"I pronounce *ze* 'ze', as it should be. You speak with warm marbles in your mouth. You have an Indian accent."

"You speak as if your tongue were a saw and English words were made of wood. You have a French accent."

It was utterly incongruous. Richard Parker was born in Bangladesh and raised in Tamil Nadu, so why should he have a French accent? Granted, Pondicherry was once a French colony, but no one would have me believe that some of the zoo animals had frequented the Alliance Française on rue Dumas.

It was very perplexing. I fell into a fog again.

I woke up with a gasp. Someone was there! This voice coming to my ears was neither a wind with an accent nor an animal speaking up. It was someone *else!* My heart beat fiercely, making one last go at pushing some blood through my worn-out system. My mind made a final attempt at being lucid.

"Only an echo, I fear," I heard, barely audibly.

"Wait, I'm here!" I shouted.

"An echo at sea . . ."

"No, it's me!"

"That this would end!"

"My friend!"

"I'm wasting away . . ."

"Stay, stay!"

I could barely hear him.

I shrieked.

He shrieked back.

It was too much. I would go mad.

I had an idea.

"MY NAME," I roared to the elements with my last breath, "IS PISCINE MOLITOR PATEL." How could an echo create a name? "Do you hear me? I am Piscine Molitor Patel, known to all as Pi Patel!"

"What? Is someone there?"

"Yes, someone's there!"

"What! Can it be true? Please, do you have any food? Anything at all. I have no food left. I haven't eaten anything in days. I must have something. I'll be grateful for whatever you can spare. I beg you."

"But I have no food either," I answered, dismayed. "I haven't eaten anything in days myself. I was hoping *you* would have food. Do you have water? My supplies are very low."

"No, I don't. You have no food at all? Nothing?"

"No, nothing."

There was silence, a heavy silence.

"Where are you?" I asked.

"I'm here," he replied wearily.

"But where is that? I can't see you."

"Why can't you see me?"

"I've gone blind."

"What?" he exclaimed.

"I've gone blind. My eyes see nothing but darkness. I blink for nothing. These last two days, if my skin can be trusted to measure time. It only can tell me if it's day or night."

I heard a terrible wail.

"What? What is it, my friend?" I asked.

He kept wailing.

"Please answer me. What is it? I'm blind and we have no food and water, but we have each other. That is something. Something precious. So what is it, my dear brother?"

"I too am blind!"

"What?"

"I too blink for nothing, as you say."

He wailed again. I was struck dumb. I had met another blind man on another lifeboat in the Pacific!

"But how could you be blind?" I mumbled.

"Probably for the same reason you are. The result of poor hygiene on a starving body at the end of its tether."

We both broke down. He wailed and I sobbed. It was too much, truly it was too much.

"I have a story," I said, after a while.

"A story?"

"Yes."

"Of what use is a story? I'm hungry."

"It's a story about food."

"Words have no calories."

"Seek food where food is to be found."

"That's an idea."

Silence. A famishing silence.

"Where are you?" he asked.

"Here. And you?"

"Here."

I heard a splashing sound as an oar dipped into water. I reached for one of the oars I had salvaged from the wrecked raft. It was so heavy. I felt with my hands and found the closest oarlock. I dropped the oar in it. I pulled on the handle. I had no strength. But I rowed as best I could.

"Let's hear your story," he said, panting.

"Once upon a time there was a banana and it grew. It grew until it was large, firm, yellow and fragrant. Then it fell to the ground and someone came upon it and ate it."

He stopped rowing. "What a beautiful story!"

"Thank you."

"I have tears in my eyes."

"I have another element," I said.

"What is it?"

"The banana fell to the ground and someone came upon it and ate it—and afterwards that person *felt better*."

"It takes the breath away!" he exclaimed.

"Thank you."

A pause.

"But you don't have any bananas?"

"No. An orang-utan distracted me."

"A what?"

"It's a long story."

"Any toothpaste?"

"No."

"Delicious on fish. Any cigarettes?"

"I ate them already."

"You *ate* them?"

"I still have the filters. You can have them if you like."

"The filters? What would I do with cigarette filters without the tobacco? How could you *eat* cigarettes?"

"What should I have done with them? I don't smoke."

"You should have kept them for trading."

"Trading? With whom?"

"With me!"

"My brother, when I ate them I was alone in a lifeboat in the middle of the Pacific."

"So?"

"So, the chance of meeting someone in the middle of the Pacific with whom to trade my cigarettes did not strike me as an obvious prospect."

"You have to plan ahead, you stupid boy! Now you have nothing to trade."

"But even if I had something to trade, what would I trade it for? What do you have that I would want?"

"I have a boot," he said.

"A boot?"

"Yes, a fine leather boot."

"What would I do with a leather boot in a lifeboat in the middle of the Pacific? Do you think I go for hikes in my spare time?"

"You could eat it!"

"Eat a boot? What an idea."

"You eat cigarettes—why not a boot?"

"The idea is disgusting. Whose boot, by the way?"

"How should I know?"

"You're suggesting I eat a complete stranger's boot?"

"What difference does it make?"

"I'm flabbergasted. A boot. Putting aside the fact that I am a Hindu and we Hindus consider cows sacred, eating a leather boot conjures to my mind eating all the filth that a foot might exude in addition to all the filth it might step in while shod."

"So no boot for you."

"Let's see it first."

"No."

"What? Do you expect me to trade something with you sight unseen?"

"We're both blind, may I remind you."

"Describe this boot to me, then! What kind of a pitiful salesman are you? No wonder you're starved for customers."

"That's right. I am."

"Well, the boot?"

"It's a leather boot."

"What *kind* of leather boot?"

"The regular kind."

"Which means?"

"A boot with a shoelace and eyelets and a tongue. With an inner sole. The regular kind."

"What colour?"

"Black."

"In what condition?"

"Worn. The leather soft and supple, lovely to the touch."

"And the smell?"

"Of warm, fragrant leather."

"I must admit—I must admit—it sounds tempting!"

"You can forget about it."

"Why?"

Silence.

"Will you not answer, my brother?"

"There's no boot."

"No boot?"

"No."

"That makes me sad."

"I ate it."

"You ate the boot?"

"Yes."

"Was it good?"

"No. Were the cigarettes good?"

"No. I couldn't finish them."

"I couldn't finish the boot."

"Once upon a time there was a banana and it grew. It grew until it was large, firm, yellow and fragrant. Then it fell to the ground and someone came upon it and ate it and afterwards that person felt better."

"I'm sorry. I'm sorry for all I've said and done. I'm a worthless person," he burst out.

"What do you mean? You are the most precious, wonderful person on earth. Come, my brother, let us be together and feast on each other's company."

"Yes!"

The Pacific is no place for rowers, especially when they are weak and blind, when their lifeboats are large and unwieldy, and when the wind is not cooperating. He was close by; he was far away. He was to my left; he was to my right. He was ahead of me; he was behind me. But at last we managed it. Our boats touched with a bump even sweeter-sounding than a turtle's. He threw me a rope and I tethered his boat to mine. I opened my arms to embrace him and to be embraced by him. My eyes were brimming with tears and I was smiling. He was directly in front of me, a presence glowing through my blindness.

"My sweet brother," I whispered.

"I am here," he replied.

I heard a faint growl.

"Brother, there's something I forgot to mention."

He landed upon me heavily. We fell half onto the tarpaulin, half onto the middle bench. His hands reached for my throat.

"Brother," I gasped through his overeager embrace, "my heart is with you, but I must urgently suggest we repair to another part of my humble ship."

"You're damn right your heart is with me!" he said. "And your liver and your flesh!"

I could feel him moving off the tarpaulin onto the middle bench and, fatally, bringing a foot down to the floor of the boat.

"No, no, my brother! Don't! We're not—"

I tried to hold him back. Alas, it was too late. Before I could say the word *alone*, I was alone again. I heard the merest clicking of claws against the bottom of the boat, no more than the sound of a pair of spectacles falling to the floor, and the next moment my dear brother shrieked in my face like I've never heard a man shriek before. He let go of me.

This was the terrible cost of Richard Parker. He gave me a life, my own, but at the expense of taking one. He ripped the flesh off the man's frame and cracked his bones. The smell of blood filled my nose. Something in me died then that has never come back to life.

CHAPTER 91

I climbed aboard my brother's boat. With my hands I explored it. I found he had lied to me. He had a little turtle meat, a dorado head, and even—a supreme treat—some biscuit crumbs. And he had water. It all went into my mouth. I returned to my boat and released his.

Crying as I had done did my eyes some good. The small window at the top left of my vision opened a crack. I rinsed my eyes with sea water. With every rinsing, the window opened further. My vision came back within two days.

I saw such a vision that I nearly wished I had remained blind. His butchered, dismembered body lay on the floor of the boat. Richard Parker had amply supped on him, including on his face, so that I never saw who my brother was. His eviscerated torso, with its broken ribs curving up like the frame of a ship, looked like a miniature version of the lifeboat, such was its blood-drenched and horrifying state.

I will confess that I caught one of his arms with the gaff and used his flesh as bait. I will further confess that, driven by the extremity of my need and the madness to which it pushed me, I ate some of his flesh. I mean small pieces, little strips that I meant for the gaff's hook that, when dried by the sun, looked like ordinary animal flesh. They slipped into my mouth nearly unnoticed. You must understand, my suffering was unremitting and he was already dead. I stopped as soon as I caught a fish.

I pray for his soul every day.

CHAPTER 92

I made an exceptional botanical discovery. But there will be many who disbelieve the following episode. Still, I give it to you now because it's part of the story and it happened to me.

I was on my side. It was an hour or two past noon on a day of quiet sunshine and gentle breeze. I had slept a short while, a diluted sleep that had brought no rest and no dreams. I turned over to my other side, expending as little energy as possible in doing so. I opened my eyes.

In the near distance I saw trees. I did not react. I was certain it was an illusion that a few blinks would make disappear.

The trees remained. In fact, they grew to be a forest. They were part of a low-lying island. I pushed myself up. I continued to disbelieve my eyes. But it was a thrill to be deluded in such a high-quality way. The trees were beautiful. They were like none I had ever seen before. They had a pale bark, and equally distributed branches that carried an amazing profusion of leaves. These leaves were brilliantly green, a green so bright and emerald that, next to it, vegetation during the monsoons was drab olive.

I blinked deliberately, expecting my eyelids to act like lumberjacks. But the trees would not fall.

I looked down. I was both satisfied and disappointed with what I saw. The island had no soil. Not that the trees stood in water. Rather, they stood in what appeared to be a dense mass of vegetation, as sparkling green as the leaves. Who had ever heard of land with no soil? With trees growing out of pure vegetation? I felt satisfaction because such a geology confirmed that I was right, that this island was a chimera, a play of the mind. By the same token I felt disappointment because an island, any island, however strange, would have been very good to come upon.

Since the trees continued to stand, I continued to look. To take in green, after so much blue, was like music to my eyes. Green is a lovely colour. It is the colour of Islam. It is my favourite colour.

The current gently pushed the lifeboat closer to the illusion. Its shore could not be called a beach, there being neither sand nor pebbles, and there was no pounding of surf either, since the waves that fell upon the island simply vanished into its porosity. From a ridge some three hundred yards inland, the island sloped to the sea and, forty or so yards into it, fell off precipitously, disappearing from sight into the depths of the Pacific, surely the smallest continental shelf on record.

I was getting used to the mental delusion. To make it last I refrained from putting a strain on it; when the lifeboat nudged the island, I did not move, only continued to dream. The fabric of the island seemed to be an intricate, tightly webbed mass of tube-shaped seaweed, in diameter a little thicker than two fingers. What a fanciful island, I thought.

After some minutes I crept up to the side of the boat. "Look for green," said the survival manual. Well, this was green. In fact, it was chlorophyll heaven. A green to outshine food colouring and flashing neon lights. A green to get drunk on. "Ultimately, a foot is the only good judge of land," pursued the manual. The island was within reach of a foot. To judge—and be disappointed—or not to judge, that was the question.

I decided to judge. I looked about to see if there were sharks. There were none. I turned on my stomach, and holding on to the tarpaulin, I slowly brought a leg down. My foot entered the sea. It was pleasingly cool. The island lay just a little further down, shimmering in the water. I stretched. I expected the bubble of illusion to burst at any second.

It did not. My foot sank into clear water and met the rubbery resistance of something flexible but solid. I put more weight down. The illusion would not give. I put my full weight on my foot. Still I did not sink. Still I did not believe.

Finally, it was my nose that was the judge of land. It came to my olfactory sense, full and fresh, overwhelming: the smell of vegetation. I gasped. After months of nothing but salt-water-bleached smells, this reek of vegetable organic matter was intoxicating. It was then that I believed, and the only thing that sank was my mind; my thought process became disjointed. My leg began to shake.

"My God! My God!" I whimpered.

I fell overboard.

The combined shock of solid land and cool water gave me the strength to pull myself forward onto the island. I babbled incoherent thanks to God and collapsed.

But I could not stay still. I was too excited. I attempted to get to my feet. Blood rushed away from my head. The ground shook violently. A dizzying blindness overcame me. I thought I would faint. I steadied myself. All I seemed able to do was pant. I managed to sit up.

"Richard Parker! Land! Land! We are saved!" I shouted.

The smell of vegetation was extraordinarily strong. As for the greenness, it was so fresh and soothing that strength and comfort seemed to be physically pouring into my system through my eyes.

What was this strange, tubular seaweed, so intricately entangled? Was it edible? It seemed to be a variety of marine algae, but quite rigid, far more so than normal algae. The feel of it in the hand was wet and as of something crunchy. I pulled at it. Strands of it broke off without too much effort. In cross-section it consisted of two concentric walls: the wet, slightly rough outer wall, so vibrantly green, and an inner wall midway between the outer wall and the core of the algae. The division in the two tubes that resulted was very plain: the centre tube was white in colour, while the tube that surrounded it was decreasingly green as it approached the inner wall. I brought a piece of the algae to my nose. Beyond the agreeable fragrance of the vegetable, it had a neutral smell. I licked it. My pulse quickened. The algae was wet with fresh water.

I bit into it. My chops were in for a shock. The inner tube was bitterly salty—but the outer was not only edible, it was delicious. My tongue began to tremble as if it were a finger flipping through a dictionary, trying to find a long-forgotten word. It found it, and my eyes closed with pleasure at hearing it: *sweet*. Not as in *good*, but as in *sugary*. Turtles and fish are many things, but they are never, ever sugary. The algae had a light sweetness that outdid in delight even the sap of our maple trees here in Canada. In consistency, the closest I can compare it to is water chestnuts.

Saliva forcefully oozed through the dry pastiness of my mouth. Making loud noises of pleasure, I tore at the algae around me. The inner and outer tubes separated cleanly and easily. I began stuffing the sweet outer into my mouth. I went at it with both hands, force-feeding my mouth and setting it to work harder and faster than it had in a very long time. I ate till there was a regular moat around me.

A solitary tree stood about two hundred feet away. It was the only tree downhill from the ridge, which seemed a very long way off. I say *ridge*; the word perhaps gives an incorrect impression of how steep the rise from the shore was. The island was low-lying, as I've said. The rise was gentle, to a height of perhaps fifty or sixty feet. But in the state I was in, that height loomed like a mountain. The tree was more inviting. I noticed its patch of shade. I tried to stand again. I managed to get to a squatting position but as soon as I made to rise, my head spun and I couldn't keep my balance. And even if I hadn't fallen over, my legs had no strength left in them. But my will was strong. I was determined to move forward. I crawled, dragged myself, weakly leapfrogged to the tree.

I know I will never know a joy so vast as I experienced when I entered that tree's dappled, shimmering shade and heard the dry, crisp sound of the wind rustling its leaves. The tree was not as large or as tall as the ones inland, and for being on the wrong side of the ridge, more exposed to the elements, it was a little scraggly and not so uniformly developed as its mates. But it was a tree, and a tree is a blessedly good thing to behold when you've been lost at sea for a long, long time. I sang that tree's glory, its solid, unhurried purity, its slow beauty. Oh, that I could be like it, rooted to the ground but with my every hand raised up to God in praise! I wept.

As my heart exalted Allah, my mind began to take in information about Allah's works. The tree did indeed grow right out of the algae, as I had seen from the lifeboat. There was not the least trace of soil. Either there was soil deeper down, or this species of tree was a remarkable instance of a commensal or a parasite. The trunk was about the width of a man's chest. The bark was greyish green in colour, thin and smooth, and soft enough that I could mark it with my fingernail. The cordate leaves were large and broad, and ended in a single point. The head of the tree had the lovely full roundness of a mango tree, but it was not a mango. I thought it smelled somewhat like a lote tree, but it wasn't a lote either. Nor a mangrove. Nor any other tree I had ever seen. All I know was that it was beautiful and green and lush with leaves.

I heard a growl. I turned. Richard Parker was observing me from the lifeboat. He was looking at the island, too. He seemed to want to come ashore but was afraid. Finally, after much snarling and pacing, he leapt from the boat. I brought the orange whistle to my mouth. But he didn't have aggression on his mind. Simple balance was enough of a challenge; he was as wobbly on his feet as I was. When he advanced, he crawled close to the ground and with trembling limbs, like a newborn cub. Giving me a wide berth, he made for the ridge and disappeared into the interior of the island.

I passed the day eating, resting, attempting to stand and, in a general way, bathing in bliss. I felt nauseous when I exerted myself too much. And I kept feeling that the ground was shifting beneath me and that I was going to fall over, even when I was sitting still.

I started worrying about Richard Parker in the late afternoon. Now that the setting, the territory, had changed, I wasn't sure how he would take to me if he came upon me.

Reluctantly, strictly for safety's sake, I crawled back to the lifeboat. However Richard Parker took possession of the island, the bow and the tarpaulin remained my territory. I searched for something to moor the lifeboat to. Evidently the algae covered the shore thickly, for it was all I could find. Finally, I resolved the problem by driving an oar, handle first, deep into the algae and tethering the boat to it.

I crawled onto the tarpaulin. I was exhausted. My body was spent from taking in so much food, and there was the nervous tension arising from my sudden change of fortunes. As the day ended, I hazily remember hearing Richard Parker roaring in the distance, but sleep overcame me.

I awoke in the night with a strange, uncomfortable feeling in my lower belly. I thought it was a cramp, that perhaps I had poisoned myself with the algae. I heard a noise. I looked. Richard Parker was aboard. He had returned while I was sleeping. He was meowing and licking the pads of his feet. I found his return puzzling but thought no further about it—the cramp was quickly getting worse. I was doubled over with pain, shaking with it, when a process, normal for most but long forgotten by me, set itself into motion: defecation. It was very painful, but afterwards I fell into the deepest, most refreshing sleep I had had since the night before the *Tsimtsum* sank.

When I woke up in the morning I felt much stronger. I crawled to the solitary tree in a vigorous way. My eyes feasted once more upon it, as did my stomach on the algae. I had such a plentiful breakfast that I dug a big hole.

Richard Parker once again hesitated for hours before jumping off the boat. When he did, mid-morning, as soon as he landed on the shore he jumped back and half fell in the water and seemed very tense. He hissed and clawed the air with a paw. It was curious. I had no idea what he was doing. His anxiety passed, and noticeably surer-footed than the previous day, he disappeared another time over the ridge.

That day, leaning against the tree, I stood. I felt dizzy. The only way I could make the ground stop moving was to close my eyes and grip the tree. I pushed off and tried to walk. I fell instantly. The ground rushed up to me before I could move a foot. No harm done. The island, coated with such tightly woven, rubbery vegetation, was an ideal place to relearn how to walk. I could fall any which way, it was impossible to hurt myself.

The next day, after another restful night on the boat—to which, once again, Richard Parker had returned—I was able to walk. Falling half a dozen times, I managed to reach the tree. I could feel my strength increasing by the hour. With the gaff I reached up and pulled down a branch from the tree. I plucked off some leaves. They were soft and unwaxed, but they tasted bitter. Richard Parker was attached to his den on the lifeboat—that was my explanation for why he had returned another night.

I saw him coming back that evening, as the sun was setting. I had retethered the lifeboat to the buried oar. I was at the bow, checking that the rope was properly secured to the stem. He appeared all of a sudden. At first I didn't recognize him. This magnificent animal bursting over the ridge at full gallop couldn't possibly be the same listless, bedraggled tiger who was my companion in misfortune? But it was. It was Richard Parker and he was coming my way at high speed. He looked purposeful. His powerful neck rose above his lowered head. His coat and his muscles shook at every step. I could hear the drumming of his heavy body against the ground.

I have read that there are two fears that cannot be trained out of us: the startle reaction upon hearing an unexpected noise, and vertigo. I would like to add a third, to wit, the rapid and direct approach of a known killer.

I fumbled for the whistle. When he was twenty-five feet from the lifeboat I blew into the whistle with all my might. A piercing cry split the air.

It had the desired effect. Richard Parker braked. But he clearly wanted to move forward again. I blew a second time. He started turning and hopping on the spot in a most peculiar, deer-like way, snarling fiercely. I blew a third time. Every hair on him was raised. His claws were full out. He was in a state of extreme agitation. I feared that the defensive wall of my whistle blows was about to crumble and that he would attack me.

Instead, Richard Parker did the most unexpected thing: he jumped into the sea. I was astounded. The very thing I thought he would never do, he did, and with might and resolve. He energetically paddled his way to the stern of the lifeboat. I thought of blowing again, but instead opened the locker lid and sat down, retreating to the inner sanctum of my territory.

He surged onto the stern, quantities of water pouring off him, making my end of the boat pitch up. He balanced on the gunnel and the stern bench for a moment, assessing me. My heart grew faint. I did not think I would be able to blow into the whistle again. I looked at him blankly. He flowed down to the floor of the lifeboat and disappeared under the tarpaulin. I could see parts of him from the edges of the locker lid. I threw myself upon the tarpaulin, out of his sight—but directly above him. I felt an overwhelming urge to sprout wings and fly off.

I calmed down. I reminded myself forcefully that this had been my situation for the last long while, to be living with a live tiger hot beneath me.

As my breathing slowed down, sleep came to me.

Sometime during the night I awoke and, my fear forgotten, looked over. He was dreaming: he was shaking and growling in his sleep. He was loud enough about it to have woken me up.

In the morning, as usual, he went over the ridge.

I decided that as soon as I was strong enough I would go exploring the island. It seemed quite large, if the shoreline was any indication; left and right it stretched on with only a slight curve, showing the island to have a fair girth. I spent the day walking—and falling—from the shore to the tree and back, in an attempt to restore my legs to health. At every fall I had a full meal of algae.

When Richard Parker returned as the day was ending, a little earlier than the previous day, I was expecting him. I sat tight and did not blow the whistle. He came to the water's edge and in one mighty leap reached the side of the lifeboat. He entered his territory without intruding into mine, only causing the boat to lurch to one side. His return to form was quite terrifying.

The next morning, after giving Richard Parker plenty of advance, I set off to explore the island. I walked up to the ridge. I reached it easily, proudly moving one foot ahead of the other in a gait that was spirited if still a little awkward. Had my legs been weaker, they would have given way beneath me when I saw what I saw beyond the ridge.

To start with details, I saw that the whole island was covered with the algae, not just its edges. I saw a great green plateau with a green forest in its centre. I saw all around this forest hundreds of evenly scattered, identically sized ponds with trees sparsely distributed in a uniform way between them, the whole arrangement giving the un-mistakable impression of following a design.

But it was the meerkats that impressed themselves most indelibly on my mind. I saw in one look what I would conservatively estimate to be hundreds of thousands of meerkats. The landscape was covered in meerkats. And when I appeared, it seemed that all of them turned to me, astonished, like chickens in a farmyard, and stood up.

We didn't have any meerkats in our zoo. But I had read about them. They were in the books and in the literature. A meerkat is a small South African mammal related to the mongoose; in other words, a carnivorous burrower, a foot long and weighing two pounds when mature, slender and weasel-like in build, with a pointed snout, eyes sitting squarely at the front of its face, short legs, paws with four toes and long, non-retractile claws, and an eight-inch tail. Its fur is light brown to grey in colour with black or brown bands on its back, while the tip of its tail, its ears and the characteristic circles around its eyes are black. It is an agile and keen-sighted creature, diurnal and so-cial in habits, and feeding in its native range—the Kalahari Desert of southern Africa—on, among other things, scorpions, to whose venom it is completely immune. When it is on the lookout, the meerkat has the peculiarity of standing perfectly upright on the tips of its back legs, balancing itself tripod-like with its tail. Often a group of meerkats will take the stance collectively, standing in a huddle and gazing in the same direction, looking like commuters waiting for a bus. The earnest expression on their faces, and the way their front paws hang before them, make them look either like children self-consciously posing for a photographer or patients in a doctor's office stripped naked and demurely trying to cover their genitals.

That is what I beheld in one glance, hundreds of thousands of meerkats—more, a million—turning to me and standing at attention, as if saying, "Yes, sir?" Mind you, a standing meerkat reaches up eighteen inches at most, so it was not the height of these creatures that was so breathtaking as their unlimited multitude. I stood rooted to the spot, speechless. If I set a million meerkats fleeing in terror, the chaos would be indescribable. But their interest in me was short-lived. After a few seconds, they went back to doing what they had been doing before I appeared, which was either nibbling at the algae or staring into the ponds. To see so many beings bending down at the same time reminded me of prayer time in a mosque.

The creatures seemed to feel no fear. As I moved down from the ridge, none shied away or showed the least tension at my presence. If I had wanted to, I could have touched one, even picked one up. I did nothing of the sort. I simply walked into what was surely the largest colony of meerkats in the world, one of the strangest, most wonderful experiences of my life. There was a ceaseless noise in the air. It was their squeaking, chirping, twittering and barking. Such were their numbers and the vagaries of their excitement that the noise came and went like a flock of birds, at times very loud, swirling around me, then rapidly dying off as the closest meerkats fell silent while others, further off, started up.

Were they not afraid of me because I should be afraid of them? The question crossed my mind. But the answer—that they were harmless—was immediately apparent. To get close to a pond, around which they were densely packed, I had to nudge them away with my feet so as not to step on one. They took to my barging without any offence, making room for me like a good-natured crowd. I felt warm, furry bodies against my ankles as I looked into a pond.

All the ponds had the same round shape and were about the same size—roughly forty feet in diameter. I expected shallowness. I saw nothing but deep, clear water. The ponds seemed bottomless, in fact. And as far down as I could see, their sides consisted of green algae. Evidently the layer atop the island was very substantial.

I could see nothing that accounted for the meerkats' fixed curiosity, and I might have given up on solving the mystery had squeaking and barking not erupted at a pond nearby. Meerkats were jumping up and down in a state of great ferment. Suddenly, by the hundreds, they began *diving* into the pond. There was much pushing and shoving as the meerkats behind vied to reach the pond's edge. The frenzy was collective; even tiny meerkittens were making for the water, barely being held back by mothers and guardians. I stared in disbelief. These were not standard Kalahari Desert meerkats. Standard Kalahari Desert meerkats do not behave like frogs. These meerkats were most definitely a subspecies that had specialized in a fascinating and surprising way.

I made for the pond, bringing my feet down gingerly, in time to see meerkats swimming—actually swimming—and bringing to shore fish by the dozens, and not small fish either. Some were dorados that would have been unqualified feasts on the lifeboat. They dwarfed the meerkats. It was incomprehensible to me how meerkats could catch such fish.

It was as the meerkats were hauling the fish out of the pond, displaying real feats of teamwork, that I noticed something curious: every fish, without exception, was already dead. Freshly dead. The meerkats were bringing ashore dead fish they had not killed.

I kneeled by the pond, pushing aside several excited, wet meerkats. I touched the water. It was cooler than I'd expected. There was a current that was bringing colder water from below. I cupped a little water in my hand and brought it to my mouth. I took a sip.

It was fresh water. This explained how the fish had died—for, of course, place a saltwater fish in fresh water and it will quickly become bloated and die. But what were seafaring fish doing in a freshwater pond? How had they got there?

I went to another pond, making my way through the meerkats. It too was fresh. Another pond; the same. And again with a fourth pond.

They were all freshwater ponds. Where had such quantities of fresh water come from, I asked myself. The answer was obvious: from the algae. The algae naturally and continuously desalinated sea water, which was why its core was salty while its outer surface was wet with fresh water: it was oozing the fresh water out. I did not ask myself why the algae did this, or how, or where the salt went. My mind stopped asking such questions. I simply laughed and jumped into a pond. I found it hard to stay at the surface of the water; I was still very weak, and I had little fat on me to help me float. I held on to the edge of the pond. The effect of bathing in pure, clean, salt-free water was more than I can put into words. After such a long time at sea, my skin was like a hide and my hair was long, matted and as silky as a fly-catching strip. I felt even my soul had been corroded by salt. So, under the gaze of a thousand meerkats, I soaked, allowing fresh water to dissolve every salt crystal that had tainted me.

The meerkats looked away. They did it like one man, all of them turning in the same direction at exactly the same time. I pulled myself out to see what it was. It was Richard Parker. He confirmed what I had suspected, that these meerkats had gone for so many generations without predators that any notion of flight distance, of flight, of plain fear, had been genetically weeded out of them. He was moving through them, blazing a trail of murder and mayhem, devouring one meerkat after another, blood dripping from his mouth, and they, cheek to jowl with a tiger, were jumping up and down on the spot, as if crying, "My turn! My turn! My turn!" I would see this scene time and again. Nothing distracted the meerkats from their little lives of pond staring and algae nibbling. Whether Richard Parker skulked up in masterly tiger fashion before landing upon them in a thunder of roaring, or slouched by indifferently, it was all the same to them. They were not to be ruffled. Meekness ruled.

He killed beyond his need. He killed meerkats that he did not eat. In animals, the urge to kill is separate from the urge to eat. To go for so long without prey and suddenly to have so many—his pent-up hunting instinct was lashing out with a vengeance.

He was far away. There was no danger to me. At least for the moment.

The next morning, after he had gone, I cleaned the lifeboat. It needed it badly. I won't describe what the accumulation of human and animal skeletons, mixed in with innumerable fish and turtle remains, looked like. The whole foul, disgusting mess went overboard. I didn't dare step onto the floor of the boat for fear of leaving a tangible trace of my presence to Richard Parker, so the job had to be done with the gaff from the tarpaulin or from the side of the boat, standing in the water. What I could not clean up with the gaff—the smells and the smears—I rinsed with buckets of water.

That night he entered his new, clean den without comment. In his jaws were a number of dead meerkats, which he ate during the night.

I spent the following days eating and drinking and bathing and observing the meerkats and walking and running and resting and growing stronger. My running became smooth and unselfconscious, a source of euphoria. My skin healed. My pains and aches left me. Put simply, I returned to life.

I explored the island. I tried to walk around it but gave up. I estimate that it was about six or seven miles in diameter, which means a circumference of about twenty miles. What I saw seemed to indicate that the shore was unvarying in its features. The same blinding greenness throughout, the same ridge, the same incline from ridge to water, the same break in the monotony: a scraggly tree here and there. Exploring the shore revealed one extraordinary thing: the algae, and therefore the island itself, varied in height and density depending on the weather. On very hot days, the algae's weave became tight and dense, and the island increased in height; the climb to the ridge became steeper and the ridge higher. It was not a quick process. Only a hot spell lasting several days triggered it. But it was unmistakable. I believe it had to do with water conservation, with exposing less of the algae's surface to the sun's rays.

The converse phenomenon—the loosening of the island—was faster, more dramatic, and the reasons for it more evident. At such times the ridge came down, and the continental shelf, so to speak, stretched out, and the algae along the shore became so slack that I tended to catch my feet in it. This loosening was brought on by overcast weather and, faster still, by heavy seas.

I lived through a major storm while on the island, and after the experience, I would have trusted staying on it during the worst hurricane. It was an awe-inspiring spectacle to sit in a tree and see giant waves charging the island, seemingly preparing to ride up the ridge and unleash bedlam and chaos—only to see each one melt away as if it had come upon quicksand. In this respect, the island was Gandhian: it resisted by not resisting. Every wave vanished into the island without a clash, with only a little frothing and foaming. A tremor shaking the ground and ripples wrinkling the surface of the ponds were the only indications that some great force was passing through. And pass through it did: in the lee of the island, considerably diminished, waves emerged and went on their way. It was the strangest sight, that, to see waves *leaving* a shoreline. The storm, and the resulting minor earthquakes, did not perturb the meerkats in the least. They went about their business as if the elements did not exist.

Harder to understand was the island's complete desolation. I never saw such a stripped-down ecology. The air of the place carried no flies, no butterflies, no bees, no insects of any kind. The trees sheltered no birds. The plains hid no rodents, no grubs, no worms, no snakes, no scorpions; they gave rise to no other trees, no shrubs, no grasses, no flowers. The ponds harboured no freshwater fish. The seashore teemed with no weeds, no crabs, no crayfish, no coral, no pebbles, no rocks. With the single, notable exception of the meerkats, there was not the least foreign matter on the island, organic or inorganic. It was nothing but shining green algae and shining green trees.

The trees were not parasites. I discovered this one day when I ate so much algae at the base of a small tree that I exposed its roots. I saw that the roots did not go their own independent way into the algae, but rather joined it, became it. Which meant that these trees either lived in a symbiotic relationship with the algae, in a giving-and-taking that was to their mutual advantage, or, simpler still, were an integral part of the algae. I would guess that the latter was the case because the trees did not seem to bear flowers or fruit. I doubt that an independent organism, however intimate the symbiosis it has entered upon, would give up on so essential a part of life as reproduction. The leaves' appetite for the sun, as testified by their abundance, their breadth and their superchlorophyll greenness, made me suspect that the trees had primarily an energy-gathering function. But this is conjecture.

There is one last observation I would like to make. It is based on intuition rather than hard evidence. It is this: that the island was not an island in the conventional sense of the term—that is, a small landmass rooted to the floor of the ocean—but was rather a free-floating organism, a ball of algae of leviathan proportions. And it is my hunch that the ponds reached down to the sides of this huge, buoyant mass and opened onto the ocean, which explained the otherwise inexplicable presence in them of dorados and other fish of the open seas.

It would all bear much further study, but unfortunately I lost the algae that I took away.

Just as I returned to life, so did Richard Parker. By dint of stuffing himself with meerkats, his weight went up, his fur began to glisten again, and he returned to his healthy look of old. He kept up his habit of returning to the lifeboat at the end of every day. I always made sure I was there before him, copiously marking my territory with urine so that he didn't forget who was who and what was whose. But he left at first light and roamed further afield than I did; the island being the same all over, I generally stayed within one area. I saw very little of him during the day. And I grew nervous. I saw how he raked the trees with his forepaws—great deep gouges in the trunks, they were. And I began to hear his hoarse roaring, that *aaonh* cry as rich as gold or honey and as spine-chilling as the depths of an unsafe mine or a thousand angry bees. That he was searching for a female was not in itself what troubled me; it was that it meant he was comfortable enough on the island to be thinking about producing young. I worried that in this new condition he might not tolerate another male in his territory, his night territory in particular, especially if his insistent cries went unanswered, as surely they would.

One day I was on a walk in the forest. I was walking vigorously, caught up in my own thoughts. I passed a tree—and practically ran into Richard Parker. Both of us were startled. He hissed and reared up on his hind legs, towering over me, his great paws ready to swat me down. I stood frozen to the spot, paralyzed with fear and shock. He dropped back on all fours and moved away. When he had gone three, four paces, he turned and reared up again, growling this time. I continued to stand like a statue. He went another few paces and repeated the threat a third time. Satisfied that I was not a menace, he ambled off. As soon as I had caught my breath and stopped trembling, I brought the whistle to my mouth and started running after him. He had already gone a good distance, but he was still within sight. My running was powerful. He turned, saw me, crouched—and then bolted. I blew into the whistle as hard as I could, wishing that its sound would travel as far and wide as the cry of a lonely tiger.

That night, as he was resting two feet beneath me, I came to the conclusion that I had to step into the circus ring again.

The major difficulty in training animals is that they operate either by instinct or by rote. The shortcut of intelligence to make new associations that are not instinctive is minimally available. Therefore, imprinting in an animal's mind the artificial connection that if it does a certain action, say, roll over, it will get a treat can be achieved only by mind-numbing repetition. It is a slow process that depends as much on luck as on hard work, all the more so when the animal is an adult. I blew into the whistle till my lungs hurt. I pounded my chest till it was covered with bruises. I shouted "Hep! Hep! Hep!"—my tiger-language command to say "Do!"—thousands of times. I tossed hundreds of meerkat morsels at him that I would gladly have eaten myself. The training of tigers is no easy feat. They are considerably less flexible in their mental make-up than other animals that are commonly trained in circuses and zoos—sea lions and chimpanzees, for example. But I don't want to take too much credit for what I managed to do with Richard Parker. My good fortune, the fortune that saved my life, was that he was not only a young adult but a pliable young adult, an omega animal. I was afraid that conditions on the island might play against me, that with such an abundance of food and water and so much space he might become relaxed and confident, less open to my influence. But he remained tense. I knew him well enough to sense it. At night in the lifeboat he was unsettled and noisy. I assigned this tension to the new environment of the island; any change, even positive, will make an animal tense. Whatever the cause, the strain he was under meant that he continued to show a readiness to oblige; more, that he felt a *need* to oblige.

I trained him to jump through a hoop I made with thin branches. It was a simple routine of four jumps. Each one earned him part of a meerkat. As he lumbered towards me, I first held the hoop at the end of my left arm, some three feet off the ground. When he had leapt through it, and as he finished his run, I took hold of the hoop with my right hand and, my back to him, commanded him to return and leap through it again. For the third jump I knelt on the ground and held the hoop over my head. It was a nerve-racking experience to see him come my way. I never lost the fear that he would not jump but attack me. Thankfully, he jumped every time. After which I got up and tossed the hoop so that it rolled like a wheel. Richard Parker was supposed to follow it and go through it one last time before it fell over. He was never very good at this last part of the act, either because I failed to throw the hoop properly or because he clumsily ran into it. But at least he followed it, which meant he got away from me. He was always filled with amazement when the hoop fell over. He would look at it intently, as if it were some great fellow animal he had been running with that had collapsed unexpectedly. He would stay next to it, sniffing it. I would throw him his last treat and move away.

Eventually I quit the boat. It seemed absurd to spend my nights in such cramped quarters with an animal who was becoming roomy in his needs, when I could have an entire island. I decided the safe thing to do would be to sleep in a tree. Richard Parker's nocturnal practice of sleeping in the lifeboat was never a law in my mind. It would not be a good idea for me to be outside my territory, sleeping and defenceless on the ground, the one time he decided to go for a midnight stroll.

So one day I left the boat with the net, a rope and some blankets. I sought out a handsome tree on the edge of the forest and threw the rope over the lowest branch. My fitness was such that I had no problem pulling myself up by my arms and climbing the tree. I found two solid branches that were level and close together, and I tied the net to them. I returned at the end of the day.

I had just finished folding the blankets to make my mattress when I detected a commotion among the meerkats. I looked. I pushed aside branches to see better. I looked in every direction and as far as the horizon. It was unmistakable. The meerkats were abandoning the ponds—indeed, the whole plain—and rapidly making for the forest. An entire nation of meerkats was on the move, their backs arched and their feet a blur. I was wondering what further surprise these animals held in store for me when I noticed with consternation that the ones from the pond closest to me had surrounded my tree and were climbing up the trunk. The trunk was disappearing under a wave of determined meerkats. I thought they were coming to attack me, that here was the reason why Richard Parker slept in the lifeboat: during the day the meerkats were docile and harmless, but at night, under their collective weight, they crushed their enemies ruthlessly. I was both afraid and indignant. To survive for so long in a lifeboat with a 450-pound Bengal tiger only to die up a tree at the hands of two-pound meerkats struck me as a tragedy too unfair and too ridiculous to bear.

They meant me no harm. They climbed up to me, over me, about me—and past me. They settled upon every branch in the tree. It became *laden* with them. They even took over my bed. And the same as far as the eye could see. They were climbing every tree in sight. The entire forest was turning brown, an autumn that came in a few minutes. Collectively, as they scampered by in droves to claim empty trees deeper into the forest, they made more noise than a stampeding herd of elephants.

The plain, meanwhile, was becoming bare and depopulated.

From a bunk bed with a tiger to an overcrowded dormitory with meerkats—will I be believed when I say that life can take the most surprising turns? I jostled with meerkats so that I could have a place in my own bed. They snuggled up to me. Not a square inch of space was left free.

They settled down and stopped squeaking and chirping. Silence came to the tree. We fell asleep.

I woke up at dawn covered from head to toe in a living fur blanket. Some meerkittens had discovered the warmer parts of my body. I had a tight, sweaty collar of them around my neck—and it must have been their mother who had settled herself so contentedly on the side of my head—while others had wedged themselves in my groin area.

They left the tree as briskly and as unceremoniously as they had invaded it. It was the same with every tree around. The plain grew thick with meerkats, and the noises of their day started filling the air. The tree looked empty. And I felt empty, a little. I had liked the experience of sleeping with the meerkats.

I began to sleep in the tree every night. I emptied the lifeboat of useful items and made myself a nice treetop bedroom. I got used to the unintentional scratches I received from meerkats climbing over me. My only complaint would be that animals higher up occasionally relieved themselves on me.

One night the meerkats woke me up. They were chattering and shaking. I sat up and looked in the direction they were looking. The sky was cloudless and the moon full. The land was robbed of its colour. Everything glowed strangely in shades of black, grey and white. It was the pond. Silver shapes were moving in it, emerging from below and breaking the black surface of the water.

Fish. Dead fish. They were floating up from deep down. The pond—remember, forty feet across—was filling up with all kinds of dead fish until its surface was no longer black but silver. And from the way the surface kept on being disturbed, it was evident that more dead fish were coming up.

By the time a dead shark quietly appeared, the meerkats were in a fury of excitement, shrieking like tropical birds. The hysteria spread to the neighbouring trees. It was deafening. I wondered whether I was about to see the sight of fish being hauled up trees.

Not a single meerkat went down to the pond. None even made the first motions of going down. They did no more than loudly express their frustration.

I found the sight sinister. There was something disturbing about all those dead fish.

I lay down again and fought to go back to sleep over the meerkats' racket. At first light I was stirred from my slumber by the hullabaloo they made trooping down the tree. Yawning and stretching, I looked down at the pond that had been the source of such fire and fluster the previous night.

It was empty. Or nearly. But it wasn't the work of the meerkats. They were just now diving in to get what was left.

The fish had disappeared. I was confounded. Was I looking at the wrong pond? No, for sure it was that one. Was I certain it was not the meerkats that had emptied it? Absolutely. I could hardly see them heaving an entire shark out of water, let alone carrying it on their backs and disappearing with it. Could it be Richard Parker? Possibly in part, but not an entire pond in one night.

It was a complete mystery. No amount of staring into the pond and at its deep green walls could explain to me what had happened to the fish. The next night I looked, but no new fish came into the pond.

The answer to the mystery came sometime later, from deep within the forest.

The trees were larger in the centre of the forest and closely set. It remained clear below, there being no underbrush of any kind, but overhead the canopy was so dense that the sky was quite blocked off, or, another way of putting it, the sky was solidly green. The trees were so near one another that their branches grew into each other's spaces; they touched and twisted around each other so that it was hard to tell where one tree ended and the next began. I noted that they had clean, smooth trunks, with none of the countless tiny marks on their bark made by climbing meerkats. I easily guessed the reason why: the meerkats could travel from one tree to another without the need to climb up and down. I found, as proof of this, many trees on the perimeter of the heart of the forest whose bark had been practically shredded. These trees were without a doubt the gates into a meerkat arboreal city with more bustle in it than Calcutta.

It was here that I found the tree. It wasn't the largest in the forest, or in its dead centre, or remarkable in any other way. It had good level branches, that's all. It would have made an excellent spot from which to see the sky or take in the meerkats' nightlife.

I can tell you exactly what day I came upon the tree: it was the day before I left the island.

I noticed the tree because it seemed to have fruit. Whereas elsewhere the forest canopy was uniformly green, these fruit stood out black against green. The branches holding them were twisted in odd ways. I looked intently. An entire island covered in barren trees—but for one. And not even all of one. The fruit grew from only one small part of the tree. I thought that perhaps I had come upon the forest equivalent of a queen bee, and I wondered whether this algae would ever cease to amaze me with its botanical strangeness.

I wanted to try the fruit, but the tree was too high. So I returned with a rope. If the algae was delicious, what would its fruit be like?

I looped the rope around the lowest limb of the tree and, bough by bough, branch by branch, made my way to the small, precious orchard.

Up close the fruit were dull green. They were about the size and shape of oranges. Each was at the centre of a number of twigs that were tightly curled around it—to protect it, I supposed. As I got closer, I could see another purpose to these curled twigs: support. The fruit had not one stem, but dozens. Their surfaces were studded with stems that connected them to the surrounding twigs. These fruit must surely be heavy and juicy, I thought. I got close.

I reached with a hand and took hold of one. I was disappointed at how light it felt. It weighed hardly anything. I pulled at it, plucking it from all its stems.

I made myself comfortable on a sturdy branch, my back to the trunk of the tree. Above me stood a shifting roof of green leaves that let in shafts of sunlight. All round, for as far as I could see, hanging in the air, were the twisting and turning roads of a great suspended city. A pleasant breeze ran through the trees. I was keenly curious. I examined the fruit.

Ah, how I wish that moment had never been! But for it I might have lived for years—why, for the rest of my life—on that island. Nothing, I thought, could ever push me to return to the lifeboat and to the suffering and deprivation I had endured on it—nothing! What reason could I have to leave the island? Were my physical needs not met here? Was there not more fresh water than I could drink in all my lifetime? More algae than I could eat? And when I yearned for variety, more meerkats and fish than I could ever desire? If the island floated and moved, might it not move in the right direction? Might it not turn out to be a vegetable ship that brought me to land? In the meantime, did I not have these delightful meerkats to keep me company? And wasn't Richard Parker still in need of improving his fourth jump? The thought of leaving the island had not crossed my mind once since I had arrived. It had been many weeks now—I couldn't say how many exactly—and they would stretch on. I was certain about that.

How wrong I was.

If that fruit had a seed, it was the seed of my departure.

The fruit was not a fruit. It was a dense accumulation of leaves glued together in a ball. The dozens of stems were dozens of leaf stems. Each stem that I pulled caused a leaf to peel off.

After a few layers I came to leaves that had lost their stems and were flatly glued to the ball. I used my fingernails to catch their edges and pull them off. Sheath after sheath of leaf lifted, like the skins off an onion. I could simply have ripped the "fruit" apart—I still call it that for lack of a better word—but I chose to satisfy my curiosity in a measured way.

It shrunk from the size of an orange to that of a mandarin. My lap and the branches below were covered with thin, soft leaf peelings.

It was now the size of a rambutan.

I still get shivers in my spine when I think of it.

The size of a cherry.

And then it came to light, an unspeakable pearl at the heart of a green oyster.

A human tooth.

A molar, to be exact. The surface stained green and finely pierced with holes.

The feeling of horror came slowly. I had time to pick at the other fruit.

Each contained a tooth.

One a canine.

Another a premolar.

Here an incisor.

There another molar.

Thirty-two teeth. A complete human set. Not one tooth missing. Understanding dawned upon me.

I did not scream. I think only in movies is horror vocal. I simply shuddered and left the tree.

I spent the day in turmoil, weighing my options. They were all bad.

That night, in bed in my usual tree, I tested my conclusion. I took hold of a meerkat and dropped it from the branch.

It squeaked as it fell through the air. When it touched the ground, it instantly made for the tree.

With typical innocence it returned to the spot right next to me. There it began to lick its paws vigorously. It seemed much discomforted. It panted heavily.

I could have left it at that. But I wanted to know for myself. I climbed down and took hold of the rope. I had made knots in it to make my climbing easier. When I was at the bottom of the tree, I brought my feet to within an inch of the ground. I hesitated.

I let go.

At first I felt nothing. Suddenly a searing pain shot up through my feet. I shrieked. I thought I would fall over. I managed to take hold of the rope and pull myself off the ground. I frantically rubbed the soles of my feet against the tree trunk. It helped, but not enough. I climbed back to my branch. I soaked my feet in the bucket of water next to my bed. I wiped my feet with leaves. I took the knife and killed two meerkats and tried to soothe the pain with their blood and innards. Still my feet burned. They burned all night. I couldn't sleep for it, and from the anxiety.

The island was carnivorous. This explained the disappearance of the fish in the pond. The island attracted saltwater fish into its subterranean tunnels—how, I don't know; perhaps fish ate the algae as gluttonously as I did. They became trapped. Did they lose their way? Did the openings onto the sea close off? Did the water change salinity so subtly that it was too late by the time the fish realized it? Whatever the case, they found themselves trapped in fresh water and died. Some floated up to the surface of the ponds, the scraps that fed the meerkats. At night, by some chemical process unknown to me but obviously inhibited by sunlight, the predatory algae turned highly acidic and the ponds became vats of acid that digested the fish. This was why Richard Parker returned to the boat every night. This was why the meerkats slept in the trees. This was why I had never seen anything but algae on the island.

And this explained the teeth. Some poor lost soul had arrived on these terrible shores before me. How much time had he—or was it she?—spent here? Weeks? Months? *Years?* How many forlorn hours in the arboreal city with only meerkats for company? How many dreams of a happy life dashed? How much hope come to nothing? How much stored-up conversation that died unsaid? How much loneliness endured? How much hopelessness taken on? And after all that, what of it? What to show for it?

Nothing but some enamel, like small change in a pocket. The person must have died in the tree. Was it illness? Injury? Depression? How long does it take for a broken spirit to kill a body that has food, water and shelter? The trees were carnivorous too, but at a much lower level of acidity, safe enough to stay in for the night while the rest of the island seethed. But once the person had died and stopped moving, the tree must have slowly wrapped itself around the body and digested it, the very bones leached of nutrients until they vanished. In time, even the teeth would have disappeared.

I looked around at the algae. Bitterness welled up in me. The radiant promise it offered during the day was replaced in my heart by all the treachery it delivered at night.

I muttered, "Nothing but teeth left! TEETH!"

By the time morning came, my grim decision was taken. I preferred to set off and perish in search of my own kind than to live a lonely half-life of physical comfort and spiritual death on this murderous island. I filled my stores with fresh water and I drank like a camel. I ate algae throughout the day until my stomach could take no more. I killed and skinned as many meerkats as would fit in the locker and on the floor of the lifeboat. I reaped dead fish from the ponds. With the hatchet I hacked off a large mass of algae and worked a rope through it, which I tied to the boat.

I could not abandon Richard Parker. To leave him would mean to kill him. He would not survive the first night. Alone in my lifeboat at sunset I would know that he was burning alive. Or that he had thrown himself in the sea, where he would drown. I waited for his return. I knew he would not be late.

When he was aboard, I pushed us off. For a few hours the currents kept us near the island. The noises of the sea bothered me. And I was no longer used to the rocking motions of the boat. The night went by slowly.

In the morning the island was gone, as was the mass of algae we had been towing. As soon as night had fallen, the algae had dissolved the rope with its acid.

The sea was heavy, the sky grey.

CHAPTER 93

I grew weary of my situation, as pointless as the weather. But life would not leave me. The rest of this story is nothing but grief, ache and endurance.

High calls low and low calls high. I tell you, if you were in such dire straits as I was, you too would elevate your thoughts. The lower you are, the higher your mind will want to soar. It was natural that, bereft and desperate as I was, in the throes of unremitting suffering, I should turn to God.

CHAPTER 94

When we reached land, Mexico to be exact, I was so weak I barely had the strength to be happy about it. We had great difficulty landing. The lifeboat nearly capsized in the surf. I streamed the sea anchors—what was left of them—full open to keep us perpendicular to the waves, and I tripped them as soon as we began riding a crest. In this way, streaming and tripping the anchors, we surfed in to shore. It was dangerous. But we caught one wave at just the right point and it carried us a great distance, past the high, collapsing walls of water. I tripped the anchors a last time and we were pushed in the rest of the way. The boat hissed to a halt against the sand.

I let myself down the side. I was afraid to let go, afraid that so close to deliverance, in two feet of water, I would drown. I looked ahead to see how far I had to go. The glance gave me one of my last images of Richard Parker, for at that precise moment he jumped over me. I saw his body, so immeasurably vital, stretched in the air above me, a fleeting, furred rainbow. He landed in the water, his back legs splayed, his tail high, and from there, in a few hops, he reached the beach. He went to the left, his paws gouging the wet sand, but changed his mind and spun around. He passed directly in front of me on his way to the right. He didn't look at me. He ran a hundred yards or so along the shore before turning in. His gait was clumsy and uncoordinated. He fell several times. At the edge of the jungle, he stopped. I was certain he would turn my way. He would look at me. He would flatten his ears. He would growl. In some such way, he would conclude our relationship. He did nothing of the sort. He only looked fixedly into the jungle.

Then Richard Parker, companion of my torment, awful, fierce thing that kept me alive, moved forward and disappeared forever from my life.

I struggled to shore and fell upon the sand. I looked about. I was truly alone, orphaned not only of my family, but now of Richard Parker, and nearly, I thought, of God. Of course, I wasn't. This beach, so soft, firm and vast, was like the cheek of God, and somewhere two eyes were glittering with pleasure and a mouth was smiling at having me there.

After some hours a member of my own species found me. He left and returned with a group. They were six or seven. They came up to me with their hands covering their noses and mouths. I wondered what was wrong with them. They spoke to me in a strange tongue. They pulled the lifeboat onto the sand. They carried me away. The one piece of turtle meat I had brought from the boat they wrenched from my hand and threw away.

I wept like a child. It was not because I was overcome at having survived my ordeal, though I was. Nor was it the presence of my brothers and sisters, though that too was very moving. I was weeping because Richard Parker had left me so unceremoniously. What a terrible thing it is to botch a farewell. I am a person who believes in form, in the harmony of order. Where we can, we must give things a meaningful shape. For example—I wonder—could you tell my jumbled story in exactly one hundred chapters, not one more, not one less? I'll tell you, that's one thing I hate about my nickname, the way that number runs on forever. It's important in life to conclude things properly. Only then can you let go. Otherwise you are left with words you should have said but never did, and your heart is heavy with remorse. That bungled goodbye hurts me to this day. I wish so much that I'd had one last look at him in the lifeboat, that I'd provoked him a little, so that I was on his mind. I wish I had said to him then—yes, I know, to a tiger, but still—I wish I had said, "Richard Parker, it's over. We have survived. Can you believe it? I owe you more gratitude than I can express. I couldn't have done it without you. I would like to say it formally: Richard Parker, thank you. Thank you for saving my life. And now go where you must. You have known the confined freedom of a zoo most of your life; now you will know the free confinement of a jungle. I wish you all the best with it. Watch out for Man. He is not your friend. But I hope you will remember me as a friend. I will never forget you, that is certain. You will always be with me, in my heart. What is that hiss? Ah, our boat has touched sand. So farewell, Richard Parker, farewell. God be with you."

The people who found me took me to their village, and there some women gave me a bath and scrubbed me so hard that I wondered if they realized I was naturally brown-skinned and not a very dirty white boy. I tried to explain. They nodded and smiled and kept on scrubbing me as if I were the deck of a ship. I thought they were going to skin me alive. But they gave me food. Delicious food. Once I started eating, I couldn't stop. I thought I would never stop being hungry.

The next day a police car came and brought me to a hospital, and there my story ends.

I was overwhelmed by the generosity of those who rescued me. Poor people gave me clothes and food. Doctors and nurses cared for me as if I were a premature baby. Mexican and Canadian officials opened all doors for me so that from the beach in Mexico to the home of my foster mother to the classrooms of the University of Toronto, there was only one long, easy corridor I had to walk down. To all these people I would like to extend my heartfelt thanks.

PART THREE

Benito Juárez Infirmary, Tomatlán, Mexico

Mr. Tomohiro Okamoto, of the Maritime Department in the Japanese Ministry of Transport, now retired, told me that he and his junior colleague at the time, Mr. Atsuro Chiba, were in Long Beach, California—the American western seaboard's main container port, near L.A.— on unrelated business when they were advised that a lone survivor of the Japanese ship Tsimtsum, *which had vanished without a trace in Pacific international waters several months before, was reported to have landed near the small town of Tomatlán, on the coast of Mexico. They were instructed by their department to go down to contact the survivor and see if any light could be shed on the fate of the ship. They bought a map of Mexico and looked to see where Tomatlán was. Unfortunately for them, a fold of the map crossed Baja California over a small coastal town named Tomatán, printed in small letters. Mr. Okamoto was convinced he read Tomatlán. Since it was less than halfway down Baja California, he decided the fastest way to get there would be to drive.*

They set off in their rented car. When they got to Tomatán, eight hundred kilometres south of Long Beach, and saw that it was not Tomatlán, Mr. Okamoto decided that they would continue to Santa Rosalía, two hundred kilometres further south, and catch the ferry across the Gulf of California to Guaymas. The ferry was late and slow. And from Guaymas it was another thirteen hundred kilometres to Tomatlán. The roads were bad. They had a flat tire. Their car broke down and the mechanic who fixed it surreptitiously cannibalized the motor of parts, putting in used parts instead, for the replacement of which they had to pay the rental company and which resulted in the car breaking down a second time, on their way back. The second mechanic overcharged them. Mr. Okamoto admitted to me that they were very tired when they arrived at the Benito Juárez Infirmary in Tomatlán, which is not at all in Baja California but a hundred kilometres south of Puerto Vallarta, in the state of Jalisco, nearly level with Mexico City. They had been travelling non-stop for forty-one hours. "We work hard," Mr. Okamoto wrote.

He and Mr. Chiba spoke with Piscine Molitor Patel, in English, for close to three hours, taping the conversation. What follows are excerpts from the verbatim transcript. I am grateful to Mr. Okamoto for having made available to me a copy of the tape and of his final report. For the sake of clarity I have indicated who is speaking when it is not immediately apparent. Portions printed in a different font were spoken in Japanese, which I had translated.

CHAPTER 96

"Hello, Mr. Patel. My name is Tomohiro Okamoto. I am from the Maritime Department in the Japanese Ministry of Transport. This is my assistant, Atsuro Chiba. We have come to see you about the sinking of the ship *Tsimtsum*, of which you were a passenger. Would it be possible to talk to you now?"

"Yes, of course."

"Thank you. It is very kind of you. *Now, Atsuro-kun, you're new at this, so pay attention and seek to learn.*"

"*Yes, Okamoto-san.*"

"*Is the tape recorder on?*"

"*Yes, it is.*"

"*Good. Oh, I'm so tired! For the record, today is February 19th,*"

Are you comfortable, Mr. Patel?"

"Yes, I am. Thank you. And you?"

"We are very comfortable."

"You've come all the way from Tokyo?"

"We were in Long Beach, California. We drove down."

"Did you have a good trip?"

"We had a wonderful trip. It was a beautiful drive."

"I had a terrible trip."

"Yes, we spoke to the police before coming here and we saw the lifeboat."

"I'm a little hungry."

"Would you like a cookie?"

"Oh, yes!"

"Here you go."

"Thank you!"

"You're welcome. It's only a cookie. Now, Mr. Patel, we were wondering if you could tell us what happened to you, with as much detail as possible."

"Yes. I'd be happy to."

CHAPTER 97

The story.

CHAPTER 98

Mr. Okamoto: "Very interesting."

    Mr. Chiba: "What a story."

"He thinks we're fools. Mr. Patel, we'll take a little break and then we'll come back, yes?"

"That's fine. I'd like another cookie."

"Yes, of course."

Mr. Chiba: "He's already had plenty and most he hasn't even eaten. They're right there beneath his bedsheet."

"Just give him another one. We have to humour him. We'll be back in a few minutes."

CHAPTER 99

Mr. Okamoto: "Mr. Patel, we don't believe your story."

"Sorry—these cookies are good but they tend to crumble. I'm amazed. Why not?"

"It doesn't hold up."

"What do you mean?"

"Bananas don't float."

"I'm sorry?"

"You said the orang-utan came floating on an island of bananas."

"That's right."

"Bananas don't float."

"Yes, they do."

"They're too heavy."

"No, they're not. Here, try for yourself. I have two bananas right here."

Mr. Chiba: "Where did those come from? What else does he have under his bedsheet?"

Mr. Okamoto: "Damn it. No, that's all right."

"There's a sink over there."

"That's fine."

"I insist. Fill that sink with water, drop these bananas in, and we'll see who's right."

"We'd like to move on."

"I absolutely insist."

[Silence]

Mr. Chiba: "What do we do?"

Mr. Okamoto: "I feel this is going to be another very long day."

[Sound of a chair being pushed back. Distant sound of water gushing out of a tap]

Pi Patel: "What's happening? I can't see from here."

Mr. Okamoto [distantly]: "I'm filling the sink."

"Have you put the bananas in yet?"

[Distantly] "No."

"And now?"

[Distantly] "They're in."

"And?"

[Silence]

Mr. Chiba: "Are they floating?"

[Distantly] "They're floating."

"So, are they floating?"

[Distantly] "They're floating."

"What did I tell you?"

Mr. Okamoto: "Yes, yes. But it would take a lot of bananas to hold up an orang-utan."

"It did. There was close to a ton. It still makes me sick when I think of all those bananas floating away and going to waste when they were mine for the picking."

"It's a pity. Now, about—"

"Could I have my bananas back, please?"

Mr. Chiba: "I'll get them."

[Sound of a chair being pushed back]

[Distantly] "Look at that. They really do float."

Mr. Okamoto: "What about this algae island you say you came upon?"

Mr. Chiba: "Here are your bananas."

Pi Patel: "Thank you. Yes?"

"I'm sorry to say it so bluntly, we don't mean to hurt your feelings, but you don't really expect us to believe you, do you? Carnivorous trees? A fish-eating algae that produces fresh water? Tree-dwelling aquatic rodents? These things don't exist."

"Only because you've never seen them."

"That's right. We believe what we see."

"So did Columbus. What do you do when you're in the dark?"

"Your island is botanically impossible."

"Said the fly just before landing in the Venus flytrap."

"Why has no one else come upon it?"

"It's a big ocean crossed by busy ships. I went slowly, observing much."

"No scientist would believe you."

"These would be the same who dismissed Copernicus and Darwin. Have scientists finished coming upon new plants? In the Amazon basin, for example?"

"Not plants that contradict the laws of nature."

"Which you know through and through?"

"Well enough to know the possible from the impossible."

Mr. Chiba: "I have an uncle who knows a lot about botany. He lives in the country near Hita-Gun. He's a bonsai master."

Pi Patel: "A what?"

"A bonsai master. You know, bonsai are little trees."

"You mean shrubs."

"No, I mean trees. Bonsai are little trees. They are less than two feet tall. You can carry them in your arms. They can be very old. My uncle has one that is over three hundred years old."

"Three-hundred-year-old trees that are two feet tall that you can carry in your arms?"

"Yes. They're very delicate. They need a lot of attention."

"Whoever heard of such trees? They're botanically impossible."

"But I assure you they exist, Mr. Patel. My uncle—"

"I believe what I see."

Mr. Okamoto: "Just a moment, please. Atsuro, with all due respect for your uncle who lives in the country near Hita-Gun, we're not here to talk idly about botany."

"I'm just trying to help."

"Do your uncle's bonsai eat meat?"

"I don't think so."

"Have you ever been bitten by one of his bonsai?"

"No."

"In that case, your uncle's bonsai are not helping us. Where were we?"

Pi Patel: "With the tall, full-sized trees firmly rooted to the ground I was telling you about."

"Let us put them aside for now."

"It might be hard. I never tried pulling them out and carrying them."

"You're a funny man, Mr. Patel. Ha! Ha! Ha!"

Pi Patel: "Ha! Ha! Ha!"

Mr. Chiba: "Ha! Ha! Ha! It wasn't that funny."

Mr. Okamoto: "Just keep laughing. Ha! Ha! Ha!"

Mr. Chiba: "Ha! Ha! Ha!"

Mr. Okamoto: "Now about the tiger, we're not sure about it either."

"What do you mean?"

"We have difficulty believing it."

"It's an incredible story."

"Precisely."

"I don't know how I survived."

"Clearly it was a strain."

"I'll have another cookie."

"There are none left."

"What's in that bag?"

"Nothing."

"Can I see?"

Mr. Chiba: "There goes our lunch."

Mr. Okamoto: "Getting back to the tiger . . ."

Pi Patel: "Terrible business. Delicious sandwiches."

Mr. Okamoto: "Yes, they look good."

Mr. Chiba: "I'm hungry."

"Not a trace of it has been found. That's a bit hard to believe, isn't it? There are no tigers in the Americas. If there were a wild tiger out there, don't you think the police would have heard about it by now?"

"I should tell you about the black panther that escaped from the Zurich Zoo in the middle of winter."

"Mr. Patel, a tiger is an incredibly dangerous wild animal. How could you survive in a lifeboat with one? It's—"

"What you don't realize is that we are a strange and forbidding species to wild animals. We fill them with fear. They avoid us as much as possible. It took centuries to still the fear in some pliable animals— *domestication* it's called—but most cannot get over their fear, and I doubt they ever will. When wild animals fight us, it is out of sheer desperation. They fight when they feel they have no other way out. It's a very last resort."

"In a lifeboat? Come on, Mr. Patel, it's just too hard to believe!"

"Hard to believe? What do you know about hard to believe? You want hard to believe? I'll give you hard to believe. It's a closely held secret among Indian zookeepers that in 1971 Bara the polar bear escaped from the Calcutta Zoo. She was never heard from again, not by police or hunters or poachers or anyone else. We suspect she's living freely on the banks of the Hugli River. Beware if you go to Calcutta, my good sirs: if you have sushi on the breath you may pay a high price! If you took the city of Tokyo and turned it upside down and shook it, you'd be amazed at all the animals that would fall out: badgers, wolves, boa constrictors, Komodo dragons, crocodiles, ostriches, baboons, capybaras, wild boars, leopards, manatees, ruminants in untold numbers. There is no doubt in my mind that feral giraffes and feral hippos have been living in Tokyo for generations without being seen by a soul. You should compare one day the things that stick to the soles of your shoes as you walk down the street with what you see lying at the bottom of the cages in the Tokyo Zoo—then look up! And you expect to find a tiger in a Mexican jungle! It's laughable, just plain laughable. Ha! Ha! Ha!"

"There may very well be feral giraffes and feral hippos living in Tokyo and a polar bear living freely in Calcutta. We just don't believe there was a tiger living in your lifeboat."

"The arrogance of big-city folk! You grant your metropolises all the animals of Eden, but you deny my hamlet the merest Bengal tiger!"

"Mr. Patel, please calm down."

"If you stumble at mere believability, what are you living for? Isn't love hard to believe?"

"Mr. Patel—"

"Don't you bully me with your politeness! Love is hard to believe, ask any lover. Life is hard to believe, ask any scientist. God is hard to believe, ask any believer. What is your problem with hard to believe?"

"We're just being reasonable."

"So am I! I applied my reason at every moment. Reason is excellent for getting food, clothing and shelter. Reason is the very best tool kit. Nothing beats reason for keeping tigers away. But be excessively reasonable and you risk throwing out the universe with the bathwater."

"Calm down, Mr. Patel, calm down."

Mr. Chiba: "**The bathwater? Why is he talking about bathwater?**"

"How can I be calm? You should have seen Richard Parker!"

"Yes, yes."

"Huge. Teeth like this! Claws like scimitars!"

Mr. Chiba: "**What are scimitars?**"

Mr. Okamoto: "**Chiba-san, instead of asking stupid vocabulary questions, why don't you make yourself useful? This boy is a tough nut to crack. Do something!**"

Mr. Chiba: "Look! A chocolate bar!"

Pi Patel: "Wonderful!"

[Long silence]

Mr. Okamoto: "**Like he hasn't already stolen our whole lunch. Soon he'll be demanding tempura.**"

[Long silence]

Mr. Okamoto: "We are losing sight of the point of this investigation. We are here because of the sinking of a cargo ship. You are the sole survivor. And you were only a passenger. You bear no responsibility for what happened. We—"

"Chocolate is so good!"

"We are not seeking to lay criminal charges. You are an innocent victim of a tragedy at sea. We are only trying to determine why and how the *Tsimtsum* sank. We thought you might help us, Mr. Patel."

[Silence]

"Mr. Patel?"

[Silence]

Pi Patel: "Tigers exist, lifeboats exist, oceans exist. Because the three have never come together in your narrow, limited experience, you refuse to believe that they might. Yet the plain fact is that the *Tsimtsum* brought them together and then sank."

[Silence]

Mr. Okamoto: "What about this Frenchman?"

"What about him?"

"Two blind people in two separate lifeboats meeting up in the Pacific—the coincidence seems a little far-fetched, no?"

"It certainly does."

"We find it very unlikely."

"So is winning the lottery, yet someone always wins."

"We find it *extremely* hard to believe."

"So did I."

"**I knew we should have taken the day off**. You talked about food?"

"We did."

"He knew a lot about food."

"If you can call it food."

"The cook on the *Tsimtsum* was a Frenchman."

"There are Frenchmen all over the world."

"Maybe the Frenchman you met was the cook."

"Maybe. How should I know? I never saw him. I was blind. Then Richard Parker ate him alive."

"How convenient."

"Not at all. It was horrific and it stank. By the way, how do you explain the meerkat bones in the lifeboat?"

"Yes, the bones of a small animal were—"

"More than one!"

"—of *some* small animals were found in the lifeboat. They must have come from the ship."

"We had no meerkats at the zoo."

"We have no proof they were meerkat bones."

Mr. Chiba: "Maybe they were banana bones! Ha! Ha! Ha! Ha! Ha!"

"Atsuro, shut up!"

"I'm very sorry, Okamoto-san. It's the fatigue."

"You're bringing our service into disrepute!"

"Very sorry, Okamoto-san."

Mr. Okamoto: "They could be bones from another small animal."

"They were meerkats."

"They could be mongooses."

"The mongooses at the zoo didn't sell. They stayed in India."

"They could be shipboard pests, like rats. Mongooses are common in India."

"Mongooses as shipboard pests?"

"Why not?"

"Who swam in the stormy Pacific, several of them, to the lifeboat? That's a little hard to believe, wouldn't you say?"

"Less hard to believe than some of the things we've heard in the last two hours. Perhaps the mongooses were already aboard the lifeboat, like the rat you mentioned."

"Simply amazing the number of animals in that lifeboat."

"Simply amazing."

"A real jungle."

"Yes."

"Those bones are meerkat bones. Have them checked by an expert."

"There weren't that many left. And there were no heads."

"I used them as bait."

"It's doubtful an expert could tell whether they were meerkat bones or mongoose bones."

"Find yourself a forensic zoologist."

"All right, Mr. Patel! You win. We cannot explain the presence of meerkat bones, if that is what they are, in the lifeboat. But that is not our concern here. We are here because a Japanese cargo ship owned by Oika Shipping Company, flying the Panamanian flag, sank in the Pacific."

"Something I never forget, not for a minute. I lost my whole family."

"We're sorry about that."

"Not as much as I am."

[Long silence]

Mr. Chiba: "What do we do now?"

Mr. Okamoto: "I don't know."

[Long silence]

Pi Patel: "Would you like a cookie?"

Mr. Okamoto: "Yes, that would be nice. Thank you."

Mr. Chiba: "Thank you."

[Long silence]

Mr. Okamoto: "It's a nice day."

Pi Patel: "Yes. Sunny."

[Long silence]

Pi Patel: "Is this your first visit to Mexico?"

Mr. Okamoto: "Yes, it is."

"Mine too."

[Long silence]

Pi Patel: "So, you didn't like my story?"

Mr. Okamoto: "No, we liked it very much. Didn't we, Atsuro? We will remember it for a long, long time."

Mr. Chiba: "We will."

[Silence]

Mr. Okamoto: "But for the purposes of our investigation, we would like to know what really happened."

"What really happened?"

"Yes."

"So you want another story?"

"Uhh . . . no. We would like to know what really happened."

"Doesn't the telling of something always become a story?"

"Uhh . . . perhaps in English. In Japanese a story would have an element of *invention* in it. We don't want any invention. We want the 'straight facts', as you say in English."

"Isn't telling about something—using words, English or Japanese—already something of an invention? Isn't just looking upon this world already something of an invention?"

"Uhh . . ."

"The world isn't just the way it is. It is how we understand it, no? And in understanding something, we bring something to it, no? Doesn't that make life a story?"

"Ha! Ha! Ha! You are very intelligent, Mr. Patel."

Mr. Chiba: "What is he talking about?"

"I have no idea."

Pi Patel: "You want words that reflect reality?"

"Yes."

"Words that do not contradict reality?"

"Exactly."

"But tigers don't contradict reality."

"Oh please, no more tigers."

"I know what you want. You want a story that won't surprise you. That will confirm what you already know. That won't make you see higher or further or differently. You want a flat story. An immobile story. You want dry, yeastless factuality."

"Uhh . . ."

"You want a story without animals."

"Yes!"

"Without tigers or orang-utans."

"That's right."

"Without hyenas or zebras."

"Without them."

"Without meerkats or mongooses."

"We don't want them."

"Without giraffes or hippopotamuses."

"We will plug our ears with our fingers!"

"So I'm right. You want a story without animals."

"We want a story without animals that will explain the sinking of the *Tsimtsum*."

"Give me a minute, please."

"Of course. I think we're finally getting somewhere. Let's hope he speaks some sense."

[Long silence]

"Here's another story."

"Good."

"The ship sank. It made a sound like a monstrous metallic burp. Things bubbled at the surface and then vanished. I found myself kicking water in the Pacific Ocean. I swam for the lifeboat. It was the hardest swim of my life. I didn't seem to be moving. I kept swallowing water. I was very cold. I was rapidly losing strength. I wouldn't have made it if the cook hadn't thrown me a lifebuoy and pulled me in. I climbed aboard and collapsed.

"Four of us survived. Mother held on to some bananas and made it to the lifeboat. The cook was already aboard, as was the sailor.

"He ate the flies. The cook, that is. We hadn't been in the lifeboat

303

a full day; we had food and water to last us for weeks; we had fishing gear and solar stills; we had no reason to believe that we wouldn't be rescued soon. Yet there he was, swinging his arms and catching flies and eating them greedily. Right away he was in a holy terror of hunger. He was calling us idiots and fools for not joining him in the feast. We were offended and disgusted, but we didn't show it. We were very polite about it. He was a stranger and a foreigner. Mother smiled and shook her head and raised her hand in refusal. He was a disgusting man. His mouth had the discrimination of a garbage heap. He also ate the rat. He cut it up and dried it in the sun. I—I'll be honest—I had a small piece, very small, behind Mother's back. I was so hungry. He was such a brute, that cook, ill-tempered and hypocritical.

"The sailor was young. Actually, he was older than me, probably in his early twenties, but he broke his leg jumping from the ship and his suffering made him a child. He was beautiful. He had no facial hair at all and a clear, shining complexion. His features—the broad face, the flattened nose, the narrow, pleated eyes—looked so elegant. I thought he looked like a Chinese emperor. His suffering was terrible. He spoke no English, not a single word, not *yes* or *no*, *hello* or *thank you*. He spoke only Chinese. We couldn't understand a word he said. He must have felt very lonely. When he wept, Mother held his head in her lap and I held his hand. It was very, very sad. He suffered and we couldn't do anything about it.

"His right leg was badly broken at the thigh. The bone stuck out of his flesh. He screamed with pain. We set his leg as best we could and we made sure he was eating and drinking. But his leg became infected. Though we drained it of pus every day, it got worse. His foot became black and bloated.

"It was the cook's idea. He was a brute. He dominated us. He whispered that the blackness would spread and that he would survive only if his leg were amputated. Since the bone was broken at the thigh, it would involve no more than cutting through flesh and setting a tourniquet. I can still hear his evil whisper. He would do the job to save the sailor's life, he said, but we would have to hold him. Surprise would be the only anaesthetic. We fell upon him. Mother and I held his arms while the cook sat on his good leg. The sailor writhed and screamed. His chest rose and fell. The cook worked the knife quickly. The leg fell off. Immediately Mother and I let go and moved away. We thought that if the restraint was ended, so would his struggling. We thought he would lie calmly. He didn't. He sat up instantly. His screams were all the worse for being unintelligible. He screamed and we stared, transfixed. There was blood everywhere. Worse, there was the contrast between the frantic activity of the poor sailor and the gentle repose of his leg at the bottom of the boat. He kept looking at the limb, as if imploring it to return. At last he fell back. We hurried into action. The cook folded some skin over the bone. We wrapped the stump in a piece of cloth and we tied a rope above the wound to stop the bleeding. We laid him as comfortably as we could on a mattress of life jackets and kept him warm. I thought it was all for nothing. I couldn't believe a human being could survive so much pain, so much butchery. Throughout the evening and night he moaned, and his breathing was harsh and uneven. He had fits of agitated delirium. I expected him to die during the night.

"He clung to life. At dawn he was still alive. He went in and out of consciousness. Mother gave him water. I caught sight of the amputated leg. It cut my breath short. In the commotion it had been shoved aside and forgotten in the dark. It had seeped a liquid and looked thinner. I took a life jacket and used it as a glove. I picked the leg up.

"'What are you doing?' asked the cook.

"'I'm going to throw it overboard,' I replied.

"'Don't be an idiot. We'll use it as bait. That was the whole point.'

"He seemed to regret his last words even as they were coming out, for his voice faded quickly. He turned away.

"'The *whole point*?' Mother asked. 'What do you mean by that?'

"He pretended to be busy.

"Mother's voice rose. 'Are you telling us that we cut this poor boy's leg off not to save his life but to get *fishing bait*?'

"Silence from the brute.

"'Answer me!' shouted Mother.

"Like a cornered beast he lifted his eyes and glared at her. 'Our supplies are running out,' he snarled. 'We need more food or we'll die.'

"Mother returned his glare. 'Our supplies are *not* running out! We have plenty of food and water. We have package upon package of biscuits to tide us over till our rescue.' She took hold of the plastic container in which we put the open rations of biscuits. It was unexpectedly light in her hands. The few crumbs in it rattled. 'What!' She opened it. 'Where are the biscuits? The container was full last night!'

"The cook looked away. As did I.

"'You selfish monster!' screamed Mother. 'The only reason we're running out of food is because you're gorging yourself on it!'

"'He had some too,' he said, nodding my way.

"Mother's eyes turned to me. My heart sank.

"'Piscine, is that true?'

"'It was night, Mother. I was half asleep and I was so hungry. He gave me a biscuit. I ate it without thinking . . .'

"'Only one, was it?' sneered the cook.

"It was Mother's turn to look away. The anger seemed to go out of her. Without saying another word she went back to nursing the sailor.

"I wished for her anger. I wished for her to punish me. Only not this silence. I made to arrange some life jackets for the sailor's comfort so that I could be next to her. I whispered, 'I'm sorry, Mother, I'm sorry.' My eyes were brimming with tears. When I brought them up,

I saw that hers were too. But she didn't look at me. Her eyes were gazing upon some memory in mid-air.

"'We're all alone, Piscine, all alone,' she said, in a tone that broke every hope in my body. I never felt so lonely in all my life as I did at that moment. We had been in the lifeboat two weeks already and it was taking its toll on us. It was getting harder to believe that Father and Ravi had survived.

"When we turned around, the cook was holding the leg by the ankle over the water to drain it. Mother brought her hand over the sailor's eyes.

"He died quietly, the life drained out of him like the liquid from his leg. The cook promptly butchered him. The leg had made for poor bait. The dead flesh was too decayed to hold on to the fishing hook; it simply dissolved in the water. Nothing went to waste with this monster. He cut up everything, including the sailor's skin and every inch of his intestines. He even prepared his genitals. When he had finished with his torso, he moved on to his arms and shoulders and to his legs. Mother and I rocked with pain and horror. Mother shrieked at the cook, 'How can you do this, you monster? Where is your humanity? Have you no decency? What did the poor boy do to you? You monster! You monster!' The cook replied with unbelievable vulgarity.

"'At least cover his face, for God's sake!' cried my mother. It was unbearable to have that beautiful face, so noble and serene, connected to such a sight below. The cook threw himself upon the sailor's head and before our very eyes scalped him and pulled off his face. Mother and I vomited.

"When he had finished, he threw the butchered carcass overboard. Shortly after, strips of flesh and pieces of organs were lying to dry in the sun all over the boat. We recoiled in horror. We tried not to look at them. The smell would not go away.

"The next time the cook was close by, Mother slapped him in the face, a full hard slap that punctuated the air with a sharp crack. It was something shocking coming from my mother. And it was heroic. It was an act of outrage and pity and grief and bravery. It was done in memory of that poor sailor. It was to salvage his dignity.

"I was stunned. So was the cook. He stood without moving or saying a word as Mother looked him straight in the face. I noticed how he did not meet her eyes.

"We retreated to our private spaces. I stayed close to her. I was filled with a mix of rapt admiration and abject fear.

"Mother kept an eye on him. Two days later she saw him do it. He tried to be discreet, but she saw him bring his hand to his mouth. She shouted, 'I saw you! You just ate a piece! You said it was for bait! I knew it. You monster! You animal! How could you? He's *human*! He's your own kind!' If she had expected him to be mortified, to spit it out and break down and apologize, she was wrong. He kept chewing. In fact, he lifted his head up and quite openly put the rest of the strip in his mouth. 'Tastes like pork,' he muttered. Mother expressed her indignation and disgust by violently turning away. He ate another strip. 'I feel stronger already,' he muttered. He concentrated on his fishing.

"We each had our end of the lifeboat. It's amazing how willpower can build walls. Whole days went by as if he weren't there.

"But we couldn't ignore him entirely. He was a brute, but a practical brute. He was good with his hands and he knew the sea. He was full of good ideas. He was the one who thought of building a raft to help with the fishing. If we survived any time at all, it was thanks to him. I helped him as best I could. He was very short-tempered, always shouting at me and insulting me.

"Mother and I didn't eat any of the sailor's body, not the smallest morsel, despite the cost in weakness to us, but we did start to eat what the cook caught from the sea. My mother, a lifelong vegetarian, brought herself to eat raw fish and raw turtle. She had a very hard time of it. She never got over her revulsion. It came easier to me. I found hunger improved the taste of everything.

"When your life has been given a reprieve, it's impossible not to feel some warmth for the one to whom you owe that reprieve. It was very exciting when the cook hauled aboard a turtle or caught a great big dorado. It made us smile broadly and there was a glow in our chests that lasted for hours. Mother and the cook talked in a civil way, even joked. During some spectacular sunsets, life on the boat was nearly good. At such times I looked at him with—yes—with tenderness. With love. I imagined that we were fast friends. He was a coarse man even when he was in a good mood, but we pretended not to notice it, even to ourselves. He said that we would come upon an island. That was our main hope. We exhausted our eyes scanning the horizon for an island that never came. That's when he stole food and water.

"The flat and endless Pacific rose like a great wall around us. I never thought we would get around it.

"He killed her. The cook killed my mother. We were starving. I was weak. I couldn't hold on to a turtle. Because of me we lost it. He hit me. Mother hit him. He hit her back. She turned to me and said, 'Go!' pushing me towards the raft. I jumped for it. I thought she was coming with me. I landed in the water. I scrambled aboard the raft. They were fighting. I did nothing but watch. My mother was fighting an adult man. He was mean and muscular. He caught her by the wrist and twisted it. She shrieked and fell. He moved over her. The knife appeared. He raised it in the air. It came down. Next it was up—it was red. It went up and down repeatedly. I couldn't see her. She was at the bottom of the boat. I saw only him. He stopped. He raised his head and looked at me. He hurled something my way. A line of blood struck me across the face. No whip could have inflicted a more painful lash. I held my mother's head in my hands. I let it go. It sank in a cloud of blood, her tress trailing like a tail. Fish spiralled down towards it until a shark's long grey shadow cut across its path and it vanished. I looked up. I couldn't see him. He was hiding at the bottom of the boat. He appeared when he threw my mother's body overboard. His mouth was red. The water boiled with fish.

"I spent the rest of that day and the night on the raft, looking at him. We didn't speak a word. He could have cut the raft loose. But he didn't. He kept me around, like a bad conscience.

"In the morning, in plain sight of him, I pulled on the rope and boarded the lifeboat. I was very weak. He said nothing. I kept my peace. He caught a turtle. He gave me its blood. He butchered it and laid its best parts for me on the middle bench. I ate.

"Then we fought and I killed him. He had no expression on his face, neither of despair nor of anger, neither of fear nor of pain. He gave up. He let himself be killed, though it was still a struggle. He knew he had gone too far, even by his bestial standards. He had gone too far and now he didn't want to go on living any more. But he never said 'I'm sorry.' Why do we cling to our evil ways?

"The knife was all along in plain view on the bench. We both knew it. He could have had it in his hands from the start. He was the one who put it there. I picked it up. I stabbed him in the stomach. He grimaced but remained standing. I pulled the knife out and stabbed him again. Blood was pouring out. Still he didn't fall over. Looking me in the eyes, he lifted his head ever so slightly. Did he mean something by this? I took it that he did. I stabbed him in the throat, next to the Adam's apple. He dropped like a stone. And died. He didn't say anything. He had no last words. He only coughed up blood. A knife has a horrible dynamic power; once in motion, it's hard to stop. I stabbed him repeatedly. His blood soothed my chapped hands. His heart was a struggle—all those tubes that connected it. I managed to get it out. It tasted delicious, far better than turtle. I ate his liver. I cut off great pieces of his flesh.

"He was such an evil man. Worse still, he met evil in me—selfishness, anger, ruthlessness. I must live with that.

"Solitude began. I turned to God. I survived."

[Long silence]

"Is that better? Are there any parts you find hard to believe? Anything you'd like me to change?"

Mr. Chiba: "What a horrible story."

[Long silence]

Mr. Okamoto: "Both the zebra and the Taiwanese sailor broke a leg, did you notice that?"

"No, I didn't."

"And the hyena bit off the zebra's leg just as the cook cut off the sailor's."

"Ohhh, Okamoto-san, you see a lot."

"The blind Frenchman they met in the other lifeboat—didn't he admit to killing a man and a woman?"

"Yes, he did."

"The cook killed the sailor and his mother."

"Very impressive."

"His stories match."

"So the Taiwanese sailor is the zebra, his mother is the orang-utan, the cook is . . . the hyena—which means he's the tiger!"

"Yes. The tiger killed the hyena—and the blind Frenchman—just as he killed the cook."

Pi Patel: "Do you have another chocolate bar?"

Mr. Chiba: "Right away!"

"Thank you."

Mr. Chiba: "But what does it mean, Okamoto-san?"

"I have no idea."

"And what about the island? Who are the meerkats?"

"I don't know."

"And those teeth? Whose teeth were those in the tree?"

"I don't know. I'm not inside this boy's head."

[Long silence]

Mr. Okamoto: "Please excuse me for asking, but did the cook say anything about the sinking of the *Tsimtsum*?"

"In this other story?"

"Yes."

"He didn't."

"He made no mention of anything leading up to the early morning of July 2nd that might explain what happened?"

"No."

"Nothing of a nature mechanical or structural?"

"No."

"Nothing about other ships or objects at sea?"

"No."

"He could not explain the sinking of the *Tsimtsum* at all?"

"No."

"Could he say why it didn't send out a distress signal?"

"And if it had? In my experience, when a dingy, third-rate rust-bucket sinks, unless it has the luck of carrying oil, lots of it, enough to kill entire ecosystems, no one cares and no one hears about it. You're on your own."

"When Oika realized that something was wrong, it was too late. You were too far out for air rescue. Ships in the area were told to be on the lookout. They reported seeing nothing."

"And while we're on the subject, the ship wasn't the only thing that was third-rate. The crew were a sullen, unfriendly lot, hard at work when officers were around but doing nothing when they weren't. They didn't speak a word of English and they were of no help to us. Some of them stank of alcohol by mid-afternoon. Who's to say what those idiots did? The officers—"

"What do you mean by that?"

"By what?"

"'Who's to say what those idiots did?'"

"I mean that maybe in a fit of drunken insanity some of them released the animals."

Mr. Chiba: "Who had the keys to the cages?"

"Father did."

Mr. Chiba: "So how could the crew open the cages if they didn't have the keys?"

"I don't know. They probably used crowbars."

Mr. Chiba: "Why would they do that? Why would anyone want to release a dangerous wild animal from its cage?"

"I don't know. Can anyone fathom the workings of a drunken man's mind? All I can tell you is what happened. The animals were out of their cages."

Mr. Okamoto: "Excuse me. You have doubts about the fitness of the crew?"

"Grave doubts."

"Did you witness any of the officers being under the influence of alcohol?"

"No."

"But you saw some of the crew being under the influence of alcohol?"

"Yes."

"Did the officers act in what seemed to you a competent and professional manner?"

"They had little to do with us. They never came close to the animals."

"I mean in terms of running the ship."

"How should I know? Do you think we had tea with them every day? They spoke English, but they were no better than the crew. They made us feel unwelcome in the common room and hardly said a word to us during meals. They went on in Japanese, as if we weren't there. We were just a lowly Indian family with a bothersome cargo. We ended up eating on our own in Father and Mother's cabin. 'Adventure beckons!' said Ravi. That's what made it tolerable, our sense of adventure. We spent most of our time shovelling excrement and rinsing cages and giving feed while Father played the vet. So long as the animals were all right, we were all right. I don't know if the officers were competent."

"You said the ship was listing to port?"

"Yes."

"And that there was an incline from bow to stern?"

"Yes."

"So the ship sank stern first?"

"Yes."

"Not bow first?"

"No."

"You are sure? There was a slope from the front of the ship to the back?"

"Yes."

"Did the ship hit another ship?"

"I didn't see another ship."

"Did it hit any other object?"

"Not that I saw."

"Did it run aground?"

"No, it sank out of sight."

"You were not aware of mechanical problems after leaving Manila?"

"No."

"Did it appear to you that the ship was properly loaded?"

"It was my first time on a ship. I don't know what a properly loaded ship should look like."

"You believe you heard an explosion?"

"Yes."

"Any other noises?"

"A thousand."

"I mean that might explain the sinking."

"No."

"You said the ship sank quickly."

"Yes."

"Can you estimate how long it took?"

"It's hard to say. Very quickly. I would think less than twenty minutes."

"And there was a lot of debris?"

"Yes."

"Was the ship struck by a freak wave?"

"I don't think so."

"But there was a storm?"

"The sea looked rough to me. There was wind and rain."

"How high were the waves?"

"High. Twenty-five, thirty feet."

"That's quite modest, actually."

"Not when you're in a lifeboat."

"Yes, of course. But for a cargo ship."

"Maybe they were higher. I don't know. The weather was bad enough to scare me witless, that's all I know for sure."

"You said the weather improved quickly. The ship sank and right after it was a beautiful day, isn't that what you said?"

"Yes."

"Sounds like no more than a passing squall."

"It sank the ship."

"That's what we're wondering."

"My whole family died."

"We're sorry about that."

"Not as much as I am."

"So what happened, Mr. Patel? We're puzzled. Everything was normal and then . . . ?"

"Then normal sank."

"Why?"

"I don't know. You should be telling me. You're the experts. Apply your science."

"We don't understand."

[Long silence]

Mr. Chiba: *Now what?*

Mr. Okamoto: *We give up. The explanation for the sinking of the Tsimtsum is at the bottom of the Pacific.*

[Long silence]

Mr. Okamoto: *Yes, that's it. Let's go.* Well, Mr. Patel, I think we have all we need. We thank you very much for your cooperation. You've been very, very helpful."

"You're welcome. But before you go, I'd like to ask you something."

"Yes?"

"The *Tsimtsum* sank on July 2nd, 1977."

"Yes."

"And I arrived on the coast of Mexico, the sole human survivor of the *Tsimtsum*, on February 14th, 1978."

"That's right."

"I told you two stories that account for the 227 days in between."

"Yes, you did."

"Neither explains the sinking of the *Tsimtsum*."

"That's right."

"Neither makes a factual difference to you."

"That's true."

"You can't prove which story is true and which is not. You must take my word for it."

"I guess so."

"In both stories the ship sinks, my entire family dies, and I suffer."

"Yes, that's true."

"So tell me, since it makes no factual difference to you and you can't prove the question either way, which story do you prefer? Which is the better story, the story with animals or the story without animals?"

Mr. Okamoto: "That's an interesting question . . ."

Mr. Chiba: "The story with animals."

Mr. Okamoto: "Yes. The story with animals is the better story."

Pi Patel: "Thank you. And so it goes with God."

[Silence]

Mr. Chiba: "What did he just say?"

Mr. Okamoto: "I don't know."

Mr. Chiba: "Oh look—he's crying."

[Long silence]

Mr. Okamoto: "We'll be careful when we drive away. We don't want to run into Richard Parker."

Pi Patel: "Don't worry, you won't. He's hiding somewhere you'll never find him."

Mr. Okamoto: "Thank you for taking the time to talk to us, Mr. Patel. We're grateful. And we're really very sorry about what happened to you."

"Thank you."

"What will you be doing now?"

"I guess I'll go to Canada."

"Not back to India?"

"No. There's nothing there for me now. Only sad memories."

"Of course, you know you will be getting insurance money."

"Oh."

"Yes. Oika will be in touch with you."

[Silence]

Mr. Okamoto: "We should be going. We wish you all the best, Mr. Patel."

Mr. Chiba: "Yes, all the best."

"Thank you."

Mr. Okamoto: "Goodbye."

Mr. Chiba: "Goodbye."

Pi Patel: "Would you like some cookies for the road?"

Mr. Okamoto: "That would be nice."

"Here, have three each."

"Thank you."

Mr. Chiba: "Thank you."

"You're welcome. Goodbye. God be with you, my brothers."

"Thank you. And with you too, Mr. Patel."

Mr. Chiba: "Goodbye."

Mr. Okamoto: "I'm starving. Let's go eat. You can turn that off."

CHAPTER 100

Mr. Okamoto, in his letter to me, recalled the interrogation as having been "difficult and memorable." He remembered Piscine Molitor Patel as being "very thin, very tough, very bright."

His report, in its essential part, ran as follows:

Sole survivor could shed no light on reasons for sinking of Tsimtsum. Ship appears to have sunk very quickly, which would indicate a major hull breach. Important quantity of debris would support this theory. But precise reason of breach impossible to determine. No major weather disturbance reported that day in quadrant. Survivor's assessment of weather impressionistic and unreliable. At most, weather a contributing factor. Cause was perhaps internal to ship. Survivor believes he heard an explosion, hinting at a major engine problem, possibly the explosion of a boiler, but this is speculation. Ship twenty-nine years old (Erlandson and Skank Shipyards, Malmö, 1948), refitted in 1970. Stress of weather combined with structural fatigue a possibility, but conjecture. No other ship mishap reported in area on that day, so ship-ship collision unlikely. Collision with debris a possibility, but unverifiable. Collision with a floating mine might explain explosion, but seems fanciful, besides highly unlikely as sinking started at stern, which in all likelihood would mean that hull breach was at stern too. Survivor cast doubts on fitness of crew but had nothing to say about officers. Oika Shipping Company claims all cargo absolutely licit and not aware of any officer or crew problems.

Cause of sinking impossible to determine from available evidence. Standard insurance claim procedure for Oika. No further action required. Recommend that case be closed.

As an aside, story of sole survivor, Mr. Piscine Molitor Patel, Indian citizen, is an astounding story of courage and endurance in the face of extraordinarily difficult and tragic circumstances. In the experience of this investigator, his story is unparalleled in the history of shipwrecks. Very few castaways can claim to have survived so long at sea as Mr. Patel, and none in the company of an adult Bengal tiger.